COMOROS

JUMHURIYAT AL-QUMUR AL-ITTIHADIYAH AL-ISLAMIYAH;
FEDERAL ISLAMIC REPUBLIC OF THE COMOROS

COUNTRY STUDY GUIDE

International Business Publications, USA
Washington, DC, USA - Comoros

COMOROS

COUNTRY STUDY GUIDE

Editorial content: International Business Publications, USA

Editor-in-Chief: Dr. Igor S. Oleynik
Editor: Natasha Alexander
Managing Editor: Karl Cherepanya

Published by
International Business Publications, USA
P.O.Box 15343, Washington, DC 20003
Phone: (202) 546-2103, Fax: (202) 546-3275.
E-mail: rusric@erols.com

UPDATED ANNUALLY

We express our sincere appreciation to all government agencies and international organizations which provided information and other materials for this guide

Databases & Information: International Business Publications, USA
Cover Design: International Business Publications, USA

ISBN 0-7397-4293-0

For customer service and information, please contact:
in the USA: International Business Publications, USA
P.O.Box 15343, Washington, DC 20003
Phone: (202) 546-2103, Fax: (202) 546-3275.
E-mail: rusric@erols.com

Printed in the USA

COMOROS

COUNTRY STUDY GUIDE

TABLE OF CONTENTS

STRATEGIC & DEVELOPMENT PROFILES

Population: 580,000 (estimate July 2000).
Surface area : 1,862 km² (three main islands and a great number of islets distant 300 km/190 miles from the eastern coast of Africa).
Comparison with a European country : *2/3 of Luxemburg.*
Capital : Moroni.
Languages: Comori=Shimasiwa is related to Swahili (national language); French and Arabic (official languages).
Religions: Sunni Muslims (98.9%) / Christians (1.1%)
Administrative Divisions : three islands; Grande Comore (Njazidja), Anjouan (Nzwani), and Moheli (Mwali).
Population Density : 500/km² (2000).
Young people under 15 years old : 43% (estimate 2000).
Population Growth: 2,7% (estimate 2000).
Ethnic Background : Antalote, Cafre, Makoa, Oimatsaha, Sakalava.
Urban Population : 35% (1999).
Net Migration Rate : 0 migrant(s)/1,000 population (2000 estimate).
Birth Rate : 41 births/1,000 population (estimate 2000).
Death Rate : 9.6 deaths/1,000 population (estimate 2000).
Infant Mortality Rate : 86 deaths/1,000 live births (estimate 2000).
Life Expectancy at Birth : 60 years old.
Life Expectancy per Sex : *Males* 58 years old, *Females* 62 years old (estimate 2000).
Literacy Rate : Total Population 57.3%, *Males*64.2%, *Females* 50.4%.
Currency : 1 Comoran franc (KMF) = 100 Centimes.
Market Exchange Rate : 1 $ = 545 KMF (Market Exchange Rate September 2000).
Labour Force by Sector of Activity : *Agriculture* 77%, *Industry and Services* 23% (2000).
Nominal Gross Domestic Product GDP : 89 Million KMF (Source : IMF 1999).
Inflation Rate - Consumer Prices : 4% (1999).
Gross Domestic Product Per Capita : $ 725.-- purchasing power parity (1997).
Industries : Tourism, perfume distillation, textiles, furniture, jewelry, construction materials, soft drinks.
Agriculture Products : Vanilla, cloves, perfume essences, copra, coconuts, bananas, cassava (tapioca).
Population below the Poverty Line : NA%.
HDI (Human Development Index, UNDP figures 1999): within the 174 Countries selected in the Human Development Report of the UNDP the Comoros archipelago is ranked 139.
Total External Debt Outstanding and Disbursed: US $ 145 Million.
Major Trading Partners : Mainly France.
Major Export Products : vanilla, ylang-ylang, cloves, perfume oil, copra.

Major Import Products : rice and other foodstuffs, consumer goods, petroleum products, cement, transport equipment.
Year of Independence : 6 July 1975 from France.
Political System : Independent Republic.
Conventional Name : Federal Islamic Republic of the Comoros/Republique Federale Islamique des Comores.
Year of independence: 1975 from France.
Admitted in the United Nations in: 1975.
Member i.a. of: League of Arab States, Organization of the Islamic Conference (OIC), Common Market of East and Southern Africa (COMESA), ACCT, ACP, AfDB, AFESD, AL, CCC, ECA, FAO, FZ, G-77, IBRD, ICAO, IDA, IDB, IFAD, IFC, IFRCS (associate), ILO, IMF, InOC, Intelsat, IOC, ITU, NAM, OAU, OIC, OPCW, UN, UNCTAD, UNESCO, UNIDO, UPU, WHO, WMO.
Political system: Federal Islamic Republic / multiparty system.
President: Assoumani AZZALI (since 6 May 1999).
Head of government Prime Minister : Bianrifi TARMIDI (since 2 December 1999).
Minister of Economy, Trade, Industry, & Cottage Industry: Assoumani ABOUDOU.
Minister of Foreign Affairs & Cooperation: Souefou Mohamed EL AMINE.
Minister of Transport, Tourism, Posts, & Telecommunications: Sad Dhoiffir BOUNOU.

Some features :

- The Comoros became a member of the Arab League in 1993.
- In 1976 Mayotte, the fourth of the main islands in the archipelago, opted to remain under French sovereignty.
- Since independence in 1975, the Comoros experienced 18 coups d'etat or attempted coups d'etat.
- Three of these coup d'état were led by a French mercenary, Bob Denard.
- The most recent military coup abruptly removed from office a civilian government on 30th April 1999.
- The latest crisis started in August 1997 when the islands of Anjouan and Moheli declared their independence and self determination from the main island of Grand Comore.
- Peace talks held in Madagascar under the auspices of the Organization of African Unity (OAU) reached a deal in April 1999 according to which the three islands would have their own parliament and would become a Republic named "Union of Comoran islands". The Presidency would rotate between them every three years.
- Chronical instability have left the islands disadvantaged and unable to develop a flourishing touristic industry that would boost the Economy (only 27.000 tourists visited Comoros in 1998).

The Comoros are highly dependent on imported food which usually represents 40% of all imports.
France has remained by far the most important trading partner.

- The country is not self sufficient for food import.
- Governement is trying to curb population growth and to privatize, reconvert the economy from an agricultural self sufficient model into an industrial and diversified one.
- The regular financial debt is usually covered by France.
- The country's debt has been restructured by the International Monetary Fund (IMF), and the government has been forced to accept a "structural adjustment package". The original structural adjustment package covered the period of 1991 to 1993, but it was renewed in 1993. A further agreement with the IMF was reached in 1994. Since 1981 the currency has been the Comorian franc. The Comorian franc had a fixed exchange rate with the French franc of 50 to 1 until 1994, when the rate was changed to 75 Comorian francs to 1 French franc. In 1998, the Comorian franc exchanged at an average of 443 to the U.S. dollar.

GENERAL OVERVIEW

Located in a strategic position at the northern end of the Mozambique Channel, the Comoro Islands once played a major role in a thriving world economy of the western Indian Ocean.

The archipelago arose from the seabed of the western Indian Ocean as the result of volcanic activity. The four major islands: Ngazidja, Mwali, Nzwani, and Mayotte (Maore), are of varying age with distinct topograhical characteristics. Mayotte, the oldest of the islands, is highly eroded with slow, meandering streams. Ngazidja, the youngest of the islands, is closest to Africa, has a massive volcano, and marked by fresh lava flows. In October, 2000, the volcano showed signs of increased seismic activity.

The islands possess a variety of animal life with several species unique to the Comoros or rarely found elsewhere. The famous Coelacanth, a fish once thought to be extinct for millions of years, is found very much alive in Comorian waters. Livingstone's flying fox, a giant fruit bat with a wing span over four feet, is found nowhere else in the world. Several varieties of insects, including the butterfly pictured at left, and over a dozen species of birds are unique to the islands. Many of these species are now being threatened with extinction.

Communities on the islands are mentioned in ancient documents. Domoni, one of these communities, for example, was described as a major trading center in the fifteenth century with trade contacts in Africa and Asia. We know from archaeological evidence that it traded with places as far away as Japan. After the Portuguese appeared in the Indian Ocean and before the opening of the Suez Canal, many European and American vessels stopped in the islands for supplies.

Today, the Comoros are "Forgotten Islands" with the prospects and problems many small countries in the world are experiencing.

Comoros has had difficulty in achieving political stability, having endured 18 coups or attempted coups since receiving independence from France in 1975. Most recently, in August 1997, the islands of Anjouan and Moheli declared their independence from Comoros. An attempt in September 1997 by the government to reestablish control over the rebellious islands by force failed, and presently the Organization of African Unity is brokering negotiations to effect a reconciliation.

GEOGRAPHY

Area: 2,171 sq. km. (838 sq. mi.); slightly less than half the size of Delaware.
Major islands: Grande Comore (1,025 sq. km.), Anjouan (424 sq. km.), Mayotte (374 sq. km.), and Moheli (211 sq. km.).
Cities: Capital--Moroni (pop. 30,000). Mutsamudu (pop. 20,000).
Terrain: Rugged.
Climate: Tropical marine.

Location: Southern Africa, group of islands in the Mozambique Channel, about two-thirds of the way between northern Madagascar and northern Mozambique

Geographic coordinates: 12 10 S, 44 15 E

Map references: Africa

Area:
total: 2,170 sq km
land: 2,170 sq km
water: 0 sq km

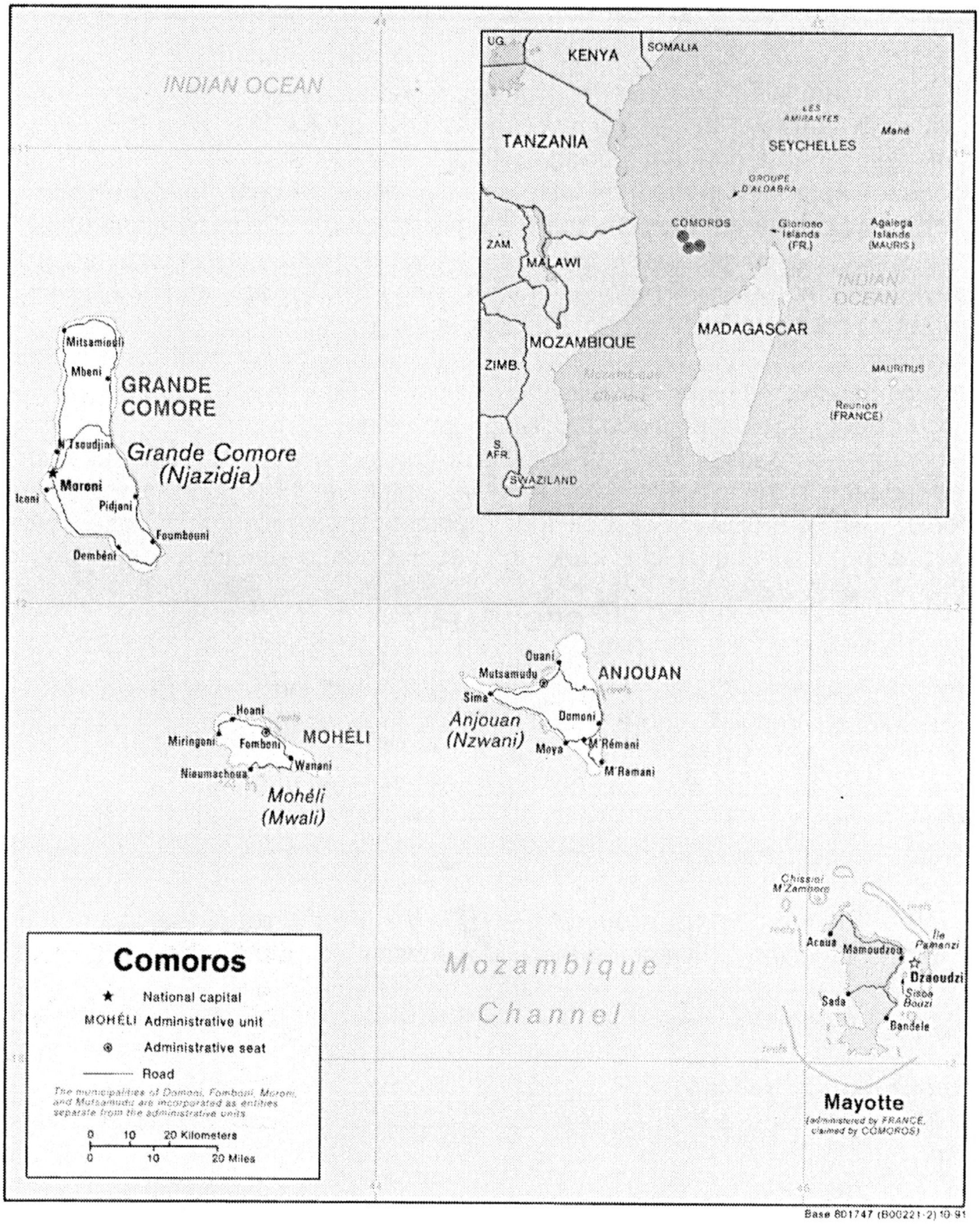
INDIAN OCEAN
U.G.
KENYA
SOMALIA
TANZANIA
SEYCHELLES
COMOROS
Glorioso Islands (FR.)
Agalega Islands (MAURIS.)
ZAM.
MALAWI
INDIAN OCEAN
MADAGASCAR
MOZAMBIQUE
ZIMB.
MAURITIUS
Reunion (FRANCE)
S. AFR.
SWAZILAND
Mitsamiouli
Mbeni
GRANDE COMORE
N'Tsoudjini
Grande Comore (Njazidja)
Moroni
Pidjani
Foumbouni
Dembéni
Ouani
Mutsamudu
ANJOUAN
Sima
Anjouan (Nzwani)
Domoni
Moya
M'Rémani
M'Ramani
Hoani
Miringoni
Fomboni
MOHÉLI
Wanani
Nioumachoua
Mohéli (Mwali)
Chissioi M'Zamboro
Acoua
Mamoudzou
Dzaoudzi
Pamanzi
Sada
Bandele
Mozambique Channel
Comoros
National capital
MOHÉLI Administrative unit
Administrative seat
Road
0 10 20 Kilometers
0 10 20 Miles
Mayotte
(administered by FRANCE, claimed by COMOROS)
Base 801747 (B00221-2) 10-91

Area—comparative: slightly more than 12 times the size of Washington, DC

Land boundaries: 0 km

Coastline: 340 km

Maritime claims:
exclusive economic zone: 200 nm
territorial sea: 12 nm

Climate: tropical marine; rainy season (November to May)

Terrain: volcanic islands, interiors vary from steep mountains to low hills

Elevation extremes:
lowest point: Indian Ocean 0 m
highest point: Le Kartala 2,360 m

Natural resources: NEGL

Land use:
arable land: 35%
permanent crops: 10%
permanent pastures: 7%
forests and woodland: 18%
other: 30% (1993 est.)

Irrigated land: NA sq km

Natural hazards: cyclones possible during rainy season (December to April); Le Kartala on Grand Comore is an active volcano

Environment—current issues: soil degradation and erosion results from crop cultivation on slopes without proper terracing; deforestation

Environment—international agreements:
party to: Biodiversity, Climate Change, Desertification, Endangered Species, Hazardous Wastes, Law of the Sea, Ozone Layer Protection
signed, but not ratified: none of the selected agreements

Geography—note: important location at northern end of Mozambique Channel

PEOPLE

Population: 562,723 (July 1999 est.)

Age structure:
0-14 years: 43% (male 120,397; female 119,945)
15-64 years: 54% (male 150,851; female 154,990)
65 years and over: 3% (male 7,878; female 8,662) (1999 est.)

Population growth rate: 3.11% (1999 est.)

Birth rate: 40.29 births/1,000 population (1999 est.)

Death rate: 9.23 deaths/1,000 population (1999 est.)

Net migration rate: 0 migrant(s)/1,000 population (1999 est.)

Sex ratio:
at birth: 1.03 male(s)/female
under 15 years: 1 male(s)/female
15-64 years: 0.97 male(s)/female
65 years and over: 0.91 male(s)/female
total population: 0.98 male(s)/female (1999 est.)

Infant mortality rate: 81.63 deaths/1,000 live births (1999 est.)

Life expectancy at birth:
total population: 60.85 years
male: 58.39 years
female: 63.38 years (1999 est.)

Total fertility rate: 5.43 children born/woman (1999 est.)

Nationality:
noun: Comoran(s)
adjective: Comoran

Ethnic groups: Antalote, Cafre, Makoa, Oimatsaha, Sakalava

Religions: Sunni Muslim 86%, Roman Catholic 14%

Languages: Arabic (official), French (official), Comoran (a blend of Swahili and Arabic)

Literacy:
definition: age 15 and over can read and write
total population: 57.3%
male: 64.2%
female: 50.4% (1995 est.)

GOVERNMENT

Country name:
conventional long form: Federal Islamic Republic of the Comoros
conventional short form: Comoros
local long form: Republique Federale Islamique des Comores
local short form: Comores

Data code: CN

Government type: independent republic

INDEPENDENCE

Unilateral declaration of independence 6 July 1975. France renounced sovereignty 3 Jan 1976 -- except in Mayotte.

Capital: Moroni

Administrative divisions: three islands; Grande Comore (Njazidja), Anjouan (Nzwani), and Moheli (Mwali)
note: there are also four municipalities named Domoni, Fomboni, Moroni, and Moutsamoudou

Independence: 6 July 1975 (from France)

National holiday: Independence Day, 6 July (1975)

Constitution: 20 October 1996

Legal system: French and Muslim law in a new consolidated code

Suffrage: 18 years of age; universal

Executive branch:
chief of state: Interim President TADJIDDINE Ben Said Massounde (since 6 November 1998); note—President Mohamed TAKI Abdulkarim died in office 6 November 1998 and was succeeded by Interim President MASSOUNDE
head of government: Prime Minister Abbas DJOUSSOUF (since 22 November 1998)
cabinet: Council of Ministers appointed by the president
elections: president elected by popular vote to a five-year term; election last held 16 March 1996 (next to be held NA); prime minister appointed by the president
election results: Mohamed TAKI Abdulkarim elected president; percent of vote—64%

note: the Comoran constitution stipulates that upon the death of the president, a new president is to be elected within 90 days; however, Interim President TADJIDDINE has stated that a new election cannot be held until Anjouan is reunited with the rest of the country

Legislative branch: bicameral legislature consists of the Senate (15 seats; members selected by regional councils for six-year terms) and a Federal Assembly or Assemblee Federale (43 seats; members elected by popular vote to serve four-year terms)
elections: Federal Assembly—last held 1 and 8 December 1996 (next to be held NA)
election results: Federal Assembly—percent of vote by party—NA; seats by party—RND 39, RND candidate running as independent 1, FNJ 3

Judicial branch: Supreme Court or Cour Supremes, two members are appointed by the president, two members are elected by the Federal Assembly, one by the Council of each island, and former presidents of the republic

Political parties and leaders: Rassemblement National pour le Development or RND, party of the government [leader NA]; Front National pour la Justice or FNJ, Islamic party in opposition [leader NA]
note: under a new constitution ratified in October 1996, a two-party system was established; former President Mohamed TAKI Abdulkarim called for all parties to dissolve and join him in creating the RND; the constitution stipulates that only parties that win six seats in the Federal Assembly (two from each island) are permitted to be in opposition, but if no party accomplishes that the second most successful party will be in opposition; in the elections of December 1996 the FNJ appeared to qualify as opposition

International organization participation: ACCT, ACP, AfDB, AFESD, AL, CCC, ECA, FAO, FZ, G-77, IBRD, ICAO, IDA, IDB, IFAD, IFC, IFRCS (associate), ILO, IMF, InOC, Intelsat (nonsignatory user), IOC, ITU, NAM, OAU, OIC, OPCW, UN, UNCTAD, UNESCO, UNIDO, UPU, WHO, WMO, WTrO (applicant)

Diplomatic representation in the US:
chief of mission: Ambassador-designate Ahmed DJABIR (ambassador to the US and Canada and permanent representative to the UN)
chancery: (temporary) care of the Permanent Mission of the Federal and Islamic Republic of the Comoros to the United Nations, 336 East 45th Street, 2nd Floor, New York, NY 10017
telephone: [1] (212) 349-2030

Diplomatic representation from the US: the US does not have an embassy in Comoros; the ambassador to Mauritius is accredited to Comoros

Flag description: green with a white crescent in the center of the field, its points facing downward; there are four white five-pointed stars placed in a line between the points of the crescent; the crescent, stars, and color green are traditional symbols of Islam; the four stars represent the four main islands of the archipelago—Mwali, Njazidja, Nzwani, and Mayotte (a territorial collectivity of France, but claimed by Comoros); the design, the most recent of several, is described in the constitution approved by referendum on 7 June 1992

ECONOMY

Economy—overview: One of the world's poorest countries, Comoros is made up of three islands that have inadequate transportation links, a young and rapidly increasing population, and few natural resources. The low educational level of the labor force contributes to a subsistence level of economic activity, high unemployment, and a heavy dependence on foreign grants and technical assistance. Agriculture, including fishing, hunting, and forestry, is the leading sector of the economy. It contributes 40% to GDP, employs 80% of the labor force, and provides most of the exports. The country is not self-sufficient in food production; rice, the main staple, accounts for the bulk of imports. The government is struggling to upgrade education and technical training, to privatize commercial and industrial enterprises, to improve health services, to diversify exports, to promote tourism, and to reduce the high population growth rate. Continued foreign support is essential if the goal of 4% annual GDP growth is to be maintained.

GDP: purchasing power parity—$400 million (1997 est.)

GDP—real growth rate: 3.5% (1997 est.)

GDP—per capita: purchasing power parity—$700 (1997 est.)

GDP—composition by sector:
agriculture: 40%
industry: 14%
services: 46% (1996 est.)

Population below poverty line: NA%

Household income or consumption by percentage share:
lowest 10%: NA%
highest 10%: NA%

Inflation rate (consumer prices): 2.5% (1997)

Labor force: 144,500 (1996 est.)

Labor force—by occupation: agriculture 80%, government 3%

Unemployment rate: 20% (1996 est.)

Budget:
revenues: $48 million
expenditures: $53 million, including capital expenditures of $NA (1997)

Industries: tourism, perfume distillation, textiles, furniture, jewelry, construction materials, soft drinks

Industrial production growth rate: NA%

Electricity—production: 15 million kWh (1996)

Electricity—production by source:
fossil fuel: 86.67%
hydro: 13.33%
nuclear: 0%
other: 0% (1996)

Electricity—consumption: 15 million kWh (1996)

Electricity—exports: 0 kWh (1996)

Electricity—imports: 0 kWh (1996)

Agriculture—products: vanilla, cloves, perfume essences, copra, coconuts, bananas, cassava (tapioca)

Exports: $11.4 million (f.o.b., 1996 est.)

Exports—commodities: vanilla, ylang-ylang, cloves, perfume oil, copra

Exports—partners: France 43%, US 43%, Germany 7% (1996)

Imports: $70 million (f.o.b., 1996 est.)

Imports—commodities: rice and other foodstuffs, consumer goods; petroleum products, cement, transport equipment

Imports—partners: France 59%, South Africa 15%, Kenya 6% (1996)

Debt—external: $219 million (1996 est.)

Economic aid—recipient: $43.3 million (1995)

Currency: 1 Comoran franc (CF) = 100 centimes

Exchange rates: Comoran francs (CF) per US$1—420.01 (December 1998), 442.46 (1998), 437.75 (1997), 383.66 (1996), 374.36 (1995), 416.40 (1994)

Fiscal year: calendar year

COMMUNICATIONS

Telephones: 8,000

Telephone system: sparse system of microwave radio relay and HF radiotelephone communication stations
domestic: HF radiotelephone communications and microwave radio relay
international: HF radiotelephone communications to Madagascar and Reunion

Radio broadcast stations: AM 2, FM 1, shortwave 0

Radios: 81,000 (1994)

Television broadcast stations: 0 (1998)

Televisions: 200 (1994

TRANSPORTATION

Railways: 0 km

Highways:
total: 880 km
paved: 673 km
unpaved: 207 km (1996 est.)

Ports and harbors: Fomboni, Moroni, Moutsamoudou

Merchant marine: none

Airports: 4 (1998 est.)

Airports—with paved runways:
total: 4
2,438 to 3,047 m: 1
914 to 1,523 m: 3 (1998 est.)

MILITARY

Military branches: Comoran Security Force

Military manpower—availability:
males age 15-49: 132,969 (1999 est.)

Military manpower—fit for military service:
males age 15-49: 79,224 (1999 est.)

Military expenditures—dollar figure: $3 million (1994 est.)

Military expenditures—percent of GDP: NA%

TRANSNATIONAL ISSUES

Disputes—international: claims French-administered Mayotte; the islands of Anjouan (Nzwani) and Moheli (Mwali) have moved to secede from Comoros.

NARCOTICS

Comoros is neither a major producer, nor a significant consumer of narcotics. Nevertheless, Comoros officials expressed concern in 1999 over a perceived increase in domestic consumption of cannabis and Mandrax. Comoros is a transshipment route to South Africa and Europe for cannabis and cocaine from Madagascar and heroin from Southwest Asia. There is no evidence of transshipment to the U.S. The amount of trafficking is unknown, but political instability, exacerbated by a military coup in April, the ongoing secession of Anjouan Island, and weak law enforcement make this three-island nation a vulnerable target for drug traffickers. The Comoran police have a small anti-narcotics unit, which has received assistance and training in the past from France. Comoros is not a party to any of the UN drug conventions. Money laundering is not criminalized, but given the small size of the financial sector (one bank), it is not thought to be a major problem.

IMPORTANT INFORMATION FOR UNDERSTANDING COMOROS

GEOGRAPHY & NATURE

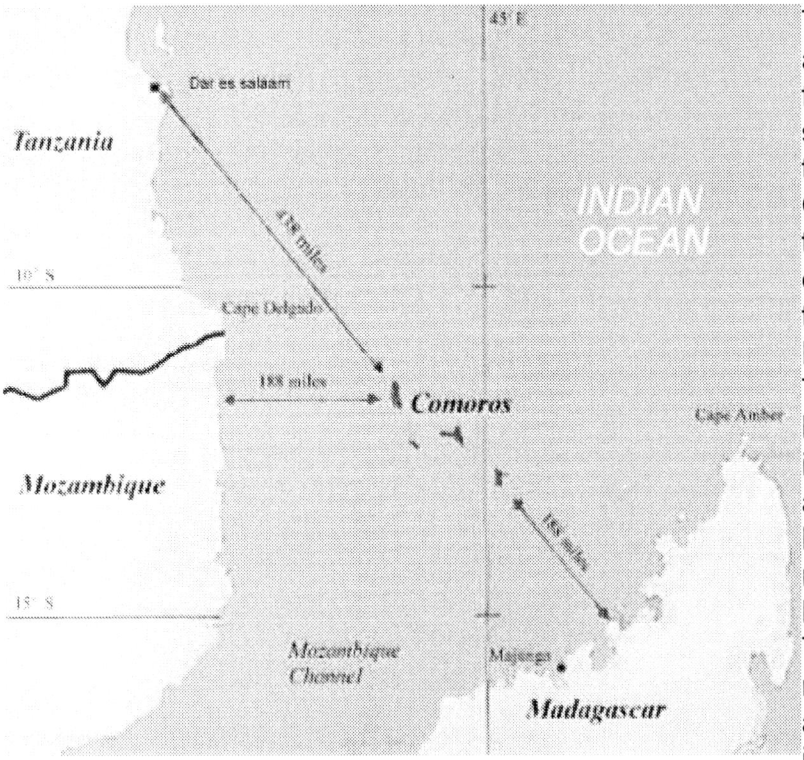

The Comoro Islands are an archipelago of four islands and several islets located in the western Indian Ocean about ten to twelve degrees south of the Equator and less than 200 miles off the East African coast. They lie approximately halfway between the island of Madagascar and northern Mozambique at the northern end of the Mozambique Channel. The archipelago is the result of volcanic action along a fissure in the seabed running west-northwest to east-southeast. The total area of the four islands is 785 square miles (2,034 square kilometers).

The four major islands are Ngazidja, Mwali, Nzwani, and Mayotte (Maore). Ngazidja is the largest and the youngest island in the archipelago. It is the most westerly of the islands, lying 188 miles from Mozambique. Ngazidja has an active volcano that rises to a height of 7,746 feet (2,361 meters) above sea level.

Mwali, 28 miles south-southeast of Ngazidja, is the smallest of the islands with a central mountain range that rises 2,556 feet (790 meters) above sea level. Nzwani lies about twenty-five miles easterly of Mwali, has a central peak that rises 5,072 feet (1,575 meters) above sea level. It also has several swift running streams that cascade down to long, sandy beaches. Forty-four miles to the southeast of Nzwani is Mayotte (Maore), the oldest of the islands. It is almost surrounded by a barrier reef and is fairly flat with slow meandering streams and mangrove swamps.

COMOROS ISLANDS

NGAZIDJA

Referred to by the French as Grande Comore, Ngazidja is the site of Moroni, the capital city of the Republic, and is the largest of the islands in the Comoro archipelago. It has an area of 442 square miles (1,146 square kilometers). The northern two-thirds of the island are dominated by a rocky plain known as La Grille. The southern third of the island is dominated by an active volcano, Karthala, which stands over 7700 feet (2361 meters) high. Karthala's crater is nearly a mile in diameter, making it the largest active crater in the world. Since 1857 there have been over a dozen eruptions with lava flows; the most extensive was that of 1918. The most recent serious eruption was in 1977.

The island's over 200,000 inhabitants are predominantly descended from Arab and African ancestors. Agriculture on the island is generally limited to areas lower than 2,000 feet in altitude. Above this altitude is the remnants of a dense tropical forest (in the south) and an area of grassy plain (in the center and north).

European sailing ships stopped for provisions at Ngazidja as early as 1570 when the island was ruled by 12 sultans. Although each was independent of the others, they generally recognized a principal sultan, whose rights and responsibilities were primarily conciliatory in inter-regional disputes, and accorded him or her the title of Sultan Thibe. There was frequent conflict over the right to use this title, especially after the Europeans appeared on the scene, as these latter generally assumed that the title indicated sovereignty over the entire island.

The best documented of the conflicts between sultans is the long and complicated struggle between the rulers of the towns of Bambao and Itsandra during the nineteenth century. This eventually led to the establishment of a French protectorate over the island and the ceding of Ngazidja to France.

The names of the islands and of the capital city in the Comoros, Moroni, has raised interest among members of The Church of Jesus Christ of Latter-day Saints. In the Book of Mormon there is reference to the angel Moroni, son of Mormon, and to the hill, Cumorah. They play central roles in the Book of Mormon and there is some question about the possible relationship between these names in the Book of Mormon and those in the Indian Ocean.

The name of the town in the Comoros and the name of the islands themselves predate Joseph Smith and the Book of Mormon. 'Moroni' has a meaning in the local language, viz. "at the place of fire." It is constructed of the root 'moro,' which means "fire" or "heat" and the locative '-ni,' which means "at the place of" or "in." This is a logical name constructed from the morphemes of the language reflecting the fact that the community is located at the base of an immense, active volcano. Likewise, the name 'Comoro' has a meaning. It is composed of an old Swahili locative 'ko-' and the word 'moro.' It's meaning is also "the place of fire."

Whether the relationship between the terms in the Book of Mormon and the names in the islands is coincidental or there is some historical relationship between the two is uncertain at present. It is possible that Joseph Smith had heard of Moroni and the Comoro Islands since numbers of American whaling ships had visited the islands in the early part of the nineteenth century and their names were probably known throughout the northeastern United States at the time Smith had his vision.

MWALI

Mwali is the smallest of the islands in the Comoro archipelago. Referred to by the French as Moheli, it has an area of 81 square miles (211 square kilometers). The island has rich soil, magnificent forests and fine pasture lands. The valleys and slopes of the island are covered with coconut trees, coffee trees, cacao and ylang-ylang trees, and a wide variety of crops. Three small islets on the south side of the island near the harbor of Nioumachoua provide a natural sheltering place for sailing ships during inclement weather. In the past, one of these islands--Shisiwa Unefu--was used as a leper colony. With a population of approximately 30,000, Mwali is the least densely populated (370 inhabitants per square mile) of the four islands. In September 1997, a group of secessionists declared the island independent of the Comoro Republic but this claim has been rejected by the Republic.

NZWANI

Referred to by the French as Anjouan and by early English visitors as Johanna, Nzwani has been called the "pearl" of the Indian Ocean. With forested hillsides and rivers tumbling to the sea it is a beautiful island. It is essentially a triangle with approximately 50 kilometers on each side and a total area of 164 square miles (424 square kilometers).

With a population of more than 210,000 people it is the most densely populated island in the Comoro archipelago (over 1,280 persons per square mile). Most live in small communities found throughout the island. The major towns are Mutsamudu on the western side of the island and Domoni on the eastern shore. Mutsamudu is the present capital and site of the seaport for the island. Domoni is an ancient capital and seaport. Other ancient communities are Sima and Ouani.

Its volcanic peak, Mount Ntingi, 1,575 meters high, is covered with vegetation, including large ferns, tropical mahoganies, and wild orchids, in contrast with the three points of the triangle, which are less luxuriant due to centuries of cultivation. Nzwani is the premiere producer of essential oils including ylang-ylang, jasmine, cassis, basilic, palmarosa, and orange flower.

Arabic-style sultanates developed in Nzwani as early as the sixteenth century with different areas of the island first ruled by chiefs known as Fani. Later, the chiefs were involved in conflicts and appealed to Europeans to intercede on their behalf. Eventually, in 1886, the island became a French protectorate and was formally annexed by France to its possessions in 1909.

In 1975, Nzwani was one of the three islands to make up the newly formed independent republic of the Comoro Islands. The first president of the independent country, Ahmed Abdallah, was from Nzwani and his shrine is in his hometown of Domoni, the ancient walled community on the east coast of the island. The third president, Said Mohamed Djohar, was also a resident of Domoni and a schoolmate of Ahmed Abdallah. Presently, there is an active secessionist movement on the island that declared, in 1997, the Island's independence from the Comoro Republic and hopes to reattach the island to France, like Mayotte.

MAYOTTE

Mayotte, also known by its Comorian name, Maore (or Mahore), is closest to the island of Madagascar and is geologically the oldest of the Comoro Islands. It is the most eroded and has slow moving, muddy streams. The island, along with several satellite islets, is surounded by a coral reef which is about a mile wide. Only two passages permit the entrance of large ships, thus providing a secure harbor. With an overall size of 144 square miles (374 square kilometers), it has a population of more than 35,000 inhabitants. Largely agricultural, the island produces more than 3,000 hectares (8,000 acres) of sugar cane. Vanilla, ylang-ylang, cloves, copra, and cinnamon are also produced. In recent years, Mayotte has produced the majority of the archipelago's cinnamon. A particular variety of fragrant dry rice is also grown and cattle production is an important part of its economy.

Mayotte's towns are quite different from those of the other islands. There are few of the walled cities with narrow, winding streets between multistoried stone houses found commonly on the other islands. Instead, towns are primarily comprised of wattle-and-daub or tressed coconut-frond huts ranged along wide, open streets. The architecture is more reminiscent of Madagascar than the other Comoro islands, testimony to the historical relationships between the island and Madagascar.

The Portuguese were the first Europeans to see Mayotte, having sailed to the island in the early years of the sixteenth century. Soon after, in 1595, an Englishman landed on the island, but it was the French who became the dominant European influence. Mayotte was the first of the Comoro islands to become a protectorate of France. In 1841 the Sakalava king Andriantsouli, who had declared himself sultan of Mayotte, ceded it to the French in exchange for an annual rent of 5,000 francs and the French education of his two sons. It is an administrative territory of France today.

TOPOGRAPHY

The islands are of volcanic origin and are mountainous.

The highest point on the islands is the summit of Kartala, an active volcano on Njazidja (Grand Comore) Island, which is 2361m (7746 ft) above sea level.

CLIMATE

The Comoros climate is tropical with a monsoom season from November to April. The range of annual rainfall is from 109 to 551 cm (43 to 217 in); there are frequent cyclones.

Located a little more than 10 degrees below the equator in the western Indian Ocean the islands have a maritime tropical climate.

In the wet season from October to April, the predominant northerly winds of the Indian Ocean bring moist, warm air to the region. Heaviest rainfall occurs during the period from December to April and amounts can reach as high as 15 inches (390 mm) in a month. The mean temperature during the wet season is in the high seventies with the hottest month, March, averaging temperatures in the middle eighties (fahrenheit).

From May to September southerly winds dominate the region. These are cooler and drier and temperatures in the islands average around 66 degrees fahrenheit (19 degrees celsius).

Rainfall and temperature vary from island to island during any month and even vary on an island due to the topography. The central, higher areas of an island are often cooler and more moist than the coastal regions. This variation results in microecologies on the islands with distinct flora and fauna.

The Comoros archipelago consists of four main islands aligned along a northwest-southeast axis at the north end of the Mozambique Channel, between Mozambique and the island of Madagascar. Still widely known by their French names, the islands officially have been called by their Swahili names by the Comoran government. They are Njazidja (Grande Comore), Mwali (Mohéli), Nzwani (Anjouan), and Mahoré (Mayotte). The islands' distance from each other-Njazidja is some 200 kilometers from Mahoré, forty kilometers from Mwali, and eighty kilometers from Nzwani-along with a lack of good harbor facilities, make transportation and communication difficult. The islands have a total land area of 2,236 square kilometers (including Mahoré), and claim territorial waters of 320 kilometers.

Njazidja is the largest island, sixty-seven kilometers long and twenty-seven kilometers wide, with a total area of 1,146 square kilometers. The most recently formed of the four islands in the archipelago, it is also of volcanic origin. Two volcanoes form the island's most prominent topographic features: La Grille in the north, with an elevation of 1,000 meters, is extinct and largely eroded; Kartala in the south, rising to a height of 2,361 meters, last erupted in 1977. A plateau averaging 600 to 700 meters high connects the two mountains. Because Njazidja is geologically a relatively new island, its soil is thin and rocky and cannot hold water. As a result, water from the island's heavy rainfall must be stored in catchment tanks. There are no coral reefs along the coast, and the island lacks a good harbor for ships. One of the largest remnants of Comoros' once-extensive rain forests is on the slopes of Kartala. The national capital has been at Moroni since 1962.

Nzwani, triangular shaped and forty kilometers from apex to base, has an area of 424 square kilometers. Three mountain chains-Sima, Nioumakele, and Jimilime-emanate from a central peak, Mtingui (1,575 meters), giving the island its distinctive shape. Older than Njazidja, Nzwani has deeper soil cover, but overcultivation has caused serious erosion. A coral reef lies close to shore; the island's capital of Mutsamudu is also its main port.

Mwali is thirty kilometers long and twelve kilometers wide, with an area of 290 square kilometers. It is the smallest of the four islands and has a central mountain chain reaching 860 meters at its highest. Like Njazidja, it retains stands of rain forest. Mwali's capital is Fomboni.

Mahoré, geologically the oldest of the four islands, is thirty-nine kilometers long and twenty-two kilometers wide, totaling 375 square kilometers, and its highest points are between 500 and 600 meters above sea level. Because of greater weathering of the volcanic rock, the soil is relatively rich in some areas. A well-developed coral reef that encircles much of the island ensures protection for ships and a habitat for fish. Dzaoudzi, capital of Comoros until 1962 and now Mahoré's administrative center, is situated on a rocky outcropping off the east shore of the main island. Dzaoudzi is linked by a causeway to le Pamanzi, which at ten kilometers in area is the largest of several islets adjacent to Mahoré. Islets are also scattered in the coastal waters of Njazidja, Nzwani, and Mwali.

Comoran waters are the habitat of the coelacanth, a rare fish with limblike fins and a cartilaginous skeleton, the fossil remains of which date as far back as 400 million years and which was once thought to have become extinct about 70 million years ago. A live specimen was caught in 1938 off southern Africa; other coelacanths have since been found in the vicinity of the Comoro Islands.

Several mammals are unique to the islands themselves. The macao, a lemur found only on Mahoré, is protected by French law and by local tradition. Another, Livingstone's fruit bat, although plentiful when discovered by explorer David Livingstone in 1863, has been reduced to a population of about 120, entirely on Nzwani. The world's largest bat, the jet-black Livingstone fruit bat has a wingspan of nearly two meters. A British preservation group sent an expedition to Comoros in 1992 to bring some of the bats to Britain to establish a breeding population. Humboldt's flycatcher is perhaps the best known of the birds native to Comoros. .

Partly in response to international pressures, Comorans in the 1990s have become more concerned about the environment. Steps are being taken not only to preserve the rare fauna, but also to counteract degradation of the environment, especially on densely populated Nzwani. Specifically, to minimize the cutting down of trees for fuel, kerosene is being subsidized, and efforts are being made to replace the loss of the forest cover caused by ylang-ylang distillation for perfume. The Community Development Support Fund, sponsored by the International Development Association (IDA -a World Bank affiliate) and the Comoran government, is working to improve water supply on the islands as well.

The climate is marine tropical, with two seasons: hot and humid from November to April, the result of the northeastern monsoon, and a cooler, drier season the rest of the year. Average monthly temperatures range from 23° C to 28° C along the coasts. Although the average annual precipitation is 2,000 millimeters, water is a scarce commodity in many parts of Comoros. Mwali and Mahoré possess streams and other natural sources of water, but Njazidja and Nzwani, whose mountainous landscapes retain water poorly, are almost devoid of naturally occurring running water. Cyclones, occurring during the hot and wet season, can cause extensive damage, especially in coastal areas. On the average, at least twice each decade houses, farms, and harbor facilities are devastated by these great storms.

FLORA & FAUNA

Plant and animal life on the islands are very similar to that of Madagascar.

POPULATION

The most recent official census by the Comoran government, conducted in 1999, put the islands' population, exclusive of Mahoré, at 468,313. Official counts put the population of Mahoré at 94,410 in 1999.

Average population density in Comoros was 183 persons per square kilometer in 1980. This figure concealed a great disparity between the republic's most crowded island, Nzwani, which had a density of 470 persons per square kilometer in 1991; Njazidja, which had a density of 250 persons per square kilometer in 1991; and Mwali, where the 1991 population density figure was 120 persons per square kilometer. Overall population density increased to about 285 persons per square kilometer by 1997. Mahoré's population density went from 179 persons per square kilometer in 1985 to 256 per square kilometer in 1997.

By comparison, estimates of the population density per square kilometer of the Indian Ocean's other island microstates ranged from 241 (Seychelles) to 690 (Maldives) in 1996. Given the rugged terrain of Njazidja and Nzwani, and the dedication of extensive tracts to agriculture on all three islands, population pressures on Comoros are becoming increasingly critical. A similar situation obtains on Mahoré.

The age structure of the population of Comoros is similar to that of many developing countries, in that the republic has a very large proportion of young people. In 1989, 46.4 percent of the population was under fifteen years of age, an above-average proportion even for sub-Saharan Africa. The population's rate of growth was a relatively high 3.11 percent per annum in the mid-1990s , up substantially from 3.4 percent in the mid-1980s and 3.0 percent in the mid-1970s.

In 1983 the Abdallah regime borrowed US$2.85 million from the IDA to devise a national family planning program. However, Islamic reservations about contraception made forthright advocacy and implementation of birth control programs politically hazardous, and consequently little was done in the way of public policy.

The Comoran population has become increasingly urbanized in recent years. In 1996 the percentage of Comorans residing in cities and towns of more than 5,000 persons was about 32 percent, up from 25 percent in 1985 and 23 percent in 1980. Comoros' largest cities were the capital, Moroni, with about 35,000 people, and the port city of Mutsamudu, on the island of Nzwani, with about 26,000 people. Mahoré's capital, Dzaoudzi, had a population of 5,865 according to the latest census; the island's largest town, Mamoudzou, had 12,026 people.

Migration among the various islands is relatively small. Natives of Njazidja often settle in less crowded Mwali, and before independence people from Nzwani commonly moved to Mahoré. In 1977 Mahoré expelled peasants from Njazidja and Nzwani who had recently settled in large numbers on the island. Some were allowed to reenter starting in 1981 but solely as migrant labor.

The number of Comorans living abroad has been estimated at between 80,000 and 100,000; most of them lived in Tanzania, Madagascar, and other parts of

East Africa. The number of Comorans residing in Madagascar was drastically reduced after anti-Comoran rioting in December 1976 in Mahajanga, in which at least 1,400 Comorans were killed. As many as 17,000 Comorans left Madagascar to seek refuge in their native land in 1977 alone. About 40,000 Comorans live in France; many of them had gone there for a university education and never returned. Small numbers of Indians, Malagasy, South Africans, and Europeans live on the islands and play an important role in the economy.

The total population of the Comoro Islands is estimated to be over 600,000 people today. Over 27% live in urban areas. A 1980 estimate of the average density was 182.5 persons per square kilometer, varying between 65.5 persons per square kilometer in Mwali and 349.1 persons per square kilometer in Nzwani. Today the densities are much higher.

In recent decades the population was increased by the forced evacuation of Comorians from Madagascar and Zanzibar. These peoples resettled in the Comoros adding to an already difficult situation. Earlier, changes in politics in the area had reduced the opportunities for Comorian men to go abroad; one means that had effectively eased population pressures. There still are a number of Comorians living abroad. Comorians can be found living in many parts of the world but most of the emigrants are in Europe or in Kenya and Zanzibar along the East African coast. There are an estimated 60,000 Comorians or people of Comorian descent living in France today.

The present population increase is an estimated 3.5% per year with an annual birth rate of 47 births per 1,000 and an annual death rate of 12 deaths per 1,000 population. The most recent estimate of the total fertility rate is 6.8 children born per woman. Life expectancy at birth is 54 years for males and 59 years for females.

The inhabitants are a blend of various peoples of the Indian Ocean littoral. African, Malagasy, and Arabic features are clearly evident. Maritime commerce before entry of Europeans into the Indian Ocean brought Comorians into contact with peoples from southern Africa to southeast Asia. Since the end of the fifteenth century European influence has also impacted upon Comorian life.

The dominant religion in the islands is Islam. Outside of Mayotte, where there are a number of Catholics, islanders are predominantly Sunni Muslims conforming to the Shafii rite.

SOCIETY

A number of ethnically distinguishable groups are found: the Arabs, descendants of Shirazi settlers, who arrived in significant numbers in the fifteenth century; the Cafres, an African group that settled on the islands before the coming of the

Shirazi; a second African group, the Makoa, descendants of slaves brought by the Arabs from the East African coast; and three groups of Malayo-Indonesian peoples-the Oimatsaha, the Antalotes, and the Sakalava, the latter having settled largely on Mahoré. Intermarriage has tended to blur the distinctions among these groups, however. Creoles, descendants of French settlers who intermarried with the indigenous peoples, form a tiny but politically influential group on Mahoré, numbering no more than about 100 on that island. They are predominantly Roman Catholic and mainly cultivate small plantations. In addition, a small group of people descended in part from the Portuguese sailors who landed on the Comoro Islands at the beginning of the sixteenth century are reportedly living around the town of Tsangadjou on the east coast of Njazidja.

Shirazi Arab royal clans dominated the islands socially, culturally, and politically from the fifteenth century until the French occupation. Eleven such clans lived on Njazidja, where their power was strongest, and their leaders, the sultans or sharifs, who claimed to be descendants of the Prophet Muhammad, were in a continual state of war until the French occupation. Two similar clans were located on Nzwani, and these clans maintained vassals on Mahoré and Mwali after the Sakalava wiped out the local nobles in the late eighteenth and early nineteenth centuries . Although the clan system was weakened by the economic and social dislocations of the colonial era, the descendants of clan nobles continue to form a major portion of the educated and propertied classes. The pre-independence rivalry of Said Mohamed Cheikh and Prince Said Ibrahim, leaders, respectively, of the conservative Parti Vert and the Parti Blanc, was interpreted by some as a revival of old clan antagonisms. Yet many descendants of nobles live in poverty and apparently have less influence socially and politically on Nzwani than on Njazidja.

The present-day elite, although composed in part of those of noble ancestry who took advantage of the opportunities of the cash crop economy established by the French, is mainly defined in terms of wealth rather than caste or descent. This focus on wealth is not unusual, considering that the original Shirazi settlers themselves were traders and that the precolonial sultans were actively involved in commerce. Conspicuous consumption continues to mark the lifestyle of the elite.

Especially well regarded are those individuals who hold the *grand mariage*, often after a lifetime of scrimping and saving. This wedding ceremony, which can cost as much as the equivalent of US$20,000 to US$30,000, involves an exchange of expensive gifts between the couple's families and feasts for an entire village. Although the gift giving and dancing that accompany the *grand mariage* have helped perpetuate indigenous arts in silversmithing, goldsmithing, folk song, and folk dance, the waste involved has disastrous consequences for an economy already short on domestic resources. A ban or curb on the *grand mariage* was on the agenda of many reformers in the period preceding the radical regime of Ali

Soilih, who himself had taken the almost unheard-of step of declining to participate in the ritual. However, the efforts of the Soilih government to restrict the custom aroused great resentment, and it was restored to its preeminent place in Comoran society almost immediately after Soilih was deposed in 1978. Although its expense limits the number of families that can provide their sons and daughters a *grand mariage*, the ritual is still used as a means of distinguishing Comoran society's future leaders. Only by participating in the ceremony is a Comoran man entitled to participate in his village's assembly of notables and to wear the *mharuma*, a sash that entitles him to enter the mosque by a special door. Few, if any, candidates win election to the National Assembly without a *grand mariage* in their pasts. For these reasons in particular, critics of traditional Comoran society condemn the *grand mariage* as a means of excluding people of modest resources from participating in the islands' political life.

Those who can afford the pilgrimage to Mecca are also accorded prestige. The imams who lead prayers in mosques form a distinct elite group.

Despite the weakening of the position of the Shirazi elite, one observer reports that in many subtle ways old distinctions persist. The descendants of slaves, formally emancipated in 1904, are mostly sharecroppers or squatters, working the land that belonged to their ancestors' former owners, although some have gone abroad as migrant laborers (a greatly restricted option since Madagascar's expulsion of thousands of Comorans in the late 1970s). Men of "freeborn" families choose "freeborn" wives, holding, if possible, a *grand mariage*; but if they take second wives, these women often are of slave ancestry.

LANGUAGE

The official languages of The Federal Islamic Republic of the Comoro Islands are French and Arabic. French is the language of government while Arabic is the language of Islam, the major religion on the Islands.

In daily life, most people speak one or more varieties of Comorian, the language group indigenous to the Islands. It is closely related to the Swahili of the East African coast. Comorian is typical of a Bantu language with a large number of noun classes and an elaborate set of verb tenses and aspects. For centuries, people have used Arabic script to write Comorian and there is an attempt presently to normalize an orthography for writing the varieties of the language in Roman script.

The rich vocabulary of Comorian has been enhanced by the borrowing of words from many other languages. Since Comorians have been involved in maritime trade for a thousand years or more, they have come into contact with a number of different peoples and their language reflects this contact. Words of Indian,

Persian, Arabic, Portuguese, English, and French origin have been added to those of African ancestry.

There are four varieties of Comorian spoken in the Islands: Shingazidja, Shimwali, Shinzwani, and Shimaore, each one named for the primary island on which it is spoken.

Comorian*(COMORES SWAHILI, KOMORO, COMORO)* 493,220 in Comoros Islands together with Shingazidja Comorian (1995); 92,806 in Mayotte (1995); 17,000 in Réunion (1995); 25,000 in Madagascar (1995); 628,000 in all countries. Islands of Mohéli and Anjouan. Also in Madagascar. Niger-Congo, Atlantic-Congo, Volta-Congo, Benue-Congo, Bantoid, Southern, Narrow Bantu, Central, Swahili. Dialects: SHINDZWANI (ANJOUAN), SHIMAORE (MAYOTTE). 25% literate. Second languages are Swahili, French, Arabic. Vanilla, perfume production. Muslim, Christian.

Comorian, Shingazidja*(GRANDE COMORE)* Grande Comore Island. Niger-Congo, Atlantic-Congo, Volta-Congo, Benue-Congo, Bantoid, Southern, Narrow Bantu, Swahili. Dialect: SHIMWALI (MOHELI). Nationalism affects language attitudes. Muslim.

French 1,700 in Comoros Islands (1995); Indo-European, Italic, Romance, Italo-Western, Western, Gallo-Romance. Language of all formal education except Koranic. National language.

Malagasy 700 in Comoros Islands (1995); 13,939,000 in all countries. Primarily in Madagascar. Also in Mayotte and Reunion. Austronesian, Malayo-Polynesian, Western Malayo-Polynesian, Borneo, Barito, East, Malagasy. Dialect: SAKALAVA. It is spoken by a substantial number of residents of Madagascar origin. Most are bilingual in Comorian. Traditional religion, Christian, Muslim.

RELIGION, CULTURE AND EDUCATION

Islam and its institutions help to integrate Comoran society and provide an identification with a world beyond the islands' shores. As Sunni Muslims, the people follow religious observances conscientiously and strictly adhere to religious orthodoxy. During the period of colonization, the French did not attempt to supplant Islamic customs and practices and were careful to respect the precedents of Islamic law as interpreted by the Shafii school (one of the four major legal schools in Sunni Islam, named after Muhammad ibn Idris ash Shafii, it stresses reasoning by analogy). Hundreds of mosques dot the islands.

Practically all children attend Quranic school for two or three years, starting around age five; there they learn the rudiments of the Islamic faith and some classical Arabic. When rural children attend these schools, they sometimes move away from home and help the teacher work his land.

France established a system of primary and secondary schools based on the French model, which remains largely in place. Comoran law requires all children to complete eight years of schooling between the ages of seven and fifteen. The system provides six years of primary education for students ages six to twelve, followed by seven years of secondary school. In recent years, enrollment has expanded greatly, particularly at the primary level. About 21,350 pupils, or roughly 75 percent of primary-school-age children were enrolled in 1997, up from about 46 percent in the late 1970s. About 17 percent of the secondary school-age population was enrolled, up from an estimated 7 percent fifteen to twenty years earlier. Teacher-student ratios also improved, from 47:1 to 36:1 in the primary schools and from 26:1 to 25:1 in secondary schools. The increased attendance was all the more significant given the population's high percentage of school-age children. Improvement in educational facilities was funded in 1997 by loans from the Organization of the Petroleum Exporting Countries (OPEC) and the African Development Bank. Despite the spread of education, adult literacy in 1997 has been estimated at no better than 50 percent.

Comoros has no university but post-secondary education, which in 1997 involved 443 students, is available in the form of teacher training, agricultural education training, health sciences, and business. Those desiring higher education must study abroad; a "brain drain" has resulted because few university graduates are willing to return to the islands. Teacher training and other specialized courses are available at the M'Vouni School for Higher Education, in operation since 1981 at a site near Moroni. Few Comoran teachers study overseas, but the republic often cannot give its teachers all the training they need. Some international aid has been provided, however, to further teacher training in the islands themselves. For example, in 1987 the IDA extended credits worth US$7.9 million to train 3,000 primary and 350 secondary school teachers. In 1986 the government began opening technology training centers offering a three-year diploma program at the upper secondary level. The Ministry of National Education and Professional Training is responsible for education policy.

As elsewhere in Comoran society, political instability has taken a toll on the education system. Routinely announced reductions in force among the civil service, often made in response to international pressure for fiscal reform, sometimes result in teacher strikes. When civil service cutbacks result in canceled classes or examinations, students have at times taken to the streets in protest. Students have also protested, even violently, against government underfunding or general mismanagement of the schools-the World Bank stated in 1996 that the quality of education resulted in high rates of repetition and dropouts such that the average student needed fourteen years to complete the six-year primary cycle.

MUSIC

Located at the northern end of the Mozambique channel, and at the eastern edge of the Bantu linguistic area, the Comoros are at a unique cultural and musical crossroads. Involved in the western Indian Ocean trade for over a thousand years, the islands have absorbed cultural and musical influences from East Africa, the Middle East, Madagascar, and southern India. As a result there is a remarkably wide range of musical styles in the Comoros: solo and choral, through composed and stanzaic, improvised and rehearsed, accompanied and acapella.

Contemporary Artists in the Islands and in Europe have been utilizing traditional sounds and themes and putting them in a modern idiom to produce some very interesting music.

Traditional instruments include gongs, drums, tambourines, rattles, oboes, zithers, and five-stringed lutes. The musical example below is a zither-and-rattle selection typical of social events such as womens' wedding dances. It is performed by Shirontro, a well-known singer and instrumentalist from Nzwani.

Comores: Musiques traditionnelles de l'ile d'Anjouan, a CD from INEDIT, Paris, (1) 45 44 72 30.

LANGUAGE

The official languages of The Federal Islamic Republic of the Comoro Islands are French and Arabic. French is the language of government while Arabic is the language of Islam, the major religion in the Republic. French is used as the official language on the island of Mayotte.

In daily life, most people speak one or more varieties of Comoria group indigenous to the Islands. It is closely related to the Swahili African coast. Comorian is typical of a Bantu language with a large n noun classes and an elaborate set of verb tenses and aspects. For ce people have used Arabic script to write Comorian and there is an attemp presently to normalize an orthography for writing the varieties of the langu Roman script.

The rich vocabulary of Comorian has been enhanced by the borrowing of words from many other languages. Since Comorians have been involved in maritime trade for a thousand years or more, they have come into contact with a number of different peoples and their language reflects this contact. Words of Indian, Persian, Arabic, Portuguese, English, and French origin have been added to those of African ancestry.

There are four varieties of Comorian spoken in the Islands: Shingazidja, Shimwali, Shinzwani, and Shimaore, each one named for the primary island on which it is spoken.

HISTORY

EARLY HISTORY

The Comoros Islands were very likely inhabited by Malayo-Polynesian sailors as early as the sixth century AD. Arabs and Africans were later arrivals.

For hundreds of years, the islands were a centre for traffic in slaves and spices. Between the 10th and 15th centuries, people from the areas around the Red Sea and the Persian Gulf came to the islands and established Islam. These people set up rival sultanates and while no political stability or unity was achieved, Islam gave the people homogeneity and it has subsequently dominated all aspects of the islands' social life.

FRENCH RULE

The present culture of the Comoros is very similar to that of the Swahili people on the African coast from Somalia to Mozambique.

Because of rival sultanates on the islands, in the nineteenth century France was able to exploit the situation and establish a presence. In 1886 the Comoros became a French protectorate and in 1912 France officially proclaimed them colonies.

Until the 1960s the islands were more or less totally isolated from the world. France maintained a situation which forbade political organisation and a local press. In December 1961, however, in response to increased demands from the people of the islands, a system of internal autonomy was set up.

RISE OF NATIONALISM

In 1968 there was a students' strike and in the atmosphere following it, concessions were made by the French government and the first political parties were formed in the country.

Some parties urged immediate independence from France; others were for a less-than-total break and there was even one party based in Mahoré (Mayotte), the Mouvement Populaire Mahorais (MPM), which opposed independence

INDEPENDENCE

From 1971 to 1973 there was great political unrest in the islands. In December 1972 a union of pro-independence parties won 34 seats, while the MPM won only five. The French government submitted a document to the Comorian ministers which was endorsed by them in Paris on 15 July 1973. Under the terms of the document, independence was to be granted after a delay of five years and then only after a referendum on an island-by-island basis.

There was considerable resistance to these terms in the islands and when the French Colonial Secretary visited the Comoros in September, he was greeted by hostile demonstrations. In December 1974, a referendum produced a 94.6% vote for independence but in Mahoré (Mayotte), there was a 64% vote against independence. Following this on 6 July 1975, Ahmed Abdallah, the leader of one of the major political parties, announced a unilateral declaration of independence. The five deputies, however, from Mahoré (Mayotte) rejected independence but nonetheless on 7 July, Ahmed Abdallah was elected head of state and on 18 July, the OAU (Organisation of African Unity) accepted the Comoros' membership.

POST-INDEPENDENCE

Almost as soon as he became leader, Ahmed Abdallah was deposed by Ali Solih, the leader of an opposing political party. This occurred on 3 August 1975 and Ali Solih retained a more or less tenuous hold on the country until a coup, with the help of white mercenaries led by Bob Denard, restored Ahmed Abdallah to power on 13 May 1978.

The mercenaries helped consolidate the rule of Ahmed Abdallah but their presence in the Comoros was not looked upon kindly by neighbouring countries. And in fact, the Comorian Foreign Minister was expelled from an OAU Foreign Ministers' Conference in Khartoum in July 1978. Intense diplomatic efforts were set in motion and the OAU re-accepted Comoros' membership in the organisation in February 1979.

THE MERCENARY COUP

Opposition to Ahmed Abdallah's rule was considerable both within his party and outside it. As all party politics were banned, the opposition was necessarily low-key.

After a generally unpopular tenure as leader of the country, on 27 November 1989 President Ahmed Abdallah was killed by members of his armed forces. Even though the acting president, Said Mohammed Djohar, was required to hold an election within 40 days, real power remained in the hands of Denard and his mercenaries.

In December, Denard surrendered to French forces and left the island. Subsequent elections in March 1990 saw Said Mohammed Djohar become president for a six-year term with 55.1% of the vote.

THE MILITARY COUP

In 1997 Anjouan seceded from the Comoros. Two opposing factions took control of the island and although both factions agreed to secede from Comoros they disagreed as to whether they should join France or declare independence. Fierce fighting broke out in the island.

On 23 April 1999, the Anjouan representatives refused to sign an agreement by the Organisation of African Unity (OAU) which proposed broad autonomy for the three islands under a central administration. What followed was an escalation of violence which spread to the main island and the capital Moroni.

In order to stop the spreading violence, Col. Assoumani Azzali staged a bloodless coup and ousted President Mohamed Tadjidine Ben Said Massounde and the government of his Prime Minister Abbas Djoussouf on 30 April 1999. The new leader promised that he will stay in power for one year only, and that elections will be held within that time period.

EARLY VISITORS AND SETTLERS

Little is known of the first inhabitants of the archipelago, although a sixth-century settlement has been uncovered on Nzwani by archaeologists. Historians speculated that Indonesian immigrants used the islands as stepping stones on the way to Madagascar prior to A.D. 1000. Because Comoros lay at the juncture of African, Malayo-Indonesian, and Arab spheres of influence, the present ulation reflects a blend of these elements in its physical characteristics, iguage, culture, social structure, and religion.

Local legend cites the first settlement of the archipelago by two families from Arabia after the death of Solomon. Legend also tells of a Persian king, Husain ibn Ali, who established a settlement on Comoros around the beginning of the eleventh century. Bantu peoples apparently moved to Comoros before the fourteenth century, principally from the coast of what is now southern Mozambique; on the island of Nzwani they apparently encountered an earlier group of inhabitants, a Malayo-Indonesian people. A number of chieftains bearing African titles established settlements on Njazidja and Nzwani, and by the fifteenth century they probably had contact with Arab merchants and traders who brought the Islamic faith to the islands.

A watershed in the history of the islands was the arrival of the Shirazi Arabs in the fifteenth and sixteenth centuries. The Shirazi, who originated from the city of Shiraz in what is now Iran, were Sunni Muslims adhering to the legal school of Muhammad ibn Idris ash Shafii, an eighth-century Meccan scholar who followed a middle path in combining tradition and independent judgment in legal matters. The Shirazi Arabs traveled and traded up and down the East African coast and as far east as India and Maldives. A legend is recounted on Comoros and on the East African coast of seven Shirazi brothers who set sail in seven ships, landed on the coast of northwest Madagascar and on Njazidja and Nzwani, and established colonies in the fifteenth century. The Shirazi, who divided Njazidja into eleven sultanates and Nzwani into two, extended their rule to Mahoré and Mwali, although the latter in the nineteenth century came under the control of Malagasy rulers. The Shirazi built mosques and established Islam as the religion of the islands. They also introduced stone architecture, carpentry, cotton weaving, the cultivation of a number of fruits, and the Persian solar calendar. By the sixteenth century, the Comoros had become a center of regional trade, exporting rice, ambergris, spices, and slaves to ports in East Africa and the Middle East in exchange for opium, cotton cloth, and other items.

The first Europeans to visit the islands were the Portuguese, who landed on Njazidja around 1505. The islands first appear on a European map in 1527, that of Portuguese cartographer Diogo Roberos. Dutch sixteenth-century accounts describe the Comoros sultanates as prosperous trade centers with the African coast and Madagascar. Intense competition for this trade, and, increasingly, for European commerce, resulted in constant warfare among the sultanates, a situation that persisted until the French occupation. The sultans of Njazidja only occasionally recognized the supremacy of one of their number as *tibe*, or supreme ruler.

By the early seventeenth century, slaves had become Comoros' most important export commodity, although the market for the islands' other products also continued to expand, mainly in response to the growing European presence in the region. To meet this increased demand, the sultans began using slave labor themselves, following common practice along the East African coast.

Beginning in 1785, the Sakalava of the west coast of Madagascar began slaving raids on Comoros. They captured thousands of inhabitants and carried them off in outrigger canoes to be sold in French-occupied Madagascar, Mauritius, or Reunion to work on the sugar plantations, many of which French investors owned. The island of Mahoré, closest of the group to Madagascar, was virtually depopulated. Comoran pleas for aid from the French and the other European powers went unanswered, and the raids ceased only after the Sakalava kingdoms were conquered by the Merina of Madagascar's central highlands. After the Merina conquest, groups of Sakalava and Betsimisaraka peoples left Madagascar and settled on Mahoré and Mwali.

Prosperity was restored as Comoran traders again became involved in transporting slaves from the East African coast to Reunion and Madagascar. Dhows carrying slaves brought in huge profits for their investors. On Comoros, it was estimated in 1865 that as much as 40 percent of the population consisted of slaves. For the elite, owning a large number of slaves to perform fieldwork and household service was a mark of status. On the eve of the French occupation, Comoran society consisted of three classes: the elite of the Shirazi sultans and their families, a middle class of free persons or commoners, and a slave class consisting of those who had been brought from the African coast or their descendants.

FRENCH COLONIZATION

France's presence in the western Indian Ocean dates to the early seventeenth century. The French established a settlement in southern Madagascar in 1634 and occupied the islands of Reunion and Rodrigues; in 1715 France claimed Mauritius (Île de France), and in 1756 Seychelles. When France ceded Mauritius, Rodrigues, and Seychelles to Britain in 1814, it lost its Indian Ocean ports; Reunion, which remained French, did not offer a suitable natural harbor. In 1840 France acquired the island of Nosy-Be off the northwestern coast of Madagascar, but its potential as a port was limited. In 1841 the governor of Réunion, Admiral de Hell, negotiated with Andrian Souli, the Malagasy ruler of Mayotte, to cede Mayotte to France. Mahoré offered a suitable site for port facilities, and its acquisition was justified by de Hell on the grounds that if France did not act, Britain would occupy the island.

Although France had established a foothold in Comoros, the acquisition of the other islands proceeded fitfully. At times the French were spurred on by the threat of British intervention, especially on Nzwani, and other times, by the constant anarchy resulting from the sultans' wars upon each other. In the 1880s,

Germany's growing influence on the East African coast added to the concerns of the French. Not until 1908, however, did the four Comoro Islands become part of France's colony of Madagascar and not until 1912 did the last sultan abdicate. Then, a colonial administration took over the islands and established a capital at Dzaoudzi on Mahoré. Treaties of protectorate status marked a transition point between independence and annexation; such treaties were signed with the rulers of Njazidja, Nzwani, and Mwali in 1886.

The effects of French colonialism were mixed, at best. Colonial rule brought an end to the institution of slavery, but economic and social differences between former slaves and free persons and their descendants persisted. Health standards improved with the introduction of modern medicine, and the population increased about 50 percent between 1900 and 1960. France continued to dominate the economy. Food crop cultivation was neglected as French *sociétés* (companies) established cash crop plantations in the coastal regions. The result was an economy dependent on the exporting of vanilla, ylang-ylang, cloves, cocoa, copra, and other tropical crops. Most profits obtained from exports were diverted to France rather than invested in the infrastructure of the islands. Development was further limited by the colonial government's practice of concentrating public services on Madagascar. One consequence of this policy was the migration of large numbers of Comorans to Madagascar, where their presence would be a long-term source of tension between Comoros and its giant island neighbor.

The Shirazi elite continued to play a prominent role as large landowners and civil servants. On the eve of independence, Comoros remained poor and undeveloped, having only one secondary school and practically nothing in the way of national media. Isolated from important trade routes by the opening of the Suez Canal in 1869, having few natural resources, and largely neglected by France, the islands were poorly equipped for independence.

In 1946 the Comoro Islands became an overseas department of France with representation in the French National Assembly. The following year, the islands' administrative ties to Madagascar were severed; Comoros established its own customs regime in 1952. A Governing Council was elected in August 1957 on the four islands in conformity with the *loi-cadre* (enabling law) of June 23, 1956. A constitution providing for internal self-government was promulgated in 1961, following a 1958 referendum in which Comorans voted overwhelmingly to remain a part of France. This government consisted of a territorial assembly having, in 1975, thirty-nine members, and a Governing Council of six to nine ministers responsible to it.

THE BREAK WITH FRANCE

Politics in the 1960s were dominated by a social and economic elite--largely descendants of the precolonial sultanate ruling families--which was conservative and pro-French. During Comoros' period of self-government as an overseas department, there were two main conservative political groupings: the Parti Vert (Green Party), which later became known as the Comoros Democratic Union (Union Démocratique des Comores-UDC), and the Parti Blanc (White Party), later reconstituted as the Democratic Assembly of the Comoran People (Rassemblement Démocratique du Peuple Comorien- RDPC). Dr. Said Mohamed Cheikh, president of the Parti Vert and of the Governing Council, was, until his death in 1970, the most important political leader in the islands. The Parti Blanc, under Prince Said Ibrahim, provided the opposition, endorsing a progressive program that included land reform and a loosening of the monopoly on Comoran cash crops enjoyed by the foreign-owned plantation *sociétés*. The second most powerful member of the Parti Vert, Ahmed Abdallah, a wealthy plantation owner and representative to the French National Assembly, succeeded Cheikh as president of the Governing Council soon after Cheikh died.

Well into the 1960s, the two established parties were concerned primarily with maintaining a harmonious relationship with France while obtaining assistance in economic planning and infrastructure development. Given this consensus, politically active Comorans often based their allegiance on personal feelings toward the doctor and the prince who led the two main parties and on whatever patronage either party could provide.

The independence movement started not in the Comoro Islands but among Comoran expatriates in Tanzania, who founded the National Liberation Movement of Comoros (Mouvement de la Libération Nationale des Comores--Molinaco) in 1962. Molinaco actively promoted the cause of Comoran independence abroad, particularly in the forum of the Organization of African Unity (OAU), but not until 1967 did it begin to extend its influence to the islands themselves, engaging in largely clandestine activities. The Socialist Party of Comoros (Parti Socialiste des Comores--Pasoco), established in 1968, was largely supported by students and other young people.

A growing number of politically conscious Comorans, resenting what they perceived as French neglect of the Comoro Islands, supported independence. Independence-minded Comorans, especially younger ones, were energized by dramatic events across the Mozambique Channel on the African mainland. Tanganyika had gained its independence from Britain in 1961 and soon adopted a government based on "African socialism." Zanzibar, another longtime British colony, became independent in 1963 and overthrew the ruling Arab elite in a violent revolution the following year; the island state then merged with Tanganyika to form the new nation of Tanzania. Meanwhile, nationalists were beginning uprisings in the Portuguese colony of Mozambique.

Abdallah, although a conservative politician, saw independence as a "regrettable necessity," given the unsatisfactory level of French support and the growing alienation of an increasingly radicalized younger generation. The violent suppression of a student demonstration in 1968 and the death of Said Mohammed Cheikh in 1970 provided further evidence of the erosion of the existing order. In 1972 leaders of the Parti Vert (now the UDC) and the Parti Blanc (now the RDPC) agreed to press for independence, hoping at the same time to maintain cordial relations with France. A coalition of conservative and moderate parties, the Party for the Evolution of Comoros (Parti pour l'Évolution des Comores), was in the forefront of the independence effort. The coalition excluded Pasoco, which it perceived as violently revolutionary, but it cooperated for a time with Molinaco. During 1973 and 1974, the local government negotiated with France, and issued a "Common Declaration" on June 15, 1973, defining the means by which the islands would gain independence. Part of the backdrop of the negotiations was a proindependence riot in November 1973 in Moroni in which the buildings of the Chamber of Deputies were burned. A referendum was held on December 22, 1974. Voters supported independence by a 95 percent majority, but 65 percent of those casting ballots on Mahoré chose to remain as a French department.

Twenty-eight days after the declaration of independence, on August 3, 1975, a coalition of six political parties known as the United National Front overthrew the Abdallah government, with the aid of foreign mercenaries. Some observers claimed that French commercial interests, and possibly even the French government, had helped provide the funds and the matériel to bring off the coup. The reasons for the coup remain obscure, although the belief that France might return Mahoré if Abdallah were out of power appears to have been a contributing factor. Abdallah fled to Nzwani, his political power base, where he remained in control with an armed contingent of forty-five men until forces from Moroni recaptured the island and arrested him in late September 1975. After the coup, a three-man directorate took control. One of the three, Ali Soilih, was appointed minister of defense and justice and subsequently was made head of state by the Chamber of Deputies on January 3, 1976. Four days earlier, on December 31, 1975, France had formally recognized the independence of Comoros (minus Mahoré), but active relations, including all aid programs, which amounted to more than 40 percent of the national budget, remained suspended.

THE SOILIH REGIME

Originally an agronomist, Ali Soilih had become politically active as a supporter of RDPC leader Said Ibrahim in 1970. Lasting from January 1976 to May 1978, his rule was marked by continued hostility between France and Comoros. The main issues were the status of Mahoré (particularly after France held a second referendum on the island, on February 7, 1976, in which 99.4 percent of the voters endorsed continued status as a French department) and a radical reform program designed to break the hold of traditional values and French influence on Comoran life. Soilih envisioned accomplishing his revolution in three phases, beginning with independence from France.

The second phase, a "social revolution," would abolish such customs as the wearing of veils, the costly *grand mariage* (great wedding; in Swahili *ndola nkuu*), and traditional funeral ceremonies. Comoran citizens, including young women, would be mobilized to serve in revolutionary militia and army units in an attempt to create something resembling the Red Guards of China's Cultural Revolution of the late 1960s. The third phase would decentralize government administration by establishing thirty-four local *moudirias*, or provinces. These would serve not only as administrative centers but would also provide post and telephone service and consumer goods for localities of about 9,000 people on the model of the Chinese people's communes.

Soilih emphasized the central role of young people in the revolution, lowering the voting age to fourteen. He mobilized Comoran youth into a special revolutionary militia (the Moissy), which particularly in the villages, launched violent attacks on conservative elders in Red Guard style.

After the withdrawal of French financial subsidies, the treasury was soon emptied, and in a move having budgetary as well as ideological implications, some 3,500 civil servants were dismissed in 1977. Soilih made a more than symbolic break with the past in 1976 by burning French government archives, which had been kept since the acquisition of Mahoré 135 years before. Tanzanian officers trained the Comoran Armed Forces, and the Democratic People's Republic of Korea (North Korea), Saudi Arabia, and other countries provided limited aid.

Soilih, who described himself as a devout Muslim, advocated a secular state and limitations on the privileges of the muftis, or Muslim jurists who interpret Islamic law. These reforms, which were perceived as attacks on Comoran traditions, combined with a deepening economic crisis to erode support for his government. Several attempts were made on Soilih's life, and in a referendum held in October 1977, only 55 percent of the voters supported a new constitution proposed by his government. Attacks by the Moissy on real and imagined political opponents escalated; raids on mosques were common; a number of refugees fled to Mahoré.

The eruption of Kartala in April 1977 and the influx of refugees from Madagascar following a massacre of resident Comorans there exacerbated the situation. In March 1978, some fishers in the town of Iconi, south of Moroni, were killed after protesting the government's policy on compulsory sale of their catch to the state. Severe food shortages in 1976-77 required the government to seek aid internationally and forced the young nation to divert its already limited export earnings from economic development to purchases of rice and other staples.

Popular support had dwindled to such a level that when a mercenary force of fifty, consisting largely of former French paratroopers, landed at Itsandra Beach north of the capital on May 12, 1978 the regular armed forces offered no resistance. The mercenaries were led by French-born Bob Denard (an alias for Gilbert Bourgeaud, also known as Said Mustapha M'Hadjou) a veteran of wars of revolution, counterrevolution, and separatism from Indochina to Biafra. (Ironically, Denard had played a role in the 1975 coup that had enabled Soilih to come to power.) Most Comorans supported the coup and were happy to be free of Soilih's ineffective and repressive regime. The deposed head of state was killed under mysterious circumstances on May 29, 1978. The official explanation was that he had attempted to escape.

THE ABDALLAH REGIME

Following a few days of provisional government, the two men who had financed the coup, former president Ahmed Abdallah (himself the victim of the 1975 coup) and former vice president Mohamed Ahmed, returned to Moroni from exile in Paris and installed themselves as joint presidents. Soon after, Abdallah was named sole executive.

The continued presence of the mercenaries impeded Abdallah's early efforts to stabilize Comoros. Denard seemed interested in remaining in Comoros, and he and his friends were given financially rewarding appointments with the new government. In reaction to Denard's involvement with Abdallah, the OAU revoked Comoros' OAU membership, Madagascar severed diplomatic relations, and the United Nations (UN) threatened economic sanctions against the regime. France also exerted pressure for Denard to leave, and in late September-temporarily, as it developed-he departed the islands.

Abdallah consolidated power, beginning with the writing of a new constitution. The document combined federalism and centralism. It granted each island its own legislature and control over taxes levied on individuals and businesses resident on the island (perhaps with an eye to rapprochement with Mahoré), while reserving strong executive powers for the president. It also restored Islam as the state religion, while acknowledging the rights of those who did not observe the Muslim faith. The new constitution was approved by 99 percent of Comoran voters on October 1, 1978. The Comorans also elected Abdallah to a six-year term as president of what was now known as the Federal Islamic Republic of the Comoros.

Although Abdallah had been president when Comoros broke away from France in 1975, he now moved to establish a relationship much more to France's liking.

Upon Denard's departure, he gave a French military mission responsibility for training Comoros' defense force. He also signed an agreement with France to allow its navy full use of Comoran port facilities.

Making the most of Comoros' new presidential system, Abdallah induced the nation's National Assembly to enact a twelve-year ban on political parties, a move that guaranteed his reelection in 1984. In 1979 his government arrested Soilih regime members who had not already left or been killed during the 1978 coup. Four former ministers of the Soilih government disappeared and allegedly were murdered, and about 300 other Soilih supporters were imprisoned without trial. For the next three years, occasional trials were held, in many cases only after France had insisted on due process for the prisoners.

Although the restoration of good relations with France represented a sharp break with the policies of the previous regime, Abdallah built on Soilih's efforts to find new sources of diplomatic and economic support. Thanks in large part to aid from the European Community (EC) and the Arab states, the regime began to upgrade roads, telecommunications, and port facilities. The government also accepted international aid for programs to increase the cultivation of cash crops and food for domestic consumption. Abdallah endeavored to maintain the relations established by Soilih with China, Nigeria, and Tanzania, and to expand Comoros' contacts in the Islamic world with visits to Libya and the Persian Gulf states.

Despite international assistance, economic development was slow. Although some Comorans blamed the French, who had yet to restore technical assistance to pre-1975 levels, others suspected that Abdallah, who owned a large import-export firm, was enriching himself from development efforts with the assistance of Denard, who continued to visit Comoros.

Opposition to the Abdallah regime began to appear as early as 1979, with the formation of an exile-dominated group that became known as the United National Front of Comorans-Union of Comorans (Front National Uni des Komoriens--Union des Komoriens-FNUK- Unikom). In 1980 the Comoran ambassador to France, Said Ali Kemal, resigned his position to form another opposition group, the National Committee for Public Safety (Comité National de Salut Public). A failed coup in February 1981, led by a former official of the Soilih regime, resulted in arrests of about forty people.

In regard to Mahoré, Abdallah offered little more than verbal resistance to a 1979 decision of the French government to postpone action on the status of the island until 1984. At the same time, he kept the door open to Mahoré by writing a large measure of autonomy for the component islands of the republic into the 1978 constitution and by appointing a Mahorais as his government's minister of finance. Having established an administration that, in comparison with the Soilih years, seemed tolerable to his domestic and international constituencies, Abdallah proceeded to entrench himself. He did this through domestic and international policies that would profoundly compromise Comoros' independence and create the chronic crisis that continued to characterize Comoran politics and government in mid-1990s.

THE UNDERMINING OF THE POLITICAL PROCESS

In February 1982, Comoros became a one-party state. The government designated Abdallah's newly formed Comoran Union for Progress (Union Comorienne pour le Progrès-UCP) as the republic's sole political party. Although unaffiliated individuals could run for local and national office, the only party that could organize on behalf of candidates henceforth would be the UCP. In March 1982 elections, all but one of Abdallah's handpicked UCP candidates won. UCP candidates likewise dominated the May 1983 National Assembly elections, and opposition candidates attempting to stand for election in balloting for the three islands' legislative councils in July were removed from the lists by the Ministry of Interior. Abdallah himself was elected to a second six-year term as head of state in September 1984, winning more than 99 percent of the vote as the sole candidate. During the National Assembly elections of March 22, 1987, the Abdallah regime arrested 400 poll watchers from opposition groups. A state radio announcement that one non-UCP delegate had been elected was retracted the next day.

Abdallah also kept opponents from competing with him in the arena of legitimate politics by reshuffling his government and amending the 1978 constitution. As part of what one observer wryly called the process of "remov[ing] his most avid successors from temptation," Abdallah pushed through a constitutional amendment in 1985 that abolished the post of prime minister, a move that made the president both head of state and head of the elected government. The amendment also diminished the status of Ali Mroudjae, the erstwhile prime minister and a likely future candidate for president. Another 1985 amendment took away many of the powers of the president of the National Assembly, including his right to become interim head of state in the event of the incumbent's death. The amendment transferred the right of succession to the president of the Supreme Court, an appointee of the head of state. Feeling the effect of this second amendment was assembly president Mohamed Taki, another man generally regarded as presidential timber.

Mroudjae's subsequent career in the Abdallah government illustrated the way in which Abdallah used frequent reshufflings of his cabinet to eliminate potential challengers. Mroudjae's next job was to share duties as minister of state with four other people; he was removed from the government altogether in another reshuffle four months later.

Looking to the end of his second (and, according to the constitution, final) term as head of state, Abdallah created a commission in 1988 to recommend changes to the constitution. These changes, among other things, would permit him to run yet again in 1990. A referendum on revisions to the constitution was scheduled for November 4, 1989.

A weak, divided, and opportunistic opposition facilitated Abdallah's efforts to undermine the political process. The character of Comoran politics ensured that opposition would be sustained by an unwieldy group of strong personalities. As the personal stock of these would-be leaders rose and fell, coalitions coalesced and just as quickly fell apart in a process that engendered distrust and cynicism. The ban on opposition political organizations at home--brutally upheld, when necessary, by the Presidential Guard (Garde Presidentelle-GP) and the Comoran military--further undercut efforts to organize against the head of state. The French government's displeasure at intrigues of Comoran exiles in Paris also complicated opposition efforts.

Given the absence of an ideological basis for resisting the regime, it was also not surprising that some opposition leaders were willing to ally themselves with the head of state if such a move appeared likely to advance them personally. For example, Mouzaoir Abdallah, leader of the opposition Union for a Democratic Republic in Comoros (Union pour une Rèpublique Dèmocratique aux Comores-URDC), appeared with the president at independence day celebrations in July 1988 amid rumors that the URDC chief was being considered for a reconstituted prime minister's office. In September 1988 another opposition leader, Said Hachim, agreed to join the commission considering revisions to the constitution.

The credibility of Abdallah's opponents was also damaged by the efforts of one opposition leader, former ambassador to France Said Ali Kemal, to recruit mercenaries to help overthrow the Abdallah government. Arrested in Australia in late 1983, six of the mercenaries gave testimony discrediting Kemal.

MERCENARY RULE

Abdallah complemented his political maneuvers by employing a GP officered by many of the same mercenaries who had helped him take power in 1978. Denard led this force, and also became heavily involved in Comoran business activities, sometimes acting in partnership with President Abdallah or as a front for South African business interests, which played a growing role in the Comoran economy during the Abdallah regime.

Although Denard had made a ceremonial departure from Comoros following the 1978 coup, by the early 1980s he was again openly active in the islands. The GP, whose numbers were reported to range from 300 to 700 members, primarily indigenous Comorans, were led by about thirty French and Belgian mercenaries, mostly comrades of Denard's in the post-World War II conflicts that accompanied the decolonization of Africa and Asia. Answerable only to the president, the GP operated outside the chain of command of the French-trained 1,000-member Comoran Armed Forces, a situation that caused resentment among the regular military, Comoran citizens, and other African states.

The GP's primary missions were to protect the president and to deter attempts to overthrow his government. During the July 1983 elections to the three islands' legislative councils, the GP beat and arrested demonstrators protesting the republic's singleparty system. During elections to the National Assembly in March 1987, the GP-which had become known as *les affreux*, "the frighteners"--replaced several hundred dissident poll watchers who had been arrested by the army. On March 8, 1985, one of the most serious attempts to overthrow the Abdallah government began as a mutiny by about thirty Comoran troops of the GP against their European officers. The disaffected guards had formed ties to the Democratic Front (Front Démocratique-FD), one of the more nationalistic of the republic's many banned political parties. The mutiny was quickly squelched; three of the rebellious guards were killed, and the rest were taken prisoners.

President Abdallah used the uprising as an opportunity to round up dissidents, primarily FD members, whose leadership denied involvement in the coup attempt. Later in 1985, seventyseven received convictions; seventeen, including the FD's secretary general, Mustapha Said Cheikh, were sentenced to life imprisonment at hard labor. Most of the prisoners were released in 1986 following Amnesty International charges of illegal arrests, torture, and other abuses. France had also exerted pressure by temporarily withholding new aid projects and purchases of Comoran vanilla.

Perhaps the most notorious action of the GP on behalf of the Abdallah government occurred in November 1987. After an apparent attempt by dissidents to free some political prisoners, an event quickly labeled a coup attempt by the Abdallah regime, the GP arrested fourteen alleged plotters and tortured seven of them to death. Officials of the Comoran government apparently were not allowed to participate in the prisoners' interrogation. President Abdallah was on a state visit to Egypt at the time.

With Abdallah's acquiescence and occasional participation, Denard and the other GP officers used their connections to the head of state to make themselves important players in the Comoran economy. Denard was a part owner of Établissements Abdallah et Fils, Comoros' largest import-export firm, whose primary owner was President Abdallah. Denard also owned and operated a highly profitable commercial shuttle between South Africa and Comoros, and owned Sogecom, a private security firm with contracts to protect South African hotels being built in the islands.

The GP officers, sympathetic to South Africa's apartheid government, established themselves as a conduit of South African investment and influence in Comoros. An official South African trade representative conceded that a number of his country's investment projects, including a 525-hectare experimental farm, housing, road construction, and a medical evacuation program, were brokered and managed by guard officers at the mercenaries' insistence.

The GP also arranged for South African commercial aircraft to fly in the Middle East and parts of Africa under the aegis of the Comoran national airline, in contravention of international sanctions against South Africa. Furthermore, the GP provided for South African use of Comoran territory as a base for intelligence gathering in the Mozambique Channel and as a staging area for the shipment of arms to rightist rebels in Mozambique. The GP was widely understood to be funded by South Africa, at the rate of about US$3 million per year.

COMOROS AS CLIENT STATE: THE ECONOMICS OF ABDALLAH

President Abdallah generally put his personal interests ahead of national interests in making economic policy. The result was the creation of a client state whose meager and unpredictable cash crop earnings were supplemented with increasing infusions of foreign aid.

Throughout the 1980s, export earnings from Comoros' four main cash crops-vanilla, ylang-ylang, cloves, and copra--experienced a wrenching sequence of booms and collapses because of weather and market factors, or else steadily dwindled. The regime's principal form of response was to apply the president's considerable diplomatic skills to developing an extensive network of governments and international organizations willing to extend loans and donate aid. The main suppliers were France, South Africa, the EC, the conservative Arab states, the World Bank and related organs, and regional financial institutions such as the Arab Bank for Economic Development in Africa and the African Development Bank. Some assistance went to projects of indisputable value, such as efforts to create independent news media and improve telephone communications with the outside world. Much of the aid, however, was questionable--for example, loans and grants to help the republic meet the payroll for its oversized civil service. Other more plausible projects, such as the protracted development of a seaport at the town of Mutsamudu, construction of paved ring roads linking each island's coastal settlements, and the building of power stations, nonetheless tended to be instances of placing the cart before the horse.

That is, capital-intensive improvements to infrastructure had not been coordinated with local development projects; hence, little, if any, domestic commerce existed to benefit from road networks, electrical power, and world-class port facilities. The importation of huge quantities of building materials and construction equipment provided immediate benefits to importexport firms in the islands, of which Établissements Abdallah et Fils was the largest. In the meantime, the projects were of little immediate use to Comorans and were likely to go underused for years to come.

Throughout the Abdallah period, rice imports drained as much as 50 percent of Comoran export earnings. Projects to increase food self-sufficiency, as one observer noted, "fail[ed] to respond to the largesse" provided by international sponsors such as the European Development Fund and the International Fund for Agricultural Development. The president joined with vanilla growers in resisting international pressure to divert vanillaproducing land to the cultivation of corn and rice for domestic consumption. He also declined to heed World Bank advice to impose tariffs and domestic taxes on imported rice. Abdallah's importexport firm was heavily involved in vanilla exports, as well as in the importation of Far Eastern rice at three times its price at the source.

Abdallah's firm, whose co-owners included Denard and Kalfane and Company, a Pakistani concern, also profited from managing the importation of materials used by South African firms in developing tourist hotels. Little of the material used in building these resorts was of Comoran origin. Also, once completed, the resorts would be almost entirely owned and managed by non-Comorans. Although tourism, mainly by South Africans who were unwelcome in other African resorts, was widely considered the only promising new industry in Comoros, Abdallah guided its development so that resorts benefited few Comorans other than himself and his associates.

Under Abdallah's tutelage, the Comoran economy finished the 1980s much as it had started the decade-poor, underdeveloped, and dependent on export earnings from cash crops of unpredictable and generally declining value. The critical difference, with enormous implications for the republic's capacity to have some say in its own destiny, was its new status as a nation abjectly in debt. By 1988, the last full year of the Abdallah regime, 80 percent of annual public expenditures were funded by external aid.

THE DEMISE OF ABDALLAH, 1989

Only weeks before the violent end of the Abdallah regime in late 1989, one observer noted that "Comoros is still run like a village, with a handful of tough men in charge and supported by foreign aid." As Comorans prepared for a November 4, 1989, referendum on constitutional changes that would enable President Abdallah to run for a third term in 1990, human rights remained in precarious condition, and the only avenue of economic advancement for most islanders-the civil service-faced cutbacks at the urging of the World Bank and the International Monetary Fund (IMF). Even those who would keep their government jobs, however, were not guaranteed economic security. As often occurred whenever export earnings slid, civil servants had not been paid since mid-summer.

The official result of the referendum was a 92.5 percent majority in favor of the amendments proposed by Abdallah, which now created "the conditions for a life presidency," warned one opposition leader. Balloting was marked by the now customary manipulation by the government. Opposition groups reported that polling places lacked private voting booths, government officials blocked the entry of opposition poll watchers, and the army and police removed ballot boxes before voting ended. Reaction to these abuses was unusually angry. In Njazidja voters smashed ballot boxes rather than have them carted away by the army; the governor's office was set on fire in Nzwani, and a bomb was found outside the home of the minister of finance in Moroni. More than 100 people were arrested following the election, and in subsequent weeks the international media described a deteriorating situation in the islands; the head of state claimed that France "authorizes terrorism in the Comoros," and leaders of the banned opposition in bold public statements questioned the legitimacy of the referendum.

President Abdallah was shot to death on the night of November 26-27, reportedly while asleep in his residence, the Beit el Salama (House of Peace). At first his death was seen as a logical outcome of the tense political situation following what was, in effect, his self-appointment as head of state for life. The recently dismissed head of the Comoran military was duly blamed for the murder.

Evidence emerged subsequently that Abdallah's assassination resulted from the late president's proposed actions with regard to the GP. In September 1989, Abdallah had engaged a French military consultant, who determined that the GP should be absorbed into the regular army. Following consultations among Abdallah, the French government, and South Africa's Ministry of Foreign Affairs, a decision was made to expel Denard and his fellow officers of the GP by the end of 1989. Denard and his second in command were seen walking with Abdallah only hours before he died. Although the mercenary initially blamed the assassination on the Comoran army, he later conceded that he was in Abdallah's office when the president was killed, but called the shooting "an accident due to the general state of mayhem" in the Beit al Salama.

Two days later, on November 29, the real reasons for the assassination emerged when Denard and the GP seized control of the government in a coup. Twenty-seven police officers were killed, hundreds of people were arrested, and all journalists were confined to their hotels. The mercenaries disarmed the regular army, ousted provisional president Haribon Chebani, who as chief of the Supreme Court had succeeded Abdallah, and installed Mohamed Said Djohar, who just three days earlier had become chief of the Supreme Court, as Comoros' third president in less than a week.

The immediate reaction of the republic's two main supporters, France and South Africa, was to isolate Denard. South Africa, admitting years of funding of the GP, cut off all aid. France began a military build-up on Mahoré and likewise suspended aid. On December 7, anti-Denard demonstrations by about 1,000 students and workers were violently broken up by the protests. By then the islands' school system had shut down, and the civil service had gone on strike. Faced with an untenable situation, Denard surrendered to French forces without a fight on December 15. Along with about two dozen comrades, he was flown to Pretoria and put under house arrest. The French government later announced that Denard would remain in detention in South Africa pending the outcome of a French judicial inquiry into Abdallah's death. In February 1993 he returned to France, where he was initially arrested, tried, and exonerated of involvement in the death of Abdallah.

THE ISSUE OF MAHORÉ

One of the touchiest issues in the negotiations between Comoros and France over independence in the early 1970s had been whether the 1974 referendum would be considered for the Comoros archipelago as a whole or on an island-by-island basis. Opposition to independence on Mahoré was organized by the Mayotte Popular Movement (Mouvement Populaire Mahorais-MPM), an organization that had been founded in the 1960s by Zeina M'Dere, a spokeswoman for Mahoré shopkeepers, mostly women, who had been affected economically when the colonial capital was moved from the Mahoré town of Dzaoudzi to Moroni on Njazidja in 1962.

The reasons behind Mahoré's 65 percent vote against independence were several. First, the people of Mahoré considered themselves culturally, religiously, and linguistically distinct from those of the other three islands; they felt that their long association with France (since 1841) had given their island a distinct Creole character like that of Reunion or Seychelles. Second, given Mahoré's smaller population, greater natural resources, and higher standard of living, the Mahorais thought that their island would be economically viable within a French union and ought not to be brought down to the level of the other three poorer islands. Third, most Mahorais apparently felt that Mahoré's future within a Comoran state would not be a comfortable one, given a perception of neglect that had begun with the much resented transfer of the capital.

In France and among conservatives on Reunion, the 1974 vote on Mahoré in favor of continued association with France was greeted with great enthusiasm. Comoran leaders, in contrast, accused the MPM and its leader, Marcel Henri, of fabricating the illusion of Mahorais "uniqueness" to preserve the power of Mahoré's non-Muslim, Creole elite. The issue poisoned Comoran relations with France, particularly because the Indian Ocean lobby, whose leaders included Reunion's deputy to the French National Assembly, Michel Debré, pushed for a

"Mayotte française" (French Mayotte). Apparently leaning toward the interpretation that the December 1974 referendum was an island-by-island plebiscite, the French legislature voted in June 1975 to postpone independence for six months and hold a second referendum. The Abdallah government responded by declaring independence unilaterally on July 6, 1975, for all Comoro Islands, including Mahoré. France reacted by cutting off financial aid, which provided 41 percent of the national budget. Fearing a Comoran attempt to assert control of Mahoré forcibly, France sent members of the Foreign Legion from Reunion and a fleet of three vessels to patrol the waters around the island on July 6-7. On November 12, 1975, the UN General Assembly passed a resolution giving Comoros UN membership and recognized its claims to Mahoré, which France opposed.

French policy toward Mahoré had been, in the words of one observer, "to cultivate a more or less honest majority for reunification among the uncooperative Mahorais," particularly after the forthrightly anti-French regime of Ali Soilih ended in 1978. By contrast, the Mahorais' objective appeared to be full departmental status such as that of Reunion, where residents enjoyed full rights as French citizens. In a 1976 referendum, the Mahorais expressed dissatisfaction with their status as an overseas territory. France then created a new classification for Mahoré-territorial community (*collectivité territoriale*)-under which Mahoré was administered by a prefect appointed by the French government. Local government consisted of a popularly elected seventeen-member General Council. The island was entitled to send elected representatives to Paris, one each to the National Assembly and the Senate. The French franc served as the currency of the island. This status still applied in 1993.

After it appeared that Mahoré would not be tempted by the federalist design of Ahmed Abdallah's 1978 constitution to join the Republic of the Comoros, the National Assembly in Paris decided in 1979 to prolong the existence of the *collectivité territoriale* until a 1984 plebiscite, resolving meanwhile to study the situation and consult with the islanders. In late 1984, with an overwhelming vote to remain associated with France in the offing, the French government postponed the plebiscite indefinitely. By late 1993, it had still not been held, the Mahorais apparently still eager to remain part of France and as disinclined as ever to reunite with the three troubled islands to their immediate west.

Although many politically conservative French relished the Mahorais' popular vow that *nous resterons français pour rester libre* ("we will remain French to remain free"), the Mahoré situation caused some discomfort for France internationally. Every year, resolutions calling on France to relinquish Mahoré to Comoros passed with near unanimity in the UN, and the OAU likewise issued annual condemnations. Although Comoran official distaste for the situation became more muted in the 1980s and 1990s, the Comoran government continued to draw French attention to the issue. In May 1990, newly elected president Said Mohamed Djohar called for peaceful dialogue and French review of Mahoré's status. But feeling obligated not to change the Mahorais' status against their will, the French could do little. Anti-Comoran riots and demonstrations, and the formation of an anti-immigrant paramilitary group on Mahoré in response to the presence of illegal Comoran immigrants, were also sources of embarrassment to France.

The economy of Mahoré in some ways resembles that of Comoros. Rice, cassava, and corn are cultivated for domestic consumption; ylang-ylang and vanilla are the primary exports. The main imports, whose value far outstripped that of exports, are foodstuffs, machinery and appliances, transport equipment, and metals. Construction, primarily of French-funded public works, is the only industrial activity.

A five-year development plan (1986-91) focused on large-scale public projects, principally construction of a deepwater port at Longoni and an airport at the capital, Dzaoudzi. The plan and its two main projects were later extended through 1993. Despite Mahoré's great natural beauty, tourism was inhibited by a dearth of hotel rooms and the island's isolated location.

Under French administration, Mahoré had generally enjoyed domestic peace and stability, although tensions appeared to be rising by the early 1990s. In the summer of 1991, the relocation of people from their homes to allow the expansion of the airport met with vociferous protests, mostly by young people. The protests soon grew into violent demonstrations against the local government's administration of the island. Paramilitary attacks on Comoran immigrants occurred in June 1992, and a February 1993 general strike for higher wages ended in rioting. Security forces from Reunion and France were called in to restore order.

The first Federal Assembly elected in 1992 was dissolved by Djohar after a year; polls for its successor in December 1993 returned the pro-Djohar Rassemblement pour la Démocratie et le Renouveau (RDR) with a two-seat majority. Djohar had originally been thought to enjoy the Comoros Islands' nemesis, Bob Denard. However, in September 1995 Denard launched yet another mercenary coup. It was overturned a week later by French troops despatched from Réunion. By March 1996, the situation had calmed sufficiently for scheduled presidential elections to take place. The RDR candidate, Mohammed Taki won comfortably while his party also secured a large majority in the National Assembly elections held the following December. Taki's period in office was dominated by the secession of the outlying island of Nzwani, which sought independence from the Comoros group.

Military intervention to crush the rebellion was followed by the dismissal by Taki of the elected government and assumption of absolute power. The ensuing political crisis eventually led to a military coup in May 1999 by Colonel Assumani Azzali. Despite strong protestations by the international community, Azzali has steadily consolidated control of the islands. It is less certain, however, whether he can bring political stability to the troubled islands.

After a coup d'état on 30 April 1999, Colonel Azali Assoumani proclaimed himself President of the Islamic Federal Republic of the Comoros. At that point press freedom was curbed. It has become impossible to mention the army without risking severe reprisals, as the week-long detention in October of one of the country's most influential journalists illustrated. On the island of Anjouan, which proclaimed its independence in 1997 but is still not recognised by the international community, expression in the media of any separatist idea is met by the intransigence of the military regime.

In August, Radio Ushababi, a private station hosted by young journalists in Anjouan, was the victim of administrative and police harassment (summonses and arrests). On 9 August, under pressure from the authorities, the team running the radio station decided to suspend its programmes and left the premises. Physical threats from groups of separatist militia were stepped up shortly before the legislative elections. In 1997 the same team had launched the newspaper Ushababi which had to cease publication following similar threats.

On 17 August two journalists from the Gazette des Comores, a Moroni private newspaper started in July, were refused entry to Anjouan at Ouani airport. Aboubacar Mchangama, publishing manager of the weekly L'Archipel and correspondent for Agence France-Presse and Reporters Without Borders, was arrested on 14 October. Two days later he was charged with «spreading false information» and remanded in custody at Moroni central prison. The journalist had refused to reveal the name of an officer cited in an article in his newspaper, who had mentioned tension in the army between partisans and opponents of Colonel Azali Assoumani. The officer stated that he was «not prepared to be shot in the back for Colonel Azali». The journalist was released on 21 October but may not leave the island of Njazídja until his trial or further summons by the judge investigating the case.

PEOPLE

Nationality: Noun and adjective--Comorian(s).
Population (1995 est.): 550,000. Mayotte (1990 est.)--70,000.
Annual growth rate (1995 est.): 3.56%.
Ethnic groups: Antalote, Cafre, Makoa, Oimatsaha, Sakalava.
Religions: Sunni Muslim 98%, Roman Catholic 2%.
Languages: Shikomoro (a Swahili-Arab), Malagasy, French.
Education: Attendance-62% primary, 32% secondary. Literacy--48%.

Health: Life expectancy--58 yrs. Infant mortality rate--77/1,000.
Work force (1994): 200,000. Agriculture--80%. Government--3%.

The Comorians inhabiting Grande Comore, Anjouan, and Moheli (86% of the population) share African-Arab origins. Islam is the dominant religion, and Koranic schools for children reinforce its influence. Although Arab culture is firmly established throughout the archipelago, a substantial minority of the citizens of Mayotte (the Mahorais) are Catholic and have been strongly influenced by French culture.

The most common language is Shikomoro, a Swahili dialect. French and Malagasy are also spoken. About 48% of the population is literate.

DEMOGRAPHICS

The people of the islands are of mixed descent: African, Arab and Malagasy.

Although Arabic and French are the official languages, the primary spoken tongue is the Comorian dialect of Swahili.

The great majority of the people, except on Mahoré (Mayotte) where Christianity is common, are Muslim.

GOVERNMENT AND POLITICAL SYSTEM

- **Nature and Structure of Government:**
- **Capital: Moroni**
- **Type: Independent republic**
- **Long Form of Name: Federal Islamic Republic of the Comoros**
- **Independence: 31 December 1975 (from France)**
- **Administrative Regions: Three islands; Njazidja, Nzwani, and Mwali, formerly Grand Comore, Anjouan, and Moheli respectively; note - there are also four municipalities named Domoni, Fomboni, Moroni, and Mutsamudu**
- **Constitution: 1 October 1978, amended October 1982 and January 1985**
- **National Holiday: Independence Day, 6 July (1975)**
- **Legal System: French and Muslim law in a new consolidated code**
- **Executive Branch: President, Council of Ministers (cabinet)**
- **Legislative Branch: Unicameral Federal Assembly (Assemblee Federale)**
- **Judicial Branch: Supreme Court (Cour Supreme)**
- **Suffrage: Universal at age 18**
- **Leaders: Chief of State and Head of Government: President Said Mohamed DJOHAR (since 11 March 1990); Prime Minister: Ahmed Ben Cheikh ATTOUMANE**

  Elections: Federal Assembly: last held 22 March 1987 (next were held March 1992); results - percent of vote by party NA; seats - (42 total) Udzima 42 President: last held 11 March 1990 (next to be held March 1996); results - Said Mohamed DJOHAR (Udzima) 55%, Mohamed TAKI Abdulkarim (UNDC) 45%
- **Military Branches: Comoran Security Forces (FCS), Federal Gendarmerie (GFC)**
- **Manpower Availability: Males 15-49, 105,022; 62,808 fit for military service**

The Federal Islamic Republic of the Comoro Islands

The islands became a French colony following the agreement between Great Britain, Germany, and France at the Berlin conference in the 1880s. Three of the islands: Ngazidja, Mwali, and Nzwani, declared themselves independent of France in 1975 and became the Federal Islamic Republic of the Comoro Islands. The fourth major island of the archipelago, Mayotte (Maore), continues to be administered by France although it is claimed by the Comoro Republic and this claim has been recognized by the United Nations General Assembly. In 1997, separatists on Nzwani and Mwali declared these islands to be independent from the Republic but this status has not been recognized and is being contested today.

Mr. HAMADA MADI BOLERO

Interim President

OFFICIAL NAME: FEDERAL ISLAMIC REPUBLIC OF COMOROS

Type: Republic.
Independence: July 6, 1975 (Mayotte remains under French administration).
Constitution: Adopted by referendum in 1978 and since amended.
Branches: Executive--president. Legislative--National Assembly. Judicial--traditional Muslim and codified law from French sources.
Political parties: 17 political parties.
Suffrage: universal adult.

NEW INTERIM GOVERNMENT OF NATIONAL UNION

Through a N° 02-022/CE decret of the Head of State, Colonel Azali Assoumani, a transition Government of National Union is formed on saturday 20, 2002 to manage the establishing of the new institutions for the Union of the Comoros

This Transition Government is formed as follows:

Prime Minister, Mister HAMADA MADI BOLERO

Deputy Prime Minister, Mister DJANFAR Salim, (Anjouan Authority)

Minister of Transports, Tourism, Postes and Telecommunications, Mister Hassane Ahmed BARWANE (opposition)

Minister of Culture, Youth, Sports and Information, Speaker of the Gouvernment, Mister Ali TOIHIR (Ruling Party)

Minister of Finance, Budget and Privatization, Mister Assoumany ABOUDOU (Ruling Party)

Minister of Economy, Commerce, Handcraft and Investissements, Mister CHABANE Bacar (opposition)

Minister of Production and Environment, Mister SAID ALI Boina Ali (Ruling Party)

Minister of Equipment, Energy and Urbanism, in charge of Relations with the Legislative Council, Mister Mohamed Ali Attoumane (Ruling Party)

Minister of Foreign Affairs And Cooperation, Mister HALIDY Charif (Anjouan Authority)

Minister of National Education, Professional Training and Human Rights, Mister Omar ACHIRAFF (opposition)

Minister of Home Affairs and Decentralization, Mister MOHAMED Ali Soilihi (Opposition)

Minister of Public Health, Social Affairs and Women Condition, Mister MCHAMI Mohamed (Ruling Party)

Minister of Public Administration, Employment and Work, Mister Mohamed ALI HAMIDI (opposition)

Unfortunately for national unity, on saturday 22, 2002, Moroni time, opposition leaders presented the resignation of ministers issued from opposition. The main cause of this decision would be the refusal of the Head of the Government to appoint a new minister of finance from the opposition, a change that would be badly understood by IMF and the World Bank who consider that the difficulties of the Comoros finance are due mostly to frequent changes of Finance Ministers and that this habit should be given up from now on.

A Board of Ministers meeting was held on monday, january 21st, in which Colonel Azali Assoumani resigned from all his responsabilities according to his commitments.

Upon the 28th of January, none of the resigned Ministers had confirmed their resignation.

The National Union Transition Governement is composed as mentionned above.

NATIONAL SECURITY

The military resources of the Comoros consist of a small standing army and a 500-member police force, as well as a 500-member defense force. A defense treaty with France provides naval resources for protection of territorial waters, training of Comorian military personnel, and air surveillance. France maintains a small troop presence in Comoros at government request. France maintains a small maritime base and a foreign legion contingent on Mayotte.

ECONOMY

GDP (purchasing power parity): $370 million.
Annual growth rate: 2.5% between 1980 and 1993; 0.9% in 1994.
Per capita income: $770.
Agriculture (40% of GDP): Products--perfume essences, copra, coconuts, cloves, vanilla, cinnamon, yams, bananas.
Services (25% of GDP): commerce, tourism.
Industry (6% of GDP): Types--perfume distillation.
Trade: Exports (1993 est.)--$13.7 million: vanilla, cloves, perfume essences, copra. Major markets--United States 44%, France 40%, Germany 6%, Africa 5%. Imports (1993 est.)--$40.9 million: rice, petroleum, meat, wheat flour, cotton textiles, cement. Major suppliers--France 34%, South Africa 14%, Kenya 8%, Japan 4%.
US Economic Aid: FY96 assistance totaled $120,000: $20,000 in self-help, $25,000 in democracy/human rights funds and $75,000 in international military education and training (IMET). The Peace Corps ended its programs in Comoros in 1995.
Exchange rate (1996): 428 Comorian franc = U.S. $1.

Comoros, with an estimated gross domestic product (GDP) per capita income of about $700, is among the world's poorest and least developed nations. Although the quality of the land differs from island to island, most of the widespread lava-encrusted soil formations are unsuited to agriculture. As a result, most of the inhabitants make their living from subsistence agriculture and fishing.

Agriculture, involving more than 80% of the population and 40% of the gross domestic product, provides virtually all foreign exchange earnings. Services including tourism, construction, and commercial activities constitute the remainder of the GDP. Plantations engage a large proportion of the population in producing the islands' major cash crops for export: vanilla, cloves, perfume essences, and copra. Comoros is the world's leading producer of essence of ylang-ylang, used in manufacturing perfume. It also is the world's second largest producer of vanilla. Principal food crops are coconuts, bananas, and cassava. Foodstuffs constitute 34% of total imports.

The country lacks the infrastructure necessary for development. Some villages are not linked to the main road system or at best are connected by tracks usable only by four-wheel-drive vehicles. The islands' ports are rudimentary, although a deep-water facility was recently completed on Anjouan. Only small vessels can approach the existing quays in Moroni on Grande Comore, despite recent improvements. Long-distance, ocean-going ships must lie offshore and be unloaded by smaller boats; during the cyclone season, this procedure is dangerous, and ships are reluctant to call at the island. Most freight is sent first to Mombasa or Reunion and transshipped from there.

France, Comoros' major trading partner, also provides direct budgetary support essential to the government's daily operations. The United States receives a growing percentage of Comoros' exports but supplies only a negligible fraction of its imports (less than 1%).

Comoros has an international airport at Hahaya on Grande Comore. It is a member of the franc zone (Communaute Financiere Africaine--CFA), with an exchange rate of 428 CFA francs = U.S. $1 (1991).

FOREIGN RELATIONS

In November 1975, Comoros became the 143d member of the United Nations. The new nation was defined as consisting of the entire archipelago, despite the fact that France maintains control over Mayotte.

Comoros also is a member of the Organization of African Unity, the European Development Fund, the World Bank, the International Monetary Fund, the Indian Ocean Commission, and the African Development Bank.

U.S.-COMORIAN RELATIONS

The United States recognized the Comorian Government in 1977. The two countries enjoy friendly relations. The United States closed its embassy in Moroni in 1993 and is now represented by a non-resident ambassador in neighboring Mauritius.

PRINCIPAL U.S. EMBASSY OFFICIALS

Ambassador--Harold W. Geisel (resident in Port Louis, Mauritius)
Administrative/Consular Officer--vacant

The address of the United States embassy in Mauritius is Rogers House, John F. Kennedy Street, Port Louis. (tel: 230-208-2347; fax: 230-208-9534). The mailing address for the embassy is Department of State, Washington, DC 20521-2520.

PRE-INDEPENDENCE

Until 1974, the Comoros were controlled by France. In that year, the majority of the population except on Mahoré (Mayotte) voted for independence. Independence was unilaterally declared in July 1975 although in 1976 the mainly French-speaking inhabitants of Mahoré (Mayotte), as a result of their own referendum, chose to remain under French rule.

THE 1992 CONSTITUTION

According to the 1992 constitution, the head of state is a president elected by universal suffrage for a term of five years. There is in addition a legislative branch of government -- the Federal Assembly -- with 42 members elected for four-year terms, and a Senate with 15 members chosen by an electoral college for six-year terms.

The government is headed by a prime minister who represents the majority party in parliament Njazidja has an international airport; the other islands have small airports.

The islands are served by Air Comores, Air Madagascar, Air Mauritius, Air France and South African Airways.

The Constitution of the Federal Islamic Republic of the Comoros was approved by referendum on June 7, 1992. It replaced the constitution of 1978, as amended in 1982 and 1985. Among the general principles enumerated in the preamble are the recognition of Islam as the state religion and respect for human rights as set forth in the UN Universal Declaration of Human Rights. All citizens are declared equal before the law.

The president is elected by direct universal suffrage to a five-year term and is limited to two terms. All persons over the age of eighteen who possess full civil and political rights may vote. The president may be elected to no more than two terms. The president is both head of state and head of government. The president nominates ministers to form the Council of Government, which had twelve members in the latter half of 1994. The ministries, which are routinely reshuffled, merged, eliminated, and resurrected, consisted of the following at that time: the prime minister, who also served as minister of civil service; Economy, Plan, Industry, and Handicrafts; Equipment, Energy, Urbanization, and Housing; Finance and Budget; Foreign Affairs and Cooperation; Information, Culture, Youth, Sports, and Posts and Telecommunication; Islamic Affairs and Justice;

National Education and Technical and Professional Teaching; Public Health; Rural Development, Fisheries, and the Environment; Social Affairs, Work, and Employment; and Transportation and Tourism. The president also nominates governors for each of the three islands for five-year terms. If the presidency becomes vacant, the president of the Supreme Court serves as interim president until an election can be held.

The constitution provides for a bicameral legislature. The forty-two members of the "lower" house, the Federal Assembly, represent electoral wards for four-year terms. The Federal Assembly meets for two forty-five-day sessions per year, in April and October. The upper house, the Senate, has fifteen members, five from each island, who are chosen by an Electoral College. The post of prime minister is held by a member of the party holding a majority of seats in the Federal Assembly. The number of political parties may be regulated by federal law. In 1994 more than twenty political parties were active. Areas subject to federal legislation include defense, communications, law, international trade, federal taxation, economic planning, and social services.

As a federal republic, Comoros assigns autonomy to the three constituent islands in matters that, in accordance with the constitution, do not come within the purview of the national government. Each island has a council whose members are elected to represent electoral wards for four-year terms. Normally, each council meets twice yearly, in March and December, for a fifteenday session (see Political Dynamics , this ch.).

The judiciary is considered independent of the executive and legislature. The Supreme Court examines constitutional issues and supervises presidential elections. The high court also arbitrates when the government is accused of malpractice. The Supreme Court normally consists of at least seven members: two chosen by the president, two elected by the Federal Assembly, and three chosen by the respective island councils. Former presidents also may serve on the high court.

POLITICAL DYNAMICS

In the immediate aftermath of the Abdallah assassination and subsequent events of late 1989, a limited amount of political healing occurred in Comoros. Denard and his fellow mercenaries were expelled, although the fate of their vast financial holdings in the islands remained unclear. With the South African government temporarily out of the picture, French officials now oversaw the police and the army, and the remnants of the GP were under the watchful eye of French paratroopers. Among those released in a general amnesty for political prisoners was Mustapha Said Cheikh, leader of the opposition FD who had been imprisoned for four years for alleged involvement in the unsuccessful March 1985 coup. He was quickly proposed as a possible presidential candidate. Also suggested was Mohamed Taki, one-time National Assembly president whose power had been diminished by Abdallah's constitutional maneuvers; he had subsequently gone into exile in France, where his entourage reportedly included two mercenary bodyguards. Also announcing for the presidency was Said Ali Kemal, who had been living in quiet exile in Paris since being exposed as the sponsor of Australian mercenaries who had plotted to overthrow the Abdallah government in 1983. In late December 1989, members of the formerly banned opposition, along with President Djohar, decided to form a provisional "national unity" government and to hold a multiparty presidential election in 1990.

In an awkward but somehow effective campaign to keep himself in power, Djohar spent much of the early 1990s playing a political shell game with the opposition. He moved election dates backward and forward and sanctioned irregularities, giving his opponents little choice but to condemn the balloting as invalid. Djohar began this strategy within weeks of his installation as interim president, rescheduling the presidential election set for January 14, 1990 to February 18. Djohar's decision was met with demonstrations and violence that marked an abrupt end to the post-Abdallah period of national unity, hardly three weeks after Bob Denard had been expelled from the country. The February 18 balloting broke down shortly after the polls opened. The government was accused of widespread fraud, including issuing multiple voting cards to some voters and opening the polls to voters who looked well below the minimum age of eighteen.

Elections were rescheduled for March 4, 1990 with a runoff on March 11; Djohar was the official victor, claiming 55 percent of the vote over runner-up Mohamed Taki's 45 percent. Djohar had run under the banner of the Union Comorienne pour le Progrès (Udzima- -Comoran Union for Progress), basically a recycled version of Ahmed Abdallah's old UCP, whereas Taki had represented the National Union for Comoran Democracy (Union Nationale pour la Démocratie Comorien--UNDC). As would be the case in other Comoran elections in the 1990s, the sole major issue appeared to be the character and ability of the incumbent president rather than any matter of public policy or ideology. The Supreme Court certified the results of the election, despite strong evidence that the Ministry of Interior had altered the vote count, especially in the first round, to favor Djohar at Taki's expense.

In March 1992, with two of the government's Udzima ministers having broken away to form a new party and conflict among the remaining Udzima ministers growing, Djohar headed off the complete collapse of his government by convening a multiparty constitutional convention. He scheduled a referendum on the new document in May, with general elections in June and balloting for local offices in July. After one postponement, the referendum was held on June 7. The Constitution of 1992 passed with about 74 percent of the vote, despite intensive campaigning against it by the FD and Udzima, which by this point opposed

President Djohar. Among the new document's elements were articles calling for a bicameral legislature and a limit on presidential tenure to two five-year terms.

The legislative elections, postponed several times, finally were held on November 22 and 29, 1992. They were preceded in late September by an attempted coup by junior army officers, allegedly with the support of opposition politicians. Possible motives for the coup were an unpopular restructuring program mandated by the World Bank, which entailed sharp reductions in the number of civil servants, and President Djohar's ambiguous threat on September 10 that his main opponents would "not be around for the elections." Djohar used the coup attempt as an opportunity to jail six military men and six opposition leaders "under conditions of extreme illegality," according to the Comoran Association of Human Rights (Association Comorienne des Droits Humains--ACDH).

Although a trio of French public officials sent to observe the balloting judged the election generally democratic, President Djohar's most prominent and determined opponents spent the voting days either in hiding or in jail. Two of the most important of the republic's twenty-four political parties, Udzima and the UNDC, boycotted the election. Given the president's own lack of party support, he spent most of 1993 cobbling together one government after another; at one point, in late spring 1993, he formed two governments in the space of three weeks.

The events of a single day in July 1993 perhaps summed up the near-term prospects of politics in Comoros. On July 23, heeding demands that he call legislative elections (he had dissolved parliament on June 18 because of its inability to agree to a candidate for prime minister and because of the lack of a government majority) or else face the prospect of "other forms of action" by the opposition, Djohar scheduled voting for late October. That same day, his government arrested two opposition leaders for public criticism of the president.

The scheduled elections were again postponed--for the fourth time--until December 1993. On November 17, 1993, Djohar created a new National Electoral Commission, said to be appropriately representative of the various political parties. Meanwhile Djohar had established a new progovernment party, the Rally for Democracy and Renewal (Rassemblement pour la Démocratie et le Renouveau--RDR). In the first round of elections on December 12, which featured twenty-four parties with 214 candidates for fortytwo seats, various voting irregularities occurred, including the failure to issue voting cards to some 30 percent of eligible voters. The government announced that Djohar's party had won twenty-one seats with three seats remaining to be contested. Most opposition parties stated that they would not sit in the assembly and also refused to participate in the postponed second stage elections, which were supervised by the Ministry of Interior and the gendarmerie after the National Electoral

Commission disintegrated. As a result, the RDR gained a total of twenty-two seats, and Djohar appointed RDR secretary general Mohamed Abdou Madi as prime minister.

Denouncing the proceedings, on January 17, 1994, thirteen opposition parties formed a combined Forum for National Recovery (Forum pour le Redressement National--FRN). The Udzima Party began broadcasting articles about Comoros appearing in the *Indian Ocean Newsletter*, including criticisms of the RDR. In consequence, its radio station, Voix des Îles (Voice of the Islands) was confiscated by the government in mid-February 1994-- in September 1993, the radio station belonging to Abbas Djoussouf, who later became leader of the RDR, had been closed. Tensions increased, and in March 1994 an assassination attempt against Djohar occurred. At the end of May, civil service employees went on strike, including teachers, and violence erupted in mid-June when the FRN prepared to meet.

FOREIGN AFFAIRS

Comoros' most significant international relationship is that with France. The three years of estrangement following the unilateral declaration of independence and the nationalistic Soilih regime were followed during the conservative Abdallah and Djohar regimes by a period of growing trade, aid, cultural, and defense links between the former colony and France, punctuated by frequent visits to Paris by the head of state and occasional visits by the French president to Moroni. The leading military power in the region, France has detachments on Mahoré and Reunion, and its Indian Ocean fleet sails the waters around the islands. France and Comoros signed a mutual security treaty in 1978; following the mercenary coup against Abdallah in 1989, French troops restored order and took responsibility for reorganizing and training the Comoran army. With Mahoré continuing to gravitate politically and economically toward France, and Comoros increasingly dependent on the French for help with its own considerable social, political, and economic problems, the issue of Mahoré diminished somewhat in urgency.

The close relationship Comoros developed with South Africa in the 1980s was much less significant to both countries in the 1990s. With the reform of its apartheid government, South Africa no longer needed Comoros as evidence of its ostensible ability to enjoy good relations with a black African state; the end of the Cold War had also diminished Comoros' strategic value to Pretoria. Although South Africa continued to provide developmental aid, it closed its consulate in Moroni in 1992. Since the 1989 coup and subsequent expulsion of South Africanfinanced mercenaries, Comoros likewise turned away from South Africa and toward France for assistance with its security needs.

The government fostered close relationships with the more conservative (and oil-rich) Arab states, such as Saudi Arabia and Kuwait. It frequently received aid from those countries and the regional financial institutions they influenced, such as the Arab Bank for Economic Development in Africa and the Arab Fund for Economic and Social Development. In October 1993, Comoros joined the League of Arab States, after having been rejected when it applied for membership initially in 1977.

Regional relations generally were good. In 1985 Madagascar, Mauritius, and Seychelles agreed to admit Comoros as the fourth member of the Indian Ocean Commission (IOC), an organization established in 1982 to encourage regional cooperation. In 1993 Mauritius and Seychelles had two of the five embassies in Moroni, and Mauritius and Madagascar were connected to the republic by regularly scheduled commercial flights.

Comoros also hosted an embassy of China, which established relations during the Soilih regime. The Chinese had long been a source of aid and apparently wished to maintain contact with Comoros to counterbalance Indian and Soviet (later Russian) influence in the Indian Ocean. Comoran relations with Japan were also significant because Japan was the second largest provider of aid, consisting of funding for fisheries, food, and highway development. The United States established diplomatic relations in 1977 but in September 1993 closed it embassy in Moroni. The two countries enjoy friendly relations.

In November 1975, Comoros became the 143d member of the UN. In the 1990s, the republic continued to represent Mahoré in the UN. Comoros was also a member of the OAU, the EDF, the World Bank, the IMF, the IOC, and the African Development Bank.

Comoros thus cultivated relations with various nations, both East and West, seeking to increase trade and obtain financial assistance. In 1994, however, it was increasingly facing the need to control its expenditures and reorganize its economy so that it would be viewed as a sounder recipient of investment. Comoros also confronted domestically the problem of the degree of democracy the government was prepared to grant to its citizens, a consideration that related to its standing in the world community.

* * *

The reader seeking works on the history, politics, and society of Comoros also needs to consult a number of publications that cover the republic as one of many African or Indian Ocean countries. These include *Africa Analysis*, *Africa Contemporary Record*, *Africa Events*, *Africa Research Bulletin*, and *Africa South of the Sahara*. Other periodically issued sources include the annual country-by-country *Amnesty International Report* and the newsletters *Africa Confidential* and *Indian Ocean Newsletter*. Whereas the *Times* of London, *New York Times*, and *Washington Post* report Comoros' more serious upheavals, more regular coverage is provided by *Le Monde*. Useful social and economic data can be obtained from World Bank publications. One such publication in particular, *Social Indicators of Development*, an annual, provides country-by-country tables of data on indicators of poverty and resources and expenditures. Books such as Thierry Flobert's 1976 work, *Les Comores: Évolution juridique et socio-politique*, the World Bank 1979 publication *The Comoros: Problems and Prospects of a Small, Island Economy*, and Malyn Newitt's *The Comoro Islands: Struggle Against Dependency in the Indian Ocean*, provide useful background despite their growing datedness.

PARLIAMENT

The Parliament of Comoros is unicameral.

- Name of Parliament: Federal Assembly *(Assemblée Fédérale)*
- Number of Seats: 43
- Term of legislature: 4 years
- Required age for voting: 18
- Required age for membership: 21

The 43 members of the Federal Assembly are directly elected in 43 single-member constituencies by a majority vote in two rounds. A candidate is elected if he obtains an absolute majority at the first round or a simple majority at the second. Voting is not compulsory.

Last legislative elections: 1 and 8 December 1996.

Party	seats (total of 43)
National Rally for Development RND (presidential)	36
National Front for Justice FNJ (islamist, supporting the RND)	3
Independents	4

On 20 October 1996, a new Constitution was approved by referendum. A few days later, the opposition political forces, united in a "Forum Federation" announced that they would boycott the elections.

The opposition parties characterized these elections as a *"masquerade"*.

There is no woman in this Assembly.

SECURITY AND ARMED FORCES[1]

Comoros faces no external threats. However, during the 1970s and 1980s, various groups of European mercenaries, all supposedly supported by foreign powers, played a significant role in Comorian domestic politics.

Since independence the Comorian government has contended with several internal threats. This domestic instability reflects the weakness of the island's central government, the unpopularity of its rulers, and the presence of European mercenaries. On July 6, 1975, the Comorian Chamber of Deputies approved a unilateral declaration of independence from France, named Ahmed Abdallah as president, and constituted itself as the National Assembly. On August 3, 1975, a group of notables, radicals, and technocrats overthrew the Abdallah regime. These individuals replaced the National Assembly with a National Executive Council, led by Prince Said Mohammed Jaffar. In January 1976, Ali Soilih succeeded Jaffar as president.

Soilih embarked on a revolutionary program, based on Maoist and Islamic philosophies, to facilitate the development of an economically self-sufficient and ideologically progressive state. Apart from alienating France, which terminated its aid and technical assistance programs to Comoros, Soilih's policies aroused resentment among the island's traditional leaders. To make matters worse, Soilih established his version of Mao's Red Guards, the Commando Moissi. These vigilantes, trained by Tanzanian military advisers, further alienated Comorian society by acting as a repressive political police. Growing popular discontent resulted in four unsuccessful coup attempts against the Soilih regime during its two and a half-year existence.

On May 12-13, 1978, a fifty-member European mercenary unit, hired by Ahmed Abdallah in France and led by French Colonel Robert Denard, finally overthrew Soilih. Two weeks later, security personnel killed Soilih, allegedly while he was trying to escape from house arrest. Ahmed Abdallah and his former deputy, Muhammad Ahmed, then became co-presidents. Although it initially experienced some opposition because of the role played by Denard and his mercenaries in the coup, the new government eventually gained popular support. Its popularity rested on its ability to restore relations with France, which resumed economic, military, and cultural aid to the island, and to gain assistance from the European Community and several Arab countries, including Saudi Arabia, Iraq, and Kuwait. On October 22, 1978, Abdallah was elected to a six-year term as president.

Despite the influx of foreign aid, political conditions in Comoros remained unsettled, largely because Abdallah failed to establish a government that included adequate representation for the people who lived on the outlying islands

[1] This section based on the materials of the US Library of Congress

of Njazidja, Nzwani, and Mwali. Moreover, Abdallah frequently used repressive methods against his real and imagined adversaries. In this turbulent atmosphere, opponents of Abdallah's regime made at least four unsuccessful attempts to overthrow his government.

In February 1981, loyal Presidential Guard (Garde Presidentielle--GP) units crushed an army mutiny on the main island of Grande Comore and the authorities subsequently arrested about 150 people. In December 1983, another plot surfaced after the arrest of a group of British mercenaries in Australia. According to the Comorian government, they had planned to overthrow Abdallah on behalf of a former Comorian diplomat, Said Ali Kemal. A March 1985 plot against Abdallah by the GP also failed and resulted in seventeen people being sentenced to forced labor for life and fifty others being imprisoned for their part in the coup attempt. In November 1987, French mercenaries and South African military advisers, based in Comoros, reportedly thwarted a coup by a small number of GP and armed forces personnel.

On November 27-27, 1989, the Abdallah regime finally fell after members of the GP, which included several European advisers under Colonel Denard's command, assassinated the president. As outlined in the constitution, the Supreme Court president, Said Mohamed Djohar, became interim head of state, pending a presidential election. However, Colonel Denard and his associates engineered a coup against Djohar, disarmed the army, and killed at least twenty-seven police. Growing French and South African pressure forced Colonel Denard to leave Comoros for South Africa. In April 1990, the Comorian government announced that France would maintain a military team on the islands for two years to train local security forces.

Despite the presence of French troops and a general amnesty for all political prisoners, Comoros continued to suffer from internal instability. On August 18-19, 1990, armed rebels unsuccessfully tried to overthrow Djohar by attacking various French installations on the island of Njazidja. A small group of European mercenaries allegedly the coup attempt and believed that the Djohar regime would fall if they could force the French to withdraw from the islands. The authorities detained more that twenty people in connection with the uprising. Another coup attempt occurred on September 26, 1992, when Lieutenant Said Mohamed and 100 Comorian army personnel tried to overthrow Djohar. According to plotters, the coup's purpose was "to ensure state security and to put in place a true democracy." Troops loyal to Djohar quickly crushed this coup attempt. Since then, political instability has continued to plague Comoros, largely because of opposition to Djohar and growing demands for democratization.

THE MILITARY AND THE GOVERNMENT

Until independence, Comoros had no armed forces. Since then, the government has maintained a small military establishment, which, by international standards, possesses minimal capabilities. However, despite the lack of a strong military tradition, the armed forces has played a significant role in the country's political life. In particular, the GP, which is the best trained and best armed of all security services, has repeatedly intervened in politics and eventually controlled Comoros. Such activities understandably have attracted considerable attention, especially because the GP includes European mercenaries in its ranks and in senior positions. Over the years, there have been numerous reports, some of which remain unconfirmed, that foreign powers such as France, Britain, or South Africa provided these mercenaries with money and weapons. By the early 1990s, most Western observers believed that as long as French military forces remained in the islands, the Comorian armed forces were unlikely to maintain a high political profile.

Little information exists about Comorian defense economics. In 1987, the most recent year for which figures were available, the government budgeted about 910 Comoros francs for defense expenditures.

ARMED FORCES

The national army, the Comorian Armed Forces (Forces Armées Comoriennes--FAC), maintains a personnel strength of approximately 700 to 800 men. The FAC inventory includes an array of small arms and light military vehicles. A small military aviation element operates a Cessna 402B and an AS-350B Écureuil. The aircraft are used for VIP transport. Comoros lacks a navy. Most military training occurs in Comoros; however, a small number of army personnel have received some foreign training, primarily in France and the United States. Historically, army morale has been low, largely because of the GP's predominance and influence. After taking control of the island in December 1989, France dissolved the Comorian army and unveiled plans to train and organize a new Comorian armed forces.

STATE SECURITY SERVICES

The 600-member GP reports to the president's office. However, after the assassination of President Abdallah on November 26, 1989, the GP, under Colonel Denard's command, controlled the country. After assuming responsibility for Comorian security in December 1989, France announced that the GP would be limited to a representative role with a reduced number of troops. The 500-member National Police Force (Force de Police Nationale) is headquartered in Moroni, with detachments in the other islands.

FOREIGN MILITARY ASSISTANCE

Since independence, Comoros has received foreign military assistance from Tanzania, France, South Africa, and the United States. However, by early 1994, only France and the United States continued to provide military aid to Comoros.

Tanzania hoped to keep Comoros away from Western influence by providing military aid to President Soilih. However, apart from deploying about 100 military advisers to the islands to train the army and the Commando Moissi, Tanzania lacks the resources to make a significant long-term impact on the Comorian armed forces.

Historically, France has been the most important military player in Comoros. It sought to protect its strategic interests in the Indian Ocean and its military installations on the islands of Reunion and Mayotte. Even before independence, France and Comoros signed a defense agreement in 1973; five years later, the two nations concluded a technical military assistance agreement. After the downfall of the Soilih regime in 1978, French military advisers replaced European mercenaries and guaranteed Comorian security. On November 10, 1978, Paris and Moroni signed a military agreement that provided French training for Comorian armed forces and French military assistance in case of an attack on the islands. By January 1985, seventy-six Comorian military personnel had received training in France, and the French military had stationed twenty-three advisers in Comoros.

After the assassination of President Abdullah, France deployed 140 troops from the 21st Marine Paratroop Regiment and fifty officers and warrant officers from the Military Assistance and Instruction Detachment. According to a December 16, 1989, statement by President Djohar, the latter unit was supposed to remain on the islands for one to two years to train and to reorganize the Comorian armed forces. However, by early 1994, France continued to maintain a military presence in Comoros.

During the late 1980s, South Africa and Comoros maintained a discreet but significant military relationship. The South African government constructed a radio-monitoring station on the islands. Also, according to *Indian Ocean Newsletter*, Comoros was a transshipment point for arms shipments from South Africa to Iran and to the Mozambican National Resistance (Resistência Nacional Moçambicano--Renamo) rebel movement in Mozambique. Additionally, South Africa funded the GP, under Colonel Denard's command. In late 1989, South Africa severed its connection to the GP and Colonel Denard, thereby allowing France to become the dominant foreign military power on the islands.

Since the late 1980s, the United States has maintained a small IMET program in Comoros. Initially, five to six Comorian officers received basic military training and English language instruction in the United States. In 1989 the IMET program was expanded to include professional military education and technical training courses for a small number of Comorian military personnel. By the early 1990s, the IMET program complemented the ongoing French effort to reorganize the Comorian armed forces.

PENAL SYSTEM

The Comorian legal system rests on Islamic law and an inherited French legal code. Village elders or civilian courts settle most disputes. The judiciary is independent of the legislative and the executive. The Supreme Court acts as a Constitutional Council in resolving constitutional questions and supervising presidential elections. As High Court of Justice, the Supreme Court also arbitrates in cases where the government is accused of malpractice. The Supreme Court consists of two members selected by the president, two elected by the Federal Assembly, and one by the council of each island.

STUDYING COUNTRY THROUGH THE CONSTITUTION

COMOROS CONSTITUTION

PREAMBLE

The preamble affirms the will of the Comoran people to derive from the state religion, Islam, inspiration for the principles and laws that the State and its institutions govern, to adhere to the principles laid down by the Charters of the UN, the Organization of African Unity and the Organization of the Islamic Conference and by the Treaty of the League of Arab States, and to guarantee the rights of all citizens, without discrimination, in accordance with the UN Declaration of Human Rights and the African Charter of Human Rights

PRESIDENT OF THE REPUBLIC

The President is the Head of State and is elected by direct universal suffrage for n six-year term, which is renewable for an unrestricted number of mandates. He is also Head of the Armed Forces and ensures the legitimate functioning of public powers and the continuation of the State. He is the guarantor of national independence, the unity of the Republic, the autonomy of the islands, territorial integrity and adherence to international agreements. Candidates for the presidency must be aged between 40 and 75 years, of Comoran nationality by birth, and resident in the archipelago for at least 12 consecutive months prior to elections. The President presides over the Council of Ministers. He is empowered to ask the Federal Assembly to reconsider a Bill. The President can, having consulted with the Prime Minister and the Presidents of the Federal Assembly and the High Council of the Republic in writing, dissolve the Federal

Assembly. The President determines and implements the Republic's foreign policy.

LEGISLATIVE POWER

Legislative power is vested in the Federal Assembly, which represents the Comoran nation. Deputies in the Federal Assembly are elected for five years by direct suffrage. Legislative elections take place between 30 and 90 days after the expiry of the mandate of the incumbent Federal Assembly. The electoral law dictates the number of members of the Federal Assembly, but there is a minimum of five deputies from each island.

The deputies elect the President of the Federal Assembly at the beginning of their mandate. The Federal Assembly sits for two sessions each year and, if necessary, for extraordinary sessions. Matters covered by federal legislation include constitutional institutions, defence, posts and telecommunications, transport, civil and penal law, public finance, external trade, federal taxation, long-term economic planning, education and health.

HIGH COUNCIL OF THE REPUBLIC

The High Council of the Republic considers constitutional sass and the control of public finance, and acts as a High Court of J It has a renewable mandate of seven years and is composed members appointed by the President, three members elected by Federal Assembly and one member elected by the Council of eaach Island. The High Council oversees and proclaims the re presidential and legislative elections and referendums.

ISLAND INSTITUTIONS

While respecting the unity of the Republic, each island is autonomous territorial entity which freely controls its own administration through a Governor and a Council, The Governor of each appointed by the President of the Republic, from three candidates proposed by the Council of the island. The Council of each island is composed of the mayors of the communes and sits for not more than 15 days at a time, in March and December, and, if necessary, for extraordinary sessions. The Council is responsible for such matters as the budget of the island, taxes, culture, health, primary education and the environment.

GENERAL PROVISIONS

The Comoros archipelago constitutes a federal Islamic republic. Sovereignty belongs to the people, and is exercised through their elected representatives or by the process of referendum. There is universal secret suffrage, which can be direct or indirect, for all citizens who are over the age of 18 and in full possession of their civil and political rights.

Political parties and groups operate freely, respecting national sovereignty, democracy and territorial integrity. However, political parties which are not represented by at least two deputies from each island, as a result of the first legislative election to follow the adoption of the Constitution, will be dissolved, unless those parties merge with others which are legitimately represented in the Federal Assembly. If only one political party has representation in the Federal Assembly, the party which has obtained the second highest number of votes will continue to operate freely. Only political parties and groups active throughout the Republic may participate in national elections. Political parties must be democratic both in their internal structure and their activities

THE GOVERNMENT

The President appoints the Prime Minister, and on his recommendations, the other members of the Government. Under the authority of the President of the Republic, the Council of Ministers determines and implements domestic policy.

JUDICIAL POWER

Judicial power is independent of executive and legislative power The President is the guarantor of the independence of the judicial system and chairs the Higher Council of the Magistracy (Conseil Supérieur de la Magistrature), of which the Minister of Justice is Vice-President.

COUNCIL OF THE ULÉMAS

The Council of the Ulémas offers opinions on projects for 1st ordinances and decrees. The President of the Republic, the Minister, the President of the Federal Assembly, the Presidents the Councils and the Governors of the islands may consult Council of the Ulémas on any religious issue. The Council of Ulémas may submit recommendations to the Federal Assembly, the Government or the Governors of the islands if it considers legislation to be in contravention of the principles of Islam.

REVISION OF THE CONSTITUTION

The power to initiate constitutional revision is vested in the President of the Republic. However, one-third of the members of Federal Assembly may propose amendments to the President Constitutional revision must be approved by a majority of the deputies in the Federal Assembly, and is subject to approval by national referendum. However, the President of the Republic may decide to promulgate a constitutional project, without submitting it to a referendum, if it has been adopted at a congress of deputies and the councillors of the islands, by a majority of two-thirds. The Republican and Islamic nature of the State cannot be revised.

DEMOCRACY AND HUMAN RUGHTS[2]

The Federal Islamic Republic of the Comoros is ruled by Colonel Assoumani Azali, who took power in a coup in April. The country consists of three islands (Grande Comore, Anjouan, and Moheli) and claims a fourth, Mayotte, which is governed by France. Comoros has been prone to coups and political insurrection since independence in 1975. On April 29 and 30, army commander Colonel Azali staged a bloodless coup and overthrew President Tadjiddine Ben Said Massounde, the Interim President who had held office since the death of democratically elected President Mohamed Taki Abdoulkarim in November 1998. Colonel Azali justified the coup and his subsequent self-designation as president by stating that the previous government was unable to maintain law and order on Grande Comore or to solve the Anjouan secession crisis. Colonel Azali said that he would step down on April 14, 2000 and relinquish power to a democratically elected president.

However, his vow was conditioned on Anjouan's return to the republic and participation in the elections. On May 6, Azali decreed a new Constitution that gives him both executive and legislative powers. While the Cabinet is predominantly civilian, three-quarters of the regime's directorate, where the real power is thought to reside, is composed of members of the military. In December in response to international criticism, Azali appointed a civilian prime minister, Bianrifi Tarmidi; however, Azali remains the Head of State and army commander in chief. The judiciary was the only federal institution to survive the coup intact. Its nominal independence was not tested during the year; however, in the past, both the executive and other elites have influenced the outcome of court cases.

The Anjouan secession crisis entered its third year. In April Anjouanais representatives were the only parties who refused to sign a reunification accord brokered by the Organization for African Unity's (OAU), which was negotiated in Antananarivo, Madagascar. The Anjouanais leadership had not signed the accords by year's end. In August legislative elections were held on Anjouan, in which the faction led by Lieutenant Colonel Said Abeid won an overwhelming majority. Opposition parties alleged that most of their candidates were disqualified unfairly. Several opposition leaders were expelled to Mayotte in September, then imprisoned when they were sent back to Anjouan by French authorities. The OAU observer force departed the country after the coup. The OAU General Assembly and Council of Ministers both have criticized the coup, and the General Assembly threatened sanctions if constitutional government was not restored before the next OAU summit.

---

[2] Bureau of Democracy, Human Rights, and Labor U.S. Department of State

The Comorian Defense Force (FCD) and the gendarmerie are responsible for internal security and are under Azali's direct control. Security forces committed some human rights abuses.

The economy of this extremely poor country is dominated by agriculture. Revenues from the main crops--vanilla, essence of ylang-ylang, and cloves--continue to fall while the population of 547,600 has been growing at a rate of 2.7 percent annually. Per capita income was approximately $400 per year in 1997. The national accounts have not been updated since 1998. The country depends heavily on foreign assistance from the European Union and Arab countries, including Bahrain, Kuwait, Qatar, Saudi Arabia, and the United Arab Emirates.

The human rights situation remained poor, and worsened in several areas. Citizens do not have the right to change their government. Police regularly threatened Christians, prison conditions remain poor, and police sometimes arbitrarily arrested and detained persons. There were some infringements on freedom of the press and academic freedom. The military regime limits freedom of religion. Societal discrimination against women and Christians continued to be serious problems. There were some instances of forced child labor. Prior to the coup, nongovernmental political factions harassed and beat Anjouanais residents throughout Grande Comore after Anjouanais representatives refused to sign the Antananarivo accords in April.

On at least one occasion, quasi-police authorities known as embargoes on Anjouan beat and detained Christians. Political violence on Anjouan resulted in a number of deaths.

RESPECT FOR HUMAN RIGHTS

RESPECT FOR THE INTEGRITY OF THE PERSON, INCLUDING FREEDOM

A. POLITICAL AND OTHER EXTRAJUDICIAL KILLING

There were no reports of political or extrajudicial killings by the authorities on Grande Comore.

Between May 11 and 13, 1998, police clashed with protestors on Grand Comore over the May 6 government closure of the opposition party's Radio Tropique. Police seriously injured several persons, but the only death reportedly was due to a traffic accident caused by the fighting. No police officers were held responsible for their actions during the protests.

In addition to the police and the military, there are many groups throughout Anjouan that are armed, including paramilitary forces, militias, and civilians. Battles between rival militias resulted in about a dozen deaths.

In May a Paris, France court acquitted Bob Denard, a 70-year-old mercenary, of charges that he killed President Ahmed Abdallah in 1989.

b. Disappearance

There were no reports of politically motivated disappearances.

c. Torture and Other Cruel, Inhuman, or Degrading Treatment or Punishment

The new Constitution declared by Colonel Azali does not specifically prohibit torture or other cruel, inhuman, or degrading treatment or punishment; however, while there were no reports of security force brutality, police regularly threatened Christians (see Section 2.c.).

In April just prior to the coup, nongovernmental political factions and gangs of youths harassed and beat hundreds of Anjouanais on the main island of Grand Comore after representatives from Anjouan refused to sign a reunification accord.

In April embargoes arrested, beat, and detained three local Christians (see Section 2.c.). Prison conditions continued to be poor. A lack of proper sanitation, overcrowding, inadequate medical facilities, and poor diet are common problems. The military regime has not taken action to remedy these problems.

The military regime permits prison visit by independent monitors; however, no such visits occurred during the year.

d. Arbitrary Arrest, Detention, or Exile

The Constitution does not prohibit arbitrary arrest and detention specifically, and there were instances in which authorities arbitrarily arrested and detained citizens. Three opposition politicians, including former interim Prime Minister Abbas Djoussouf, were arrested and detained briefly following minor street demonstrations in September. In September the courts dismissed charges against all three. In October authorities arrested a journalist for writing an article that suggested that there was discord within the army over Azali's rule (see Section 2.a.).

In April embargoes on Anjouan arrested, beat, and detained for a day three local Christians (see Sections 1.c. and 2.c.). Usually the authorities hold those detained for a few days and often attempt to convert them forcibly to Islam. This incident was not investigated, nor was any action taken against the persons responsible. Anjouan authorities also detained political opponents. In September secessionist authorities on Anjouan exiled a score of opponents to Mayotte, then imprisoned several of the group's leaders when they were sent back to Anjouan by French authorities. The opponents were released from prison in early October, and no charges were filed against them.

The Constitution does not prohibit forced exile, but the military regime did not use it.

E. Denial of Fair Public Trial

The Constitution provides for an independent judiciary enforced by the Head of State; however, while the nominal independence of the judiciary was not tested during the year, in the past, the executive and other elites have exercised influence over court cases. The Head of State names magistrates by decree.

The High Council, made up of four members appointed by the President, three members elected by the Federal Assembly, and a member of each island council, also serves as the High Court of the Republic and rules on cases of constitutional law. The May Constitution does not provide for equality before the law of all citizens. It does not mention the right to counsel. Trials are open to the public except for limited exceptions defined by law. The legal system incorporates Islamic law as well as French legal codes. There are very few lawyers in the country, making it difficult to obtain legal representation. The military regime does not provide legal counsel to the accused. Most disputes are presented to village elders for possible resolution before being taken to court.

There were no reports of political prisoners.

F. Arbitrary Interference with Privacy, Family, Home, or Correspondence

There were no known cases of arbitrary interference with privacy or correspondence. Former President Taki's bans on alcohol and immodest dress no longer remained in effect. Alcohol can be imported and sold with a permit from the military regime.

SECTION 2 RESPECT FOR CIVIL LIBERTIES, INCLUDING:

A. Freedom of Speech and Press

The Constitution does not provide specifically for freedom of the press, and on at least one occasion authorities infringed on this right. In early October, a freelance correspondent with Agence France Presse, Aboubacar Mchangama, was arrested and detained for reporting about unease within the army between supporters and opponents of Colonel Azali. He reportedly was released on bail on October 21. Nevertheless, small independent newspapers exist side-by-side with the semiofficial weekly Al-Watwan, and some of the independent newspapers criticized the regime freely.

The regime-controlled radio station, Radio Comoros, was the only national radio station until the opposition radio station Radio Tropique resumed operations in June. In addition there are at least 10 regional and local stations, some of which are openly critical of the regime. Residents also receive broadcasts from Mayotte Radio, as well as from French television, without government interference. A national television station is under construction with assistance from the Chinese Government. There are several private local television stations, and satellite antennas are popular. Amateur radio licenses have been issued without hindrance in the past.

Foreign newspapers are available, as are books from abroad. Internet service was introduced by the Taki Government in September 1998.

In August an independent radio station on Anjouan, Radio Ushababi, which was opposed to the independence movement, reportedly was forced to cease broadcasting after being harassed by police and threatened on several occasions by a group of separatist militiamen.

There is no university, but secondary students and teachers speak freely and criticize the regime openly. Public schools no longer are closed on Grand Comore. In order to pressure the Anjouan authorities into signing the Antananarivo accords, the Azali military regime prevented Anjouanais students who traveled to Grande Comore from taking their baccalaureate exams.

B. Freedom of Peaceful Assembly and Association

The Constitution does not provide specifically for freedom of assembly and association, but the regime generally respected these rights in practice.

C. Freedom of Religion

The Constitution does not prohibit discrimination based on religion or religious belief specifically, and authorities infringed on this right. An overwhelming majority of the population is Sunni Muslim. Authorities restricted the right of Christians to practice their faith. Police regularly threatened and sometimes detained practicing Christians. Usually, the authorities hold those detained for a few days and often attempt to convert them to Islam forcibly. In October two citizens were arrested, tried, and convicted of " anti-Islamic activity" in part because they possessed Christian books and audiovisual material. One of the citizens was sentenced to 18 months in prison, while the other was sentenced to 4 months. Local government officials attempted to force Christians to attend services at mosques against their will.

There are two Roman Catholic churches and one Protestant church. However, prior to the April coup, the former military regime restricted the use of these three churches to noncitizens. There was no information available as to whether the new military regime continued this practice. Many Christians practice their faith in private residences. The regime permits Christian missionaries to work in local hospitals and schools, but does not permit them to proselytize.

The Ulamas council, which had advised the President, Prime Minister, President of the Federal Assembly, the Council of Isles, and the island governors on whether bills, ordinances, decrees, and laws are in conformity with the principles of Islam, no longer exists.

In April embargoes on Anjouan arrested, beat, and detained for a day three local Christians. Some community authorities on Anjouan banned Christians from attending any community events and banned Christian burials in a local cemetery.

d. Freedom of Movement Within the Country, Foreign Travel, Emigration, and Repatriation

The Constitution does not specifically provide for these rights; however, the military regime generally respected them in practice. There is no longer a curfew in effect. Air links that had been severed since December 1998 between Grande Comore and Anjouan were restored in April. Passports were again available.

The regime has not formulated a policy regarding refugees, asylees, or first asylum.

RESPECT FOR POLITICAL RIGHTS

THE RIGHT OF CITIZENS TO CHANGE THEIR GOVERNMENT

According to the Constitution's preamble and in practice, citizens do not have the right to change their government. The Constitution states that national sovereignty belongs to the nation's citizens who may exercise it through referendums; however, the regime had not scheduled a referendum by year's end.

According to the Constitution, the Head of State--self-appointed President Azali--has legislative power, which he exercises through ordinances, and executive power, which he exercises through decrees. On April 30, Colonel Azali said that he would step down on April 14, 2000, and relinquish power to a democratically elected president if Anjouan returns to the Republic and participates in the elections.

There are no bans in effect on political parties, which continue openly to criticize the regime without penalty.

Village chiefs and Muslim religious leaders tend to dominate local politics. Traditional social, religious, and economic institutions also affect the country's political life in important ways.

Although women have the right to vote and to run for office, they are underrepresented severely in national politics. At least two women hold senior government positions: one is the Minister for National Education and the other holds the second highest position on the State Council, which advises the Cabinet.

GOVERNMENTAL ATTITUDE REGARDING INTERNATIONAL AND NONGOVERNMENTAL INVESTIGATION OF ALLEGED VIOLATIONS OF HUMAN RIGHTS

The military regime did not prevent the operation of human rights nongovernmental organizations (NGO's), and a number of NGO's operated in the country. However, the Comoros Human Rights Association, established in 1990, was on the verge of disintegration due to a lack of funds.

The military regime cooperated with international NGO's, and a few international NGO's operated in the country.

DISCRIMINATION BASED ON RACE, SEX, RELIGION, DISABILITY, LANGUAGE, OR SOCIAL STATUS

The Constitution does not prohibit discrimination based on these factors specifically, but only states that the judiciary is the guardian of individual liberties. Local communities discriminate against and harass Christians, and Islamic fundamentalism is growing in popularity as more students return to the country after pursuing Islamic studies abroad.

WOMEN

Violence against women occurs, but medical authorities, the police, and women's groups believe that it is rare. In theory a woman could seek protection through the courts in the case of violence, but in fact the problem is addressed most often within the extended family or at the village level.

Men have the dominant role in society. A matriarchal African tradition affords women some rights, especially in terms of landholding. Societal discrimination against women was most apparent in rural areas where women have onerous farming and child-rearing duties, with fewer opportunities for education and wage employment. In contrast an improvement in the status of women was most evident in the major towns, where growing numbers of women are in the labor force and generally earn wages comparable to those of men engaged in similar work; however, few women hold positions of responsibility in business. While legal discrimination exists in some areas, in general inheritance and property rights do not disfavor women. For example, the house that the father of the bride traditionally provides to the couple at the time of their marriage remains her property in the event of divorce.

CHILDREN

The regime has not commented on the protection of children's rights and welfare, nor has it taken any action to protect or promote children's welfare. Population pressure and poverty force some families to place their children in the homes of others. These children, often as young as 7 years of age, typically work long hours as domestic servants in exchange for food and shelter (see Section 6.c.). Legal provisions that address the rights and welfare of children are not enforced because of a lack of inspectors.

Female genital mutilation, which is widely condemned by international health experts as damaging to both physical and psychological health, generally is not practiced. Child abuse appears to be rare.

PEOPLE WITH DISABILITIES

There is no evidence of widespread discrimination against the disabled in the provision of education or other services. No legislation is in force concerning accessibility to public buildings or services for persons with disabilities.

RELIGIOUS MINORITIES

There is widespread societal discrimination against Christians in all sectors of life. Attempts have been made to isolate Christians from village life. Christians face insults and threats of violence from members of their communities. Christians have been harassed by mobs in front of mosques and summoned for questioning by religious authorities. In some instances, families forced Christian members out of their homes or threatened them with a loss of financial support. Some Christians have had their Bibles taken by family members. Local government officials, religious authorities, and family members have attempted to force Christians to attend services at mosques against their will.

Community members and authorities in Lingoni, Anjouan, banned Christians from attending any community events, and in Mremeni, Anjouan, they banned Christian burials in the local cemetery.

WORKER RIGHTS

A. THE RIGHT OF ASSOCIATION

The Constitution does not provide for the right to unionize and strike, but these rights are practiced freely. Farming on small land holdings, subsistence fishing, and petty commerce make up the daily activity of most of the population. The wage labor force is small, and numbers less than 7,000 including government employees, and less than 2,000 excluding them. Teachers, civil servants, and dockworkers are unionized. Unions are independent of the regime. Teachers and hospital workers strike intermittently, mostly because they often are not paid for months at a time. There are no laws protecting strikers from retribution, but there were no known instances of retribution.

There are no restrictions on unions joining federations or affiliating with international bodies.

B. THE RIGHT TO ORGANIZE AND BARGAIN COLLECTIVELY

Unions have the right to bargain collectively, and strikes are legal. Wages are set by employers in the small private sector and by the Government, especially the Ministries of Finance and Labor, in the larger public sector. The Labor Code, which is enforced only loosely, does not include a system for resolving labor disputes, and it does not prohibit antiunion discrimination by employers.

There are no export processing zones.

C. PROHIBITION OF FORCED OR COMPULSORY LABOR

The Constitution does not mention forced or compulsory labor, but it generally is not practiced; however, some families place their children in the homes of others where they work long hours in exchange for food or shelter (see Section 5).

D. STATUS OF CHILD LABOR PRACTICES AND MINIMUM AGE FOR EMPLOYMENT

The Labor Code defines the minimum age for employment as 15 years of age. The Ministry of Labor has few resources to enforce this provision, but, except for domestic work, child labor is not a problem due to the general lack of wage employment opportunities. There were some instances of forced or bonded labor by children (see Section 5 and 6.c.). Children generally help with the work of their families in the subsistence farming and fishing sectors (see Section 5).

E. ACCEPTABLE CONDITIONS OF WORK

There is no minimum wage.

Previous governments periodically have reminded employers to respect the Labor Code, which specifies 1 day off per week plus 1 month of paid vacation per year, but the regime has not set a standard workweek.

There are no safety or health standards for the minuscule manufacturing sector.

TRAFFICKING IN PERSONS

The law does not prohibit trafficking in persons; however, there were no reports that persons were trafficked in, to, or from the country.

FREEDOM OF RELIGION

The 1996 Constitution, which was suspended by the military after a coup on April 30, 1999, prohibited discrimination on the basis of religion or religious belief; however, during 1998 the Government infringed on the freedom of religion of non-Muslims to some extent. The 1996 Constitution also established an Ulamas Council, which advised the President, Prime Minister, President of the Federal Assembly, the Council of Isles, and the island governors on whether bills, ordinances, decrees, and laws were in conformity with the principles of Islam. The Constitution promulgated by the head of the military after the April 30, 1999, coup provides that the National Army of Development uphold individual and collective liberties; however, it does not provide specifically for freedom of religion. The three federal governments that held power between January 1, 1999 and June 30, 1999 discouraged the practice of religions other than Islam; Christians, in particular, faced restrictions on their ability to practice their faith. The Constitution written by the separatist leadership of the island of Anjouan provides for freedom of religion; however, the Anjouan separatist leadership discouraged the practice of religions other than Islam.

An overwhelming majority--almost 99 percent--of the population are Sunni Muslim. Fewer than 300 persons--less than 1 percent of the population--are Christian; all of whom reportedly converted to Christianity within the last 5 years. There is a very small population (less than five families) of Indian descent. There was no information available to indicate whether any members of this population practice Hinduism.

There are two Roman Catholic churches, one in Moroni on the island of Grande Comore and one in Mutsamudu on the island of Anjouan. There is one Protestant church in Moroni. However, prior to the April 1999 coup, the Government restricted the use of these three churches to noncitizens. There was no information available on whether the new Government has continued this practice. Many Christians practice their faith in private residences. Christian missionaries work in local hospitals and schools, but they are not allowed to proselytize.

Police regularly threatened and sometimes detained practicing Christians. Most detentions occurred on the island of Anjouan where the practicing Christian population is more open. In 1998 in Anjouan, police reportedly arrested and beat a Christian and demolished a house that had been used as a meeting place for Christians. There were also reports that the secessionist Anjouan's quasi-police authorities, known as embargoes, arrested and detained nine Christians. In April 1999, embargoes arrested, beat, and detained for a day three local Christians. Usually, the authorities hold those detained for a few days and often attempt forcibly to convert them to Islam. None of the above incidents were investigated, nor was action taken against the persons responsible. One Anjouanais Christian estimates that around 50 Christians, both men and women, have been detained in Anjouan by the embargoes during the period covered by this report.

Local government officials have attempted to force Christians to attend services at mosques against their will (see Section II). Some community authorities on Anjouan banned Christians from attending any community events and banned Christian burials in a local cemetery (see Section II).

There is Islamic instruction in public schools for students at the middle school level that coincides with Arabic instruction. Almost all children between 4 and 7 years of age go to Koranic schools outside of normal school hours in order to learn to read the Koran.

Former President Taki's bans on alcohol and immodest dress remain in effect, but reportedly are not enforced. Alcohol can be imported and sold with a permit from the Government.

There was no change in the status of at times limited respect for freedom of religion.

There were no reports of the forced religious conversions of minor U.S. citizens who had been abducted or illegally removed from the United States, or of the Government's refusal to allow such citizens to be returned to the United States.

SOCIETAL ATTITUDES

There is widespread societal discrimination against Christians in all sectors of life. Attempts have been made to isolate Christians from village life. Community members and authorities in Lingoni, Anjouan, banned Christians from attending any community events and, in Mremeni, Anjouan, banned Christian burials in the local cemetery. Christians face insults and threats of violence from members of their communities. Christians have been harassed by mobs in front of mosques and called in for questioning by religious authorities. In some instances, families have forced Christian family members out of their homes or threatened them with a loss of financial support. Some Christians have had their Bibles taken by family members. Local government officials, religious authorities, and family members have attempted to force Christians to attend services at mosques against their will.

Islamic fundamentalism is growing in popularity as more students return to the country after studying Islamic subjects in foreign countries.

U.S. GOVERNMENT POLICY

The U.S. Embassy discusses religious freedom issues with the Government in the overall context of the promotion of human rights.

STRATEGIC ECONOMIC AND BUSINESS INFORMATION

ECONOMY & ECONOMIC DEVELOPMENT

Agriculture, including fishing, hunting, and forestry - is the predominant sector of comoross' economy. It contributes 40 percent to GDP and employs 80 percent of the labor force. The export business is largely dominated by French companies and a few businessmen, the islands' export crops are copra, vanilla, coffee, cocoa, cloves and ylang-ylang, though external demand for copra, vanilla and ylang-ylang is now shrinking. However, the country is not self-sufficient in food production, and rice, the country's main staple, accounts for 90 percent of imports. Tourism has started to develop, but its growth has been hampered by an unstable political environment.

Because of sluggish economic growth and depressed world market prices of comoross's main export crops, in particular vanilla and cloves, real per capita incomes have declined during the past decade. Chronic financial problems emerged and public finance deficits, including grants, reached about 7 percent of GDP in 1997, reflecting weak revenue effort. Domestic and external arrears have accumulated and civil servant salaries have not been paid on a regular basis. The external current account deficit remained high at 15 percent of GDP in 1997. The inflation rate declined to about 2 percent by end-1997, as a result of prudent monetary policy and stagnating economic activity.

Selected economic indicators
GNP (1997) - US$ 194mn
Consumer price inflation (average), (1997): 2.5%
Population (1997) - 696, 000
Trade balance (1997)
Export, fob - US$ 8.8 mn
Import, fob - US$ 46.2 mnCurrent account balance (1997) - US$-13.4mn
Total external debt, (1996) - US$ 206mn
Exchange rate (1997 av. Cfr/US$) - 437.8
Principle exports - Vanilla, Ylang ylang, cloves
Principle imports - Rice, petroleum products
Major food crops - rice, cassava, coconut, bananas, sweet potatoes, pulses, and corn.
Major export crops - Vanilla, ylang-ylang, cloves, and copra

Currency - Comorian franc

Traditionally, seaborne trade played an important role in the Islands' economy. Today, agriculture is the principal economic activity with crops grown both for domestic consumption and export. The major food crops are cassava, coconut, bananas, rice, sweet potatoes, pulses, and corn. Vanilla, ylang-ylang, cloves, and copra have been the major export crops.

The Comoros were the world's leading producer of the essence of ylang-ylang, an oil widely used in the perfume industry. The Islands were also the world's second-largest producer of vanilla. The market demands for these products have decreased significantly in the past decade, however. In 1996, for example, there was a 60% drop in the value of vanilla and exports declined by 42.7% from the previous year. During the same year, the volume of ylang-ylang essence declined by 15.8% and the value of the exports dropped by 24.6%.

Some animal husbandry is undertaken by individual farmers and a small scale fishing industry exists. Coelecanth specimens provided some income for fishermen and the government. This fish was thought by western scientists to have been extinct for 70 million years but has been caught by local fishermen for years. At one time it was sold to the local government and resold to museums and research centers all over the world.

There is a small tourist industry on the Islands which has been recently promoted by South African interests.

France has been the major trading partner of the Comoros. The Islands have a relatively large negative trade balance and the government has been for many years dependent upon external aid. A number of countries in the past have provided this aid with France being the dominant donor.

The currency of the country is the Comorian franc. Its value is tied to the French franc at 75 Comorian francs to 1 French franc. There are banks on the islands of Ngazidja, Nzwani, and Maore but no bank on Mwali. The banks are open Monday through Friday mornings.

During the colonial period, the French and local leading citizens established plantations to grow cash crops for export. Even after independence, French companies, such as Société Bambao and Établissements Grimaldi--and other concerns, such as Kalfane and Company and later, President Abdallah's Établissements Abdallah et Fils--dominated the Comoran economy. These firms diverted most of their profits overseas, investing little in the infrastructure of the islands beyond what was needed for profitable management of the plantations, or what could benefit these businesses' associates or related concerns. A serious consequence of this approach has been the languishing of the food-crop agricultural sector and the resultant dependence on overseas food imports, particularly rice. In 1993 Comoros remained hostage to fluctuating prices on the international market for such crops as vanilla, ylang-ylang, and cloves.

Comoros is one of the world's poorest countries; its per capita gross national product (GNP--see Glossary) was estimated at US$400 in 1994, following the January devaluation of the Comoran franc. Although GNP increased in real terms at an average annual rate of 3.1 percent during the 1980s, rapid population growth effaced these gains and caused an average annual decrease in per capita GNP of 0.6 percent. Gross domestic product (GDP-- see Glossary) grew in real terms by 4.2 percent per year from 1980 to 1985, 1.8 percent from 1985 to 1988, and 1.5 percent in 1990. In 1991, because of its balance of payments difficulties, Comoros became eligible for the IDA's Special Program of Assistance for debt-distressed countries of sub-Saharan Africa.

The economy is based on private ownership, frequently by foreign investors. Nationalization, even during the Soilih years, has been limited. Soilih did expropriate the facilities of a foreign oil company, but only after the government of Madagascar took over the company's plants in that country. The Abdallah government, despite its openness to foreign participation in the economy, nationalized the Société Bambao and another Frenchcapitalized firm, the Comoran Meat Company (Société Comorienne des Viandes--Socovia), which specialized in sales of meat and other foods in the islands. The nationalization was short-lived, however, because Socovia and other government-held enterprises were either liquidated or privatized as part of economic restructuring efforts in 1992.

Following the Abdallah regime's rapprochement with France in 1978, the Comoran economy became increasingly dependent on infusions of French aid, along with assistance from other governments and international organizations. By 1990, the year Comoros concluded negotiations with the IMF for an economic restructuring program, the republic's total external public debt was US$162.4 million, an amount equal to about three-quarters of GNP. The government delayed implementing the structural adjustment plan and was directed by the World Bank and the IMF to do so by September 1992. The plan recommendations entailed discharging about 2,800 of 9,000 civil servants, among other unpopular measures. The IMF granted Comoros a new credit for US$1.9 million in March 1994 under the Structural Adjustment Facility. For the period 1994-96, Comoros sought an economic growth rate of 4 percent as well as an inflation rate of 4 percent for 1995-96. The growth rate for 1994, however, was estimated only at 0.7 percent and the inflation rate at 15 percent. Meanwhile, in a move designed to encourage private enterprise and reduce unemployment, in May 1993 the UN Development Programme had given Comoros a credit of US$2 million for programs in these areas. In January 1994, the European Development Fund (EDF) granted 1.3 million European Currency Units (ECUs; for value, see Glossary) to Comoros to develop small businesses. Comoros also received 5.7 million French francs from the French Aid and Cooperation Fund for agriculture and rural development.

The results of foreign aid to Comoros have been mixed at best. The purposes of the aid ranged from helping the government cover its payroll for such huge, seemingly endless projects as expanding the seaport at Moroni and developing a new port at Mutsamuda on Nzwani. Neither project had shown much promise by early 1994. Meanwhile, the islands have been unable to develop local resources or create the infrastructure needed for economic development. The few successes included the creation of national news media and limited improvements in public health, education, and telecommunications. Developmental assistance from the United States, which totaled US$700,000 in fiscal year (FY--see Glossary) 1991, was administered by CARE, the nongovernmental organization, and focused primarily on reforestation, soil conservation, and sustainable agriculture.

The overall effect of the republic's dependence on aid has been perennial trade deficits accompanied by chronic budget deficits. In 1992 total exports had a value of US$21 million, and total imports were valued at US$50 million. In 1991 receipts totaled about US$34.7 million (CF9.7 trillion; CF--Comoran franc; for value of the Comoran franc--see Glossary) whereas expenditures totaled about US$93.8 million (CF26.2 trillion). The shortfall, which equaled about 170 percent of receipts, was financed by international grants and loans, by draws upon existing lines of credit, and by debt rescheduling.

In 1991 France received 55 percent of Comoran exports, followed by the United States (19 percent) and Germany (16 percent). The main export products were vanilla, ylang-ylang, and cloves. The republic's primary suppliers were France (56 percent of imports), the Belgium-Luxembourg economic union (11 percent), and Japan (5 percent). Imports consisted of basic foodstuffs (rice and meat), petroleum, and construction materials.

Comoros has officially participated in the African Franc Zone (Communauté Financière Africaine-- CFA; see Glossary) since 1979. The CFA franc was devalued by 50 percent on January 12, 1994, causing the exchange rate to become 100 CFA francs for one French franc. Subsequently, the Comoran franc was devalued so that instead of being directly aligned with the CFA franc, seventyfive Comoran francs equaled one French franc.

The banking system consists of the Central Bank of Comoros (Banque Centrale des Comores) established in 1981; the Bank for Industry and Commerce (Banque pour l'Industrie et le Commerce-- BIC), a commercial bank established in 1990 that had six branches in 1993 and was a subsidiary of the National Bank of Paris-- International (Banque Nationale de Paris--Internationale); BIC Afribank, a BIC subsidiary; and the Development Bank of Comoros (Banque de Développement des Comores), established in 1982, which provided support for small and midsize development projects. Most of the shares in the Development Bank of Comoros were held by the Comoran government and the central bank; the rest were held by the European Investment Bank and the Central Bank for Economic Cooperation (Caisse Centrale de Coopération Économique--CCCE), a development agency of the French government. All of these banks had headquarters in Moroni.

A national labor organization, the Union of Comoran Workers (Union des Travailleurs des Comores), also had headquarters in Moroni. Strikes and worker demonstrations often occurred in response to political crises, economic restructuring mandated by international financial organizations, and the failure of the government--occasionally for months at a time--to pay civil servants.

AGRICULTURE, LIVESTOCK, AND FISHING

One of the poorest and most underdeveloped in the world, the Comorian economy is based primarily on agriculture.

The agricultural sector divides naturally into two parts: subsistence farming and farming for export. Subsistence farming, which provides the staples making up three-quarters of the islanders' diet, consists of coconuts, cassava, bananas and rice. Small quantities of fish are also eaten as well as very small amounts of meat.

Because of extensive land holdings in the hands of foreign companies and a traditional ruling elite, land for subsistence agriculture is inadequate to meet local needs; some 50% of the annual budget is spent on importing food and less than one-tenth of the active population is formally employed.

As world food prices rise and the price of Comorian exports falls, the country's trade deficit grows steadily.

Agriculture supported about 80 percent of the population and supplied about 95 percent of exports in the early 1990s. Two agricultural zones are generally defined: the coastal area, which ranges in elevation from sea level to 400 meters and which supports cash crops such as vanilla, ylang-ylang, and cloves; and the highlands, which support cultivation of crops for domestic consumption, such as cassava, bananas, rain rice, and sweet potatoes. As the population increased, food grown for domestic use met fewer and fewer of Comorans' needs. Data collected by the World Bank showed that food production per capita fell about 12 percent from 1980 to 1987. The republic imported virtually all its meat and vegetables; rice imports alone often accounted for up to 30 percent of the value of all imports.

Comoros is the world's principal producer of ylang-ylang essence, an essence derived from the flowers of a tree originally brought from Indonesia that is used in manufacturing perfumes and soaps. Ylang-ylang essence is a major component of Chanel No. 5, the popular scent for women. The republic is the world's second largest producer of vanilla, after Madagascar. Cloves are also an important cash crop. A total of 237 tons of vanilla was exported in 1991, at a price of about CF19 per kilogram. A total of 2,750 tons of cloves was exported in 1991, at a price of CF397 per kilogram. That year forty-three tons of ylang-ylang essence were exported at a price of about CF23,000 per kilogram. The production of all three commodities fluctuates wildly, mainly in response to changes in global demand and natural disasters such as cyclones. Profits--and therefore, government receipts-- likewise skyrocket and plummet, wreaking havoc with government efforts to predict revenues and plan expenditures. Stabex (Stabilization of Export Earnings--see Glossary), a system of the EC, provides aid to Comoros and other developing countries to mitigate the effects of fluctuations in the prices of export commodities.

Long-term prospects for the growth and stabilization of the markets for vanilla and ylang-ylang did not appear strong in the early 1990s. Vanilla faced increased competition from synthetic flavorings, and the preferences of perfume users were moving away from the sweet fragrance provided by ylang-ylang essence. Copra, the dried coconut meat that yields coconut oil, once an important Comoran export, had ceased to be a significant factor in the economy by the late 1980s, when the world's tastes shifted from high-fat coconut oil toward "leaner" substances such as palm oil. Although clove production and revenues also experienced swings, in the early 1990s cloves did not appear to face the same sorts of challenges confronting vanilla and ylang-ylang. Most Comoran vanilla is grown on Njazidja; Nzwani is the source of most ylangylang .

Numerous international programs have attempted to reduce the country's dependence on food imports, particularly of rice, a major drain on export earnings. Organizations initiating these rural development programs have included the EDF, the IFAD, the World Food Program, the Arab Bank for

Economic Development in Africa, the UN Food and Agriculture Organization, and the governments of France and the United States. Despite these international efforts, which numbered as many as seventeen in 1984, food production per capita actually declined in Comoros during the 1980s. The major clove and vanilla growers, whose plantations occupy the islands' fertile coastal lands, generally resisted these restructuring efforts, as did rice-importing firms, including the country's largest, Établissements Abdallah et Fils.

Crowded onto the mountain slopes by the cash crop plantations, food-crop farmers have caused deforestation and the erosion of the highlands' thin, fragile soil. In response, aid providers have dedicated an increasing amount of agricultural assistance to reforestation, soil restoration, and environmentally sensitive means of cultivation. For example, all United States agricultural aid in 1991 (US$700,000) was directed to such projects, as was a US$4 million loan from the IFAD to help initiate a small producers' support program on Nzwani.

The livestock sector is small--some 47,000 cattle, 120,000 goats, 13,000 sheep, and 4,000 asses in 1990. Comoros continues to import most domestically consumed meat.

Since the latter part of the 1980s, Comoros has made headway in developing fisheries as a source of export earnings. In 1988 the government concluded a three-year agreement with the EC by which forty French and Spanish vessels would be permitted to fish in Comoran waters, primarily for tuna. In return, Comoros would receive ECU300,000, and ECU50,000 would be invested in fisheries research. In addition, fishing vessel operators would pay ECU20 per ton of tuna netted. Although the deep waters outside the islands' reefs do not abound in fish, it has been estimated that up to 30,000 tons of fish could be taken per year from Comoran waters (which extend 320 kilometers offshore). The total catch in 1990 was 5,500 tons. Japan has also provided aid to the fishing industry. Fisheries development is overseen by a state agency, the Development Company for Small-Scale Fisheries of Comoros (Société de Développement de la Pêche Artisanale des Comores).

INDUSTRY AND INFRASTRUCTURE

Industrial activities are responsible for only a tiny portion of Comoran economic activity--about 5 percent of GDP in 1994. Principal industries are those that involve processing cash crops for export: preparing vanilla and distilling ylang-ylang into perfume essence. These activities were once controlled almost entirely by French companies, but as they closed unprofitable plantations, individual farmers set up many small, inefficient distilleries. Comorans also produce handicrafts for export. Other industries are small and geared to internal markets: sawmills, printing, carpentry, and the production of shoes, plastics, yogurt, handicrafts (such as the jewelry exchanged as part of the *grand mariage*), and small fishing boats. Several factors provide major obstacles to the growth of industry: the islands' geographically isolated position, their distance from each other, a scarcity of raw materials and skilled labor, and the high cost of electricity (energy is produced by hydropower, imported petroleum, and wood products) and transportation. Value added in industry slowly declined throughout the 1980s.

Perhaps the primary outcome of South African penetration of the Comoran economy during the Abdallah regime was the development of tourism. Although South African investors built or renovated several hotels during the 1980s (with assistance from the South African and Comoran governments), only one resort, the 182-room Galawa Beach on Njazidja, was operating by late 1992. About 100 other hotel rooms were available on the islands. Political instability, a declining South African interest in the islands as the apartheid regime was disassembled and other tropical tourism venues became more welcoming, and the need to import most construction materials and consumable supplies inhibited the growth of tourism, despite the islands' physical beauty. Nonetheless, in large part thanks to Galawa Beach, which had been closed during 1990, tourism increased from 7,627 visitors in 1990 to 16,942 in 1991. Most of these tourists were Europeans, primarily French

TRANSPORTATION AND COMMUNICATIONS

The relative isolation of the Comoro Islands had made air traffic a major means of transportation. One of President Abdallah's accomplishments was to make Comoros more accessible by air. During his administration, he negotiated agreements to initiate or enhance commercial air links with Tanzania and Madagascar. The Djohar regime reached an agreement in 1990 to link Moroni and Brussels by air. By the early 1990s, commercial flights connected Comoros with France, Mauritius, Kenya, South Africa, Tanzania, and Madagascar. The national airline was Air Comores. Daily flights linked the three main islands, and air service was also available to Mahoré; each island had airstrips. In 1986 the republic received a grant from the French government's CCCE to renovate and expand Hahaya airport, near Moroni. Because of the absence of regularly scheduled sea transport between the islands, nearly all interisland passenger traffic is by air.

More than 99 percent of freight is transported by sea. Both Moroni on Njazidja and Mutsamudu on Nzwani have artificial harbors. There is also a harbor at Fomboni, on Mwali. Despite extensive internationally financed programs to upgrade the harbors at Moroni and Mutsamudu, by the early 1990s only Mutsamudu was operational as a deepwater facility. Its harbor could accommodate vessels of up to eleven meters' draught. At Moroni, ocean-going vessels typically lie offshore and are loaded or unloaded by smaller craft, a costly and sometimes dangerous procedure. Most freight continues to be sent to

Kenya, Reunion, or Madagascar for transshipment to Comoros. Use of Comoran ports is further restricted by the threat of cyclones from December through March. The privately operated Comoran Navigation Company (Société Comorienne de Navigation) is based in Moroni, and provides services to Madagascar.)

Roads serve the coastal areas, rather than the interior, and the mountainous terrain makes surface travel difficult. In 1987 the total length of roads in Comoros was about 750 kilometers, including both paved and dirt roads.

In large part thanks to international aid programs, Moroni has international telecommunications service. Telephone service, however, is largely limited to the islands' few towns. Some 3,000 telephones were in use in 1991.

CURRENCY FLUCTUATIONS

The currency of the Comoros is the Comoros franc, divided into 100 centimes.

Along with other countries of the franc zone, the Comoros was affected by the devaluation of the French currency in January 1994. The Comoros government, however, insisted that the devaluation of its franc should be only 33% and not 50% as elsewhere. It was subsequently allowed a lesser devaluation because of its remoteness. The exchange rate became FF1=CF75, with both inflation and the price of imports rising.

The government made a commitment to the IMF (International Monetary Fund) in 1994 to attempt economic growth of 0.7% while maintaining the current account deficit at not more than 20% and inflation at 15%.

EXPORTS

Mostly in the hands of French companies and a few businessmen, the islands' export crops are copra, vanilla, coffee, cocoa, cloves and ylang-ylang.

Ylang-ylang is a tropical Asian tree of the pineapple family with fragrant greenish-yellow flowers from which a perfume is distilled.

Unfortunately, demand for copra, vanilla and ylang-ylang is now shrinking. Many former importers of vanilla and ylang-ylang now manufacture synthetic substitutes.

The cultivation and export of sisal has also been abandoned.

TRADE WITH THE US

January 2000
by 1-digit SITC commodity
In millions of dollars

1-Digit SITC Commodity	Exports	Imports
0 Food and Live Animals	(-)	0.07
5 Chemicals and Related Products, N.E.S.	(-)	(Z)
7 Machinery and Transport Equipment	(Z)	(-)
9 Commodities and Transactions, N.E.S.	(Z)	(Z)
* TOTAL *	(Z)	0.08

(-) Represents zero.
(Z) Represents less than 0.05

Source: US Census Bureau, Foreign Trade Division, Data Dissemination Branch, Phone: (301)457-2311.
Last modified: 21 Feb 2001

.

February 2000
by 1-digit SITC commodity
In millions of dollars

1-Digit SITC Commodity	Exports	Imports
5 Chemicals and Related Products, N.E.S.	(-)	(Z)
6 Manufactured Goods Classified Chiefly	(Z)	(-)
7 Machinery and Transport Equipment	0.09	(-)
9 Commodities and Transactions, N.E.S.	(Z)	(Z)
* TOTAL *	0.09	(Z)

(-) Represents zero.
(Z) Represents less than 0.05

Source: US Census Bureau, Foreign Trade Division, Data Dissemination Branch, Phone: (301)457-2311.
Last modified: 21 Feb 2001

.

March 2000
by 1-digit SITC commodity
In millions of dollars

1-Digit SITC Commodity	Exports	Imports
0 Food and Live Animals	(-)	0.11
5 Chemicals and Related Products, N.E.S.	(-)	(Z)

1-Digit SITC Commodity	Exports	Imports
7 Machinery and Transport Equipment	(Z)	(-)
9 Commodities and Transactions, N.E.S.	(Z)	(-)
* TOTAL *	(Z)	0.14

(-) Represents zero.
(Z) Represents less than 0.05

Source: US Census Bureau, Foreign Trade Division, Data Dissemination Branch, Phone: (301)457-2311.
Last modified: 21 Feb 2001

.

April 2000
by 1-digit SITC commodity
In millions of dollars

1-Digit SITC Commodity	Exports	Imports
0 Food and Live Animals	(-)	0.29
5 Chemicals and Related Products, N.E.S.	(-)	(Z)
7 Machinery and Transport Equipment	0.15	(-)
9 Commodities and Transactions, N.E.S.	(Z)	(Z)
* TOTAL *	0.15	0.30

(-) Represents zero.
(Z) Represents less than 0.05

Source: US Census Bureau, Foreign Trade Division, Data Dissemination Branch, Phone: (301)457-2311.
Last modified: 21 Feb 2001

.

May 2000
by 1-digit SITC commodity
In millions of dollars

1-Digit SITC Commodity	Exports	Imports
0 Food and Live Animals	(-)	0.08
5 Chemicals and Related Products, N.E.S.	(-)	(Z)
9 Commodities and Transactions, N.E.S.	(Z)	(Z)
* TOTAL *	(Z)	0.09

(-) Represents zero.
(Z) Represents less than 0.05

Source: US Census Bureau, Foreign Trade Division, Data Dissemination Branch, Phone: (301)457-2311.

Last modified: 21 Feb 2001

.

June 2000
by 1-digit SITC commodity
In millions of dollars

1-Digit SITC Commodity	Exports	Imports
5 Chemicals and Related Products, N.E.S.	(-)	(Z)
7 Machinery and Transport Equipment	0.16	(-)
9 Commodities and Transactions, N.E.S.	(-)	(Z)
* TOTAL *	0.16	(Z)

(-) Represents zero.
(Z) Represents less than 0.05

Source: US Census Bureau, Foreign Trade Division, Data Dissemination Branch, Phone: (301)457-2311.
Last modified: 21 Feb 2001

.

July 2000
by 1-digit SITC commodity
In millions of dollars

1-Digit SITC Commodity	Exports	Imports
0 Food and Live Animals	(-)	0.24
5 Chemicals and Related Products, N.E.S.	(-)	(Z)
7 Machinery and Transport Equipment	(Z)	(-)
9 Commodities and Transactions, N.E.S.	(Z)	(-)
* TOTAL *	(Z)	0.28

(-) Represents zero.
(Z) Represents less than 0.05

Source: US Census Bureau, Foreign Trade Division, Data Dissemination Branch, Phone: (301)457-2311.
Last modified: 21 Feb 2001

.

August 2000
by 1-digit SITC commodity
In millions of dollars

1-Digit SITC Commodity	Exports	Imports
5 Chemicals and Related Products, N.E.S.	0.18	(Z)
9 Commodities and Transactions, N.E.S.	(-)	(Z)

* TOTAL *	0.18	(Z)

(-) Represents zero.
(Z) Represents less than 0.05

Source: US Census Bureau, Foreign Trade Division, Data Dissemination Branch, Phone: (301)457-2311.
Last modified: 21 Feb 2001

.

September 2000
by 1-digit SITC commodity
In millions of dollars

1-Digit SITC Commodity	Exports	Imports
0 Food and Live Animals	(-)	0.35
5 Chemicals and Related Products, N.E.S.	(-)	(Z)
8 Miscellaneous Manufactured Articles	(-)	(Z)
9 Commodities and Transactions, N.E.S.	(Z)	(-)
* TOTAL *	(Z)	0.36

(-) Represents zero.
(Z) Represents less than 0.05

Source: US Census Bureau, Foreign Trade Division, Data Dissemination Branch, Phone: (301)457-2311.
Last modified: 21 Feb 2001

.

October 2000
by 1-digit SITC commodity
In millions of dollars

1-Digit SITC Commodity	Exports	Imports
0 Food and Live Animals	(-)	(Z)
5 Chemicals and Related Products, N.E.S.	(-)	(Z)
7 Machinery and Transport Equipment	(Z)	(-)
9 Commodities and Transactions, N.E.S.	(-)	(Z)
* TOTAL *	(Z)	(Z)

(-) Represents zero.
(Z) Represents less than 0.05

Source: US Census Bureau, Foreign Trade Division, Data Dissemination Branch, Phone: (301)457-2311.
Last modified: 21 Feb 2001

.

November 2000

by 1-digit SITC commodity
In millions of dollars

1-Digit SITC Commodity	Exports	Imports
0 Food and Live Animals	(-)	0.60
5 Chemicals and Related Products, N.E.S.	(-)	(Z)
9 Commodities and Transactions, N.E.S.	(Z)	(-)
* TOTAL *	(Z)	0.64

(-) Represents zero.
(Z) Represents less than 0.05

Source: US Census Bureau, Foreign Trade Division, Data Dissemination Branch, Phone: (301)457-2311.
Last modified: 21 Feb 2001

.

December 2000
by 1-digit SITC commodity
In millions of dollars

1-Digit SITC Commodity	Exports	Imports
0 Food and Live Animals	(-)	1.49
5 Chemicals and Related Products, N.E.S.	(-)	(Z)
7 Machinery and Transport Equipment	(Z)	(-)
9 Commodities and Transactions, N.E.S.	(-)	(Z)
* TOTAL *	(Z)	1.51

(-) Represents zero.
(Z) Represents less than 0.05

Source: US Census Bureau, Foreign Trade Division, Data Dissemination Branch, Phone: (301)457-2311.
Last modified: 21 Feb 2001

.

Year-to-Date 2000
by 1-digit SITC commodity
In millions of dollars

1-Digit SITC Commodity	Exports	Imports
0 Food and Live Animals	(-)	3.23
5 Chemicals and Related Products, N.E.S.	0.18	0.27
6 Manufactured Goods Classified Chiefly by Material	(Z)	(-)
7 Machinery and Transport Equipment	0.51	(-)
8 Miscellaneous Manufactured Articles	(-)	(Z)
9 Commodities and Transactions, N.E.S.	(Z)	(Z)

---

* TOTAL *	0.70	3.51

(-) Represents zero.
(Z) Represents less than 0.05
Source: US Census Bureau, Foreign Trade Division, Data Dissemination Branch,

ECONOMIC REFORMS STRATEGY[3]

INTRODUCTION

1. The Comoros has experienced a difficult political and economic situation in recent years. Geographically isolated, with limited natural resources, and a very small and fragmented domestic market, the Comoros is one of the poorest countries in Africa. About 60 percent of the population is estimated to live below the poverty line, and many lack access to safe water and electricity, as well as to basic government services such as education and health care. The situation was further aggravated by the secession of Anjouan in 1997 and the ensuing difficult relations between the islands. Mounting wage arrears resulted in a sharp deterioration in public services up to 1999, and external arrears and the breakdown of our political institutions in 1999 led to a decline in donor assistance.

2. Our main efforts over the past two years have been geared toward resolving the political situation. These efforts resulted in an agreement by all the parties involved in February 2001, to restore democratic political institutions and reunify the country. A Tripartite Commission, made up of representatives of the government, opposition parties, and civil society of the three islands, is drafting a new constitution, to be put to a national referendum by September 2001. Following this, a provisional government of national unity will be formed to administer the country's transition and prepare legislative and presidential elections. In each island and at the central level, new elected institutions should be in place by early 2002.

3. We have also started resolving our economic problems and regularizing our relations with donors. The functioning of the federal administration has improved, and we have taken steps toward fiscal consolidation. In 1999, we took measures—an increase in tax rates and a strengthening of collection efforts, streamlining of the database of government employees—enabling us to clear the arrears to the World Bank in January 2000, allowing the latter to resume its assistance to the Comoros. We also contacted the other creditors to reconcile

[3] Memorandum on Economic and Financial Policies of the Government of the Comoros presented to the International Monetary Fund July 2001–June 2002

the debt data and to start discussions on addressing the external arrears. However, much remains to be done.

4. With the assistance of the staffs of the IMF and the World Bank, we have prepared an economic program for the period July 2001-June 2002 to address the most pressing problems. We intend to submit this program to a meeting of "Friends of the Comoros," to be organized with the assistance of the World Bank on July 5, 2001, with a view to obtaining financial support. It will also form the basis for a medium-term program covering the period 2002–04, that will seek to accelerate economic growth and reduce poverty and that can be supported by the IMF, the World Bank, and other donors.

RECENT ECONOMIC DEVELOPMENTS

5. **On average, real GDP growth remained well below the population growth rate during the 1990s**. Private sector investment stagnated as a result of the difficult political environment and deep-seated structural problems. The production of our main export products (vanilla, cloves, and ylang-ylang) has not increased, and there has also been no expansion in capacity in the tourism sector since the opening of the only resort hotel on Grande Comore in 1989. Inflation has remained stable around 3 percent per year since 1996, but increased to 4.8 percent in 2000 following a sharp upturn in petroleum product prices.

6. **After considerable progress in 1999, the fiscal position was mixed in 2000**. Total revenue decreased by 9 percent, falling from 11.8 percent of GDP in 1999 to 10.2 percent in 2000 following technical problems in customs, tax arrears incurred by the state-owned petroleum company (*Société Comorienne des Hydrocarbures—SCH*), and the granting, in July 2000, of an exemption from import taxes on personal effects for the benefit of members of the large Comorian community living abroad. **To address the revenue shortfall, the government approved a supplementary budget in July 2000, reducing expenditure on goods and services** by 0.5 percent of GDP compared to 1999. The delay in resolving the political situation with Anjouan resulted in additional savings of about 0.5 percent of GDP compared to the original budget. As a result, domestically financed current expenditure declined from 12.7 percent of GDP in 1999 to 11.2 percent in 2000. Capital expenditure, which was almost entirely financed by foreign grants and loans, declined from 5.4 percent of GDP in 1999 to 3.9 percent in 2000 as a result of the cutback in donor support.

7. **The overall domestic budget deficit on a commitment basis**[1] remained unchanged in 2000 compared to 1999 at 0.2 percent of GDP. Given external debt service obligations equivalent to 4.3 percent of GDP and in the absence of budget support by donors and of domestic financing sources, this deficit resulted

in a further net accumulation in wage arrears by one month[2] and new arrears to suppliers (1.1 percent of GDP) and to external creditors (3.2 percent of GDP).

8. **In the context of the French franc zone, monetary policy continued to be aimed at maintaining the fixed exchange rate.**[3] Broad money growth reached 14.5 percent in 2000, while credit to the private sector rose by 14.4 percent. In view of the fact that there is only one commercial bank in the financial system of the Comoros, the monetary authorities continue to set maximum lending and minimum deposit interest rates. Since 1999, interest rates have been linked to money market rates in Europe; they remained unchanged in 2000 because of negligible movement in the European reference rates.

9. **The balance of payments showed a significant improvement in 2000** following a substantial strengthening in the terms of trade, contributing to a 55 percent increase in the total value of exports. Imports increased only by 2 percent, as higher petroleum imports were largely offset by a decline in other imports, reflecting lower donor assistance. The improvement in the services balance over the past few years continued in 2000, following an increase of around 15 percent in receipts from tourism (mainly from Comorians living abroad). Private transfers also increased, but this was more than offset by lower official grants. Reflecting these developments, the current account deficit (including grants) declined from 4.1 percent of GDP in 1999 to 0.4 percent in 2000. The surplus on the capital and financial account increased slightly as a decline in donor assistance was more than offset by a large reduction in net foreign assets of the commercial bank. The overall balance rose from a deficit of US$6 million in 1999 to a surplus of US$2 million in 2000. External debt service arrears increased by US$7 million, and gross official reserves increased by more than US$9 million to US$44 million, equivalent to eight months of imports of goods and nonfactor services.

10. **The severe fiscal problems resulted in further external debt service arrears**, especially to the African Development Bank (AfDB) and the Arab Bank for Economic Development in Africa (BADEA) and bilateral creditors. Following an informal meeting with creditors in March 2001, we were able to reconcile most of our multilateral debt and the stock of external debt was estimated at about US$225 million (111 percent of GDP) at end-2000. This included arrears estimated at US$84 million, of which US$55 million was owed to multilateral creditors, mainly the AfDB and the BADEA.

11. **Since the secession crisis in 1997, there has been no systematic collection of macroeconomic data on Anjouan**. Indications are that Anjouan has been able to continue exporting, despite the trade embargo in 2000, benefiting from the significant improvement in the international prices of ylang-ylang, cloves, and vanilla over the past two years. However, the island authorities had to assume responsibility for all 2,100 civil servants on

the island (which were previously paid by the federal government) and it hired an estimated 500 additional employees. Although comprehensive fiscal data are not yet available, the Anjouan authorities were able to pay only one month wages in 1999 and six months in 2000, indicating the seriousness of the island's fiscal position. The island authorities resumed preparing a formal budget in 2000, but public expenditure management remains very weak; the embargo prevented access to banking services, and all fiscal transactions are in cash.

ECONOMIC AND FINANCIAL POLICIES FOR 2001–02

A. Poverty Reduction and Growth

12. **Poverty is endemic in the Comoros**. Per capita income was estimated at US$356 in 2000 and the 1995 household budget survey indicated that 60 percent of the population lived below the poverty line. The incidence of poverty is more widespread on Anjouan than on Grande Comore or Mohéli and affects mainly households living on subsistence agriculture. Reflecting the negative per capita growth rates, the incidence of poverty is estimated to have increased since 1995, especially on Anjouan, with the effects mitigated on Grande Comore by higher transfers from the large Comorian community abroad.

13. **The government attaches great importance to reducing poverty, which we regard as the root cause of the political problems of recent years**. In the context of the National Reconstruction and Reconciliation Program, prepared in September 2000, and with the assistance of the United Nations Development Programme (UNDP), we have started developing a national strategy for reducing poverty and increasing economic growth. A draft strategy paper will be submitted to broad-based consultations with political representatives, representatives of the society at large, and donors, in 2002. An interim strategy paper describing the extent and the nature of poverty in the Comoros, as well as a detailed timetable for preparing the final paper and the consultation process, will be prepared by end-2001.

14. **The main requirements for reducing poverty are political stability and the acceleration of growth in a stable macroeconomic environment**. The economic and financial program for 2001–02 is designed to start addressing these issues. The World Bank recently approved the financing of a study on the outlook for accelerating growth in the Comoros, which will be completed by end-2001. We are also working with other institutions to develop policies aimed at improving the productivity of the agricultural sector, which employs more than 70 percent of the labor force but contributes only about 40 percent of GDP. With the assistance of the World Bank, the government intends to accelerate its efforts to increase the efficiency of the public sector, including the public enterprises.

B. The Macroeconomic Framework for 2001–02

15. **Our macroeconomic policies are geared toward increasing real GDP growth, while containing inflation and maintaining the fixed exchange rate parity and an adequate level of foreign exchange reserves**. After a prolonged period of decline, it will take time for structural reforms to lead to substantial and sustainable higher growth. Nevertheless, the improvement in the political situation as well as a rebound in the production of cash crops are expected to allow a small increase in real GDP in 2001. With the resumption of donor assistance, our policies will aim at a gradual increase in growth to a level at least equal to the population growth rate of about 3 percent by 2004; inflation will be maintained at about 3 percent per year. Monetary policy will continue to be conducted within the context of the French franc zone; gross official reserves are expected to decline to about 7 months of imports of goods and nonfactor services over the medium-term.

C. Fiscal Policies

16. **The budget for 2001 aimed at addressing the main fiscal difficulties.** Revenues were projected to increase by 28 percent to 12.3 percent of GDP, mainly reflecting measures to reverse the revenue shortfall in 2000: the tax exemption on personal effects was withdrawn, the problems in customs administration were resolved, and the increase in petroleum prices in September 2000 is expected to allow the SCH to avoid further arrears and to pay the arrears from 2000. In addition, the base of the consumption tax was extended to the wholesale sector. Nontax revenue was projected to increase by 1 percent of GDP, reflecting higher dividends from public enterprises, as well as the resumption of payments of royalties on the leasing of the international telephone access code for the Comoros (equivalent to 0.6 percent of GDP).

17. **Domestic expenditures were projected to increase from 10.5 percent of GDP in 2000 to 11.3 percent of GDP in 2001**, mainly reflecting a 20 percent increase in expenditure on goods and services (about half of the increase was reclassified under capital expenditure in the budget for 2001). The general civil-service wage freeze, in place since 1995, was continued, but the budget provided for a 2.8 percent increase in the wage bill, reflecting the mandatory inclusion in the civil service of some 900 long-term contractual employees. **The budget projected an improvement in the overall domestic balance (on a commitment basis)**, from the small deficit in 2000 to a surplus of 1 percent of GDP in 2001. Nevertheless, external debt service obligations amounted to 3 percent of GDP, and despite projected revenues from the sale of a cellular phone license of 0.5 percent of GDP, the residual financing gap amounted to1.8 percent of GDP, threatening new domestic and external arrears.

18. **With the support of the IMF staff, we reviewed the fiscal outlook for 2001 with the aim to avoid new domestic arrears and regularize relations with external creditors**. In line with this, we intend to issue a revised budget for 2001 by end-July, strengthening the tax effort and readjusting expenditure. This revision will also include an exceptional expenditure program to provide for the costs of the transition and reintegration of Anjouan, as well as making a start with necessary reforms, for which we intend to request donor support.

19. **The revenue effort aims at increasing revenue by 0.3 percent of GDP**. Starting July 1, 2001, we will eliminate the withholding tax on imports for the water and power company (*Compagnie d'Eau et d'Electricité—CEE*). The import taxes on alcoholic beverages will be raised from 200 percent to 250 percent and the effective import tax rates on several goods will also be raised to correct their decline in real terms over the past five years, by changing their specific into ad valorem rates. The specific rate on cement will be increased from CF 9 to CF 10 per kilo and the tax benefits granted to the CEE under the Investment Code will not be renewed beyond September 2001. In addition, we decided to postpone until 2002 the budgeting of the revenue from the cellular telephone license, given the uncertainties about the amount and the timing of this revenue. **With regard to expenditure**, we intend to reduce the budget for goods and services by 0.4 percent of GDP, at the same time preserving the allocations for basic education and health, which were increased considerably compared to 2000.

20. **The revised budget will also provide for the payment of all current obligations to multilateral creditors and interest payments for the second half of the year to bilateral creditors**. In anticipation of our eligibility for debt relief under the enhanced HIPC Initiative and unless other sources can be found quickly (the government of China has already indicated its willingness to forgive all outstanding debt, amounting to US$6.3 million), we will propose to our creditors that all arrears be rescheduled until a comprehensive solution can be found at the time of the decision point. On this basis, the overall domestic balance (on a commitment basis) before exceptional expenditure, would record a surplus of 2.1 percent of GDP, and the financing gap would narrow appreciably to only 0.3 percent of GDP.

21. **The exceptional expenditure program**, which was formulated with the assistance of the staffs of the World Bank and the IMF, aims at increasing transfers to Anjouan, covering the costs of restoring democratic institutions (the referendum and elections) and facilitating the establishment of regional administrations; in addition, it provides for urgent expenditure for rehabilitation in the key sectors of education, health, water, and rural development as well as for a reduction in domestic arrears and in the statutory advance account with the BCC. The cost of this program is estimated at about US$12.8 million for July 2001–June 2002.

22. Taking account of the increase in revenue, the expenditure readjustments, and the program of exceptional expenditure, **the overall domestic balance (on a commitment basis, including exceptional expenditure)** is expected to record a deficit in 2001 of 1.1 percent of GDP. We intend to reduce the stock of domestic arrears by CF 1 billion and the statutory advance at the BCC (in order to improve government cash flow management) by CF 200 million. Thus, including the external debt service obligations, **the exceptional financing requirement** would be CF 5.3 billion (US$8.1 million) for 2001. Although we may incur some additional principal arrears with regard to bilateral debt, we expect that most of the financing need will be met from additional concessional financing—including US$4.3 million from the World Bank under the Emergency Economic Recovery Credit (EERC) and the Post-Conflict Fund for 2001—following the upcoming donor meeting.

23. **Prospects for the federal government budget for 2002 will depend on the results of the ongoing discussions on the structure of the new Comorian entity**; in this context, the Tripartite Commission has created a third subcommittee to address the fiscal issues of decentralization. Provisional estimates based on the current situation indicate a decline in revenue to 12 percent of GDP, owing to the absence of exceptional revenue projected for 2001 and in spite of an increase in regular tax receipts. We plan to maintain the overall wage bill at a constant level until the completion of a review of employment in the government; any upward adjustment in wages will be limited to resources generated by a decline in staffing. Expenditure on goods and services will increase slightly in real terms but overall current domestic expenditure is expected to fall as the transitional process is completed and despite a projected increase in inter-regional transfers. Provisional estimates for the overall domestic balance for 2002 (on a commitment basis), including exceptional expenditure, show a substantial downturn in the domestic deficit amounting to 0.2 percent of GDP. However, including debt service, and a further reduction in domestic debt, resulted in an estimated overall financing requirement of CF 5.2 billion (US$10 million) for the year as a whole, of which CF 2.5 billion (US$4.8 million) in the first half of the year, for which we will also seek donor assistance. We intend to examine the budget for 2002 in more detail with IMF staff at the time of a review of our program, scheduled for the last quarter of 2001.

D. Fiscal Sector Reform

24. **The government is determined to strengthen government finance management** to ensure that expenditure is limited in a sustainable manner to a level consistent with the country's resources. This would require efforts in reforming the tax system, improving expenditure management, and controlling the wage bill, as well as seeking a long-term solution to the problem of domestic arrears.

25. **We intend to continue the reform of the tax system**. The objectives of the reform are to reduce reliance on import taxes—which accounted for 75 percent of all tax revenue in 2000—and to reduce customs tariffs over the medium-term, in line with our commitments under regional cooperation arrangements such as the Cross Border Initiative/Regional Integration Facility Forum, while maintaining revenue and increasing the efficiency of the tax system. Based on recent recommendations by an IMF technical assistance mission, we intend to implement further reforms in import tariffs—including the general application of ad valorem taxes starting with the budget for 2002—and to take additional measures to strengthen customs administration, including by reinforcing the large taxpayer unit and making it responsible for ex post verification of import duties. We also expect to make further improvements in the structure and administration of domestic taxes. We will revise the respective laws to make the Minister of Finance, following approval by the cabinet, the sole authority to grant tax exemptions. The government has also launched a study with a view to eliminate the tax exemptions for foreign-financed projects and to provide such tax relief through the budget, starting in 2002. The government is also reviewing the possibility of eliminating all exemptions for government institutions in the 2002 budget. It will make every effort to strengthen cooperation between the customs departments of the different islands.

26. **We will also make further improvements in expenditure management for the purposes of improved control and increased transparency**. The Cash Flow Committee, chaired by the Prime Minister or the Minister of Finance, has established a monthly plan for controlling revenue and expenditure; under this plan, implementation of the 2001 budget will have priority over paying arrears. In addition, as of 2001, expenditure can no longer be committed until the availability of resources has been verified in the cash flow plan, so as to avoid any further accumulation of arrears. Next steps will include the computerization of all payroll components and military pay, for which the government will seek support from donors. The Ministry of Finance will draw up a procedures manual by end-2001 with a view to gaining better control of budget execution.

27. **The government attaches great importance to civil service reform**, aimed at improving the efficiency and the quality of government services and maintaining the wage bill consistent with the available resources. For this purpose, since 1999, we have taken measures to stabilize and gain greater control over the wage bill; other measures are under preparation for implementation in 2001, including the introduction of regulations for the Administrative Court. In the medium term, we would like to prepare a comprehensive civil service reform program. First, with World Bank assistance, we intend to complete an assessment of the civil service legal and institutional framework in 2001. More than 53 percent of the civil service is employed in the education sector, and in light of the structural problems faced by this sector in previous years, the government, with the support of the World Bank, will carry out

a technical audit of the Ministry of Education; this will be completed in early 2002 and will represent the first phase of a review of education sector policy. We expect to further reduce the civil service by 100 employees in 2001, and the government is preparing a program for the early retirement of about 400 employees, which will be implemented when financial resources are identified over the 2001–05 period.

28. **The government has entered into negotiations with its social partners to prepare a medium-term strategy for settling the large wage arrears**. This strategy will be based on the following principles: first, a focus on achieving a comprehensive solution to this problem (no payments will be made before an overall strategy has been adopted); second, limitation of the financial impact of the payment plan, given the financial difficulties faced by our country; third, use of an external audit to ensure rigorous verification of the validity of these claims; fourth, comparable treatment on the three islands, to ensure equity; and fifth, efforts to identify possible financing for clearing arrears.

29. **As of October 2000, the government started paying off arrears to domestic suppliers**. The government has decided to restore the commission on domestic debt to prepare a complete inventory and audit of all budgetary arrears, following which a payment plan will be finalized by end-June 2002. The government will call on donors for support in financing and selecting the audit firm and discuss with the authorities of Anjouan on providing them with support in starting a similar process during 2002.

30. **Considerable effort is necessary to re-establish a basic administration and efficient expenditure management in Anjouan**. With the assistance of the central government and donors, the Anjouan authorities expect to make quick progress in this area, with a view to establishing a basic budget and expenditure management system by end-2001. The Anjouan authorities opened an account at the central bank in June 2001, and all major transactions will be carried out through this account, improving control. Since end-May 2001, Anjouan has been preparing monthly reports on its revenue, expenditure, and financing sources; these reports are submitted to the central government to allow monitoring of fiscal developments in the Comoros on a consolidated basis. Since June 1, 2001 all revenues in Anjouan are paid to the Treasury, an audit commission was also created to verify all the expenditures and revenues of the island.

E. Monetary and Financial Sector Policies

31. **The restrictions imposed by our membership in the French franc zone have enabled us to maintain low inflation, a stable exchange rate, and an adequate level of foreign exchange reserves, despite severe fiscal imbalances**. While we intend to remain within this system, we realize that it limits the monetary policy options, which are also hampered by the shallowness of our

financial system. Monetary policy will pursue its principal objective of maintaining the fixed exchange rate. It will also seek to improve the efficiency of the financial system and strengthen banking supervision, including by providing further training for staff. A proposal to amend the banking legislation to allow for the regulation of the microfinance institutions will be submitted to the government by end-2001. The government is also drafting a regulation to establish a minimum liquidity ratio for the savings bank and to separate it physically and financially from the national post and telecommunications company (SNPT). It also expects to recruit a consultant before end-2001 to start searching for a strategic partner for the national development bank.

F. External Sector

32. **The deficit on the current account of the balance of payments (excluding grants) is projected to increase to 9.2 percent of GDP in 2001.** This reflects a decline in export prices from their exceptionally high level in 2000, and a sharp increase in imports because of the government's exceptional expenditure program. However, this higher deficit is expected to be offset to a large extent by higher foreign assistance and a decline in scheduled debt repayments. Consequently, gross official reserves of the BCC are projected to slightly increase to US$45 million, although, in terms of imports of goods and nonfactor services, they are projected to decline to 7.3 months. Over the medium-term, the current account deficit, excluding grants, is projected to remain at about 7 percent of GDP, and gross official reserves at about 7 months of imports of goods and nonfactor services.

33. **The weaknesses in our external debt management system have contributed to the external debt problems**. To improve this situation, all government and government guaranteed external borrowing will be made subject to the prior authorization of the Minister of Finance, as of end-July 2001. In addition, the Ministry of Finance will request donor assistance in setting up a computerized external debt management system and in building up human resource skills devoted to this important function. Finally, throughout the period of the SMP, the government will not contract or guarantee any new external borrowing on nonconcessional terms.

G. Structural Reforms and Governance

34. **The government also intends to continue making progress in the area of structural reforms**. With the assistance of the World Bank and other donors, we intend to pursue the program of government divestiture of public enterprises. Before end-2002, the government intends to complete the privatization of the port and maritime transport company SOCOPOTRAM, restructure the SNPT, and place the SCH in concession; the national airline has been reconstituted, so that it will not require budget financing. The government also plans to review the

mechanism used to set domestic prices of petroleum products, with a view to facilitating more automatic adjustments to world market prices, in particular to avoid further arrears in payments of taxes on petroleum products. The improvements expected from the privatization of the water and power sector in 1998 have not yet materialized. The government therefore intends to seek the support of donors to carry out a review of water and power sector policy and identify measures that can improve the efficiency of the sector. To this end, the government will give any support necessary to the CEE to reduce electricity theft and improve collection.

35. **The government attaches great importance to improving governance**. We will relaunch the regular publication of the official journal by end-2001. With World Bank assistance, the government is currently strengthening the courts and the Ministry of Justice. In addition, with a view to improving transparency in government finance, we will resume publishing the budgets, starting with the supplementary budget for 2001, in July 2001. We also intend, as of 2001, to publish the annual reports of public enterprises.

36. **We realize that a major effort will be needed to improve our macroeconomic and sociodemographic statistical database**. Accordingly, we have decided to strengthen the Planning Directorate by attaching it to the Office of the Head of State and providing it with new structures and experienced staff from other administrations. We plan to ask donors for assistance to finance our contribution to AFRISTAT, and we have requested technical assistance from the IMF to carry out a broad-based review of our statistics system; this review will be used as the basis for a medium-term action plan.

PROGRAM MONITORING

37. To monitor progress in the implementation of the program, quarterly quantitative benchmarks were established on: (a) net foreign assets of the BCC; (b) domestic bank financing of the government; (c) government revenue; (d) the wage bill; (e) nonconcessional external public borrowing; and (f) public sector accumulation of external payment arrears to multilateral institutions (Table 1). Structural benchmarks have been established to serve as a guide in the implementation of basic reforms (Table 2). Implementation of the program will be reviewed in November 2001 and May 2002.

Table 1. Comoros: Quantitative Benchmarks under the Staff-Monitored Program[1]
July 2001–June 2002
(In millions of Comorian francs, unless otherwise indicated)

	2001			2002	
	June Stock	September Benchmark	December Benchmark	March Benchmark	June Benchmark
(a) Ceiling on net domestic financing of the government[2 3 4]		0	–496	–1,214	–1,214
(b) Ceiling on wage bill[5]		4,900	6,267	1,567	3,134
(c) Floor on total revenues[5]<>		11,345	14,323	3,482	8,032
(d) Floor on net foreign assets of the central bank[2 4]	22,105	308	510	620	730
(e) Ceiling on contracting or guaranteeing of external debt on nonconcessional terms[2]		0	0	0	0
(f) Ceiling on accumulation of debt service arrears towards multilateral creditors[2]		0	0	0	0

[1]The definitions of the benchmarks and the adjusters are provided under the Technical Memorandum of Understand

[2]Cumulative change since end-June 2001.

[3]Excluding IMF.

[4]The benchmark will be asjusted for a short fall in budget support as described in the TMU.

[5]Cumulative change since the beginning of the fiscal year, except where otherwise indicated.

Table 2. Comoros: Structural Benchmarks Under the Staff-Monitored Program, July 2001–June 2002

Sector	Measure	Date to Be Implemented
Governance	Publish supplementary budget for 2001	End-July 2001
	Publish 2002 budget	End-January 2002
Fiscal	Eliminate the exemption for the withholding tax (*Acompte sur Impôts et Taxes, AIT*) for the water and electricity operating company (CEE), and raise rates of specific taxes on cement and alcoholic beverages	End-July 2001
	Prepare and implement new expenditure management procedures manual	January 1, 2002
Domestic debt	Reactivate domestic debt committee and submit request to donors for financing of audit of all domestic supplier arrears, including on Anjouan	End-September 2001
External debt	Computerize and update the external debt database.	End-December 2001
Financial sector	Submit to government amendments to legislation for the regulation of micro-finance institutions	January 1, 2002

[1]Domestic balances (primary, current, overall) exclude grants, foreign-financed current and capital expenditures, technical assistance, and interest charges on the external debt.
[2]The total stock of wage arrears accumulated during 1995-2000 (excluding Anjouan after mid-1998) is estimated at CF 8.7 billion, equivalent to about 20 months of wages.
[3]Since 1994, the exchange rate is set at FF 1 = CF 75; it is expressed in euro since January 2000 at the rate of EUR 1 = CF 492.

TECHNICAL MEMORANDUM OF UNDERSTANDING FOR THE STAFF-MONITORED PROGRAM (SMP)[4]

1. This technical memorandum of understanding (TMU) contains the definitions of the quantitative benchmarks of the Comoros staff-monitored program for the period July 2001-June 2002 and describes the reporting requirements under that program. The TMU is an integral part of the documents that govern the IMF's monitoring of the Comoros program.

I. QUANTITATIVE BENCHMARKS[1]

A. Ceiling on Net Domestic Financing of the Government

2. Net domestic financing of the government (NDF) is defined as the sum of (a) the variation in the stock of federal government domestic debt to the Central Bank of the Comoros (BCC) and the commercial bank (BIC) minus its deposits held with those institutions; (b) privatization receipts; and (c) new budgetary arrears. New budgetary arrears are defined as arrears accumulated during the fiscal year on wages, domestic interest, and goods and services. Payments on salaries, wages, and pensions are deemed in arrears when they remain unpaid more than 30 days beyond the due payment date. Interest payments are in arrears when the payment is not made on the due date. Payments to suppliers are deemed to be in arrears if they have not been made within the normal grace period of 30 days or such other period as has been contractually agreed after the verified delivery of the concerned goods or services, unless the amount or the timing of the payment is subject to good faith negotiations between the government and the creditor. Domestic payment arrears include the amount to be recommitted and net payments delays (clearings, items in process of payment, expenditure committed but with no payment order issued), as defined in the table on federal government operations (TOFE).

B. Ceiling on the Wage Bill

3. The wage bill includes all wages and salaries, premiums for social insurance and pensions, indemnities, bonuses and other payments directly related to rewarding employment. Included in the wage bill are the wage expenditures of the civil service, gouvernorats, military, and Caisse de Retraite des Comores (CRC). Under the program, the ceiling on the wage bill in the budgets for 2001 and 2002 amounts to CF 6,267 million in each year.

C. Floor on Total Revenues

[4] IMF Materials. July 2001–June 2002

4. Total revenue consists of all tax and nontax revenue included in the TOFE. Under the program, total revenue for 2001 amounts to CF 14,323 million and in 2002 to CF 8,032 million for the period January-June 2002.

D. Floor on Net Foreign Assets of the BCC

5. For the purpose of the program, net foreign assets of the BCC (NFA) is defined as its usable foreign assets minus its foreign liabilities, converted in Comorian francs at the end-period exchange rates. NFA is defined consistent with the definition of the Operational Guidelines on the *Data Template on International Reserves and Foreign Currency Liquidity* template as external assets readily available to, or controlled by, the BCC. It includes the reserve position with the Fund net of outstanding use of Fund credit, but excludes any pledged or otherwise encumbered reserve assets, including, but not limited to, reserve assets used as collateral or guarantee for third-party external liabilities.

E. Ceiling on Nonconcessional External Borrowing

6. Under the program, the avoidance of nonconcessional external debt contracted or guaranteed by the government or the BCC is a continuous benchmark. Nonconcessional external debt is all debt with a concessionality level of less than 35 percent. For loans with a maturity of at least 15 years, the 10-year average "commercial interest rate reference rate" (CIRR), published by the OECD, should be used to calculate the level of concessionality. For loans with shorter maturities, the 6-month average CIRR should be used. For the purposes of the program through December 31, 2001, the 6-month and 10-year CIRRs published by the OECD in December 2000 will be used. To both the 10-year and 6-month averages, the following margins for differing repayment periods should be added: 0.75 percent for repayment periods of less than 15 years; 1 percent for 15-19 years; 1.15 percent for 20-29 years; and 1.25 percent for 30 years or more.

7. This performance criterion applies not only to debt as defined in point No. 9 of the Guidelines on Performance Criteria with Respect to Foreign Debt adopted on August 24, 2000 (Executive Board Decision No. 12274 (00/85)) but also to commitments contracted or guaranteed for which value has not been received. The definition of debt set forth in No. 9 of the guidelines is as follows:

> "(a) For the purpose of this guideline, the term "debt" will be understood to mean a current, i.e., not contingent, liability, created under a contractual arrangement through the provision of value in the form of assets (including currency) or services, and which requires the obligor to make one or more payments in the form of assets (including currency) or services, at some future point(s) in time; these payments will discharge the principal and/or interest

liabilities incurred under the contract. Debts can take a number of forms, the primary ones being as follows: (i) loans, i.e., advances of money to obligor by the lender made on the basis of an undertaking that the obligor will repay the funds in the future (including deposits, bonds, debentures, commercial loans and buyers' credits) and temporary exchanges of assets that are equivalent to fully collateralized loans under which the obligor is required to repay the funds, and usually pay interest, by repurchasing the collateral from the buyer in the future (such as repurchase agreements and official swap arrangements); (ii) suppliers' credits, i.e., contracts where the supplier permits the obligor to defer payments until some time after the date on which the goods are delivered or services are provided; and (iii) leases, i.e., arrangements under which property is provided which the lessee has the right to use for one or more specified period(s) of time that are usually shorter than the total expected service life of the property, while the lessor retains the title to the property. For the purpose of the guideline, the debt is the present value (at the inception of the lease) of all lease payments expected to be made during the period of the agreement excluding those payments that cover the operation, repair or maintenance of the property. (b) Under the definition of debt set out in point 9(a) above, arrears, penalties, and judicially awarded damages arising from the failure to make payment under a contractual obligation that constitutes debt are debt. Failure to make payment on an obligation that is not considered debt under this definition (e.g., payment on delivery) will not give rise to debt."

8. Excluded from this benchmark are (i) debt contracted in the context of rescheduling agreements; and (ii) leases of office space, equipment and housing contracted by representatives of the Comoros abroad.

F. Ceiling on External Payments Arrears to Multilateral Creditors

9. Under the program, the program, the government will not incur new payment arrears to multilateral creditors, starting from January 1, 2001. External payment arrears are defined as nonpayment in full of interest and principal obligations due to each multilateral creditor, excluding arrears resulting from nonpayment of debt service for which rescheduling negotiations are under way. Thus, the stock of arrears to each multilateral creditor should not exceed the stock outstanding as of December 2000, minus any payment of arrears existing before January 1, 2001 minus any arrears resulting from nonpayment of debt service for which rescheduling negotiations are under.

10. The stock of external debt service arrears to multilateral creditors as of end-December 2000 (in millions of U.S. dollars) was: US$0.0 million to the IDA,

US$0.0 million to the IMF, US$15.5 million to the African Development Bank (of which US$3.9 million to the African Development Fund), US$0.0 million to the European Union/European Development Fund, US$24.4 million to the Arab Bank for Economic Development in Africa (BADEA), US$0.0 million to the International Fund for Agricultural Development (IFAD), US$3.4 million to the OPEC Fund, and US$11.2 million to the Islamic Development Bank.

G. Periods Covered by the Benchmarks

11. The benchmark concerning the contracting or guaranteeing of external debt is continuous during the program period. The other quantitative benchmarks pertain to end-September 2001, end-December 2001, end-March 2002, and end-June-2002. The ceilings on net domestic financing of the government, net foreign assets of the BCC, and the contracting or guaranteeing of external debt on nonconcessional terms are defined in cumulative changes from end-June 2001. The ceilings on the wage bill and on total revenues are defined in cumulative changes from the start of the fiscal year. The benchmark on no accumulation of debt service arrears toward multilateral creditors is cumulative from January 1, 2000.

II. MONITORING OF THE STRUCTURAL BENCHMARKS

Governance

12. The authorities will provide the Fund a copy of the published supplementary budget for 2001 and the published 2002 budget.

Fiscal

13. The authorities will provide the Fund a statement by the Ministry of Finance indicating that the exemption for the withholding tax (Accompte sur Impôts et Taxes AIT) for the water and electricity operating company (CEE) has been eliminated, and rates of specific taxes on cement and alcoholic beverages have been raised. The authorities will also provide the Fund a copy of the published expenditure management procedures manual.

Domestic Debt

14. The authorities will provide the Fund a statement by the Ministry of Finance indicating that the domestic debt committee has been reactivated, and a copy of the request to donors for financing of audit of all domestic supplier arrears, including on Anjouan.

External Debt

15. The authorities will provide the Fund an Excel file with an updated external debt database.

Financial Sector

16. The authorities will provide the Fund a copy of the amendments to legislation for the regulation of the micro-finance institutions.

III. ADJUSTERS

A. Adjuster to the Benchmarks for NFA of the BCC and NDFof the Government for a Shortfall in Budget Support

17. For the purposes of the program, the benchmarks for NFA and NDF of the government will be adjusted for a shortfall in budget support compared with the projected level. The benchmark for NFA will be adjusted downward and the benchmark for NDF will be adjusted upward for the full amount of the shortfall. Budget support is defined as foreign assistance for the general financing of the federal budget that is provided unconditionally or conditional upon policy actions only, without predetermined additional current of capital expenditure counterpart.

18. Budget support for July 2001–June 2002 is projected (cumulative since July 2001) at CF 0 million by end-September 2001, CF 296 million by end-December 2001; CF 1,109 million at end-March 2002; and CF1,109 million at end-June 2002.

IV. INFORMATION AND DATA TO BE PROVIDED TO THE IMF

19. The Comorian authorities will provide Fund staff with the following information and data according to the schedule provided, either directly (e-mail or facsimile) or my airmail. The monetary data, external debt data, the consumer price index, and any information on important legislative and /or other developments (see paragraph 15) will be provided not later than one month after the date to which they pertain. The fiscal data will be provided not later than two months after the date to which they pertain.

Monthly:

- The monetary survey, and the monthly balance sheets of the BCC and the commercial bank;
- Classification of commercial bank loans by economic sector;
- Interest rates;
- TOFE data on a cash and commitment basis and the related detailed tables on revenue;

- External public debt operations (debt contracted and publicly guaranteed, settlement of external payments arrears, and debt service paid;
- Consumer price index; and
- Imports and exports, production of electricity, tourist arrivals, and any other indicators of economic activity that may be available on a monthly basis.

When available:

- National accounts data
- Balance of payments
- Quarterly production of major products (vanilla, cloves, ylang-ylang)

20. Moreover, information on important measures adopted by the government in the economic and social areas that would have an impact on program development, changes in legislation, and any other pertinent legislation will be reported to Fund staff on a timely basis for consultation or information, as appropriate[5].

INTERNATIONAL ASSISTANCE

Independent from France in 1975, the Comoros is a small archipelago nation in the Indian Ocean, with promising tourism potential. The country situation has been difficult for many years due to political instability and a weakening economy. Poor economic management coupled with weak political commitment to reforms led to deteriorating public finances and weak private sector response, exacerbated by the devaluation of the Comorian Franc in January 1994. In August 1997, two of the three main Comorian islands, Anjouan and Moheli, sought to sever links with the main island Grande Comore, citing economic mismanagement and political neglect. The government has since tried to restore order and promote national reconciliation with the mediation of the Organization of African Unity (OAU).

ECONOMY

Agriculture - including fishing, hunting, and forestry - is the predominant sector of Comoros' economy. It contributes 40 percent to GDP and employs 80 percent of the labor force. However, the country is not self-sufficient in food production, and rice, the country's main staple, accounts for 90 percent of imports. Tourism has started to develop, but its growth has been hampered by an unstable political environment.

[5] [1]The benchmarks refer to the federal government, unless otherwise indicated.

Because of sluggish economic growth and depressed world market prices of Comoros' main export crops, in particular vanilla and cloves, real per capita incomes have declined during the past decade. Chronic financial problems emerged and public finance deficits, including grants, reached about 7 percent of GDP in 1997, reflecting weak revenue effort. Domestic and external arrears have accumulated and civil servant salaries have not been paid on a regular basis. The external current account deficit remained high at 15 percent of GDP in 1997. The inflation rate declined to about 2 percent by end-1997, as a result of prudent monetary policy and stagnating economic activity. Growth will be possible with improved economic management and strengthened fiscal discipline, and with private sector involvement in reform efforts.

POLITICS

After more than a decade of one-party rule, punctuated by foreign mercenary control of government, a multi-party political system was introduced in 1990 with an open presidential election. A new constitution was approved by referendum in 1992 and the first multi-party legislative election was organized in the following year. In 1996, a second presidential and legislative election took place in a democratic manner with a peaceful political transition for the first time in the Comoros, which has had a long history of coups and mercenaries. In 1997, political crisis arose with the declaration of secession by Anjouan and Moheli islands. As of September 1998, the crisis has yet to be resolved and social tensions persist.

DEVELOPMENT PICTURE/DONOR COORDINATION

With declining real per capita incomes and a government experiencing serious financial difficulties, the village-level communities of the Comoros have become increasingly self-reliant and emerged as the primary source of hope for the country's future. These communities have demonstrated interest in the development process, willingness to pay for quality services and ability to take responsibility for management. As a result, donors have increased assistance to support community development and improve social and economic infrastructure at the village level. The Bank, UNDP, European Community, France and some Arab states are among active donors in Comoros, and donor coordination in Comoros has been good.

WORLD BANK ROLE

Bank assistance to the Comoros has centered on: economic growth with focus on poverty reduction; human capital development; and preservation of the environment, given the islands' severe deforestation and soil erosion. Because public finances have become weak, the World Bank is increasingly directing its resources toward supporting community development, focusing on projects that rely on communities themselves for successful implementation.

The Bank's portfolio for the Comoros amounts to US$47 million and consists of 6 projects funded by the International Development Association (IDA), the World Bank's interest-free lending arm for the poorest countries. Three projects (Social Fund, Health, Education) were approved in 1997-1998 and designed to help improve equity across the islands, with implementation supported by enterprising village communities. In collaboration with the IMF and other donors, the Bank will continue policy dialogue with the government on the need for sustained commitment to economic stability and key structural reforms. The World Bank is cooperating with Organization of African Unity on a national reconciliation initiative which, if successful, could lead to a stronger economy.

IFC has not yet made any investment in the Comoros, but has provided advisory assistance in the agribusiness sector. The Comoros has not yet joined MIGA.

CONTACTS

Mr. Michael Sarris
Country Director
1818 H Street NW, Washington, DC 20433 USA
Tel: (202) 473-4009
Fax: (202) 473-8564
E-mail: msarris@worldbank.org

Mr. Luca Barbone
Macroeconomic Sector Manager
1818 H Street NW, Washington, DC 20433 USA
Tel: (202) 473-2556
Fax: (202) 473-8466
E-mail: lbarbone@worldbank.org

Ms. Pisei Eap
Country Economist
1818 H Street NW, Washington, DC 20433 USA
Tel: (202) 473-4364
Fax: (202) 473-8466
E-mail: peap@worldbank.org

WORLD BANK PROJECTS

EDUCATION PROJECT

The economy is predominantly rural and highly dependent on external assistance, averaging about US$118 per capita per annum over 1989-93. Since independence in 1975, the country has experienced considerable economic change. Following a period of growth generated by externally-financed infrastructure projects, real GDP growth slowed significantly from an annual average of 4.3 percent in 1981-85 to 0.8 percent over 1991-95. The decline in economic performance is a manifestation of the country's developmental constraints, which include a narrow export base, weak institutional capacity exacerbated by poor economic management, as well as an unfavorable private sector environment.

To address its macroeconomic imbalances and remove some of the structural constraints to growth, the government launched an adjustment program in 1991, which made considerable progress in liberalizing imports, removing price controls, and improving the environment for private sector activity, as well as reducing the fiscal burden arising from the parastatal sector. Consequently, after initial delays caused by an unsettled political climate in which the fiscal situation deteriorated further, the implementation of the program accelerated and was completed at end 1994. Domestic savings improved from negative 3.7 percent of GDP in 1991 to zero percent in 1993. The budgetary deficit (before capital grants) fell from 13.1 percent of GDP in 1991 to 7.4 percent in 1993, owning to expenditure cuts through civil service reduction. The external current account deficit (before capital grants) was marginally reduced from 11.1 percent of GDP in 1991 to 10.5 percent in 1993, as imports declined in response to the reduced aggregate demand pressure, exports began to recover, and tourism receipts started to increase. The Comorian Franc was devalued by 33 percent in foreign currency in January 1994, in concert with the 50 percent devaluation that took place in other CFA countries. The economy's response to this devaluation was mixed, however, with a slow down of economic activities registered in trade and agriculture sector, which contributed to a real GDP decline averaging 2.3 percent a year in 1994-95. Export performance for traditional commodities was poor, in particular, because of the nearly 50 percent drop in export prices for vanilla in the world market.

Economic reforms in Comoros have been complicated by the parallel efforts at introducing political reforms. Recent Presidential and legislative elections held in March 1996 and December 1996 respectively represent major landmarks in the country's political transition process. The new government has recognized the need for the country to improve its economic management and performance, which include measures to improve budgetary revenues and cut expenditures, as well as create a more conducive environment for private sector investment partially through adoption of a comprehensive privatization program for the public enterprises. However, due to the political turmoil and the process of legislative elections which took place in December 1996, concrete actions have yet to be taken. In consequence, the second adjustment program to support these reforms which was to have been prepared for 1996 has been delayed. The program would be taken up once satisfactory budgetary performance has been established in the first half of 1997.

Sector Background. Finding of a World Bank Poverty Assessment (FY95) indicate that the majority of the Comorian population lives in relative poverty or at near poverty levels. Consumption is very unevenly distributed-the Gini coefficient is 76%, as rural areas in all three islands house the majority of the population (82%) and of the poor: the head count index for rural areas in Grande Comore, Anjouan, and Moheli is 92%,76%, and 85% respectively while for the country's urban areas it stands at 15%. Very preliminary estimates of the 1996 household expenditure survey show that 84% of rural households live in poverty compared to 15% of urban households. It is estimated that 75% of the poor households work in agriculture. Additional analysis confirms that poverty is higher in Anjouan and Moheli, which together account for just under half of the country's population. The survey revealed another "at risk" category as 79% of women have been unilaterally divorced by their husbands and therefore constitute another vulnerable group. The poor households are characterized by lower levels of literacy, although 67% of heads of poor households can read Comorian Arabic taught in "Koranic schools" at the community level, but only 37% have basic arithmetic skills.

The Government is aware that education is not producing the basic skills required for national development and the reduction of poverty. More than one-third of school-age children do not have access to formal schooling at primary level and, among those who complete the 6-year primary cycle on time, only one in ten continues to lower secondary schooling. In 1993-94, net enrollment ratios (the latter take out over- and under-age children and repeaters) at primary and lower and upper secondary levels were estimated to 64, 11 and 2 percent, respectively. Girls represented nearly 45 percent of enrollees at each level. However, these figures mask an inequitable distribution of services between the three islands. In 1993-94, girl's enrollment ratios were significantly lower than those of boys in 9 of the 15 school districts, especially in Anjouan. Access to primary education is constrained by limited space in existing classrooms. The vast majority of the 262 public primary schools (1996) were built more than 15 years ago, using space norms (less than 30 m2 per classroom) that are not adequate for the current size of classes (national average of 39 pupils) and site planning which does not provide for sanitary facilities and a minimum size courtyard. At secondary level, the capacity of the existing collèges (40) and lycees (9) is underutilized, mainly due to restricted entrance at lower secondary level and recent expansion of private education, and MOE has already started rationalizing the school map with the closing of 5 collèges and 1 lycees in 1994.

In addition, low internal efficiency is reflected by the gap between net and gross enrollment ratios at primary, lower and upper secondary levels, the latter estimated at 89, 27 and 15 percent, respectively by level. A cohort analysis shows that, for 1,000 children entering Grade 1, only 116 are expected to complete the primary cycle, 60 the lower secondary cycle and 13 to pass the Grade 13 examination (baccalaureat). The system must provide 14 years of schooling per student who completes the primary cycle. This situation is due in large part to the poor level of quality of public education. Sporadic teacher strikes, shortages of school materials and poor management have contributed to the deterioration of quality.

Communities in the Comoros have demonstrated their cohesiveness, dynamism, interest in the development process, ability to manage effectively community development concerns, and willingness to pay for services such as health and education,. As a result of the deteriorating conditions in public schools, a growing number of parents and local authorities, mostly in the largest villages and in dynamic communities, chose private for-profit schooling. While this development of private schooling is welcomed, it raises issues of equity, sustainability (e.g. if public schools resume normal operations) and quality assurance. Moreover, during the last two years, this development led to further deterioration of public education, especially for the poor. Teaching staff in private schools are recruited among civil servants who retain their public position but often neglect their obligations to public schools. The Government is moving prudently, considering a range of policies and measures to encourage development of quality private schooling while at the same time improving equitable access to quality education and improving efficiency of public provision of education services. Measures that are being considered include: improved accreditation system for private schools, better control of teacher assignments and presence, and cost recovery for publicly-provided services to private schools (e.g. teacher in- service training, standardized examinations).

In the Comoros, the main factor perpetuating poverty across generations is the low level of education among the poor which limits their employment and trade options as well as their mobility. In addition, relatively high wages (in foreign country terms) and low productivity contribute to poverty by making the Comoros uncompetitive in international markets. Employment is expected to benefit from changes enhancing the business environment and employment creation, such as improvement in the legal system, trade liberalization, better access to credit and better land tenure, which are supported by an FY94 IDA-financed Small Enterprise Development Project and the proposed FY97 Pilot Agriculture Services Project.

The vocational training system consists of six public training institutions which altogether have a capacity of about 1,000 students. These institutions are under the Ministries of Education (ENTP - Ecole Nationale Technique et Professionnelle; ENAC - Ecole Nationale d'Administration et de Comptabilite; and the CHA - Centre Horticole Applique), Agriculture (ENA - Ecole Nationale d'Agriculture; ENP - Ecole Nationale des Peches), and Health (ENS - Ecole Nationale de Sante). The latter three closed in recent years after having trained technicians and skilled workers who were employed mostly in government agencies. The Second Education Project assisted in the creation of ENTP and ENAC and financed civil works, equipment and development costs. Technical assistance was provided under the French and Belgian bilateral assistance programs. Private provision of training started only recently and is still embryonic. Also, community-supported apprenticeship schemes have been initiated and are supported by the Community Development Fund (FADC) supported under the IDA-financed PHRD Project.

Post-secondary education available in the Comoros consists of teacher training, agriculture, a business school and the school of health sciences, which overall provide about 200 student-places. A large number of students (estimated at more than 1,000 in 1995) go abroad for university studies. Given its priorities and resource availability, the government has agreed with donors to limit the number of scholarships abroad to those provided by donor funds.

Project Objectives. The project would support investments in the first two priority sub-sectors identified in the PRET, namely primary education and vocational training. To ensure effective and timely implementation of the project, it would also support local capacity building in the planning, execution, monitoring and evaluation of project-financed activities.

Project Description. The project would support investments in the first two priority sub-sectors identified in the Government's Program for the Reinforcement of Education and Training, namely primary education and vocational training. To ensure effective and timely implementation of the project, it would also support local capacity building in the planning, execution, monitoring and evaluation of sector management. The project would improve learning at primary level through increased participation in quality education. Participation would be improved through: (a) establishment of local school committees with financial and managerial authority on public primary schools; and (b) provision of adequate infrastructure through improvement grants to participating communities in targeted areas. Quality of the teaching-learning processes would be improved through: (a) development of better management practices to monitor delivery of the study program; (b) provision of teaching/learning materials, both for class and individual learning activities; (c) changes in the teaching-learning methods used by teachers in the classroom; (d) changes in the supervision practices to develop and monitor implementation of effective teaching practices; and (e) support to development of learning assessment and education information systems at regional and central levels of the MOE.

The project would improve competencies of skilled workers through the establishment of an autonomous, flexible and effective demand- driven training system in which training institutions and employers will get grants from the Government. The establishment of a performing vocational training system would be achieved through the creation of a small, autonomous institution - the Office for Vocational Training (OVT) - managed by an independent council. Competencies and skills would be developed through (a) support for management and the initial financing of a Vocational Training Fund (VTF) which would finance one part of the expenses of training linked to the execution of sub-projects which respond to needs identified in the labor market; (b) support for the development of training modules which lead to a qualification and the training of the trainers; and (c) support for the reorganization of existing vocational training institutions in order to develop autonomous management, as well as modular programs adapted to the labor market.

The total project cost is estimated at US$7.5 million equivalent, including contingencies and taxes. IDA would finance 7.0 million and communities' / beneficiaries' contributions is estimated at 0.2 million. The Comorian Government is expected to contribute US$0.3.

Project Implementation. In line with strategic orientations which prioritize the empowerment of school heads, on the one hand, and, on the other hand, partnership with community and employers, the management of the project will be light, but effective. It will be oriented towards the achievement of the goals of the Program for the Reinforcement of Education and Training, the achievement of measurable objectives and the evaluation of performance. In order to improve access to quality primary education and to strengthen the management of the education system, a Project Management Unit will have the task of: (a) directing local and regional teams which will negotiate contracts of activities with institutions and with parent-teacher associations; (b) coordinating the implementation of programs of activities in close collaboration with the relevant local authorities; and (c) measuring the achievement of defined objectives and evaluating the impact of measures and actions which have been introduced on learning outcomes and the enrollment of students. The PMU would be placed under the coordination of the Director of the National Center for the Management and Implementation of Education Projects (CNGEPE).

The PMU would comprise six managers engaged on contract by means of a transparent selection process and remunerated under the Credit: (a) a Project Coordinator whose office will be located in Moroni; (b) a financial manager responsible for keeping the books of the project and for managing the Credit; (c) a specialist in bidding procedures responsible for the management of purchases and contracts of goods, works and services; and (d) three regional coordinators, one officer per island, who will be responsible for planning, coordinating, monitoring and the control of activities financed under the Credit. Regional offices will comprise support staff with three administrators who will assure the functions of the Directorate secretariat and operational assistance. The professional services required for specific operations will form the object of separate contracts of employment, negotiated locally in accordance with detailed terms of reference.

Project Sustainability. In terms of financial sustainability, the investments planned under this project will require that the Government undertake a series of measures to increase public revenues, to allocate sufficient levels of public resources to education, and to rationalize expenditures in the sector. During appraisal, agreement would be sought on: (a) a sustainable Public Expenditure Program (both investment and recurrent) for the period 1997-1999; and (b) the level and composition of the recurrent budget for salary and non-salary expenditures.

COMOROS-ENVIRONMENT, WATER SUPPLIES

The proposed project addresses the need for physical infrastructure and improved sectoral management in the transport, water and urban sectors. Transport: road infrastructure in Comoros is fairly widespread, and a Road Maintenance Fund (RMF) is in place to ensure that roads are maintained. However, many areas remain unconnected to the major roads, and road ransport is dangerous due to inadequate signage, unstable road shoulders and an antiquated and poorly enforced Road Code. Inter-island transport is limited and unreliable: maritime transport is mainly provided by small, poor- quality vessels according to no fixed schedule, and is markedly unsafe; air transport is too expensive for the majority of the population and equipment is unreliable and poorly maintained. The Ministry of Transport and Tourism (MTT) is marked by weak management and enforcement capacity. The Government of Comoros (GOC) has begun to address maritime and air transport safety issues, but the measures are insufficient so far.

Water: Comoros suffers from an overall problem of inadequate access to potable water (current rates of coverage are: 30% for Grand Comore, 45% for Anjouan, and 60% for Moheli). In addition, management of water resources is scattered among multiple public sector institutions with poor technical capacity; and water infrastructure is generally limited, unmaintained and in poor condition, leading to lack of service and water loss (estimated on Grand Comore as being as high as 45%). The GOC has adopted recommendations of the UNICEF-financed National Action Plan for Water and Basic Sanitation to (a) integrate the water sector into the NEAP; (b) establish an institutional framework to monitor, plan and coordinate water sector activities; (c) concentrate on rural and periurban microprojects; (d) focus on the needs of beneficiary communities and promote and increase their contribution to service delivery; (e) use appropriate technologies to increase low-cost, sustainable access to water/sanitation; (f) standardize construction systems; and (g) strengthen water engineering capacity in Comoros. The water authority (Comoran National Electric and Water Company) is in the process of privatizing, which should improve management and delivery of services.

Urban: Comoros currently lacks policies for urban and land management, despite a high annual urban growth rate (5.5%), leading to unplanned, and environmentally detrimental, urban growth. Given this lack of urban planning and management, urban sanitation infrastructure and services are very poor: Comoros' main cities are virtually without drainage and wastewater systems, and solid waste collection is extremely limited and unsustainable due to lack of cost recovery. Urban wastes currently pose grave and growing threats to public health and the environment. The GOC has created a Department of Urban Development (DU) within the Ministry of Land Management (MAT) to address urban growth issues, however this institution is still in its infancy and needs support and an updated urban strategy to guide its work. A first priority is to develop a construction code and institute urban planning to direct urban growth.

The proposed project is an integral part of a multidonor- financed program in the Comoros, and supports the development objectives of the larger program. The main program objective is to improve living conditions and stimulate economic growth, while preserving the environment and public investments in basic infrastructure. Focusing on three priority sectors (transport, water and urban), the specific objectives of the project are to: (i) maintain road infrastructure and open up isolated villages; (ii) improve the safety of road and maritime transport; (iii) establish rapid maritime transport links to increase inter-island exchange; (iv) establish sustainable water use guidelines and significantly increase water coverage rates for populations of the 3 islands by 2002; and (v) improve management of transport, water and urban infrastructure through public awareness campaigns, stakeholder participation, cost-recovery measures and targeted support to public sector institutions.

Project Description. The proposed project is an integral component of a larger, multidonor program of support to protect the environment, develop essential infrastructure and strengthen institutions in three priority sectors. The project seeks to lay the foundation and provide opportunities for local communities, nongovernmental organizations (NGOs), and the private sector to participate in service delivery and economic growth. In transport, the project focuses on: (a) gradually privatizing regional public road maintenance workshops, and converting force-account road maintenance to private sector contracts; (b) improving the efficiency and safety of road transport through better subsector regulation and management, extension and maintenance of roads and road signs, and improved functioning of the Road Maintenance Fund; (c) promoting more reliable inter-island exchange through the development of a rapid and affordable transport mode, improving and enforcing safety regulations, and training sector personnel; and (d) strengthening the Public Works and Transport Departments (DGTP and DT) to more effectively manage the sector.

In the water sector, the project focuses on protecting water resources and improving water supply to urban and rural populations on the islands of Anjouan and Mohéli. A study will determine the feasibility of cost-recovery mechanisms and mechanisms for community participation in infrastructure maintenance to rationalize consumption and ensure the sustainability of water supply. The project will also provide institutional support to the Government to develop a general water policy and better manage the sector, and community training and public awareness campaigns to support sustainable water use.

The project will assist the newly established DU to: (a) revise the Urban and Construction Codes, with particular emphasis on environmental protection; (b) involve local communities in service delivery and infrastructure maintenance (drainage and sanitation); (c) establish a mechanism to recover costs for urban service delivery; (d) implement road and drainage works included in the Urban Master Plan for Moroni; and (e) develop urban master plans for Mutsamudu and Fomboni to ensure environmentally sound urban growth over the medium-to-long term.

The proposed IDA Credit is US$13.25 million. The GOC will contribute US$1.5 million (equivalent), and local communities are expected to contribute US$0.25 million (equivalent) in monetary and/or in-kind resources. The Fonds d'Assistance et de Coopération (FAC) will provide cofinancing of US$1.9 million to support technical assistance to the executing agencies. Parallel funding of the larger program is as follows: European Union (EU): US$21 million; Caisse Française de Dévéloppement (CFD): US$1.9 million; FAC: US$1.87 million; and Japan International Cooperation Agency (JICA): US$1.6 million. A further US$1.54 million will come from microprojects within the program, and funding for US$3.17 is still being sought.

The executing agencies are technical and sectoral departments in Ministry of Land Management and the Ministry of Transport and Tourism. The Department of Public Works (DGTP) in MAT is responsible for overall project coordination. Responsibility for implementation and management of individual project components rests with the sectoral departments as follows: the Transport Department (DT) of MTT will execute the transport components, the Department of Energy and Mineral Resources (DERM) in MAT will oversee water sector activities, and the MAT's Department of Urban Development will take responsibility for the urban components. An interministerial steering committee will be set up to coordinate donor interventions, and intersectoral activities.

The proposed project is integrated into a larger donor-supported program. The IDA Credit would support interventions that complement and amplify those of other donors. In addition, the project is based on the participation of community groups that are already involved in providing services to residents, and will develop and apply cost-recovery measures, wherever feasible.

Extending and rehabilitating road infrastructure will improve mobility and access to markets and services, stimulating agricultural production and enhancing quality of life. Reliable and affordable inter- island transport will likewise improve mobility and provide wider access to markets, jobs and services. Sustainable provision of water, sanitation and drainage will improve the health and quality of life for urban and rural residents, with particular benefits to the poor. Better urban management will improve living conditions for the urban poor by avoiding unplanned and underserved informal settlements. Providing opportunities for small and medium enterprises (SMEs) in road rehabilitation and maintenance will create employment opportunities for unskilled and semi-skilled labor.

The establishment and enforcement of environmentally-sound construction and urban development codes will protect vulnerable lands and ecosystems (particularly coastal zones) from unplanned urban expansion. Provision of urban drainage and sanitation systems will protect land from erosion, flooding, and will preserve groundwater resources from contamination. Cost-recovery measures for water and sanitation services will help rationalize the consumption of water resources.

Project Objective Categories. Environmental protection is the primary project objective. Secondary objectives include private sector development and public sector management.

THE UNITED NATIONS IN COMOROS

Implementing Agency	United Nations Development Programme
Country	Comoros Islands
Focal Area	Biodiversity
Project Title	Island Biodiversity and Participatory Conservation in the Federal Republic of Comoros
GEF Allocation	US$2.442 million

Total Financing	US$2.442 million
Dates	October 1995–Nov 2002
Environmental Problem	• Rich terrestrial and marine island biodiversity threatened by population growth and poverty
Project Goals	• Develop biodiversity management frameworks and network of protected areas • Strengthen government and NGO capacity for biodiversity conservation • Find alternative income- and benefit-generating activities for local communities
	Lying in the Western Indian Ocean between northern Mozambique and Madagascar, the three islands of the Federal Islamic Republic of the Comoros contain a rich array of biodiversity and habitats, both marine and terrestrial. This wealth, however, stands in stark contrast with the poverty of its people. Densely populated, the Comoros has a population growing at 2.7 percent annually. Recently, the nation's economy has suffered, as export earnings from spices and other agricultural products have dropped on the world market. Population pressures and poverty have led to a vicious cycle of resource overexploitation, environmental degradation, and exacerbated poverty. Natural resources are being depleted at an alarming rate. The government of Comoros has recognized the links between natural resource conservation and sustainable development. It developed and adopted a National Environmental Policy in 1993 and approved an Environmental Action Plan in 1994. Implementation of these efforts would help address some of the islands' serious environment and development issues. Unfortunately, the government has undergone many changes and reorganizations in recent years and has lacked the human and financial resources to carry out this plan.
The Project	This project, now being implemented by the Ministry of Rural Development, Fisheries, and the Environment, will contribute to the sustainable development of the Comoros and maintain the islands' unique natural heritage by implementing the biodiversity components of the National Environmental Policy and Environmental Action Plan. The government recognized that, with its limited resources, a participatory approach in which all stakeholders take part in actively managing resources is needed. The project also work with other conservation and development programs to maximize use of all

	available resources. The project's main contribution will be to promote the nation's sustainable economic development by establishing model systems to conserve biodiversity. Expansion and replication of these systems throughout the country will enable government and the people of the Comoros to protect and develop their valuable biodiversity resources. In the short term, the project will develop capacity and establish the legal, financial, institutional, and operational frameworks and essential technical skills for collaborative management and sustainable use of biodiversity. The project will play a lead role in establishing in-country capacity and frameworks for long-term biodiversity conservation, reducing further loss of unique ecosystems and valuable habitats, and establishing mechanisms that include the conservation of biodiversity resources as part of the country's sustainable development program.
Activities	• Develop and implement collaborative management frameworks for participatory biodiversity conservation • Strengthen capacity of government and nongovernmental organizations (NGOs) for biodiversity conservation through formal and experiential training • Develop and implement a legal framework and sustainable funding mechanisms for environmental conservation, emphasizing biodiversity • Initiate process for establishing a network of protected areas and facilitate an individualized collaborative management agreement and plan for one model protected area • Develop and implement species recovery plans for endemic species that are vulnerable or threatened with extinction • Increase awareness, interest, and participation in biodiversity conservation by training key partners to carry out this work as well as train others to do it • Develop sustainable income- and other benefit-generating alternatives.
Benefits	• Conserve unique island biodiversity in a framework of sustainable development • Increase government capacity at all levels to manage natural resources better • Strengthen indigenous NGO organizational and programmatic skills • Assure long-term funding for established and proposed protected areas and species protection activities.

The Global Environment Facility (GEF) is a financial mechanism that provides grants

<table>
<tr><td colspan="2">and concessional funds to developing countries for projects and activities designed to protect the global environment. GEF resources address climate change, biological diversity, international waters, and depletion of the ozone layer. Activities concerning land degradation, primarily desertification and deforestation as they relate to the four focal areas, are also eligible for funding.

GEF is a joint venture of the United Nations Development Programme (UNDP), the United Nations Environment Programme (UNEP), and the World Bank. These three agencies implement GEF projects.</td></tr>
<tr><td>For more information on this project, contact:
United Nations Development Programme
Mahenau Agha
Information Officer
One United Nations Plaza
New York NY 10017 USA
Tel: (212) 906-6112 Fax: (212) 906-6998
E-mail: mahenau.agha@undp.org
Internet Home Page: www.undp.org/gef</td><td>For more information on GEF:
GEF Headquarters
1818 H Street NW
Washington DC 20433 USA
Tel: (202) 473-0508 Fax: (202) 522-3240/522-3245
Internet Home Page: www.gefweb.com

Chief Executive Officer:
Mohamed T. El-Ashry
Senior External Relations Coordinator:
Hutton G. Archer
E-mail: harcher@worldbank.org</td></tr>
</table>

FOREIGN DEBT

Comoros major creditors have ended a meeting in the nation's capital Moroni to examine the government's request for debt relief.

The meeting grouped officials from the World Bank, the International Monetary Funds (IMF), the African Development Bank (ADB), the Arab Bank for African Development (BADEA), the Islamic Development Bank (IDB) and other creditors as well as bilateral partners such as China and France.

Opening the meeting at the weekend, the Comorian Finance and Budget Minister Ansoumany Aboudou, said it was to explain to the creditors, the county's efforts at finding a solution to the debt burden.

"The process of political reconciliation should (also) be financially backed so as not to undermine efforts made so far," the Minister added.

He said that national reconciliation could only be sustainable if financial resources was made available to the new Comorian entity as defined by its institutions.

An IMF official told PANA that the financial institution was determined to back an "intermediate and informal programme" for Comoros transition period.

Richard Wedebbae of the World Bank stressed the need for budgetary prudence to ensure that funds to be made available would be used for the agreed purposes.

Comoros external debt is estimated at 218.6 million dollars.

The meeting of creditors was organised at the initiative of the IMF, whose delegation was in Comoros for two weeks on routine consultation.

The first and only financial agreement between Moroni and the IMF was about 10 years ago, and since then, attempts for renegotiations with the international financial institution have proved abortive.

AFRICAN DEVELOPMENT BANK AND WORLD BANK PROJECTS IN EAST AFRICA

This international market insight is intended to inform companies about potential multilateral development bank (mdb) projects in East Africa. For the purpose of this IMI, East Africa includes Comoros, Djibouti, Eritrea, Ethiopia, Kenya, Madagascar, Mauritius, Seychelles, Somolia, Tanzania, and Uganda. As of August 2000, nearly 60 projects to be carried out in this region are in various stages in the African Development Bank (AfDB) and the World Bank pipelines. These projects offer U.S. companies an excellent opportunity to provide goods or services in a wide variety of sectors including agriculture, education, environment, finance, population and health, power, public sector management, social, telecommunications, transport, and urban and rural development.

An Overview of AfDB and World Bank Operations in Africa

The AfDB and World Bank are very active in meeting the development needs of Africa. The AfDB is based in Abidjan, Cote d'Ivoire and is comprised of 53 countries in Africa and 24 non-African countries, including the United States. In 1999, it approved nearly $1.7 billion in the form of loans and grants, private equity investments, debt relief, emergency operations, and loan reallocations. Approximately, $150.0 million of this was approved for East Africa in the form of 15 loans and grants covering five countries (Kenya, Madagascar, Seychelles, Tanzania, and Uganda). The fifteen were broken down as follows: five in the social sector, four in the agriculture sector, two in the transport sector, two in the multisector, one in the industry sector, and one in the public utilities sector. Private sector support is also of increasing importance to the Bank as it seeks to implement a strategy of poverty reduction and accelerated growth. Historically, over 28 percent of Bank loans and grants to East Africa have been earmarked for the agriculture sector. This has been followed by allocations in the transport and public utility sectors.

At the same time, the World Bank, with its headquarters in Washington, DC, is also placing great importance on assisting in the development of the African continent. In fiscal year 1999, the World Bank lending commitments to sub-Saharan Africa totaled approximately $2.1 billion. Multisector projects accounted for approximately one-fifth of those approved, followed by projects in the education, transport, population, health and nutrition, and agriculture sectors. It is the Bank's intention to assist in the acceleration of private-sector led growth, the promotion of peace and stability, and the enhancement of human and social development. Resources are also being allocated to improving the capacity building and leadership needs of member-states. Understanding the importance of honest and accountable government as well as limited resources, the Bank has decided to increasingly target resources on countries and sectors with supportive policy environments.

Upcoming Opportunities in the Pipelines

U.S. companies should not overlook opportunities provided through AfDB- and World Bank-financed projects. A list of projects in East Africa that are in the most-recent AfDB and World Bank pipelines can be found below. Companies interested in finding out more about these projects are encouraged to first examine the pipelines on each Bank's respective website (see end of document for website addresses). The pipelines are also published in *UN Development Business*, a bi-monthly publication that also includes general and specific procurement notices of mdb-financed projects (see contact information below).

Pipelines provide a basic description of each project, its project cost, where it is in the project cycle, the type of procurement required, and executing agency contact information. After reviewing the pipeline, companies should contact the executing ministry or agency that is carrying out the project. It is the executing agency following Bank rules and regulations that carries out the procurement. U.S. companies are encouraged to contact the executing agency early on in the project cycle to let their interest be known. They can provide detailed information on upcoming projects including the specific goods and services to be procured as well as answer any questions that arise or clarifications that are needed.

The lifespan of multilateral development bank projects can be great. From the time a project is being identified until it finishes and undergoes an evaluation process, a number of years may have passed. During this process, projects may be put on hold or their scope and needs may change and this is another reason for periodically keeping in contact with officials involved at the respective executing agencies.

Bank task managers and other staff persons may also be a valuable resource for learning about specific projects or if problems ensue with procurement. In addition to staff at headquarters, the World Bank has offices throughout Africa. In most cases, bank staff should be approached following contacts with the executing agencies.

American firms are also encouraged to contact the U.S. Department of Commerce's office of Multilateral Development Bank Operations (MDBO), and its World Bank and African Development Bank Commercial Liaison Offices. MDBO and its liaison offices are part of the U.S. Commercial Service and provide the U.S. business community with commercial information on development bank opportunities, individual counseling and guidance, and business outreach. The U.S. Commercial Service also has a Regional Office for East Africa in Nairobi, Kenya which can assist U.S. companies interested in meeting with executing agency officials, finding potential partners, and providing commercial information on the country where the project will be taking place. Contact information for all of these offices can be found at the end of this IMI.

Upcoming World Bank and African Development Bank Projects in East Africa, August 2000

Comoros

Bank	Sector	Project
World Bank	Infrastructure	Infrastructure, Water, and Enviroment

Djibouti

Bank	**Sector**	**Project**
AfDB	Agriculture	Fishing Industry Development Program
AfDB	Structural Adjustment	Structural Adjustment I
World Bank	Reconstruction/Rehabilitation	International Road Corridor Rehabilitation

Eritrea

Bank	**Sector**	**Project**
World Bank	Education/Training	Education
World Bank	Population, Health and Nutrition	Integrated Early Childhood Development
World Bank	Population, Health and Nutrition	HIV/AIDS/Malaria
World Bank	Private Sector Development	Private Sector Reconstruction
World Bank	Reconstruction/Rehabilitation	Reconstruction/Rehabilitation

World Bank	Transport	Roads
World Bank	Urban Development	Cultural Heritage
AfDB	Infrastructure	Asmara Infrastructure Development Study

Ethiopia

Bank	**Sector**	**Project**
World Bank	Population, Health and Nutrition	Conservation and Sustainable Use of Medicinal Plants
World Bank	Power	Power Distribution
World Bank	Private Sector Development	Privatization Technical Assistance
World Bank	Social	Women's Development Initiative
World Bank	Transport	Second Roads Sector Development
World Bank	Urban Development	Cultural Heritage
AfDB	Agriculture	Pastoral Areas Development Study
AfDB	Agriculture	Koga Irrigation
AfDB	Private Sector Development	Privatization Technical Assistance Project
AfDB	Transport	Ethiopian Airlines Infrastructure Facilities Project

Kenya

Bank	**Sector**	**Project**
World Bank	Agriculture	Agricultural Sector Investment
World Bank	Education/Training	Strengthening Primary and Secondary Education
World Bank	Population, Health and Nutrition	AIDS Disaster Response
World Bank	Population, Health and Nutrition	District AIDS and Reproductive Health
World Bank	Power	Emergency Energy
World Bank	Transport	District Rural Roads Network Rehabilitation--Roads 2000
AfDB	Agriculture	National Livestock Development Program
AfDB	Education/Training	Education III/Strengthening of Primary - Secondary Education
AfDB	Population, Health and Nutrition	Poverty Reduction
AfDB	Transport	Roads 2000 - Districts Rural Roads

		Rehabilitation Project

Madagascar

Project	Sector	
World Bank	Agriculture	Farmer Ownership Model
World Bank	Agriculture	Agricultural Intensification and Food Security
World Bank	Education/Training	Skills Development
World Bank	Public Sector Management	Public-Private Partnership and Information Management for Regional Development
World Bank	Social	Community Development Fund
World Bank	Social	Cultural Heritage
World Bank	Transport	Transport Sector Reform and Rehabilitation
AfDB	Water Supply/Sanitation	Projet d'Approvisionnement en Eau Potable et Assainissement (AEPA) in City of Tulear

Mauritius

Project	Sector	Project
World Bank	Finance	Financial Sector Infrastructure
World Bank	Water Supply/Sanitation	Solid Waste Management
AfDB	Transport	Mahebourg-Trou d'Eau-Belle Mare Road Project

Seychelles

Bank	Sector	Project
AfDB	Infrastructure	Infrastructure Development
AfDB	Education/Training	Education IV and Capacity Building Project

Tanzania

Bank	Sector	Project
World Bank	Population, Health and Nutrition	Health Sector Program
World Bank	Social	Social Action Fund
World Bank	Structural Adjustment	Structural Adjustment II
World Bank	Water Supply/Sanitation	Dar es Salaam Water Supply and Sanitation
AfDB	Structural Adjustment	Structural Adjustment II
AfDB	Water Supply/Sanitation	Dar es Salaam Water Supply and Sanitation

AfDB	Education/Training	Alternative Learning & Skills Development in Zanzibar

Uganda

Bank	**Sector**	**Project**
AfDB	Agriculture	Area-Based Agriculture Modernization Program
AfDB	Power	Alternative Energy Resources Assessment and Utilization Study
AfDB	Population, Health and Nutrition	Support to the Health Sector Strategic Plan
AfDB	Education/Training	Education II
AfDB	Transport	Roads Maintenance and Upgrading Project

World Bank and African Development Bank Website Information

Homepages
World Bank: http://www.worldbank.org
AfDB: http://www.afdb.org

World Bank Africa Page: http://www.worldbank.org/afr

Monthly Operational Summaries
World Bank: http://www.worldbank.org/html/opr/procure/MOS/contents.html
AfDB: http://www.afdb.org/opportunities/business.html

Contact Information:

For more information on multilateral development bank opportunities in Africa, financed by the World Bank or the African Development Bank, please contact:

Multilateral Development Bank Operations
USA Trade Center, R-MDBO
U.S. Department of Commerce
Washington, DC 20230
Tel: (202) 482-3399
Fax: (202) 482-3914
Director: Ms. Janet G. Thomas
Email: Mdbo.Banks@mail.doc.gov
Website: http://www.usatrade.gov

African Development Bank Commercial Liaison Office
Washington, DC Headquarters

USA Trade Center, R-MDBO
U.S. Department of Commerce
Washington, DC 20230
Tel: (202) 482-3399
Fax: (202) 482-3914
Senior Commercial Officer: Mr. Tapan Banerjee
e-mail: Tapan.Banerjee@mail.doc.gov

Abidjan, Cote d'Ivoire
AfDB Commercial Liaison Officer
U.S. Commercial Service
U.S. Embassy
01 B.P. 1712
Abidjan 01, Cote d'Ivoire
Tel: (225) 20-21-46-16
Fax: (225) 20-22-24-37
Commercial Liaison Officer: currently vacant

The World Bank Commercial Liaison Office
U.S. Executive Director's Office
U.S. Commercial Service Liaison Office
The World Bank
1818 H Street, NW
Washington, DC 20433
Tel: (202) 458-0120 - Senior Commercial Officer
(202) 458-0118 - Commercial Liaison
Fax: (202) 477-2967
Senior Commercial Officer: Ms. Karen Zens
e-mail: Karen.Zens@mail.doc.gov
Commercial Liaison: Ms. Janice Mazur
e-mail: Janice.Mazur@mail.doc.gov

BUSINESS CLIMATE AND CONTACTS

The Federal Islamic Republic of Comoros is an impoverished archipelago with a population of 600,000 spread across three principal islands at the northern end of the Madagascar Channel. Although currently ruled by a democratically elected president, the country has had a tumultuous political history since independence in 1975, one marked by numerous coups and coup-attempts. The country's fragile economy relies heavily on external aid, tourism, and the export of vanilla, cloves and oils used in the manufacture of perfume. Physical infrastructure is poor: Power outages are frequent, many villages lack potable water, and international transportation and communication are unreliable. The Banque Nationale de Paris Intercontinentale is the country's only international financial institution.

Foreign investment is minimal. The country's two principal hotels are owned and operated by a South African concern. A French company in mid-1997 took over management of the country's ailing electrical utility and other French companies are likely to enter the market if there are additional privatizations. Commerce between the United States and Comoros is minuscule. The government has a stated policy of welcoming foreign investment and is prepared to offer tax and other concessions to foreign investors.

France's diplomatic presence is the largest in the country. The United Nation's Development Program, the European Union, China and Libya also maintain missions in Comoros. The United States closed its embassy in Moroni in 1994 and now covers the country from its embassy in Port Louis, Mauritius. Relations between the United States and Comoros are amicable.

French is the language of business and daily life in Comoros, although some Arabic and Swahili are spoken. Comoros is a Muslim country, and visitors should observe conservative norms of dress and behavior.

U.S. AND COUNTRY CONTACTS

Mohamed Ali Soilihi
Minister of Finance
BP 324
Moroni, Comoros
Tel: 269-74-4141
Fax: 269-74-4140

Chamber of Commerce and Industry
BP 763
Moroni, Comoros
Tel: 269-73-0958

Central Bank
BP 405
Moroni, Comoros
Tel: 269-73-1002
Fax: 269-74-0349

Hotels Sun International
BP 1027
Moroni, Comoros
Tel: 269-73-8119
Fax: 269-73-2846

Comoros Vanilla Organization
BP 472
Moroni, Comoros
Tel: 269-73-2709
Fax: 269-73-2719

PRACTICAL INFORMATION FOR CONDUCTING BUSINESS

Official name	The Federal Islamic Republic of the Comoros
Surface	2236 Sq. Km
Population	670,000 inhabitants (1996)
Density	300 inhabitants per square kilometer
Capital	Moroni
Climate	The climate is tropical, hot and humid between November and May ; cooler and drier between May and October. The hottest month is March (31°C) and the coldest month is August (19°C)
Main holidays	July 6, November 27, Eid Al-Fitr*, Eid Al-Adha*, Islamic new year* and Eid Al Mawlid*
Weekly day off	§ Government and Business : Saturday p.m and Sunday § Banking : Saturday and Sunday

** Variable dates*

GENERAL INFORMATION

Languages	Arabic, French, and Comorian are official languages.
Currency	Comorian franc. 1US$ = 452,3 Cfr (January 1998)
Local time	GMT + 3 hours
Working hours	Government and Business : Monday-Thursday : From 7h30 to 12h and from 15h to 17h30- Friday : 7h30 to 11h - Saturday: From 7h30 to 12h. Banking : Monday-Thursday : From 7h to 12h and Friday 7h to 11h30

1998 Population (M): 0.5
1998 GNP (USD B): 0.2

1997/98 % annual GNP growth rate: 1
1998 GNP per capita (USD): 370
1990-98 % annual growth GDP: N/A
1990-98 % inflation: N/A

1998 Labour force (M): N/A
1998 Female % of labour force: N/A
1997 Adult illiteracy rate as % of people 15 and above (male): 45 (Male and female)
1997 % share of income or consumption (highest 10% of population / lowest 10%): N/A
1997 Telephone main lines per 1000 people: N/A

1990-98 % annual growth of gross domestic investment: N/A
1997 Private investment as % of gross domestic fixed investment: N/A
1997 Foreign direct investment (USD M): N/A
1998 Merchandise exports (USD M): N/A
1997 Present value of external debt as % of GDP: N/A

1998 Value added as % of GDP Agriculture: N/A
1998 Value added as % of GDP Industry: N/A
1998 Value added as % of GDP Services: N/A

The Comoros economy is founded on agriculture, which accounts for 40% of GDP. The country is the worlds largest producer of ylang ylang - an oil used in the perfume industry - and the second largest producer of vanilla. World demand and prices of these exports have declined sharply in the last decade, and with them foreign exchange receipts. France is the major trading partner and foreign donor. Government expenditure is heavily dependent on foreign aid.

The geography of the islands is an important asset, with the tourist industry attracting 20,000 visitors a year. There has been recent investment from South Africa, which may help to expand the sector, although it may be hampered by political instability. There are active independence movements on some of the islands, and a coup attempt was made in March 2000.

There is some population pressure, which along with concentration of land ownership has meant that the three-quarters of Comorians who live by subsistence farming do not grow enough food to support themselves. 50% of the annual budget is spent on food, substantially accounting for the large trade deficit. It is also widened by petroleum imports, necessary because there is no indigenous upstream oil industry. Electricity is provided by a parastatal. Despite a sparse telecommunications network, there is a local Internet service provider.

Recent years have seen poor economic growth, with income per head declining. Only a tenth of the population works in the formal sector.

Internet information on investing in Comoros is hard to find, so the sections on investment procedures are not included here.

LEGAL FRAMEWORK OF TRADE RELATIONS

Comoros is member of the following international organizations:

Organization of the Islamic Conference (O.I.C) ;
United Nations Organization (U.N) ;
International Monetary Fund (I.M.F) ;
The Franc Zone
Indian Ocean Commission

Comoros is among the African developing countries linked with the European Union States by A.C.P convention.

TRADE STRUCTURE

MAIN IMPORTED AND EXPORTED PRODUCTS:

Main Imported products	Main Exported products
Rice and other food stuffs	Vanilla
Petroleum Products	Ylang Ylang
Cement	Cloves
Grain	Perfume Oil
Consumer goods	Copra

PRINCIPAL TRADING PARTNERS:

Main Suppliers	Main Customers
France	U.S.A

South Africa	France
Kenya	Germany
Madagascar	

FOREIGN TRADE REGULATIONS :

IMPORTS REGULATIONS:

Product originating from EU members, Monaco and countries whose currencies are pegged to the French franc are imported freely. But imports from other countries are subject to individual licensing.

Import licenses are issued by the directorate-General of Economic Affairs in the Ministry of Economy, Industry, Commerce and Planning.

Import licenses are valid for six months, with a possibility of extension for another six-month only; Goods must be shipped prior to expiration of the license.

Some products are prohibited for imports from all countries.

The following documents are required at import level :

Commercial invoice : An ordinary commercial invoice should be provided in duplicate, giving a detailed description of the merchandise and listing all charges on a CIF basis. It should be signed and certified in the following statement by the exporter : "we certify that the goods in this shipment are of ....origin (manufactured by the undersigned) and that the above mentioned value is true and correct".

Certificate of origin : Two (2) copies must be sent if requested by the importer or letter of credit, It must be certified by a recognized chamber of commerce, which usually requires one additional notarized copy for its files.

Packing list : Packing lists are considered essential in expediting customs clearance of goods, particularly of shipments containing numerous small items, but there are not legally required.

Bill of lading : There are no regulations specifying the form or number of bills of lading required for any particular shipment. A bill of lading customarily shows the name of the shipper, the name and address of the consignee, port of destination, description of the goods, the listing of the freight and other charges, the number of bills of lading in the full set, and the date and signature of the carriers official acknowledging receipt on board of the goods for shipment. The information should correspond with that shown on the invoices and packages.

EXPORTS REGULATIONS :

In compliance with the Export regulations a sanitary certificate is required for exports of live animals, plants and plant parts.

OTHER FORMALITIES AND DOCUMENTS :

Exporters must contact the Comorian authorities to obtain information on the modalities and legalization that should be applied.

As concerns the imports :

Labeling : It's used to apply French labeling regulations

Marking : Any common shipping practice may be followed. In general, all identifying marks, including the consignee's mark with port marks, should be inscribed plainly on the packages to facilitate arrival of the shipment. Packages should be numbered unless the contents can be identified readily without numbers.

Packing : Packing material which can bring disease into the country is prohibited.

FINANCIAL REGULATIONS OF FOREIGN TRADE OPERATIONS

BANKING SYSTEM

The Banking sector is composed of the Banque Centrale des Comores (BCC, the Central Bank), the Banque de Développement des Comores (BDC, which focuses on development lending) and the Banque pour l'Industrie et le Commerce des Comores (BIC).

The BIC is linked to France's Banque Nationale de Paris and provides full international trade finance as well as local personal and business banking services.

FOREIGN EXCHANGE SYSTEM

The Central Bank of Comoros manages the exchange control. The bank has delegated some approval authority related to exchange controls to the commercial bank and the Postal Administration.

The Central Bank authorizes foreign exchange on the strength of the import license.

All import transactions must be domiciled with the authorized bank if valued at CFA/Francs 500,000 or more.

METHODS AND MEANS FOR INTERNATIONAL PAYMENT

Payments to France, Monaco, and the operations account countries are permitted freely. Payments related to authorized imports are not restricted . Invisible payments to other countries are subject to approval;

The most used method of payment is the letter of credit.

CUSTOMS TAXATION

The Comoros uses Customs Co-operation Council Nomenclature system.

APPLICABLE DUTIES AND TAXES

Ad valorem duties : Duties are levied on the CIF value.

Preferential duties : The Lome convention linking European Union members in a trade, co-operation and aid pact with African, Caribbean and Pacific developing Countries, including the Comoros, provides for preferential entry of ACP goods into EU countries. Under terms of the agreement, the ACP countries give no reverse preferences to EU goods but extend to E.U countries equal must Favored-Nation Treatment.

A preferential trade area for eastern and southern African States was formed in 1983 with plans to establish a preferential tariff treatment for a list of products. PTA members (22 countries) will establish a common market for eastern and southern Africa (COMESA), with the institution of a Zero percent tariff among member states by the year 2000.

Customs surcharges and indirect taxes : Some imports may be subject to an import tax and a consumption tax.

SPECIAL PROVISIONS :

Samples of no commercial value are imported duty-free ; but printed advertising matter and other publicity material are dutiable.

FOREIGN TRADE LOGISTIC

INTERNATIONAL TRANSPORTS :

Maritime transports : The port of Mutsamudu, on Anjouan, offers the deepest water and can accept vessels up to 25.000 tones. Freight bound for COMOROS is often routed via south Africa, or via Reunion and Mauritius, from where Comorian port authority, the societé comorienne de navigation, operates shallow-draft services. The development of the port of Moroni and the construction of a port at fomboni, on Mwali were financed by the European Union.

Air transports : The country's main international gateway is Hahaya airport on Grande Comore. There are domestic Airports on Anjouan (Omani airport) and Moheli (Bandar el salaam). Inter-island links and services to regional destinations were operated by the national carrier, Air comor, until the government has asked a French travel group to help set up a new national air line. Weekly flights are operated to Nairobi and Antananarivo. There are also flights from South Africa. The principal long-haul air link was to Paris, but Emirates Airways already operates a schedules service to Dubai (en route from Johannesburg)

Land transports : in the beginning of the 90's, there were 900 km of roads in the Comoros. About 170 km of roads on Njazidja and Nzwani has been resurfaced. The past few years have seen a rolling programme of work to upgrade roads throughout the country and improve links to rural communities.

TELECOMMUNICATIONS

State post and communications company, the société nationale des postes et télécommunications, is making serious efforts to upgrade both local and international connections. During 1994 it increased the number of main telephone lines by 12% and extended the network to cover the north-eastern districts of Moroni and several smaller communities. The waiting list of "would-be subscribers" increased by about 50%. New investments planned include the creation of an international transit centre.

FORMALITIES FOR THE CREATION OF COMPANY

DECLARATION OF EXISTENCE AT THE SOCIAL WELFARE

-Affiliation with the social provident fund

For the cover of the risks, accidents industrial and occupational diseases, the employer is held to affiliate itself with the Social Provident fund

.

Concerning the rates of the contributions, decree 74-122/ITC of February 1, 1974 distributed the professional activities in 4 branches, and with thus fixed 4 rates of contribution.

-Declaration with the Work Management

The contractor must warn the Work Management regarding the movement of his personnel, i.e. recruitments and dismissals etc...

The factory inspector intervenes in the litigations between paid and employers.

TAXES

CATEGORIES OF TAXES:

The Licence	It from now on is calculated according to the all means and branch of industry of production. It incluses a right which is a function of the nature of the activity and a right proportional which is fonction of the fixed assets of the company.
Income tax various (IBD)	the finance law 95 reduced the rate of the income tax various of 50 % to 40 % for the companies and 30 % for the one-man businesses.
General tax on income (IGR)	It is imposed by bracket income and is taxed according to a single and decreasing scale. The finance law 95 decreased the number of sections from 10 to 6. A bearing table on the scale is on sale with the Service of the Taxation of companies (SFE) to the fields.
Income tax of the transferable securities.	There strikes the dividends its rate remains unchanged, he is 15 %.

APPROVALS

the new code of the investors was promulgated on June 30 1995. its goal is to encourage the investments as well national as foreign. It grants exceptional advantages to the contractors operating in all the sectors of the economy safe in the trade.

PRELIMINARY EXPENSES

- For the creation of a company (one needs 3 specimens of the original statutes)

Pay 5% of the authorized capital to stamp the statutes at a rate of a stamp of 400 FC per page .

to register the company with the Clerc's Office of the fixed overhead Court standing 20 200 FC

proportional expenses : 1 stamp of 185 FC/page

-Indivudual company (nonobligatory statute)

inscription with the Register of Trade and the companies:
7 500 FC

Payment of the licence professional chart

- Groupings

Recording with the Clerc's Office: 7500 FC

CONTRIBUTIONS

In the event of contribution in kind it is always asked for a legal certificate of situation a document of title for the buildings and the grounds an expertise carried out by an expert sworn in with regard to the material

PROCEDURE OF HYPOTHECATION AND HYPOTHEQUE

-Legalization of signature of conventions to the Prefecture

-Recording of conventions to the Fields in the event of mortgage and payment of 0,50 % of the amount of the credit

LEGAL TYPES

Limited liability company (limited liability company) Authorized capital minimum: 1 000 000 FC. Numbers associates minimum 2
Limited company (SA)

Authorized capital minimum: 5 000 000 FC Numbers associates minimum 7
Economic grouping of interest (G.I.E) a minimum number of 2 associates can be made up without authorized capital

USEFUL ADDRESSES :

Organization and Public Establishments	Address	Tel	Fax	Telex
Ministry of the Economy, Industry, Commerce and Planning	P.O. Box. 41 – Moroni	(269) 292		240
Ministry of Finance and the Budget	P.O. Box. 324 – Moroni	(269) 2757		219
Ministry of Foreign Affairs and Co-operation	P.O. Box. 482 - Moroni	(269) 2306	(269) 2108	219
Chambre de Commerce, d'Industrie et d'Agricutlure	B.P.763 – Moroni			
Banque Centrale des Comores	B.P. 405 – Moroni	(269) 1002		

Comoros Chambers of Commerce & Industry
Union des Chambre de commerce, D'Industrie et D'Agriculture
B.P. 763
Moroni
Tel: (269) 731026
Fax: (269) 731983
Tlg: CHAMCOMER MORONI

IMPORTANT LAWS AND REGULATIONS

BUDGET OUTLINES

UNION OF THE COMOROS

UNIT - JUSTICE - PROGRESS

CABINET OF THE PRIME MINISTER

Many of actions and measure going in the direction of development were carried out under the Presidency of Colonel AZALI.

Indeed, when those which are to business are found in the opposition, the adopted slogan consists of saying that "nothing goes any more"; and when those which are in the opposition return to business, the new opposition takes up again the same slogan. Consequence: it is of good tone always to criticise the arrangement in place. When a neutral voice is raised to support actions of the Government, it is immediately suspected "of being bought".

This is why this note is wanted rather positive: it is to dare to speak about this which is better. In other words, it is to make use of the good achievements by making known them sufficiently, and the fight for the changes of mentality passes thereby.

The objective of this note is not at all polemical: It is not a question of irritating and even less to cause. It is a sales support whose aim is to support and diffuse the positive actions of the Government.

Thus, 20 fields militate for the Action of the Government:

- Wages
- Control of expenditure
- Buying power
- The slight improvement of the living conditions of most disadvantaged
- The slight improvement of the incomes as the tiny reduction of unemployment
- The reduction of the road accidents
- The diaspora
- The international recognition of the governmental action
- Education
- Mitigated results of the privatisation of certain public companies

· Found peace and national reconciliation

· Goods of the State and recovered credits
· The free exercise of trade-union freedoms and press
· Culture
· Transparency
· Youth
· The promotion of woman

- The reform of justice
- Relaunching of the administration
- Telecommunications

Let us examine each field, point by point:

1) WAGES ARE PAID REGULARLY AT EACH END OF MONTH:

This regularity became possible thanks to the following measures:

- **The wages** of **Head of State were suppressed**
- **Wages** of **the Ministers were reduced** of **20%**
- The number of stations of the ministerial cabinets is reduced
- It has there no more cabinets at the Legislative Council
- The contractors and other agents (**762 persons**) **were laid off**
- The FOP be ablenot recruit any more of individual driver of Minister, keeper or cleaner for the members of the Government
- The agents on not renewable leave or availability are regarded as resigners
- The cumulation of several allowances be ablenot exceed 50% of wages any more
- The phantom agents were suppressed FOP
- The agents having given their station are not paid any more
- The personnel of the embassies was strongly reduced
- The agents deceased were suppressed file of the FOP
- The agents recruited apart from the normal procedures were laid off
- Recruitments are really frozen
- The organic frameworks of 1994 are applied
- **Thus, average wages passed from 690 million to 420 million per month**
- The pensions of retirement were improved (they passed 1000fc to 13000fc the minima) and are versed regularly
- A plan of treasury was set up in order manage the forecasts in expenditure better

2) THE NATIONAL EXPENDITURE IS CONTROLLED

- **Expenditure of water, electricity and telephone** of the administration **passed from 500 million to 246 million**
- **The rents** of the houses rented by the State **passed from 350 million to 84 million**
- Expenses of travel and missions are limited to the budget available
- **The system** of **the tickets of essence** of the administration, which generated an unverifiable fraud, **was suppressed**
- The made savings enabled to assign to each Member of the Government a recognizable new vehicle its black colour

3) THE LOSS OF BUYING POWER WAS CONTAINED

Rising consequence of the price of the fuel,

- **The Taxes of imports** on **the essential products were reduced** and in particular on the meat.

- **Subsidies** in the form of **having as customs** even **were granted** to the importers basic products in order avoid a rise in prices.
- **The customs customs dec90** and **taxes** on **medicines** purely and were simply withdrawn in order protect the layers disadvantaged against a new rise.
- **Tax subsidies** and **exemptions were granted to the bakers** to contain the rise in price of **the bread limited to 25% instead of the 50%**
- Even thing for the trade union of carriers USUKANI in order also prevent rises in price.

- **The Single Tax** on **the petroleum products** is **0%** for **the kerosene** and raises it of this product was contained within the limits of the possible.

4) THE IMPROVEMENT OF THE LIVING CONDITIONS OF MOST DEPRIVED THE REMAINDER ONE OF PRIORITIES OF THE GOVERNMENT

Thanks to the payment of the arrears of the debt of the World Bank for 1,1 billion FC (approximately 3 months of wages), the projects showed. As follows:

- **26.000 children will be be able to attend the classrooms built or rehabilitated in the following localities : Large-comore :** Djoumoishongo, Batsa-Itsandra, Hantsambou, Hasseindje, Dzahadjou-Itsandra, Sidjou, Ouzio, Ouhozi, Trélézini, Foumbouni, Ndrouani, Mandzissani, Séléani, Bambani-hambou, Wella-hamahamet, Dzahadjou-Mbadjini, Sérêhini, Mnoungou, Chouani, Chindini, Douniani-Mboude, Pidjani, Chamle, Chouani, Serehini. **ANJOUAN** : Kiyo, Dziani, Hamchako, Kowet, Mjimandra, Daji, Salamani-Ouzini, Mrijou, Sadapoini, Nyatranga, Boungweni, Bambao Mtsanga, Mjimbia. **MOHELI:** Ngoimarumbo, Wanani,

Boingoma, Mabahoni, Mdjimbia, Djoiezi, Domoni, Salamani, Hamavouna, Ndrodroni

- **49.500 persons will benefit from the adductions from water or cisterns built in the following localities: Large-comore** : Simamboini, Diboini, Hahaya, Mitsoudje, Ifoundihe, Maweni, Séléa. **MOHELI** : Hagnamoida, Nioumachoua, Miringoni, Ouallah I.

- **44.000 persons benefit from the stations of health built or rehabilitated in the following localities: Large-comore** : Nioumamilima **ANJOUAN** : Koni Djodjo **MOHELI** : Hagnamoida, CMU of Fomboni, CHR of Wanani

- **52.500 persons will use the rural tracks arranged in the following localities: Large-comore** : Hadawa, Mboudadjou, Sambakouni, Sima-Oichili, Vanadjou, Pidjani-Toiyifa, Vouvouni-Mboude, Dzahadjou-oichili, Kouhani-Oichili, Dzahadjou, Ouzio-Trelezini, Memboimboini **ANJOUAN** : Bandrani-Vouani, Saadani

- **28.255 persons will benefit from the drainage works in the following localities: Large-comore:** Dzahadjou-Hambou, Sambabodoni **ANJOUAN:** Dzindri, Ouani, Harembo, Ngadzale **MOHELI:** Fomboni-Cente, Nioumachoua, Itsamia, Wanani

- **80.000 persons will be be able to sleep under mosquito nets** impregnated at prices studied by the authorities

- **The hospitals of major improvements will be rehabilitated and equipped Large-comore:** Mitsamiouli, Foumbouni **ANJOUAN:** Hombo, Domoni **MOHELI:** Fomboni, Wanani

- **29.872 inhabitants of MOHELI** will benefit from the program of the fight against the filariose started by the Head of the State with Hoani (Mohéli)

- **13.450** inhabitants will benefit from the Agricultural Guidance Centre (ECA) of 1.800 ha of following **Mawéni-Mboudé** and localities: Ivembeni, Helendje, Mdjoiezi, Ntsorale, Vouvouni, Djongwe

- **7.800** inhabitants will benefit from the Agricultural Guidance Centre (ECA) of following **Dimadjou** and localities: Chezani, Sadani, Madjeweni, Mbatse, Moidja, Nyadombweni, Babadjani, Hadjambou, Itsandzeni, Ngole, Mdjihari

- **10.600** inhabitants will benefit from the Agricultural Guidance Centre (ECA) of **Bahani** and from the following localities: Ouellah, Diboini, Mbambani, Vanadjou, Zivandani, Sambakouni, Dzahani, Milevani

- **7.400** inhabitants will benefit from the Agricultural Guidance Centre (ECA) of 400 ha of following **Simboussa** and localities: Badamadji Kouboini, Inani, Kové, Darissalama, Mkanga, Ndzouani, Didjoni, Mlaloikoudjou

- **16.700** inhabitants will benefit from the Agricultural Guidance Centre (ECA) of 800 ha of following **Batsa** and localities: Ouzio, Ouellah, Pidjani, Toiyifa, Memboidjou, Trelezini

- **A laboratory of medical analyses** was open to the Military Service of Health

- **The Committee of Fight against AIDS** was set up

- **L** has management **of hospital El Maarouf** de Moroni is in clear improvement: only one case, it has there no more household refuse around the hospital, new buildings are under construction....

5) THE ALLEVIATION OF UNEMPLOYMENT AND THE IMPROVEMENT OF THE INCOMES OF THE POPULATION ARE A PRIORITY OF THE GOVERNMENT

- Under the projects of construction and rehabilitation of classroom, station of health, of water conveyance, constructions of cistern, installation of rural tracks, one counts **46 contracting companies** of Large-Comore, Anjouan and Moheli obtained **1.791 FC million**

- The jobs create under these projects are of **195 established posts and 4.840 temporary jobs**

- **68 companies** benefited from the provisions of **the Code of Investments** : the State had a lost profit as customs of **768 million** representing **the exemptions granted to these companies**

- The created uses under the Code of Investment are **1.620**

- **76 companies** were financed under the Convention Girlfriend-meck for 120 million set out again in the fields of market gardening, sewing, restaurant, services...

- The created uses under this convention are **184**

- **The price of vanilla passed from 1.250 FC to 4.000 FC kg** as a floor price: this who makes it possible considerably to improve the incomes of the small peasants and the farmers thanks to this quadrupling of the price. **In June, the prices oscillated between 7.500 FC and 8.000 FC kg**

- Between 1999 and 2000, the Association for the Promotion of the Private Sector (APSP) encouraged **the creation of 26 companies**

- **The resumption of the activities in the Vanille sector generated temporary and seasonal jobs** in the field of harvest, assembly of lianas, cooking, drying, the packing and the setting with FOB of vanilla

- **1.468 persons** have already benefited or will benefit from training in the framework of projects FADC

- **85 trainees** followed a training in the trades of hotel trade

- **10 Mechanisms of Concentration of Fish (DCP)** were given to the trade union fishermen who took part in a part of financing whose total is 7 FC million

These measures, even modest, contribute to reduce unemployment

6) THE NUMBER OF ROAD ACCIDENTS STRONGLY FELL

- The wearing of **the belt** is **obligatory** for the motorists;

- **The overloads** of **passengers** and **luggage are sanctioned;**

- The validity of the driving licence and the card of insurance is henceforth due;

- Sites of car park with Moroni were affected: "KHARTALA" for the destinations and sources of the South of Ngazidja; CHALMA for the destinations and sources of Oichili, VOLO VOLO for the destinations and sources of the North of Grane-Comore;

- The technical visits are obligatory for the carriers of passengers;

- **The payment** of **the label** , now electronic, **is obligatory;**

- **Excesses** of **speeds are penalised;**

- The regular presence of the Gendarmerie and the Police force on the roads is dissuasive;

7) CONTRIBUTIONS IN CURRENCY AND EQUIPMENT DIASPORA ARE ENCOURAGED BY THE GOVERNMENT

- The Head of the State visited the diaspora residing in France to show the interest which door the Government on the diaspora;
- A direction charged with the diaspora was created to Foreign Business;
- Considerable customs advantages were granted;
- An individual treatment of favour is reserved to the members of the diaspora on arrival at the borders (airport and port);
- The equipment sent by the diaspora for the urban development and villages often benefit from customs and tax exemptions;

8) THE EFFORTS OF THE GOVERNMENT ARE RECOGNISED BY THE INTERNATIONAL COMMUNITY

- **Creditors and donors of the Comoros Islands** met 29 the Mars with Moroni to Palate of People. Took part in this meeting: the IMF, the World Bank, the ADB, the BADEA, BIsD, European Union, France and China. In the strategy of recognition of the country by the international community, this meeting is an undeniable success;
- **The European Union resolved 2.405 FC million** within the framework of funds STABEX (which one believed lost) to support the channels of revenue;
- **The French Agency of Development (AFD) resolved 321 million** of FC to promote the onion cultivation;
- **The European Union resolved 2.215 FC million** for the multiannual Program of microprojects;
- **The League of the Arab States** intend to bring a significant financing to support the Government to lead the transition until term;
- **The Conference of the Friends of the Comoros Islands** who took place in Paris allowed to the Government of furniture a financing of 12,8 dollars million for the 12 months of transition. This amount set out again as follows: 3 million are assigned to the heading "reduction of poverty"; 5,6 million to the "economic revival and financial stabilisation"; 1,8 million to

"decentralisation"; 2,4 million to "national reconciliation", without the financing of the elections. Thus, on the basis of the criteria of size of the population and incidence of poverty, it was performed an adjustment giving rise to the following distribution of the aspect "reduction of poverty": **ANJOUAN** 50%; **MOHEL** I:10% **LARGE-COMORE** : 40%;

9) THE EDUCATION OF THE CHILDREN EDUCATED AT THE PUBLIC SCHOOL IS CONTROLLED

· The spectrum of the white years disappeared;

· The frequency of the strikes in teaching is reduced;

· The school recommencement took place normally;

· The examinations of end of year proceed correctly: 3.528 candidates pass the baccalaureat;

· The first edition of the Forum of the Trades and orientation took place;

10) THE PROCESS OF PRIVATISATION OF THE PUBLIC COMPANIES KNOWS ADMITTEDLY TOPS AND BASES

- The privatisation of the EEC is, at the present time, a disaster which the Government hopes to remedy there vigorously;
- The restructuration/privatisation of Socopotram will have also to be taken in hand;

On the other hand:

· The New Airline "Continental Wings - COMOROS ISLANDS AIRLINES" emerged and ensures already the service road between Moroni-Marseilles;

11) PEACE AND NATIONAL RECONCILIATION ARE FOUND

· February 17, 2001, for Fomboni, the International Community, the Comoro Islands were to continue to live together, to have a common destiny through the Staff member Agreement of reconciliation;

· The monitoring Committee and the Tripartite Commission are the two bodies envisaged by the Staff member Agreement of reconciliation. The total cost their activities is 0,5 dollars million. The Government takes part at the expenses of their operation up to 0,3 dollars million;

· A gift "post conflict" of the World Bank of 0,8 dollars million is assigned to Anjouan for the reintegration of young people. This project aims to support CARE International to reinstate from 600 to 650 young people and to strengthen the creation of a Adapted Non-military national service who will organise 1400 young volunteers in "comites for peace and development";

· For the elections, meadows of 2 Euros million are already acquired on the part of the European Union;

12) OF THE GOODS OF THE STATE WERE RECOVERED AND OF THE CREDITS OF THE STATE WERE RECOVERED

- The illegally usurped domanial grounds were recovered;
- Wild constructions were demolished;
- The arrears accumulated by private individuals in the public companies like Onicor, BDC etc... were the subject of forced coverings energy until the imprisonment of the debtor;
- The administrative houses are busy only by having rights and the "untouchable ones" were moved house if need be, by strength;
- The rents due on the administrative houses are taken directly to the source, at the time of the payment of the salires;
- Certain administrative houses, in a state of decrepitude, projection were rehabilitated;

13) TRADE-UNION FREEDOMS AND OF PRESS ARE SAVED

· Trade-union freedoms are maintained;

· The right to strike remains, even if it is sometimes practised improperly;

· The political parties of opposition carry out their activities;

· The freedom of the newspaper industry residence;

· The free radios maintain their activity, including those held by the opposition;

14) CULTURE

· The House of the radio and of TV was produced;

· The setting up of the FESNACO as "during the night of gold Gabusi" are now an asset to be preserved;

· The setting up one cultural day "Mbae Trambwe" has to be also preserved;

· The setting up of a "school theatrical competition" should be being perpetuated;

· The Celebration of the festival of Music entered manners;

15) TRANSPARENCY IN THE CASES

The opacity which surrounded certain dossiers is dissipated:

· The contract of Galawa, long unknown of the public, press is known;

· The dossier of Code 269 and its amendments were made public through press conference and official statements;

· The Contract of the EEC is now known;

· The financing obtained from the Conference of Pars as their future use were made public during the speech programs Prime Minister;

· For the sake of transparency, the setting up of the new airline was controlled jointly with the World Bank;

16) YOUTH

· The general states of youth took place;

· The International conventions relating to the protection of youth were ratified by Colonel Azali;

· A credit of financing intended for young people is being studied;

· The Government paid contributions of the State to the various world and regional organisations of young people, after ten years of non payment;

17) THE PROMOTION OF WOMAN

· Comorian women form part maintaining of the Army and the Gendarmerie;

· Women occupy important administrative posts;

18) THE REFORM OF JUSTICE IS COMMITTED

- 3 law courts will be rehabilitated and equipped;
- **The prisoners are kept better** thanks to recourse by the State of the services of a private company of guarding;
- 3 prisons will be rehabilitated and equipped;
- 10 new magistrates will be trained for the courts of first authority;
- 6 magistrates will be selected for specialisations;
- 20 Justice of the Peace will be trained and recruited;
- 10 subject training will be given to the clerks and to ushers;
- 3 dispensaries will be set up;
- **Open audiences** now allow to accelerate the treatment numerous dossiers awaiting judgement;
- **Clandestine migration** is stopped thanks to the setting up of a new team replacing the Police force of Air and the Borders;
- **The Official Newspaper** takes up again of the service;

19) RELAUNCHING OF THE ADMINISTRATION

- The governmental matrix which serves as a program of the Government is the fruit of collective work and co-operation between Primature and the administrations concerned
- The Head of the State regularly held meetings with the persons responsible for the administrations in order make sure that the decided measures are applied

20) TELECOMMUNICATIONS

- The extension of the network of the SNPT emerged in the following localities: **Large-comore** : Itsinkoudi, Hantsindzi, Ndroude, Dembeni, Tsinimoishongo, Panda, Founga, Koimbani, Simamboini, Domoni Ya

Mboini, Domoni ya Djou, Itsandzeni . **MOHELI** : Mbatse, Kangani, Ziroudani, Miringoni

- **New exchanges** are installed to the following localities: **Large-comore** : Ivembeni, Ntsaoueni, Dembeni, Koimbani, Mtsangadjou, Sembenoit, Mitsoudje . **MOHELI** : Nioumachoua, Wanani
- **Tariffs of the telephone calls** fell twice since 1999
- **Tariffs of connection to Internet** passed from 3 Mn the unit to 6 Mn the unit
- **The project on Code 269** will allow the Comoros Islands to break the communication insulation of the country and will generate significant income for the State

IMPORTANT OFFICIAL MATERIALS

SPEECH OF THE PRIME MINISTER OF THE FEDERAL ISLAMIC REPUBLIC OF THE COMOROS

AT THE EXTRAORDINARY SUMMIT OF THE GENERAL ASSEMBLY OF THE UNITED NATIONS ON THE HIV / AIDS HELD AT THE HEADQUATERS OF OF UNITED NATIONS IN NEW YORK, ON JUNE 24 , 25 AND 26, 2001.

Excellencies Sirs Heads of states and Heads of government,
Excellencies Sir UN Secretary-General,
Excellencies Ladies and Gentlemen the Ministers,
Ladies and gentlemen,

Speaking for the first time in front of this august assembly, I would like to release first of all the pleasant duty, to pass on you the message of sympathy and solidarity of the Head of State of the Federal Islamic Republic of Comoros, Colonel AZALI Assoumani, to you, as well as his best wishes of success for our works.

I would want then, on behalf of the Comorian Government and that of the Comorian delegation that I have the honor to lead and on my own, send our sincere thanks to the General Secretary of the UN, his Excellency M. Koffi ANNAN, and to all those who contributed to the organization of this important international meeting on the epidemic of the HIV / AIDS. An initiative translating without ambiguity the commitment and the determination of the UN to call up to a bigger attention of the International Community.

It is so a meeting arousing enormous hopes to our peoples alarmed and traumatized by the distribution of the epidemic and its devastating effects on the humanity. Indeed, in the speed at which propagates the disease, it is unmistakably decades of development that are annihilated; hence the necessity of a world mobilization with the aim of an action more strengthened in this direction. It pleases me for that purpose, to resume here an extract of the Statement of the UN Secretary-General, of last April 5, in which he expressed himself in these terms and I quote: " To encourage the active participation of all the partners in the fight against the AIDS became my personal priority.

The epidemic constitutes the challenge number one for the health services of our time and we should mobilize the competence of all the sectors of the society. However, the solution does not belong exclusively to the pharmaceutical companies. I launch an appeal to a vast mobilization on the political plan and that of a massive increase of the resources which will allow a tremendous jump forward in the prevention, the coverage and the treatment ". End of quotation.

These comments which I appreciate, call up in my opinion to an awareness of several dimensions, in the management of the epidemic of the HIV / AIDS. The social dimension which they contain drives us to have in the spirit, at first the considerable losses of human lives which increase from day to day. Indeed, one can notice about 36,1 million persons living with the HIV or the AIDS in the world, 5.3 million new infections in the year 2000, 3 million persons died from the AIDS the same year and 21.8 million deathes since the beginning of the epidemic.

In this heavy report, we attend, sometimes powerless, the decimation even the depopulation of several regions. The AIDS continues, in its merciless progress, to return orphans of the millions of children many of whom the tragic and vague fate, is not less pitiful than that of those taken by the disease. Then, an economic dimension, because by affecting the human life, the AIDS, also puts in danger the future of the economic development, by affecting the most productive layers of societies, slowing down the economic growth and gobbling up a big part of the budgets of States, within the framework of the national plans of action in education, prevention and in coverage.

We need a cultural, educational dimension, I shall say also behavioral change, which requires the intensification of the actions of prevention as central element of the retort, conscious of the fact that the transmission maybe associated to behavior at risk. I shall speak about another dimension, scientific if I may tell, and make so one vibrating honoring on the initiative of the UN Secretary-General, to meet last April, six among the main world pharmaceutical companies, with the aim of defining the measures to be taken, to improve the access to the care of health, in medicines against the HIV and associated in developing countries to fight(dispute) the AIDS.

Your appeal, Sir General Secretary, launched in favour of the encouragement to the search and to the access to medicines for the poor men, translates your consideration of the element "poverty", or still " as major brake in this fight and it, Excellences, Ladies and Gentlemen, brings to evoke me another dimension, financial this time, which establishes(constitutes) a real obstacle in our actions to fight(dispute) the HIV / AIDS. The absence of adequate means, in the phases of prevention, coverage and treatment, requires(demands), as well said it so, the UN Secretary-General, a vast mobilization, notably at the level of the massive increase of the resources to be able to face the epidemic.

We should help and allow the financial accessibility of medicines in particular to the poorest. This can not be made without a real commitment at the highest level, all the authorities were involved in the management of the epidemic. Indeed, a political commitment should allow to translate our real will to fight(dispute) the HIV / AIDS, us every decision-makers of our respective countries, responsible for the medical domain, in all the rungs of the company(society), various constituents of the society(non-trading company), the non-governmental organisations and the other bodies who bring, of a way or of the other one, our support.

It is to remind, after all, the pressing appeal which is done to us, with the aim of an innovated partnership. Innovated in the sense of a revision of our approach and in health care strategy, especially in developing countries, innovated within the framework of the measures aiming at allowing the financial accessibility of medicines, in the necessity of affecting supplementary resources, to the international action of fight anti-AIDS, and innovated finally, in the attitude consisting in becoming aware that the care of lavishing on the infected persons should keep pace with an enormous support especially moral in their place. I would moreover like to seize this occasion to return a honoring deserved to the World Health Organization, to the ONUSIDA and to all the Governmental And non - governmental Organizations which contribute to the world action aiming at fighting this plague of our time, for the remarkable efforts which they display in this domain.

But it is necessary to us, at the same time, to agree that an intensification of the anti-HIV / AIDS activities is imperative itself and proves itself as being the unique alternative which offers itself to you, in front of a disease against which, no vaccine is in our reach. These efforts are to double for certain regions among which Africa, struck quite hard by the pandemic. The picture is rather dark. I do not have to return to it, the eminent speakers who preceded me in this stand detailed of it enough. I would like, however, to underline the importance that takes on, for us, the Forum 2000, held in Addis-Abeba and the Abuja Statement for the fight against the HIV / AIDS which gives concrete expression to the concern of the high officials of the continent on the problem having exceeded the medical frame today to become a social and economic problem of an unprecedented gravity.

I would like, also, to refer to the last report of the WHO of April 9, 2001 in which it is said, I quote: " In the 16 countries of sub-Saharan Africa, more than 10 % of the population in age to procreate are now infected by the HIV ". A very alarming figure and a revelation for our continent. That is why, a joint and urgent action of our governments, fund providers and all the partners in the development is to engage , because due to its revolved extreme, in the current rhythm of distribution, the AIDS constitutes a questioning of our efforts, notably those in favour of the development. It is a potential threat, for our populations, whatever is the rate of prevalencia registered in every country, because in the absence of drastic measures of fight, no sector of society in any country will be spared.

Mister President, Excellencies Ladies and Gentlemen, In the Federal Islamic Republic of the Comoro Islands, the pandemic of the HIV / AIDS is observed with the same fear and the same concern as in numerous countries which it affected seriously . Indeed, due to its insularity, its geographic position which opens it to the canal of Mozambique and to the neighbouring islands and the tourist aspect which attracts towards it the seasonal holiday-makers, the Federal Islamic Republic of the Comoro Islands receives every year thousands of guests. This situation opens the way to an ease of traffic of poeple from countries with strong prevalencia of the HIV / AIDS.

The general impoverishment of the population, the weakness of the sensitization, the weak level of apprehension of the problem which was for a long time observed within the authorities, is for us so many reasons to be afraid of a significant increase of the number of infected pople in the near future. Since the beginning of the search of the first case of AIDS in March, 1988, the country registered 61 people infected by the HIV Virus among which 25 cases of full blown aids, all ded.

In the year 2000, new cases were detected, alarmed the high national authorities. So, within the framework of the sanitary policy, and according to the National Plan of sanitary Development, the Federal Islamic Republic of Comoros set up since 1990, among other programs, a National program of fight against MST / AIDS (PNLS). This one serves as an organizational structure and as a Coordination of the fight against MST / AIDS, in intensification of the epidemiological surveillance of the HIV / AIDS, which began from the announcement of the first case, in March, 1988.

Management structures of various level are organized to assure a better coordination of the actions of the program in all the rungs of the population. At the political level, the coordination is assured by the interministerial and multisector-based committee, set up in October, 1998. This coordination is also observed until the regional and peripheral level, by the people in charge of the Programs within the Regional Directions of Health.

On the other hand, the current Comorian government, strongly worried by the dimension observed in the programming of the fight against the disease emphasized certain essential actions retained in the action plan elaborated for the period of 1999-2003, within the framework of the national policy of fight against the AIDS. This plan of activity adapt to the world strategy such as conceived by the ONUSIDA in the dynamics of the Forum 2000 and in the Action plan of Abuja Statement.

A particular attention is granted to the young people in favour of which the specific activities were identified. And so during the Workshop of restoration of the Forum 2000, organized in February, 2001 I recommended personally, among others;

-The creation of clubs anti-AIDS in schools and within the associations of young people;

- The integration of the subject " fight against the AIDS " in school programs and the sensitization of the parents on the fight against the AIDS, within the framework of parents and teachers associations .

The commitment of the Comorian State also demonstrates itself by opening a budgetory line of support for the anti-AIDS fight, the implementation of structures of fight at the level of every island, the future creation of a technical structure of coordination and follow-up placed under the custody of the presidency of the Republic, the integration of this subject in all the official speeches of the Head of State, the implication of all the sectors of society by putting in rates religious leaders, usual leaders, associations and other structures, artists, educators, the implication of the media and the encouragement of the political parties to integrate into their programs this essential topic.

In this step, following the example of other countries, the Federal Islamic republic of Comoros collides with numerous obstacles of economic and financial order, of structural order and I pass it. So, aware of the fact that the absence of adequate means, strategies of effective fight, are an enormous obstacle in any action of fight against the HIV / AIDS, my country call up once again to a bigger international solidarity which is not certainly lacking, but which requires a consequent intensification, in this crucial period that my country crosses, marked by the process of National Reconciliation.

Excellencies, Ladies and Gentlemen,

The situation which I have just described to you shows the extreme revolved by the threats which press on my country where glides the spectre of another war, more devastating, because it is about a fight delivered against an invisible enemy, and in whom we arrange a weapon only of the only prevention, at least to save those that are still spared. May this meeting constitute the best occasion to awaken more our consciousness, on this danger which invades our planet and to conjugate even more our efforts to limit the consequences of it! I thank you.

FRIENDS OF THE COMOROS CONFERENCE

PARIS, July 5, 2001 -- A Conference of the Friends of Comoros concluded today, after a day-long discussion seeking emergency financing for the next twelve months for social and economic expenditures, strengthening of economic management institutions, and basic expenditures for national reconciliation. Donor governments, organizations and representatives of the Comoros islands came together to mobilize financial support for Comoros during the crucial period of national reconciliation and transition to new institutions and democratic government.

Participants expressed strong support to the Comorian delegation for its efforts in resolving the present crisis and exercising good economic management. They emphasized the importance of maintaining the course on national reconciliation, adhering to principles of good governance, protecting the poor and maintaining good budget management, and assured them of the continued support of the international community. The Participants1 support was also expressed in financial pledges totaling approximately US$11.5 million for the 12-month transition period. The financial commitments were as follows: France $1m, Mauritius $1m, Morocco $0.3m, AfDB $0.7m, EU $1.5m, International Organization for Francophonie $0.4m, World Bank $6.8m.[1] It is anticipated that the total final assistance will be higher than this amount because various countries and organizations committed to additional short-term financial support during the meeting.

Progress in Reconciliation

The Comorian delegation declared during the meeting that the last two years had witnessed political progress towards ending the separatist crisis facing the country. Last February 17, 2001, the government, the Anjouan authorities, the opposition party and representatives of civil society came together under the auspices of the international community to sign the Fomboni Accord towards national reconciliation. The bodies put in place by the Accord to lead the transition were a Steering Committee including representatives of the international community, and a Tripartite Commission. The Commission will present a preliminary version of the constitution of the new unified Comoros around September 2001 and will prepare a referendum of this constitution. On approval of the new constitution, a transition government will prepare the country for national elections expected to take place six months thereafter.

The Economic situation

The political crisis has had a disastrous effect on the country's economic development, increasing poverty and deteriorating social systems. Comoros' strategy during the upcoming twelve-month transition period is to maintain economic viability in order to respond to the most urgent social needs, and to guarantee that the reconciliation process remains on the right path.

During the transition period, the government aims to increase spending in poverty reduction, and has outlined a program of emergency spending targeting the health, education, electricity, water and sewerage and rural development sectors. Other priorities include the strengthening of institutions, support for decentralization, and economic recovery.

The conference was chaired by Mr. Hafez Ghanem, World Bank Country Director for Madagascar, Comoros, Mauritius and the Seychelles. The delegation of Comoros was headed by Mr. Hamada Madi Bolero, Prime Minister of Comoros, and included Colonel Said Abeid Abderemane, Mr. Souef Mohammad El-Amine, Mr. Assoumany Aboudou, Mr. Bianrifi Tarmidi, Mr. Mahmoud Ahmed Bacar and Mr. Younoussa Imani.

Representatives from 16 countries and 14 organizations attended the conference.2 Participants included representatives from Algeria, China, Egypt, France, Japan, Libya, Madagascar, Mauritius, Morocco, Mozambique, Pakistan, Seychelles, South Africa, Sudan, Sweden, the United Kingdom, the United States, African Development Bank, Agence Française de Développement, the Arab League, European Investment Bank, European Union, Islamic Development Bank, International Fund for Agricultural Development, International Monetary Fund, Organization for African Unity, International Organization for Francophonie, Kuwait Fund for Arab Economic Development, Saudi Development Fund, United Nations Development Programme, World Health Organization and the World Bank. Regional neighbors were particularly well represented. Ms. Lila Ratsifandrihamanana, Minister of Foreign Affairs of Madagascar, Mr. Sushil C. Khushiram, Minister of Economic Development, Financial Services, and Corporate Affairs of Mauritius and Dr. Aziz Pahad, Deputy Minister of Foreign Affairs of South Africa led their countries' delegations.

1 The financial commitments were as follows: France $1m, Mauritius $1m, Morocco $0.3m, AfDB $0.7m, EU $1.5m, International Organization for Francophonie $0.4m, World Bank $6.8m.

2 Participants included representatives from Algeria, China, Egypt, France, Japan, Libya, Madagascar, Mauritius, Morocco, Mozambique, Pakistan, Seychelles, South Africa, Sudan, Sweden, the United Kingdom, the United States, African Development Bank, Agence Française de Développement, the Arab League, European Investment Bank, European Union, Islamic Development Bank, International Fund for Agricultural Development, International Monetary Fund, Organization for African Unity, International Organization for Francophonie, Kuwait Fund for Arab Economic Development, Saudi Development Fund, United Nations Development Programme, World Health Organization and the World Bank.

COMOROS: EMERGENCY ECONOMIC RECOVERY PROJECT

CREDIT AMOUNT: IDA—US$6 million equivalent
TERMS: Maturity = 40 years
PROJECT DESCRIPTION: This project will provide emergency assistance to the economy during the transition out of the current secessionist crisis, and will address immediate social needs in the Comoros, particularly on the island of Anjouan. Priority expenditures in the emergency program will support the creation of decentralized institutions, and the implementation of the national reconciliation agreement. The project aims at, among other things, maintaining macroeconomic stability and addressing urgent social needs. *For more information, call Sharon Cox at (202) 473-2035, fax at 473-7917, or e-mail Scox1@worldbank.org.*

COMOROS: WORLD BANK SUPPORTS COMOROS INFRASTRUCTURE, WATER AND ENVIRONMENT PROJECT

WASHINGTON, March 1, 2001--The World Bank today approved a US$11.4 million credit to assist the Islamic Federal Republic of the Comoros to improve living conditions and stimulate economic growth for its population, while protecting the environment through investments in basic infrastructure.

Focusing on two priority sectors (roads and urban water supply), the specific objectives of the **Infrastructure, Water and Environment Project** are to:

" Maintain road infrastructure and improve the safety of road transport;
" Upgrade and expand urban water infrastructure and significantly increase access to clean water for people living on the Anjouan and Moheli islands by 2004-2005; and
" Improve decentralized management of road transport and water supply through strengthening public sector institutions, increasing public awareness, beneficiary participation, and implementing cost-recovery measures.

The project will improve the management and maintenance of the road network on all three islands. This will improve the speed of transport, road safety and reduce costs of transporting people and goods. Such actions will benefit the entire population, including rural villagers, who will gain access to markets and public services, and urban producers and traders. Improving and sustaining access to convenient, safe water in the urban areas of Anjouan and Moheli will benefit the poor on these two islands, many of whom collect water from distant, contaminated sources.

The Infrastructure, Water and Environment Project will be financed by a US$11.4 million credit from the International Development Association, the World Bank's lending arm for the poorest countries. The IDA credit is on standard terms of 40 years maturity, including 10 years grace.

RENEWAL OF THE FISHERIES PROTOCOL BETWEEN EU AND COMOROS ISLANDS

The European Community and the Islamic Republic of the Comoros Islands have initialled a Protocol to the Fisheries Agreement between the two parties for a period of three years from 28 February 2001. This Agreement concerns solely tuna fisheries and the new Protocol will provide fishing possibilities for 65 vessels. There is little change in both the number of vessels involved and in the level of the financial compensation. The two parties agreed on the allocation of a substantial part of the financial contribution to targeted measures for the development of the Comoros fisheries sector and in particular in favour of the artisanal fishing sector.

The number of vessels involved under this Agreement increases slightly from 60 to 65 vessels. The number of tuna seiners goes down from 44 to 40 while the number of surface long-liners increases from 16 to 25. Vessels from Spain, France, Portugal and Italy benefit from this Agreement.

The financial compensation remains practically the same at €350,250 per year. A new development in this Protocol is the increase of the share allocated to targeted actions in favour of the local fisheries sector from 50 to 60 per cent of the compensation (€210,150 per year). 60% of that amount (€126,000 annually) will be used to help develop the Comoros artisanal sector. The rest will be allocated to scientific and technical programmes and to strengthen administrative structures in the fisheries sector as well as monitoring and control services.

The cost of fishing licences paid by vessel owners operating under the Agreement has gone up from € 1,750 for tuna seiners to € 2,250. For long-liners the cost will also increase from €750 to €1,000 for vessels under 150 GRT and to €1,375 for those over 150GRT.

The two parties have also agreed on the procedure to be followed by the Comoros inspection authorities when they request a Community vessel to accompany them to port.

TRAVEL TO COMOROS

US STATE DEPARTMENT SUGGESTIONS

COUNTRY DESCRIPTION: The Comoros is a developing island nation located in the Indian Ocean off the east coast of Africa. Facilities for tourism are limited, and telecommunication links are extremely unreliable.

ENTRY REQUIREMENT: A passport and onward/return ticket are required. A three-week entry visa, which may be extended, may be obtained upon arrival at the airport. Travelers should obtain the latest details from the Mission of the Federal Islamic Republic of the Comoros, 420 East 50th Street, New York, NY 10022; telephone number (212) 972-8010, fax (212) 983-4712. Overseas inquiries may be made at the nearest Comorian or Senegalese Embassy or Consulate.

Access to Anjouan, Comoros' second largest island, which declared itself independent in 1997, requires prior permission from authorities in Anjouan.

SAFETY/SECURITY: The Comoros Islands have experienced frequent strikes and civil unrest, resulting in violent clashes between police and demonstrators. Although foreign residents and visitors have not been targeted, the potential for further outbreaks of civil disorder remains high.

Anjouan, the second largest island in Comoros, declared itself independent in 1997. There has been fighting between various armed groups since December 1998. U.S. citizens are urged to defer non-essential travel to Anjouan, while U.S. residents are urged to review their own personal safety in determining whether to remain on the island.

In April 1999, there was a coup d'etat on Grand Comore following a week of violent protests against Anjouanais residents there. Although the situation on Grand Comore has calmed, the potential for further outbreaks of violence exists.

U.S. citizens should avoid political rallies and street demonstrations and maintain security awareness at all times.

INFORMATION ON CRIME: Petty crime is common. Pick-pocketing, purse snatching, and various types of scams are the most common forms of crime confronting U.S. travelers in crowded market areas, beaches and parks.

The loss or theft abroad of a U.S. passport should be reported immediately to local police and to the nearest U.S. Embassy or Consulate. The pamphlets *A Safe Trip Abroad* and *Tips for Travelers to Sub-Saharan Africa* provide useful information on personal security while traveling abroad and on travel in the region. Both are available from the Superintendent of Documents, U.S. Government Printing Office, Washington, D.C. 20402, via the Internet at http://www.access.gpo.gov/su_docs, or via the Bureau of Consular Affairs home page at http://travel.state.gov.

MEDICAL FACILITIES: Medical facilities in Comoros are poor. Travelers should bring their own supplies of prescription drugs and preventive medicines. Doctors and hospitals often expect immediate cash payment for health services. The Medicare/Medicaid program does not provide for payment of medical services outside the United States.

MEDICAL INSURANCE: Check with your own insurance company to confirm whether your policy applies overseas, including provision for medical evacuation. Ascertain whether payment will be made to the overseas hospital or doctor, or whether you will be reimbursed later for expenses you incur. Some insurance policies also include coverage for psychiatric treatment and for disposition of remains in the event of death. Travelers to Comoros are strongly urged to consider supplemental medical/travelers' insurance as these policies are inexpensive when compared to the costs of a medical evacuation.

Useful information on medical emergencies abroad, including overseas insurance programs, is provided in the Department of State, Bureau of Consular Affairs brochure, *Medical Information for Americans Traveling Abroad*, available via its home page at http://travel.state.gov and autofax service at (202) 647-3000.

OTHER HEALTH INFORMATION: Information on vaccinations and other health precautions may be obtained from the Centers for Disease Control and Prevention's international traveler's hotline at telephone 1-877-FYI-TRIP (1-877-394-8747); fax: 1-888-CDC-FAXX (1-888-232-3299), or by visiting the CDC Internet home page at http://www.cdc.gov.

TRAFFIC SAFETY AND ROAD CONDITIONS: While in a foreign country, U.S. citizens may encounter road conditions that differ significantly from those in the United States. The information below concerning Comoros is provided for general reference only and may not be totally accurate in a particular location or circumstance.

Safety of Public Transportation: Poor
Urban Road Conditions/Maintenance: Fair
Rural Road Conditions/Maintenance: Poor
Availability of Roadside Assistance: Poor

Roads are generally adequate, but are narrow and poorly lit at night. Travelers should exercise extreme caution when driving after dark. Taxis or a rental car and driver are preferable to public transportation.

AVIATION SAFETY OVERSIGHT: As there is no direct commercial air service at present, or economic authority to operate such service, between the U.S. and the Comoros, the U.S. Federal Aviation Administration (FAA) has not assessed Comoros's Civil Aviation Authority for compliance with international aviation safety standards for oversight of Comorian air carrier operations. For further information, travelers may contact the Department of Transportation within the U.S. at 1-800-322-7873, or visit the FAA Internet home page at http://www.faa.gov/avr/iasa/index.htm. The U.S. Department of Defense (DOD) separately assesses some foreign air carriers for suitability as official providers of air services. For information regarding the DOD policy on specific carriers, travelers may contact DOD at 618-256-4801.

CRIMINAL PENALTIES: While in a foreign country, a U.S. citizen is subject to that country's laws and regulations, which sometimes differ significantly from those in the United States and may not afford the protections available to the individual under U.S. law. Penalties for breaking the law can be more severe than in the United States for similar offenses. Persons violating the laws of Comoros, even unknowingly, may be expelled, arrested, or imprisoned. Penalties for possession, use or trafficking in illegal drugs in Comoros are strict and convicted offenders can expect jail sentences and heavy fines.

U.S. REPRESENTATION: The United States has no embassy in Comoros, but has a liaison representative in Moroni, who can be contacted at Quartier Oasis, P.O. Box 720, Moroni, telephone number (269) 73-00-11, fax (269) 73-00-12. U.S. citizens in Comoros are encouraged to register with the U.S. Embassy in Port Louis, Mauritius. Registration information and forms may be collected at the liaison office in Moroni and forwarded to the U.S. Embassy, consular section, Rogers House, fourth floor, John F. Kennedy Street, Port Louis, Mauritius; telephone numbers (230) 208-9764 through 208-2347; fax (230) 208-9534. The Embassy homepage is located at http://usis.intnet.mu; e-mail: usembass@intnet.mu.

CHILDREN'S ISSUES: For information on international adoption of children, international parental child abduction, and international child support enforcement issues, please refer to our Internet site at http://travel.state.gov/children's_issues.html or telephone in the U.S. at 202-736-7000.

IMPORTANT INFORMATION

HEALTH

Compulsory Vaccinations: None
Recommended Immunisations: *Diphtheria, hepatitis A, *hepatitis B, malaria, *meningitis, polio, *TB, tetanus, typhoid. *recommended in some circumstances, seek further advice.

PASSPORTS AND VISA

Passports
Required, but not by the following:
1) Holders of United Nations Laissez-Passer
2) Holders of a valid Seaman Book travelling on duty

Passport Validity:
Please contact nearest Embassy/Consulate

Visa
Required, but not by holders of diplomatic passports

Notes
1)Visas are issued to all foreign nationals on arrival

VISA FEES

a) Transit Visa valid 5 days free.
b) Tourist Visa valid 1-45 days KMF 2000.
c) Tourist Visa valid up to 90 days KMF 4000.
d) Exit Visa KMF 500.
e) Visa valid up to 12 months, with resident cara KMF 25000, without resident card KMF 10000

TRANSIT

Required by all except those as noted above and persons continuing their journey by the same or first connecting aircraft from the same or nearest airport.

EXIT PERMITS

Required by all except holders of diplomatic or service passports and United Nations Laissez-Passer.

GETTING THERE

Air: The national airline, *Air Comores*, has closed down. Airlines operating to the Comoros Islands are *Air Austral, Air Madagascar, Air Tanzania Corporation, South African Airways, Sudan Airlines* and *Yemenia Yemen Airways.*

Approximate flight time: To Moroni from *London* takes a minimun of 20 hours; this includes stopovers (usually in Paris and Réunion, Khartoum or Sana'a).

International airport: *Moroni International Prince Said Ibrahim (HAH)*, 25km (15.5 miles) from the city. Buses and taxis run to the town (journey time – 30-50 minutes). Airport facilities (available for international flights) include bars and light refreshments, left luggage facilities (0600-1800) and a post office.

Sea: There are irregular sailings via Madagascar, Reunion, Mauritius, Zanzibar or East Africa (Mombasa, Kenya) to Moroni or Mutsamudu. For sailings via Europe contact the Direction Générale du Tourisme et de l'Hôtellerie in Moroni for details.

TRANSPORTATION

The following airlines provide service between the Comoro Islands and other countries. (All flights are into Prince Said Ibrahim International Airport at Hahaya, north of Moroni, Ngazidja. Please note that things can change quickly. Contact your local travel agent or the airlines for schedule details, ticket prices, and the most up-to-date information.)

INTERNATIONAL SERVICE

- AIR AUSTRAL - From and to Reunion via Dzaoudzi, Mayotte.
- AIR MADAGASCAR - Links the Comoros with Kenya and Madagascar.
- YEMEN AIRWAYS - Links Yemen, the Comoros and Johannesburg.
- COMORES AIR SERVICES - To and from Majunga, Madagascar and Zanzibar.
- AIR TANZANIA - Links the Comoros with Reunion.
- LINHAS AEREAS DE MOCAMBIQUE - Inaugurated weekly flights in November, 2000 between the Comoros and Dubai and the Comoros and Maputo.

INTERISLAND SERVICE

- COMORES AIR SERVICES and COMORES AVIATION provide a number of flights daily between the islands of the Republic. Flights between islands take approximately 30 minutes.

- A number of small ships, motorized and sailing, carry passengers between the islands. Depending upon weather conditions, trips between islands may take as little as four hours via the newest and largest of the motorized vessels.

ACCOMODATION: SELECTED HOTELS

(The following list is not comprehensive. For greater details contact the Comorian Ministry of Tourism, Tel: 269 74-4242, or the Chamber of Commerce in Moroni, Tel: 269 73-0958.) Note: The country code for the Comoros is 269 you must dial that number before the numbers given below.

La Tortue Bigotu
Mayotte Comoros

Tel: 269 611132 **Fax:** 269 611135
Street: 15 Rue Marindrini

Leisure, Sports and Other Facilities
Swimmingpool, Bar, Restaurant

Room Facilities
AC, TV

Number Of Rooms	12

Price Range **$51 - 100**

Standard Single High in Season **62**

LHabitat Rose Doudou
Mayotte Comoros

Tel: 269 610448
Street: 16 Route de Majimbini

Number Of Rooms	4
Price Range	$25 - 50
Standard Single High in Season	37

LAventura
Mayotte Comoros

Tel: 269 611130 **Fax:** 269 614813

Room Facilities
Bathtub, TV

Number Of Rooms	5
Price Range	$25 - 50
Standard Single High in Season	43

Les Flamboyants
Mayotte Comoros

Tel: 269 614190

Room Facilities
TV

Number Of Rooms	4
Price Range	$25 - 50
Standard Single High in Season	33

Le Caribou
Mayotte Comoros

Tel: 269 611414 **Fax:** 269 611905
e-mail: hotelcaribou.mayotte@wanadoo.fr

Leisure, Sports and Other Facilities
Swimmingpool, Bar, Restaurant

Room Facilities
AC

Number Of Rooms	42
Price Range	$51 - 100
Standard Single High in Season	73

Le Jimaweni
Mayotte Comoros

Tel: 269 629638 **Fax:** 269 621050

Price Range	$25 - 50
Standard Single High in Season	25

Mont Combani
Mayotte Comoros

Tel: 269 629142

Price Range	$25 - 50
Standard Single High in Season	25

Le Rocher
Mayotte Comoros

Tel: 269 601010 **Fax:** 269 601444

Leisure, Sports and Other Facilities
Swimmingpool, Bar, Restaurant

Room Facilities
AC

Number Of Rooms	25
Price Range	$51 - 100
Standard Single High in Season	63

Moya Beach Hotel
Anjouan Comoros

Tel: 269 1433

Pension Kohinoor
Grade Comore Comoros

Tel: 269 2808

ension Zilimadjou
Grade Comore Comoros

Tel: 269 1696

Moifaka Studio Hotel
Grade Comore Comoros

Tel: 269 1556 **Fax:** 269 0382

Hotel Karthala
Grade Comore Comoros

Tel: 269 57 **Fax:** 269 274

The Itsandra Sun Hotel
Grade Comore Comoros

The hotel is perched dramatically on top of the cliff about 4 miles north of Moroni, with a postcard view across the Indian Ocean.The hotel has a private cove beach and provides comfortable, friendly
Tel: 269 2316 **Fax:** 269 2309

Leisure, Sports and Other Facilities
Casino

Hotel Trevani
Mayotte Comoros

Tel: 269 601383 **Fax:** 269 601171
e-mail: hotel-trevani@wanadoo.fr

Leisure, Sports and Other Facilities
Swimmingpool, Wind Surfing, Diving, Bar, Restaurant

Room Facilities
AC, TV

Number Of Rooms	29
Price Range	$25 - 50
Standard Single High in Season	34

Le Lagon Sud
Mayotte Comoros

Tel: 269 600620 **Fax:** 269 601727
Street: Boulevard des Crabes

Number Of Rooms	6
Price Range	$25 - 50
Standard Single High in Season	37

LHibiscus
Mayotte Comoros

Tel: 269 614661

Room Facilities
TV

Number Of Rooms	6
Price Range	$25 - 50
Standard Single High in Season	35

LHabitat Rose Doudou
Mayotte Comoros

Tel: 269 610448
Street: 16 Route de Majimbini

Number Of Rooms	4
Price Range	$25 - 50
Standard Single High in Season	37

Le Bacoco
Mayotte Comoros

Tel: 269 612590

Leisure, Sports and Other Facilities
Restaurant

Number Of Rooms	2
Price Range	$25 - 50
Standard Single High in Season	42

La Baie des Tortues
Mayotte Comoros

Tel: 269 626253 **Fax:** 269 626544

Leisure, Sports and Other Facilities
Restaurant

Number Of Rooms	5

La Tortue Bigotu
Mayotte Comoros

Tel: 269 611132 **Fax:** 269 611135
Street: 15 Rue Marindrini

Leisure, Sports and Other Facilities
Swimmingpool, Bar, Restaurant

Room Facilities
AC, TV

Number Of Rooms	12
Price Range	$51 - 100
Standard Single High in Season	62

LEden
Mayotte Comoros

Tel: 269 602302
Street: 19 Rue du Commerce

Room Facilities
TV

Number Of Rooms	5
Price Range	$25 - 50
Standard Single High in Season	33

Le Royal
Mayotte Comoros

Tel: 269 601245 **Fax:** 269 602121
Street: Boulevard des Crabes

Leisure, Sports and Other Facilities
Restaurant

Room Facilities
AC

Number Of Rooms	12

Hotel Relais de Singani
Moheli Comoros

Address: P.O.Box 1674
Tel: 269 249

Hotel Al Amal
Anjouan Comoros

Tel: 269 1580

Hotel Les Arcades
Grade Comore Comoros

Tel: 269 2847 **Fax:** 269 2846

Villa Raha
Mayotte Comoros

Tel: 269 620364
Street: 13 Rue du Smiam

Number Of Rooms	11
Price Range	$25 - 50
Standard Single High in Season	37

Hotel Coelacanthe

Grade Comore Comoros

Tel: 269 2575

Les Jardins
Mayotte Comoros

Tel: 269 600267
Street: 25 rue des Jardins

Les Chambres du Coin

Mayotte Comoros

Tel: 269 603374
Otherphone: 600497
Street: 87 Rue des Amoureux

Price Range	$51 - 100
Standard Single High in Season	60
Number Of Rooms	4

GETTING AROUND

Air: Each island has an airfield. Small private operators, such as *Aeromarine* and *Air Archipel*, operate services between Moroni, Mwali (Mohéli) and Nzwani (Anjouan) and between Moroni and Dzaoudzi, but check with the airline or the Direction Générale du Tourisme et de l'Hôtellerie in Moroni for details (see address section).

Sea: Mahore (Mayotte), Pamanzi and Dzaoudzi islands are linked by a regular ferry service. Travellers can hire motorboats, sailing craft and canoes in port villages and towns, and a boat can be especially useful for Mwali (Mohéli) where the road system is rudimentary.

Road: Bush taxis (*taxis-brousse*), hired vehicles or private cars are the only forms of transport on the islands. Traffic drives on the right. All the islands have tarred roads. 4-wheel-drive vehicles are advisable for the outlying islands and in the interior, especially in the rainy season. Roads are narrow and domestic animals often roam free, so drive slowly. For details of minibus services and special minibus excursions contact the Direction Générale du Tourisme et de l'Hôtellerie in Moroni (see address section).

Documentation: An International Driving Permit is required.

WHEN TO GO

The wet season between November and April is not a particularly healthy time to visit Comoros. If you don't die from dehydration or sheer frustration at the oppressively humid conditions, you might find yourself caught in a monsoonal wind (kashkazi), or cyclone. The best time to visit is in the cooler months between May and October. This also avoids Ramadan at the end of January/beginning of February, when the collective Comoran temper can suffer from the double whammy of continual fasting and oppressive heat.

Money & Costs

Currency:Comoran franc (CF) in Comoros, and the French franc (FF) in Mayotte.

Relative costs:

Budget meal: US$5-10
Moderate restaurant meal: US$15-20
Top-end restaurant meal: US$30-40

Budget room: US$10-25
Moderate hotel: US$35-60
Top-end hotel: US$250 plus

(These figures apply to Comoros. Mayotte is considerably more expensive, with the cheapest accommodation starting at US$60 a day, and snack type meals beginning at about US$4.)

The tourist industry on Comoros is woefully underdeveloped, and the Comoran franc still hogtied to the Euro dollar. This makes basic accommodation both overpriced and underwhelming, and the islands one of the more expensive destinations in the region. If you can camp, or find a modest pension, and are willing to exist on pastries, and cheap Comoran food from the local cafes, you can get by on as little as US$25 a day. Staying at self-contained bungalows, and dining on European dishes in restaurants will set you back about US$70 a day. If you go the whole paradise enchilada and stay at the boutique resorts with swimming pools, casinos, private beaches, dining rooms, and lah-di-dah service, you'll be looking at upwards of US$350 per day.

The Banque Internationale des Comores (BIC) is an efficient bank that exchanges all currencies, but the best currency to carry around and exchange is French francs. There are several branches of the BIC in both Moroni and Mutsamudu, but the only bank on Mohéli is the bank-in-a-satchel, which flies in and out of the island every second Monday. Don't get caught there without cash because it might be a long time between withdrawals. Except in upmarket hotels and restaurants, which also exchange money at vastly inflated rates, credit cards are next to useless.

In Mayotte, money can be changed at the Banque Française Commerciale Océan Indien in Mamoudzou or Dzaoudzi. The more upmarket restaurants, and most hotels, travel agencies, and car hire firms accept American Express, Mastercard, Visa and Diners Club credit cards. If you have the right kind of card, you can even withdraw money from an automatic teller machine. And you'll need plenty of it if staying in Mayotte for any length of time.

Bargaining is something of a tradition in Comoros (less so on Mayotte) and the idea of a fixed price as strange as a three dollar note, but there is an etiquette that goes with the bargaining. The process should be unhurried, and conducted in a spirit of mutual admiration for your opponent's bargaining prowess. Hostile or agitated offers will only increase the price of the item. Tipping is not the norm except in the more Frenchified environs of Mayotte, but tipping staff for good service is appreciated.

FOOD & DRINK

Like the people, the local food is based on a mixture of Arabic, French, African and Indian cooking. Curry is popular, as is seafood. A local specialty, not to be missed, is the lobster in vanilla sauce. Many of the dishes contain coconut cream, which adds an exotic flavor. Yams, aubergine, manioc, taro, peas and onions are served with chicken, mutton, goat or tuna, parrotfish, grouper and octopus. Sometimes coelecanthe or turtle meat are offered, but should be refused as these are protected species and the locals should be discouraged from depleting the numbers.

As the Comoros is an Islamic country, beer, wine and spirits can really only be purchased from the hotels or western or Chinese shops. The locals who are not traditional Muslims, drink *trembo* which is made from coconut milk, fruit juice and 12% alcohol.

ENTERTAINMENT

There are cinemas in Mamoudzou and Dzaoudzi , as well as one in Moroni. There are various discos on Grand Comore and La Derobade. On Moheli, there is an open air bar at one of the guest houses. On Mayotte, there are a few well-known bars.

SHOPPING

Not your average tourist mecca for shopping! Things to buy include beautifully hand carved wooden boxes, Koran covers, miniature models of local fishing boats, spices, embroidery, mats, basket work, sarongs and tablecloths. The best buys would be from the markets where one is advised to bargain extensively. Souvenirs are available from the hotel shops, but at extreme prices.

SHOWS & FESTIVALS

Around the time of **Ramadan**, dancing and street pageants are to be seen. Comorians love to dance - their talents are especially evident in the various dances that form an integral part of the Muslim festival. During the rest of the year there are no major festivals, but it is definitely a bonus if one is lucky enough to be visiting at the time of a traditional wedding (usually in July and August). These traditional affairs are called *Toirabs*. If you are lucky enough to be invited, do not forget that photographs should NOT be taken and conservative clothing should be worn.

PARKS & RESERVES

There are only two national parks in the Comoros, and one is the **marine reserve** for the protection of sea turtles and other marine life. The islands off Nioumachoua on Moheli are contained in the reserve. From the beach, small boats or a motorboat will transport visitors to the small islands. The once leper colony island, **Chissioua Ouenefou**, has a beautiful sandy beach which is visited by green sea turtles. It is common to camp on this island for a few days to observe the turtles, swim and fish.

The other national park is also a marine reserve, situated just off the shore of the Le Galawa Beach Hotel. It is here that a marine education program for the locals is being set up.

PLACES TO SEE

GRAND COMORE

Grand Comore (Ngazidja), the largest and youngest of the islands, lies north west of the other islands. The most remarkable feature of this island is the live volcano, **Mt Karthala**.

Due to the volcanic base of the island, there are no natural springs or rivers and water has to be collected from rainwater or from wells which are lowered into the water table.

The south of the island, nearer Mt Karthala, is the most agriculturally active area, comprising ylang-ylang, bananas, cassava and coconut plantations. Close to Mt Karthala, lies Moroni. It is perhaps not surprising that the name Moroni means 'in the heart of the fire' in Comorian.

Situated on the west coast, more densely populated than the more traditional and sparsely populated east coast, is **Moroni**, the capital of Grand Comore (10% of the population of Grand Comore live here).

The airport for the Comoros, Hahaya, lies 12 miles (19km) north of Moroni. The harbour which is one of the best in the country, was once the home of one of the sultanates and a seat of trade with Zanzibar. A visit to the museum might cast some light, or put into perspective, the era of the sultans. The natural history section of the museum contains, in a glass case, a specimen of the coelecanthe.

The attractions of Moroni would be to wander around the Old Town (Arab Quarter), the Old Market and the harbour. Entertainment features motion pictures at the Al Kamar Cinema, the Alliance Franco-Comorienne and a small video cinema, whilst dancing can be enjoyed at some venues.

Continuing north from Moroni, a visit to **Itsandra** with its notable beach, will also reveal the 15th-century ruins of the Sultans Fort and Palace, remnants of the time when this village was the ancient capital of the island.

If you are interested in a fishing trip in a local *galawa*, Hatsambou, further along the west coast is where day trips can be arranged. This is also where the vanilla bean industry can be observed.

Near **Mitsamiouli**, the second largest town on Grand Comore, are some up-market hotels which provide a myriad of entertainment, ranging from most watersports to tennis, volleyball, table tennis, soccer, aerobics , as well as a casino and evening entertainment. Deep sea fishing, parasailing and scuba diving are also offered. This is the tourist mecca of the Comoros.

For diving enthusiasts, this is the place to be. Sea conditions are best between March and November. There is wonderful wall diving, and night dives can be arranged through the diving centre.

Further along the coast, heading eastwards, you will come across **Lac Sale**. This is a sulphur rich salt water lake in a volcanic crater. Those wanting to have a scenic stroll with the opportunity of seeing bats roosting in trees, should take a walk around the rim of the crater.

Heading now towards the east coast - wilder scenery and more traditional villages - you will discover some lovely, less touristy beaches such as N'Droude (where sea turtles lay eggs between November and March), Hantsindzi, Boumi and Chomoni.

Grand Comore's third largest town is **Foumboni**. Not many tourists visit this town which houses the Comoros' largest Muslim Secondary school.

Heading westward again, having rounded the southernmost point of Grand Comore, lies the village of **Singani**. The river of lava from the last eruption of Mt Karthala in 1977 chose to flow through this village. The entire village, apart from the local school was destroyed. A benefit of the natural disaster is the soccer field which was constructed from the volcanic ash. Singani is also known for being the main producer, together with Mitsoudje, of ylang-ylang. Artisans in

Mitsoudje specialise in woodcarvings and beautiful decorative shutters, doors, boxes and furnishings.

The last coastal town worth mention is **Iconi**. This settlement has many buildings of historical interest as it is the oldest on Grand Comore. Visit the 16th-century **Palace of Kaviridjeo** and the **Mosquee du Vendredi**, as well as the Old Town, the ruins of **La Fortaleza** and the public square once used as a royal meeting place (Place de la Cuisine des Yeux). The extinct crater of **Ngouni** is close by and the **Citadel** can be seen from Iconi. A stiff climb to the remains of the wall of the Citadel Fort, lying along the rim of the extinct Ngouni crater, affords a view of Moroni, 3.7 miles (6km) to the north.

Apart from watersports, there is hiking or trekking. **La Grille** in the north and **Mt Karthala** in the south, comprise the highland centre of the island. Mt Karthala (7,746ft/2,361m high), an active volcano, affords the more demanding option, offering several choices for reaching the summit. Expeditions can be arranged through a travel agency in Moroni. Usually for a minimum of four people, expeditions can be arranged with or without own equipment. La Grille (3,556ft/1,084m) is the mountain in the north and is definitely an easier option. Several routes are possible from the villages of Ivamberi and Simboussa Maoueni and N'tsaounei on the west coast.

ANJOUAN (NDZUANI)

The island of Anjouan (Ndzuani) has a population of approximately 180,000, many descending from the 15th-century slaves from Mozambique or the original Malay - Polynesian settlers of Madagascar. There are signs of the results of severe overpopulation with deforestation and soil erosion occurring in many places on the coastline.

This island produces large amounts of ylang-ylang and vanilla, and the industry can best be seen around Bambao. Here the **Palace Bambao Mtsanga** is worth a visit, as is the distillery for perfume oils. A tour of the plant can be arranged for visitors, and the combination of old and new methods of distillation processes can be seen.

The capital, **Mutsamudu** - notable for its architecture, although run down and grubby - was founded in 1482, and houses approximately 15,000 people. Above the town is a cyclone-damaged citadel dating back to 1860, built by one of the former sultans to defend the town against pirates.

Domoni, previously the capital of the island, is now the second largest town with a about 8,000 inhabitants. This is where some of the best quality wood carving is to be found, as well as beautiful embroidery. Palaces from the 16th and 18th centuries, convoluted streets of houses and shops, beautiful door carvings, mosques and the mausoleum of President Abderemane who was assassinated in 1989, will keep the traveller interested.

Moya, the last town worth mention, has the best beach on Anjouan. Protected by a reef, it offers wonderful swimming. Here too, one can experience one of the best sunsets. There is one problem with Moya - one should be on the look out for being charged exorbitant prices specially designed to rip off tourists. Fishing from *pirogues* with locals, having local hairdos or yellow beauty masks, can be arranged through the Moya Plage Hotel. Be wary of being overcharged when utilising the services of this hotel.

MOHELI

South east of Grand Comore, lies the smallest of the islands, Moheli. Having a mere 23,000 inhabitants as opposed to Grand Comore's 220,000, the island is the most underdeveloped of all the islands.

This 15 by 30km (9 by 18.6 mile) green gem, dissected by a rocky spine, is a backwater compared to the other islands; a true tropical paradise. The lack of industry and all the accoutrements thereof, enhances the appeal to many seeking solitude and the true deserted island atmosphere. The bank comes to Moheli every 2 weeks!

Inhabited by the Livingstone bat, the rare *maki* (mongoose lemur) and the green sea turtle, Moheli also boasts a marine reserve. The boundary of the reserved encloses several islands to the south, where the largest population of the **Comorian green turtles** are to be found.

One of these small islands was once a leper colony, now one can camp on the exquisitely white, sandy beach, and experience the turtles at close quarters. Another spot to watch the turtles from is the beach near Kave Hoani on the north coast of Moheli. Perhaps the best way to see the laying process is to camp on the beach, as the *taxi-brousse* (bush taxis) stop running at a certain time, long before the 'turtle excursion' begins.

Fomboni, the capital of Moheli, is no more that a quiet village and small port. From here one can start many day walks to the centre of the island. There are beautiful waterfalls, rivers and forests. It is here that Arab sailing boats - *dhows* - are built on the beach.

If you suffer from baldness or dandruff, locals believe a walk to Lac Dziani Boundouni and bathing or washing in the lake will cure your problem! To reach the lake one has to take a *taxi brousse* to Wanani, east of Fomboni, and then walk from there. Following the coastline, past the village of Itsamia, Sambia is the next beach, and a *taxi brousse* can be found to return to Fomboni, or travel onward to Nioumachoua.

Nioumachoua is the starting point for visits to the marine reserve. The islands off Nioumachoua are contained in the reserve. From the beach, small boats will transport visitors to the small islands. The once leper colony, Chissioua Ouenefou, has a beautiful sandy beach which is visited by green sea turtles. It is common to camp on this island for a few days to observe the turtles, swim and fish.

Further along the west coast are the beaches of Kave Hoani (more turtles, as mentioned earlier), Domoni and Miringoni.

PUBLIC HOLIDAYS

Jan 1 2000 New Year's Day. **Jan 9** Eid al-Fitr (End of Ramadan). **Mar 18** Eid al-Adha (Feast of the Sacrifice). **Apr 7** Muharram (Islamic New Year). **Apr 16** Ashoura. **May 1** Labour Day. **Jun 16** Mouloud (Birth of the Prophet Muhammad). **Jul 6** Independence Day. **Oct 27** Leilat al-Meiraj (Ascension of the Prophet). **Dec (2 days)** Anniversary of the Death of Alkoutb Said Muhammad Cheikh Al Maarouf. **Dec 29** Eid al-Fitr (End of Ramadan).

Jan 1 2001 New Year's Day. **Mar 8** Eid al-Adha (Feast of the Sacrifice). **Mar 26** Muharram (Islamic New Year). **Apr 6** Ashoura. **May 1** Labour Day. **Jun 6** Mouloud (Birth of the Prophet Muhammad). **Jul 6** Independence Day. **Oct 17** Leilat al-Meiraj (Ascension of the Prophet). **Dec (2 days)** Anniversary of the Death of Alkoutb Said Muhammad Cheikh Al Maarouf. **Dec 19** Eid al-Fitr (End of Ramadan).

Note: Muslim festivals are timed according to local sightings of various phases of the Moon and the dates given above are approximations. During the lunar month of Ramadan that precedes Eid al-Fitr, Muslims fast during the day and feast at night and normal business patterns may be interrupted. Many restaurants are closed during the day and there may be restrictions on smoking and drinking. Some disruption may continue into Eid al-Fitr itself. Eid al-Fitr and Eid al-Adha may last anything from two to ten days, depending on the region.

DIVING IN COMOROS

There are two types of diving in Comoros; one on shallow, gently sloping reefs, consisting mainly of hard corals with gullies, cracks and overhangs, where vast schools of smaller reef fish and plenty of interesting reef life is seen. The second type of diving is off the wall. This type of diving entails a boat ride of an hour or two. Dolphins frequently escort the boat to the dive. Giant tuna, sharks, mantas sailfish, marlin and whale sharks are possible sightings.

Banc Vailheu off Grande Cokore
Visibility is outstanding. Giant dogtooth, tuna, sharks, schools of rainbow runners and kingfish are often encountered and mantas, whale sharks and hammerhead sharks are occasionally seen.

Hahaya Wall
Angelfish, butterflyfish, parrotfish, and schools of goldies abound. Gorgonian fans and amphora sponges dot the steeply sloping and at times sheer reefwall. Large gamefish are often spotted.

Masiwa Wreck
Large fish such as barracuda, tuna and bonito are often sighted, and living in the wreck are numerous lionfish, moray eels, and a brindle bass. A school of batfish hovers around the masts.

Other dive sites
Treasure Cove, Coral Gardens, Masiwa Reef, Tsada Beach Msanga, Drift Oasis Mosque, Shrine, Lac Sale, Parrot Point, Njamba, Chamoni, Aquarium, Ingambwe, President's Palace and Coelacanth

SUPPLEMENTS

SELECTED GOVERNMETN AND BUSINESS CONTACTS

The country code +269.

GOVERNMENT CONTACTS

British Consulate Moroni Comoros
Tel: 269 733182 **Fax:** 269 733182

CHUMA Moroni Comoros

Front Democratique Moroni Comoros
Tel: 269 73 3603
e-mail: idriss@snpt.km

Italian Vice Consulate Honorary Moroni Comoros
Tel: 269 732818 **Fax:** 269 732818

Ministry of Natioanal Education Public Health Youth and Sport Moroni Comoros
Tel: 269 73 2420

Ministry of Culture Youth Sports and Information Moroni Comoros

Ministry of Defence Moroni Comoros

Ministry of Facilities and Energy Moroni Comoros

Ministry of Finance the Budget and Planning Moroni Comoros
Tel: 269 73 2767

Ministry of finance, The Budget the Economy Trade and Investment Moroni
P.O.Box 324
Tel: 269 73 2767
Moroni , Comoros

Ministry of Foreign Affairs and Co operation Moroni Comoros
Tel: 269 73 2306 **Fax:** 269 73 2108

Ministry of Foreign Affairs and Co-opration Moroni Comoros
Tel: 269 73 2306 **Fax:** 269 73 2108
P.O.Box 482
Tel: 269 73 2306

Fax: 269 73 2108
Moroni , Comoros

Ministry of Francophone Affairs Culture Industry and Infomation Moroni Comoros

Ministry of Justice and Islamic Affairs Moroni Comoros

Ministry of National Education Professinaol and Vo Moroni Comoros
Tel: 269 73 2420

Ministry of Production and the Environment Moroni Comoros

Ministry of Production fisheries, The Environment and Crafts Moroni Comoros

Ministry of Public Health Population and the Statu Moroni Comoros

Ministry of the Civil Service Employment and Labou Moroni Comoros

Ministry of the Economy Trade, Industry and Crafts Moroni Comoros

Ministry of the Interior and the Implemantation of Moroni Comoros
Tel: 269 73 2411

Ministry of Tourism Transport and Posts and Teleco Moroni Comoros
Tel: 269 73 2098

Mouvement pour la democratie et le progres Moroni Comoros

Nguzo Moroni Comoros

Parti comorien pour la democratie et le progres Moroni Comoros
Tel: 269 73 1733 **Fax:** 269 73 0650

Parti socialiste des Comores Moroni Comoros
Tel: 269 73 1328

Societe Comorienne des Hydrocarbures Moroni Comoros
Tel: 269 73 0486 **Fax:** 269 73 1883

The Embassy of China Moroni Comoros
Tel: 269 73 2721

The Embassy of France Moroni Comoros
Tel: 269 73 0753

The Embassy of Korea, Democratic People's Republic Moroni Comoros

The Embassy of Libya Moroni Comoros

The Embassy of Mauritius Moroni Comoros

The Embassy of Seychelles Moroni Comoros

FINANCIAL INSTITUTION

Banque Centrale des Comores Moroni Comoros
Tel: 269 73 1814 **Fax:** 269 73 0349

Banque De Developpment Des Comores Moroni Comoros
Tel: 269 730818

Banque Pour Industries Et Le Commerce Comores Moroni Comoros
Tel: 269 730243

MAIN PRIVATE COMPANIES

Entreprise Generale de Terrassement	Privee	732339	732499	576
GAZCOM	Privee	733190	731919	689
Impression de Documents	Privee	732209	732212	395
(IMPREDOC)				
Tropic Tour and Travel	Privee	730202	731919	128

PARTNERSHIPS

Banque Centr	Semi-publique	731002	730349	405
(BCC)		731814		
Banque pour	Semi-publique	730243	731229	
(BIC)		731317		
		731506		
Comorienne de l'Electricite	semi-publique	733629	732359	121
et de l'Eau		730138		

STATE COMPANIES

Companies	Telephone	Fax	Postal Address
Société Nationale des Postes et Télécommunications	269 744300	269 731079	BP 5000 Moroni
Banque de Développement des Comores	269 730154	269 730397	BP 298 Moroni
Comores Hydrocarbures	269 730490 269 730971	269 731818	BP 3840 Moroni
Office National d'importation et de commercialisation du riz (ONICOR	269 735566	-----	-----
Organisation Comorienne de la vanille (OCOVA)			BP 472 Moroni

SELECTED CONTACTS

NAME	NUMBER	Lieu	Adresse	BP
Alawiya Said Youssouf	788253	Domicile	Mtsongole	289
Boat House Notique Galawa	788638	Affaires	Mitsamiouli	0
Directeur Avis Galawa	788156	Affaires	Galawa	75
Galawa Beach	788140	Affaires	Galawa	520
Hôtel Galawa	788118	Affaires	Galawa	0
NOM UTILISATEUR	NUMERO	LIEU	ADRESSE	0
Directeur régional Grande Comore	730001	Bureau	Badjanani	0
Deweer Christan	730003	Domicile	Hamramba	54
Said Ahamada Mbae	730004	Domicile	Hamramba	1382
Ag. Commerciale Poste 14	730005	Bureau		28
Ousseni Abdérémane	730007	Domicile	Zilimadjou	593
SOCOPOTRAM	730008	Affaires	Port	0
Royal Transit	730010	Affaires	Badjanani	86
Elhad Accounting Firm	730011	Affaires	Oasis	0
Elhad Accounting Firm	730012	Affaires	Oasis	324
Said Ahamada Mbae	730004	Domicile	Hamramba	1382
Ousseni Abdérémane	730007	Domicile	Zilimadjou	593
Assudine Abdallah	730013	Domicile	Poundouni	0
Zahara Abdoussoimadou	730015	Domicile	Mission Catholique	0
ZAKIAT DJAMBAE	730017	Domicile	MAVINGOUNI	0
Ibrahim Ahmed Islam	730020	Domicile	Itsandra	0
Mbechezi Youssouf	730029	Domicile	Hadoudja	14
FATIMA ABDOU	730030	Domicile	MKAZI	0
Attaché de Defense Amb.France	730031	Diplomatie	Itsambouni	0
Rajabaly Chamoune	730052	Affaires	Irougoudjani	0
SNPT(Centre INTERNET)	730000	Exploitation	Place de France	982
Directeur régional Grande Comore	730001	Bureau	Badjanani	0

NAME	NUMBER	Lieu	Adresse	BP
Service Ligne	730002	Bureau	Volo Volo	85
Deweer Christan	730003	Domicile	Hamramba	54
Ag. Commerciale Poste 14	730005	Bureau		28
SOCOPOTRAM	730008	Affaires	Port	0
Elhad Accounting Firm	730011	Affaires	Oasis	0
Elhad Accounting Firm	730012	Affaires	Oasis	324
CHATOI Chanfi	730014	Domicile	Mbouéni	0
Mbechezi Youssouf	730029	Domicile	Hadoudja	14
Office des Postes et Télécommunications (OPT)	710000	Exploitation		0
Lycée Privé Kibala	710002	Affaire	Chitsagani	0
Office des Postes et Télécommunications (OPT)	710005	Cabine	Missiri	0
Service Derangement	710013	Bureau	Mutsamudu	0
Aboubacar Abeid	710022	Affaires	M'roni	0
HOPITAL SCE MATERNITE	710024	Affaires	Hombo	0
Said Ali Bacar Ben Omar	710028	Affaires	M'Jimari	0
Echat Youssouf	710029	Domicile	Chitsangani	54
Agence Generale de Sce	710032	Affaires	Ladiguijou	0
HOPITAL SCE PEDIATRIE	710033	Affaires	Hombo	0
Abdallah Chakiri	788560	Domicile	Ntsaoueni	524
Aboubacar Sitti	788477	Domicile	Samba	0
Achata Nour Mohamed Djamal	788044	Domicile	Mitsamiouli	0
Ahamada Bacar	788487	Domicile	Mirereni	1292
Ahmed Mohamed Sambeco	788496	Domicile	Mtsongole	1008
Alaouia Charif Said(Mme)	788653	Domicile	Rue Ah. Djoumoi/Djao	0
Ali Mchangama	788735	Domicile	Mitsamiouli	627
Amina Mohamed Bacar	788517	Domicile	R/I Ntsaoueni	0
Ancha Mzé	788657	Domicile	Rahaleo	0

NAME	NUMBER	Lieu	Adresse	BP
Anchouroi Soilih	788016	Domicile	Kariaco	984
Dhakir Mhamed Ben Charaf	770055	Domicile	SNPT	0
Fatima Ben Charaf	770101	Domicile	Zirebeni	675
Echata Issa	770121	Domicile	Mbeni	847
Mutuelle Eparrgne crédit	770122	Affaire	Mbeni	0
Mutuelle Epargne crédit	770124	Affaire	Mbeni	1943
Moinaecha Massoundi	770128	Domicile	Mbeni	668
CENTRAL EXPL	770142	Exploitation	Mbeni	2226
RECEVEUR	770143	Bureau	Mbéni	226
SITTI CHARIF	770177	Domicile	Mbéni	343
Hadidja Abdou Rachid	770213	Domicile	Mbéni	500
Cabine Publique Téléfax	720000	Cabine	Mdjawache	677
Office des Postes et Télécommunications (OPT)	720001	Bureau	Mdjawache	121
Office des Postes et Télécommunications (OPT)	720002	Bureau	Mdjwache	1132
Cabine Guichet	720004	Cabine	Mdjawache	620
Office des Postes et Télécommunications (OPT)	720005	Bureau	Mdjawache	239
Office des Postes et Télécommunications (OPT)	720006	Bureau	Mdjawache	231
Chef Télécom.	720007	Bureau	Mdjoiché	1048
Abdourahamane Ben Cheick	720010	Domicile	Mdjimbia	1313
Guichet de Renseignements	720012	Exploitation	Mdjawache	37
Office des Postes et Télécommunications (OPT)	720013	Exploitation	Mdjawache	166

EXECUTIVE DIRECTORS OF THE ISLAMIC DEVELOPMENT BANK

ADDRESSES AND COUNTRIES REPRESENTED
FOR THE 8TH TERM STARTING FROM
16 DHUL QADA 1417H

No.	Executive Director	No.	Executive Director
1	Hon. Karnaen A. Perwataatmadja (Executive Director, IDB) c/o Ministry of Finance B. Building, 1st Floor, Room No.105 JL. Dr. Wahidin Raya No.1Jakarta 10710, Indonesia Tel/Fax: (622-1) 3517558 Office Tel/Fax: (622-1) 5484389 Home COUNTRIES REPRESENTED 1. Brunei Darussalam 2. Indonesia 3. Malaysia 4. Suriname	2	Hon. Mohamadou Labarang (Executive Director, IDB) Ambassador Embassy of Cameroon P.O.BOX. 94336 Riyadh 11693 Saudi Arabia Telephone::(966) 01-4880203 Fax:(966) 01- 488 14 63Tlx: 406688 AMCASA COUNTRIES REPRESENTED 1. Burkina Faso 6. Chad 2. Cameroon 7. Gabon 3. Gambia 8. Mali 4. Mauritania 9. Niger 5. Senegal 10. Togo*
3.	Alhaji Momodu Munu (Executive Director, IDB) 12200 Braxfield Court APT#8 Rockville, MD 20852 USA Tel: (01)301 231 6582 Fax: (01)703 5267910 All correspondences should be sent to this address as of 10 January 1999 COUNTRIES REPRESENTED 1. Comoros 6. Guinea 2. Guinea-Bissau 7. Morocco 3. Sudan 8. Somalia 4. Sierra Leone 9. Tunisia 5. Uganda	4.	Hon. Tarik Kivanc (Executive Director, IDB) Rafet Canitez Cad. Orman Apt. No.7-10 ANKARA - Turkey Tel: 90-312-491 0655 Fax: 90-312-491 0655 COUNTRY REPRESENTED 1. Turkey
5.	Hon. Hicham Chaar (Executive Director, IDB) Secretary General	6.	Hon. Mohammad El Zarouq Rajab (Executive Director, IDB) Chairman & General Manager

	Council of Ministers Lebanese Council of Ministers Government Palace Beirut - Lebanon Tel Office: 353615 Res. : (009611) 863765 Fax:(009611) 867593/866630 Telex: 21220 - 20900 COUNTRIES REPRESENTED 1. Bahrain 2. Iraq 3. Lebanon 4. Oman 5. Djibouti 6. Jordan 7. Maldives		Development Bank Tripoli Socialist People's Libyan Arab Jamahiriyah Telex: 20193 Fax: (21821)-606068 COUNTRY REPRESENTED 1. Libya
7.	Hon. Bader Eddine Nouioua (Executive Director, IDB) Chez Zennadi Nour-Eddine Residence Petit Hydra Hydra - Alger, Algérie Tel: 213 2 39 20 11 213 2 59 40 28 Tel in Paris: 331 – 482 8334 Fax: 213 2 73 58 41 213 2 73 56 16 COUNTRIES REPRESENTED 1. Algeria 2. Benin 3. Mozambique 4. Syria 5. Palestine 6. Yemen	8.	Hon. Jamal Nasser Rashid Lootah (Executive Director, IDB) Assistant Undersecretary for Resources and Budget Ministry of Finance & Industries P.O.Box 433 Abu Dhabi, U.A.E. Fax:(00971)2-724922 Abu Dhabi Tel:(00971)2-787910 -723261 Wed-Thu 00971-4-535213- 535129/535632 Res:00971-4-884343 Car:050527300 For DHL Tel: 925 3900 Telex: 223255 FEDFIN COUNTRY REPRESENTED 1. United Arab Emirates
9.	Hon. Dr. Morteza Gharehbaghian Vice Minister for Banking and Insurance Affairs (Executive Director, IDB) Ministry of Economic Affairs and Finance Nasser Khosrow Avenue Tehran Islamic Republic of Iran Tel:(9821) 311 55 44/ 325 25 36 Fax:(9821) 311 97 75 COUNTRY REPRESENTED	10	Hon. Faisal Abdul Aziz Al-Zamil (Executive Director, IDB) P.O.Box 28738 Safat 13148 Kuwait Tel: (965) –2403847-2403890 Fax: (965) –2403672 COUNTRY REPRESENTED 1. Kuwait

	1. Islamic Republic of Iran		
11.	Hon. Dr. Abdullah bin Ibrahim El-Kuwaiz (Executive Director for Saudi Arabia, IDB) General Manager Gulf International Bank P.O.Box 1017 Manama - Bahrain Telex: 8802 Fax: (973) 522633 - 522644 Tel: (973) 534000 - 522445 COUNTRY REPRESENTED 1. Kingdom of Saudi Arabia	12	Hon. Zaheer Sajjad Secretary, Economic Affairs Division (Executive Director, IDB) Ministry of Finance and Economic Affairs Islamabad Islamic Republic of Pakistan Fax: (92) 51-9205971 Tel : (92) 51-9210629 (92) 51-9212769 COUNTRY REPRESENTED 1. Albania 5. Bangladesh 2. Kazakhstan 6. Kyrghyz 3. Pakistan 7.Tajikistan 4. Turkmenistan
13.	Hon. Zeinhom Zahran General Director in Office of the Minister (Executive Director, IDB) Ministry of Finance Cairo – Egypt Tel: 202 – 3543201 Fax:202- 3557994 COUNTRY REPRESENTED 1. Egypt		

LIST OF MEMBER COUNTRIES OF THE ORGANIZATION OF THE ISLAMIC CONFERENCE

1.	The Hashemite kingdom of Jordan.
2.	Republic of Azerbaijan.
3.	Islamic State of Afghanistan.
4.	Republic of Albania.
5.	The State of United Arab Emirates.
6.	The Republic of Indonesia.
7.	The Republic of Uganda.

8.	The Islamic Republic of Iran.
9.	The Islamic Republic of Pakistan.
10.	The State of Bahrain.
11.	Brunei Darussalam.
12.	Burkina Faso.
13.	The People's Republic of Bangladesh.
14.	The Republic of Benin.
15.	The Republic of Turkey.
16.	The Republic of Chad.
17.	The Republic of Turkmenistan.
18.	The Republic of Tunisia.
19.	Republic of Tajikistan.
20.	The Republic of Gabon.
21.	The Republic of the Gambia.
22.	The People's Democratic Republic of Algeria.
23.	The Federal Islamic Republic of Comoros.
24.	The Republic of Djibouti.
25.	Zanzibar.
26.	The Kingdom of Saudi Arabia.
27.	The Republic of Senegal.
28.	The Republic of Sudan.
29.	The Syrian Arab Republic.
30.	The Republic of Sierra Leone.
31.	The Republic of Somalia.
32.	The Republic of Iraq.
33.	The Sultanate of Oman.
34.	The Republic of Guinea.
35.	The Republic of Guinea-Bissau.
36.	The State of Palestine.
37.	The Republic of Kyrgyz.

38.	The State of Qatar.
39.	The Republic of Cameroon.
40.	The State of Kuwait.
41.	The Republic of Lebanon.
42.	The Socialist People's Libyan Arab Jamahiriya.
43.	The Republic of Maldives.
44.	The Republic of Mali.
45.	Malaysia.
46.	The Arab Republic of Egypt.
47.	The Kingdom of Morocco.
48.	The Islamic Republic of Mauritania.
49.	The Republic of Niger.
50.	The Federal Republic of Nigeria
51.	The Republic of Yemen.
52.	The Republic of Mozambique.
53.	The Republic of Uzbekistan.
54.	The Republic of Suriname.

STRATEGIC STATISTICS

Indicator	Units		1997	1998	1999	2000	2001
Agriculture	Amount of Main Cereal Produced	Thousand metric tons	17	17	17	...	...
	Average Daily Calorie Intake Per Person	Calories per person	1824	1858	...	...	...
	Cereal Production per Person	Kilograms per person	33.9	32.3	31.8	31.8	...
	Fertiliser Use in Arable Land	Kilograms per hectare	...	103	218	...	...
	Fish Catches	Thousand metric tons	13.0	13.0	...	...	...
	Forests and Woodland Area	Thousand hectares	40	...	...	...	...
	Meat Production per Person	Kilograms per person	3.2	3.1	3.0	3.0	...
	Percentage of Arable Land Area	Percentages	34.98	34.98	34.98	...	...
	Percentage of Forests and Woodland Area	Percentages	17.94	...	...	...	...
	Population in Agriculture	Thousands	473	486	490	...	...
	Production of Fruits	Thousand metric tons	60	61	60	62	...
	Production of Vegetables	Thousand metric tons	5	5	5	6	...
	Share of Main Crop in Cereal Production	Percentages	80.95	80.95	80.95	...	...
	Total Arable Land Area	Thousand hectares	78	78	78	...	...

	Total Cereal Production	Thousand metric tons	21	21	21	21	...
	Total Heads of Cattle	Thousands	50	50	50	50	...
	Total Heads of Sheep	Thousands	19	20	20	...	...
	Total Land Area	Thousand square kilometres	2.23	2.23	2.23	2.23	...
	Total Meat Production	Thousand metric tons	2	2	2	2	...
	Total Use of Chemical Fertilisers	Thousand metric tons	...	8	17	...	...
	Crude Birth Rate	Per thousand persons	...	42	42	...	...
	Crude Death Rate	Per thousand persons	12	11	11	...	...
	Female Life Expectancy at Birth	Years	...	60	60	60	...
	Infant Mortality Rate	Per thousand	...	64	64	64	...
	Main Cereal Produced	SITC Code	042	042	042	...	...
	Male Life Expectancy at Birth	1999	...	57	58	58	...
	Natural Growth Rate of Population	Percentages	...	3.10	3.10	...	...
	Population Density	Persons per square kilometres	278	291	296	296	...
	Share of Rural Population	Percentages	69.0	68.0	68.0	67.3	...
	Share of Urban Population	Percentages	31.0	32.0	32.0	32.7	...

	Total Midyear Population	Millions	0.62	0.65	0.66	0.66	0.71
Education	Adult Literacy Rate	Percentages	57.30	55.40	55.40	...	...
Energy and Mining	Production of Electricity	Million kilowatt-hours	17	17	...	...	...
	Total Energy Consumption	Thousand metric tons of oil equivalent	23	23	...	...	...
	Total Energy Production	Thousand metric tons of oil equivalent	0	0	...	...	...
Exports	Annual Growth Rate of Exports	Percentages	27.27	-57.14	-33.33	175.00	...
	Exports to Islamic Countries	Million dollars	0	0	0	0	...
	Exports to the Rest of the World	Million dollars	14	6	4	11	...
	Total Exports	Million dollars	14	6	4	11	...
Imports	Annual Growth Rate of Imports	Percentages	1.99	-62.99	-15.79	16.67	...
	Imports From Islamic Countries	Million dollars	2	1	10	6	...
	Imports from the Rest of the World	Million dollars	152	56	38	50	...
	Total Imports	Million dollars	154	57	48	56	...
International Finance	Balance of Payments: Current Account	Million dollars	-16	-16	...	...	...
	Balance of Payments: Invisible Balance	Million dollars	124	35	...	...	...

	Balance of Payments: Trade Balance	Million dollars	-140	-51	-44	-45	...
	Debt Service Payments	Million dollars	1	2	6	7	...
	External Public Debt: Outstanding and Disbursed	Million dollars	193	181	188	180	...
	Rate of Devaluation Against the US Dollar	Percentages	6.88	14.34	-6.11	16.14	7.96
	Rate of Exchange: End of Period	National currency per US Dollar	392.780	449.100	421.650	489.720	528.710
	Rate of Exchange: Period Average	National currency per US Dollar	383.660	437.750	442.460	461.770	533.980
	Total Foreign Exchange Reserves	Million dollars	50	40	38	36	42
	Annual Growth Rate of Population	Percentages	1.64	4.84	1.54	0.00	7.58
	Share of Labour Force in Agriculture	Percentages	74.80	74.60	74.40	...	...
	Share of Labour Force in Industry and Services	Percentages	25.20	25.40	25.60	...	...
	Currency in Circulation	Million national currency	5639	5433	5418	6310	7564
	GDP Deflator	1995=100	...	...	...	...	...
	Money Supply: M1	Million national currency	13021	10603	10015	11662	14115
	Money Supply: M1 in Dollars	Million dollars	34	24	23	25	26

	Money Supply: M2	Million national currency	19508	18374	15773	18698	21415
	Money Supply: M2 in Dollars	Million dollars	51	42	36	40	40
Tourism	Balance of Foreign Travel	Million dollars	...	...	13	...	...
	Number of Hotel Beds	Number	784	742	772	778	...
	Number of Tourists	Thousands	24	26	27	24	...
	Tourism Expenditures	Million dollars	...	...	3	...	...
	Tourism Receipts	Million dollars	23	26	16	...	...
	Main Telephone Lines in Operation per 100 Persons	Number	0.79	1.00	1.00	...	...
	Merchant Shipping: Fleets	Thousand gross registered tons	2	2	1	...	...
	Television Receivers	Thousand units	1	1	1	1	...
	Television Receivers per 1,000 Persons	Number	2	2	2	...	...

Source: SESRTCIC databases, the data in which have been compiled from national statistical publications and international statistical sources.

THE CROSS-BORDER INITIATIVE IN EASTERN AND SOUTHERN AFRICA[6]

EXECUTIVE SUMMARY

The Cross-Border Initiative (CBI) comprises a common policy framework developed by fourteen participating countries in Eastern and Southern Africa and the Indian Ocean, with the support of four co-sponsors; the International Monetary Fund, the World Bank, the European Union, and the African Development Bank. The participants are Burundi, Comoros, Kenya, Madagascar, Malawi, Mauritius, Namibia, Rwanda, Seychelles, Swaziland, Tanzania, Uganda, Zambia, and Zimbabwe; Mozambique has also indicated its intention to join. The policy framework aims to facilitate cross-border economic activity by eliminating barriers to the flow of goods, services, labor, and capital, and to help integrate markets by coordinating reform programs in several key structural areas, supported by appropriate macroeconomic policies. The initiative places the responsibility for determining how to implement the agreed policy measures at the national level.

The **four key elements of the Initiative** are:

- liberalizing foreign exchange systems by eliminating restrictions on current account transactions and certain capital transactions, and establishing unified interbank spot foreign exchange markets;
- dismantling nontariff barriers on imports and exports, eliminating tariffs on trade between CBI participants, and lowering tariffs on a nonpreferential (MFN) basis to agreed or lower levels;
- strengthening domestic financial markets by, inter alia, improving prudential and supervisory capacity of central banks; and
- simplifying and liberalizing investment procedures.

The purpose of this paper is to take stock of the achievements under the CBI in each of the four areas mentioned above. The paper takes into account recent developments through end-December 1998. Regarding the **liberalization of foreign exchange systems**, most countries had removed restrictions on current account transactions by end-1998. In addition, a handful of countries liberalized substantially capital account transactions while the remaining countries took partial steps to ease such controls, including those affecting equity investments

---

6 THE INTERNATIONAL MONETARY FUND Jose Fajgenbaum, Robert Sharer, Kamau Thugge, and Hema DeZoysa July 14, 1999

among the participating countries. On the **exchange rate regime**, most countries met the CBI objective of introducing a flexible exchange rate system within the context of a unified inter-bank foreign exchange market.

On **trade liberalization and facilitation**, significant but uneven progress was achieved. Many of the participating countries made substantial progress toward meeting the CBI targets on tariffs. Although, none of the countries fully eliminated intraregional tariffs, virtually all countries implemented preference margins for other CBI participants ranging between 60—80 percent. Progress on MFN liberalization was mixed; (i) three countries met the target of lowering the maximum tariff rate to 20—25 percent; (ii) six countries met the target of reducing the number of nonzero tariff bands to no more than three; and (iii) three countries where data are available, met the target of reducing their weighted average tariff rates to no more than 15 percent. Nevertheless, tariff exemptions remained widespread, including for imports by governments, parastatals, nongovernmental organizations, and for goods related to foreign-financed projects and those under the various investment codes. The pace of trade reform reflected, in part, concerns on the potential adverse impact on fiscal revenue.

Notable progress was achieved in reducing **nontariff barriers** to imports. Most countries eliminated import quotas and bans, as well as import licensing requirements. Moreover, the monopoly power previously exercised by state marketing boards or state controlled enterprises in regard to exporting, importing, and price setting was significantly reduced in most of the countries. Although export duties and export marketing monopolies remained in place in about half the countries, only a few countries continued to maintain export restrictions. Finally, substantial progress was also achieved in some key areas of **trade facilitation**, including implementing the harmonization of road transit charges, and the introduction of the Road Customs Transit Document and of a single goods customs declaration form.

Good progress was made in reforming the **domestic financial sectors to** improve their efficiency. Most countries moved to the use of indirect monetary instruments to control monetary aggregates, and administered interest rates were phased out and replaced with market-based mechanisms. Increased attention was devoted to strengthening the powers of central banks to enforce prudential regulations and to provide autonomy in conducting monetary policy. All CBI countries had either adopted or were in the process of adopting Basle capital adequacy standards, and several countries required that the capital ratio be above the minimum 8 percent of risk-weighted assets. In addition, most of the countries had prudential limits on connected/single borrower transactions, as well as on single/aggregate foreign exchange exposures. There was a substantial increase in the number of banks in some countries, including a significant presence of foreign owned banks, but in other countries, the degree of competition in financial markets was still limited to a few operators.

Progress was made in the area of **investment deregulation**. There was substantial simplification of approval procedures (particularly through the establishment of a one-stop investment approval authority). The publication of investment codes was completed by ten participants, and substantive progress made in the remaining countries. However, with the exception of a few countries, most of the investment codes included some form of tariff exemptions. There was slow progress in concluding double taxation agreements, in the cross-listing of stocks, and in **facilitating labor mobility** (visa protocol, residence/work permits, and short-term entry permits).

I. INTRODUCTION

1. As described in earlier papers[1], the Cross-Border Initiative (CBI) comprises a common policy framework developed by fourteen participating countries in Eastern and Southern Africa and the Indian Ocean[2], with the support of four co-sponsors—the Fund, the World Bank, the European Union (EU), and the African Development Bank. The policy framework aims to facilitate cross-border activity by eliminating barriers to cross-border flows of goods, services, labor, and capital, as well as to integrate markets through a coordination of reform programs in the areas of trade, exchange systems, domestic banking and payment systems, and investment regulations, supported by appropriate macroeconomic policies. The CBI has avoided the creation of new institutions, placing responsibility at the national level for the design and implementation of measures to support the agreed policy framework.

2. To this end, a set of "core" measures were articulated in a Concept Paper[3], which was adopted at the First CBI Ministerial Meeting in Uganda in August 1993 (Box 1). A Second Ministerial Meeting, held in Mauritius in March 1995, endorsed a "Road Map" for further trade liberalization that included the elimination of tariffs on intraregional trade and the convergence of external tariffs to a trade-weighted average of 15 percent, both by October 1998. At the Third Ministerial Meeting, held in Zimbabwe in February 1998, the participating countries decided to continue and broaden the CBI, and agreed that the future focus should emphasize investment facilitation issues, and the harmonization of national and regional policies toward a conducive environment for efficient investment and trade flows. [4]

3. Under the CBI, each participating country was expected to: (i) create a Technical Working Group (TWG) comprised of representatives of the public and private sectors that would identify and report on the main impediments to the cross-border activities outlined in the Box, and would suggest a common program of action to be implemented at the national level; (ii) establish a Policy Implementation Committee (PIC), comprised of officials with the authority to design and implement a specific program of policy measures[5]; and (iii) complete a Letter of CBI Policy (LCBIP) specifying the steps that the country would take to

implement the various measures, including regulatory changes and a timetable which would be endorsed by the co-sponsors. [6]

4. As one of the co-sponsors, the Fund's role was to ensure that each LCBIP was consistent with progress toward a stable macroeconomic framework. The CBI objectives and the schedule of implementation of the various measures have been featured in staff discussions in the context of Article IV consultations and use of Fund resources, and have been taken into account in considering technical assistance requests. For countries undertaking structural adjustment in the context of Fund-supported programs, actions included in the LCBIPs have been built in, and coordinated with, the adjustment program. The CBI has also been featured in staff discussions with nonparticipating countries to apprise them of emerging policy trends with wider implications.

5. The purpose of this paper is to take stock of the achievements of the CBI since its inception in 1993. It is, of course, important to mention that measures in areas such as improving financial intermediation were underway before the CBI began and were undertaken for domestic reasons rather than considerations regarding regional cooperation and harmonization. Section II describes progress in implementing the measures specified in the four areas of the CBI policy framework as of December 1998—foreign exchange systems, trade regimes, domestic banking and payments systems, and investment regulations. Finally, Section III discusses the remaining agenda and the issues to be addressed.

Box. Key Elements of the CBI Framework

Exchange Systems

- Complete elimination of restrictions on current account transactions, and relaxation of restrictions for some capital transactions to liberalize direct investment and investment in regional equity markets.
- Establish unified interbank spot-foreign exchange markets by 1996.

Trade Liberalization and Facilitation

- Dismantle nontariff import barriers on a most-favored-nation (MFN) basis. Short negative lists for reasons of health and security could be retained. Where immediate elimination is not feasible, participants should agree with the Fund on a schedule for their removal, normally within one year.
- Eliminate all quantitative restrictions on exports to all countries, except for a short negative list.
- Eliminate tariffs on intraregional trade by October 1998 for products originating in the CBI area.

- Aim at a harmonized external tariff with no more than three nonzero bands, a maximum rate of 20—25 percent, and a weighted average rate of 15 percent by October 1998.
- Implement harmonized transit charges and introduce: a road customs transit document, a single goods declaration document, and a bond guarantee scheme.

Domestic Banking and Payments Systems

- Strengthen regulatory and prudential functions of central banks and domestic financial markets.
- Eliminate impediments to entry by regional and extraregional financial institutions, and enable specialized financial institutions—including offshore banking facilities—to participate in providing equity and export credit facilities.

Investment Regulations

- Simplify and liberalize investment approval procedures; consolidate investment codes and all regulations into a single published document.
- Establish one-stop investment centers to process investment applications within 45—60 days, with automatic approval in the absence of valid objections.
- Process residence and employment permits within four weeks; relax or eliminate visas on a reciprocal basis; allow freer movement in border areas.
- Authorize stock exchanges to list and trade equities from other stock exchanges in the region.

II. POLICY IMPLEMENTATION AND ISSUES

A. LIBERALIZATION OF FOREIGN EXCHANGE SYSTEMS

Developments

6. Under the CBI framework, participants are expected to eliminate exchange restrictions on current account transactions in a nondiscriminatory manner and to relax certain types of capital transactions. The liberalization of the capital account referred principally to transactions associated with long-term, non-debt-creating, foreign direct investments (FDI) rather than to short-term capital. The main focus of the reform was to improve the regulatory environment for investments, both domestic and foreign; progressively harmonize investment incentives; and encourage investment in regional equity markets (see Section D below). In light of the fragility of the domestic financial system (elements of which were to be addressed within the Initiative; see Section C), the liberalization of short-term

capital inflows was not perceived to be a priority. In regard to foreign exchange markets, the objective was to establish unified, interbank spot-exchange *markets* no later than 1996. Such markets would, in turn, set the stage for more diversified operations, including forward cover, and liberalization of foreign currency accounts.

7. With regard to the removal of exchange restrictions on current account transactions, 12 of the 14 CBI countries have accepted the obligations under Article VIII, sections 2, 3, and 4 as of December 1998 (compared with only two in 1993) (Table 1)[7]. Regarding the capital account, Kenya, Malawi, Mauritius, Uganda, and Zambia have substantially liberalized capital account transactions, while Comoros and Madagascar have taken steps to ease controls, including on the repatriation of portfolio outflows. Tanzania and Zimbabwe also took steps in the latter regard.

8. Exchange arrangements vary widely, with 9 participating countries maintaining a floating exchange rate system in the context of unified interbank exchange markets (Tables 2 and 3)[8]. Controls on foreign currency accounts for residents and foreign entities have been lifted, with the exception of Burundi, Comoros, Namibia, Seychelles, Swaziland, and Zimbabwe. Finally, although some progress has been made over the last three years in easing foreign exchange repatriation and surrender requirements, most countries continue to impose such controls (Table 4). Competition in foreign exchange markets has also been enhanced with the licensing of nonbank foreign exchange bureaus in nine countries. Forward cover through commercial banks and other authorized dealers is available in nine countries. In addition, Kenya, Tanzania, and Uganda (the East African Cooperation (EAC) countries) have agreed that their respective currencies be fully accepted within the EAC countries, and that the currencies be quoted by banks and foreign exchange bureaus.

B. Trade Liberalization and Facilitation

Developments

9. The CBI framework called for a coordinated and time-bound reduction of trade barriers at the regional level, and with third countries on an MFN basis. The specifics of the trade reform agenda and the timetable for implementation included: (i) effective October 1995, increasing from 60 percent to 70 percent the intraregional tariff preference for countries that had not yet done so; (ii) elimination of tariffs on intraregional trade by October 1998, with an increase in the preference rate to 80 percent by October 1996 and to 90 percent by 1997; and (iii) a harmonized external tariff to be adopted by October 1998 consisting of no more than three nonzero bands, a trade weighted average tariff rate of no more than 15 percent, and a maximum rate of 20—25 percent[9]. With regard to nontariff barriers (NTBs), countries were expected to dismantle import licensing

requirements and similar NTBs on an MFN basis, except for a short "negative list" for noneconomic reasons such as security, health, and environment. Quantitative restrictions on exports to all countries were to be eliminated, except for a small negative list for the same noneconomic reasons.

10. By end-December 1998, many of the participating CBI countries had either met or made substantial progress toward meeting CBI targets for trade liberalization (Tables 5 and 6). Significant progress on tariff reduction on intraregional trade was achieved. Although, none of the countries met the target for eliminating intraregional tariffs by end-December 1998, Kenya, Madagascar, Tanzania, Uganda, and Zimbabwe, had implemented an 80 percent preference margin, while Burundi, Comoros, Malawi, Mauritius, Rwanda, and Zambia had increased the preference margin to 60—70 percent. Moreover, Kenya, Tanzania, and Uganda have indicated a desire to accelerate tariff reductions on trade between them, in the context of the EAC Agreement. Namibia and Swaziland could not change their preference margins because they are members of the Southern African Customs Union (SACU). Seychelles has not made any progress on increasing the preference margin.

11. Regarding the reduction of the maximum tariff rate, Kenya, Uganda, and Zambia met the CBI target of 20—25 percent by end-December 1998 [10]. In addition, Madagascar, Malawi, and Tanzania reduced their maximum rates to 30 percent, while Comoros and Rwanda lowered theirs to 40 percent. Although some reductions have taken place in the remaining six countries, the maximum rates remain high in Mauritius, Namibia, and Swaziland (in the range of 70—80 percent); and substantially higher in Burundi and Zimbabwe (100 percent), and Seychelles (200 percent).

12. Comoros, Kenya, Madagascar, Rwanda, Uganda, and Zambia met the target of reducing the number of nonzero bands to no more than three, by end-December 1998—Uganda's two tariff bands went beyond the target. Burundi, Malawi, and Tanzania had 4—5 tariff bands, and the least amount of progress was recorded in the cases of Mauritius, Seychelles, and Zimbabwe with 8, 9, and 17 bands, respectively, and the SACU countries which continued to have multiple tariff bands.

13. Information on the weighted average tariff rate is not available for all countries. Among the countries with such information, the CBI target of an average tariff rate of no more than 15 percent was met with substantial margins in Kenya, Uganda, and Zambia. Using the more widely available unweighted average tariff rate, six countries (Malawi, Namibia, Rwanda, Swaziland, Uganda, and Zambia) have averages that are either around or below 15 percent. Kenya and Madagascar had unweighted average rates of about 18 percent, and the rest of the countries had unweighted average rates ranging from 21.8 percent (Tanzania) to 35 percent (Burundi). Limited progress was made in reducing other

duties and charges (ODCs) and in amalgamating them into the basic tariff structure, mainly because of revenue concerns. Malawi, Seychelles, Tanzania, and Zambia met the CBI objective, while Burundi, Comoros, Namibia, Rwanda, Uganda, and Zimbabwe had ODCs below 15 percent, and Madagascar and Mauritius had ODCs of up to 40 percent and 400 percent, respectively.

14. Although notable progress was achieved in reducing import NTBs, particularly those related to bans, quotas, and licensing requirements, the record on dismantling state monopolies and eliminating discriminatory taxes and reducing tariff exemptions has been mixed (Table 7 and 8). The CBI countries have eliminated all import quotas and bans, with the exception of Namibia (which has quotas for imports of used cars and clothing, and seasonal bans on some agricultural products), Uganda (which has a ban on cigarettes that is expected to be eliminated by July 1999), Seychelles (which has semiannual quotas on all imports) and Swaziland (which maintains seasonal bans on some agricultural products). Import licensing requirements have been eliminated in most CBI countries, with the exception of Namibia, Seychelles, and Zimbabwe. The monopoly power previously exercised by state marketing boards or state controlled enterprises with regard to exporting, importing, and price setting was significantly reduced in all countries with the exception of Comoros, Mauritius, Namibia, Seychelles, Swaziland, and Tanzania. Similarly, progress was mixed in eliminating discriminatory higher rates of excise duty and/or value-added tax on certain imports which remain in half of the CBI countries (Burundi, Kenya, Mauritius, Seychelles, Tanzania, Uganda, and Zambia). Tariff exemptions remain widespread, including for imports by governments, parastatals, nongovernmental organizations, and for goods related to foreign-financed projects and those under the various investment codes.

15. Substantial progress was achieved in reducing impediments to exports (Table 9). By end-December 1998, only Zambia and Zimbabwe maintained export bans and quotas, respectively, while export licenses were required in only three countries (Kenya, Namibia, and Zimbabwe). Export duties remained in place in Burundi, Comoros, Rwanda, Swaziland, Tanzania, and Zimbabwe, while Burundi, Namibia, Seychelles, Swaziland, and Zimbabwe still maintained marketing monopolies.

16. Substantial progress was achieved in some key areas of trade facilitation. With the exception of the SACU countries (Namibia and Swaziland) and the island economies, the rest of the CBI countries implemented the harmonization of road transit charges, and introduced the Road Customs Transit Document (Table 10)[11]. In addition, a single goods customs declaration form was introduced by most countries, except in Burundi, Malawi, and Rwanda, where information is not available. In contrast, however, no country had yet introduced a bond guarantee scheme by the end of the CBI period.

Assessment of progress

17. The extent of trade liberalization achieved in the CBI countries can be assessed using an index of aggregate trade policy restrictiveness.[12] Under the CBI, considerable progress has been made in trade reforms, mainly in the context of adjustment programs supported by the Fund and the World Bank. Five countries moved to open trade regimes, compared to zero at the inception of the initiative; another three countries had moderately restrictive trade regimes, the same number as at the beginning of the initiative; and the remaining six countries continued to have relatively restrictive trade regimes (Figure 1 and Table 11).

18. Based on the index, the most ambitious reformers were Kenya, Madagascar, Malawi, Rwanda, Uganda, and Zambia, as they reduced their restrictiveness ratings by 4—5 points and achieved open trade regimes (except Kenya which moved from the restrictive to the moderate category). In contrast, Burundi, Comoros, Seychelles, and Zimbabwe made no progress in trade liberalization; moreover, Seychelles and Zimbabwe continued to have a rating of "10" on the index.

19. As a group, the CBI countries reduced their rating on the index by an average of 2.4 points compared to 1.7 for a select group of non-CBI African countries.[13] As a result, although the CBI countries had more restrictive trade regimes at the beginning of the Initiative, by end-1998 their trade regimes were, on average, less restrictive (5.9) than those of the select group of non-CBI countries (6.2). However, the CBI countries still remain, on average, markedly more restrictive than countries in other regions. While 43 percent of the CBI countries would be classified as having highly restrictive trade regimes, only 17 percent of the economies of the rest of world (excluding non-CBI African countries) would be classified as highly restrictive (Figure 2). Similarly, only 36 percent of the CBI countries would be classified as open compared with 52 percent for the rest of the world. Of course, the rating for the rest of world masks a wide dispersion among the various regions of the world, with industrialized countries as a group having the lowest rating of 4 and the Middle Eastern countries having the highest rating of 5.5, compared with 5.9 for CBI countries.[14] It is important to note that good practice countries (Chile, Colombia, New Zealand, and Singapore) have a rating of 1.5, and that Uganda and Zambia, with ratings of 2, are very near this level.

FACTORS INFLUENCING ACHIEVEMENT OF CBI TRADE REFORM OBJECTIVES

20. Several reasons have been cited for the delay in implementing trade policy reforms. These included: civil unrest (Burundi, Comoros and Rwanda); the concern about potential adverse impact of trade reform on government revenues (Comoros, Tanzania and Zimbabwe) and hence on macroeconomic stability; and membership in other regional trading arrangements (RTAs). The fiscal impact of

trade reform depends on the nature of the reforms introduced and the specific circumstances of the country.[15] In order to offset any possible adverse effect on revenues, the reduction in tariffs should be accompanied by a tariffication of NTBs on imports and exports, and the elimination of tariff exemptions. However, even in those circumstances where trade liberalization might lead to a short-term loss in revenues, the appropriate response should be to adopt offsetting measures—if on the revenue side preferably by less-distorting and more broad-based taxes that are applied equally to both imports and domestic production.

21. The excessive number of RTAs which the CBI countries are members may indeed have interfered with the pace of trade liberalization. As shown in Figure 3 and Table 12, the CBI countries are members of five different RTAs: the Common Market for Eastern and Southern Africa (COMESA), EAC, IOC, SACU, and the Southern Africa Development Community (SADC). These countries are faced with conflicting obligations, different and uncoordinated strategies, inconsistent external liberalization goals, and different and conflicting rules and administrative procedures. For example, under the COMESA Treaty, 80 percent preferences were to have been provided by the member states to each other by 1998 and 100 percent by 2000. In contrast, under the more accelerated CBI framework, the complete elimination of intra-CBI tariffs was envisaged to take place by end-October 1998. As for the SADC, intraregional preferences are also envisaged, but over eight years beginning in 2000.

C. REFORM OF THE DOMESTIC FINANCIAL SECTOR

Developments

22. The development of a sound financial sector and efficient payment systems are viewed as essential for increasing cross-border flows and market access. To ensure the soundness of financial institutions, the CBI framework called for intensified efforts to improve prudential and supervisory capacity of central banks so as to encourage development of the commercial banking sector and other financial institutions, and to strengthen the domestic payments system. Additional measures included developing foreign trade financing instruments and establishing correspondent banking relationships within the region.

23. At the commencement of the Initiative, virtually all CBI countries relied on bank-by-bank credit ceilings and administered interest rates as key instruments of monetary policy. Government interference was prevalent, through directed credit allocations, heavy borrowing from central banks to finance large fiscal deficits, and maintenance of negative real interest rates. With respect to the institutional structure, a proper legal framework for the independence of central banks was largely absent, entry by domestic and foreign commercial banks was restricted and led to concentrated ownership structures, and regulation and supervision were inadequate to ensure the soundness of financial institutions.

24. Despite the variety of problems, there has been good progress in improving the efficiency of the financial system. In the banking system, direct monetary instruments in the form of individual bank credit ceilings and selective credit controls have been phased out in all countries except Comoros; most countries now use indirect monetary instruments such as open market operations, changes in liquidity requirements, and standing discount facilities (Table 13).[16] Administered interest rates have been phased out and replaced with market-based mechanisms in almost all countries except Comoros and Seychelles.[17]

25. Financial market developments can also be gauged by the presence of active primary and secondary markets for public debt instruments, an interbank money market, and a stock exchange. Most CBI countries, with the exception of Comoros, Rwanda, and possibly Burundi have fairly active primary markets for government and central bank securities with weekly auctions, and/or tap sales between auctions. The existence of secondary markets is more limited, with active markets being present only in Kenya, Malawi, Zambia, and Zimbabwe. Secondary markets have been slow to develop, owing in part to the existence of high liquidity requirements, the lack of infrastructure and capacity, as well as lingering doubts about the soundness of some banks. The latter factor has confined active interbank markets to Kenya, Malawi, Mauritius, Namibia, Zambia, and Zimbabwe. Stock exchanges exist in several countries, but it could be argued that only the stock exchanges in Kenya, Namibia, Zambia, and Zimbabwe are relatively active.

26. Attention has also been devoted to central banks' powers to enforce prudential regulations. To this end, legislation was enacted or revised during 1993—98 in Madagascar, Namibia, Seychelles, Swaziland, Uganda, and Zambia (Table 14). In Comoros and Zimbabwe, the supervisory and regulatory role continues to be shared by the government and the central bank. In principle, central banks have full autonomy in most countries, except in Comoros, Kenya, Tanzania, and Zambia, where autonomy is partial.[18]

27. Roughly half the CBI countries have either fully or substantially implemented financial sector reform programs. An evaluation of the development of foreign trade instruments and the removal of impediments to entry indicate that considerable progress has also been achieved in the majority of countries. The increased focus on financial sector reform issues has also coincided with an expansion of financial markets in most of the countries. Thus, the number of commercial banks has increased to more than 50 in Kenya; 21 in Zambia; 20 in Uganda and 18 in Tanzania. At the same time, all countries with the exception of Comoros and Malawi have foreign banks operating in their countries; and Kenya, Malawi, Tanzania, and Uganda have taken measures to reduce government ownership or privatize state-owned banks and to review existing licensing procedures before licensing additional new banks. The payment system appears

to be satisfactory in ten of the participating countries although efficiency is high in only a few (Mauritius, Namibia, and Swaziland).

Assessment of progress

28. Despite recent progress in several areas, the degree of competition in financial markets in a number of countries remains limited to a few operators, and there is only a thin supply of financial instruments. The market for treasury and central bank bills remains narrow in most of the participating countries, to the extent that the frequent reason attributed to the lack of secondary markets in public debt is the absence of a sufficient amount of outstanding public paper. In this context, changes in reserve and liquidity ratios have been extensively used as the preferred monetary instrument. Such uses (together with the high level of nonperforming loans) are often cited as contributing to the wide spreads between deposit and lending rates.

29. Supervisory practices have improved significantly in most of the CBI countries. All CBI countries have either adopted or are in the process of adopting the Basle standard for capital adequacy requirement of 8 percent; and in several countries the capital ratio is above the minimum requirement. Most of the countries have prudential limits on connected/single borrower transactions, as well as on single/aggregate foreign exchange exposures.

D. REFORM OF INVESTMENT REGULATIONS

30. Another major objective of the CBI involved reforming the regulatory environment for direct investments, and the progressive harmonization of the structure of investment incentives. In regard to the regulatory environment, participating countries agreed to simplify and codify all investment-related regulatory provisions into a single published document that would be widely available; establish one-stop investment centers that would process all applications between 45 days and 60 days; and grant automatic approval in the absence of objections at the end of that period. Other specific measures called for participants to conclude avoidance of double taxation agreements on a bilateral basis; authorize the cross-listing of stocks from other exchanges in the region; and expedite the processing of residence and work permits, and relax visa requirements for investors. In addition, participating countries were expected to become members of the Multilateral Investment Guarantee Agency, and where necessary, of bilateral investment guarantee agencies such as Overseas Private Investment Corporation. The ratification of a suitable amended form of the Multilateral Industrial Enterprise Charter was also encouraged.[19]

31. Overall progress in the area of investment deregulation has been mixed. There has been almost full liberalization of approval procedures (in particular establishing a one-stop investment approval authority), and the publication of

investment codes has been completed by 10 participants, and the remaining countries have made substantive progress (Table 15). However, with the exception of a few countries, most of the investment codes include tariff exemptions. With regard to the statute of limitation, only 6 participants have fully implemented it. There has also been slow progress with regard to double taxation agreements and cross-listing of stocks.

32. Overall progress in regard to the facilitation of labor market issues (visa protocol, residence/work permits, and short-term entry permits) has also been mixed. Most of the non-island economies have taken action on short-term entry permits for border residents, while the EAC countries—Kenya, Tanzania, and Uganda—no longer require visas for their citizens to travel between their countries. There has been little progress in the processing of residence and work permits except for Kenya, Namibia, Tanzania, Uganda, and Zambia.

III. THE REMAINING AGENDA

33. In the context of a gradual return to macroeconomic stability, good progress has been achieved in most of the CBI countries in the liberalization of exchange systems over the last few years. This is reflected in the widespread elimination of restrictions on external current transactions, the shift towards market-based exchange rates, and the move (mainly in respect of inflows) towards liberalizing external capital transactions related largely to FDI. The movement towards liberalization, moreover, has reduced reliance on direct controls, and correspondingly increased the role of macroeconomic policies. In particular, macroeconomic policies have become the key instruments in promoting exchange rate stability and containing inflationary pressures. Some countries, however, still need to remove the remaining restrictions on current account transactions. To strengthen investor confidence and the export environment there is also the need to further liberalize capital account transactions on FDI and to liberalize foreign exchange repatriation and surrender requirements.

34. Although some of the CBI countries have made significant progress in trade liberalization going well beyond the CBI objectives to achieve open trade regimes, others continue to have either moderately or highly restrictive trade regimes. Ideally, the countries classified as having moderately to highly restrictive trade regimes need to move to open trade regimes, say, over the next three years. Moreover, countries should continue to persevere with trade reform by lowering their maximum tariff rates to no more than 15 percent (in line with the current maximum rate for Uganda), and reducing the number of nonzero tariff bands to 2 or 3 and their unweighted average tariff rates to no more than 10 percent over the medium term.

35. The continuing existence of other duties and charges outside the basic tariff structure needs to be eliminated. The amalgamation of these charges into the

tariff structure would reduce its complexity and improve its transparency and efficiency. With regard to NTBs, much remains to be done, especially in the areas of state monopolies and discriminatory taxes. Given that NTBs are the most distortionary aspects of a trade regime, the future agenda should focus attention on eliminating them as a priority. By making the trade regimes more transparent and less distorted, such an agenda would help make these economies more efficient and competitive. More determined efforts will be needed to eliminate or reduce sharply tariff exemptions. This would serve the purpose of strengthening the fiscal position and introducing more transparency into the trade regimes.

36. The difficulties caused by overlapping RTAs needs to be addressed. Ideally, while trade liberalization should be undertaken on an MFN basis, the extension of tariff preferences to other members of RTAs is likely to enhance trade creation and lessen trade diversion, if accompanied by liberalizing on an MFN basis. In this light, it would be important that the overlapping regional trade arrangements in Eastern and Southern Africa (see Annex I) harmonize the various goals and objectives of the different RTAs, coordinate them more efficiently, and make their objectives more internally consistent so as to (i) avoid negating some of the potential gains from regionalism and undermining the potential improvement in the investment climate that arise from a larger market and improved transparency; (ii) introduce common and simple (rather than conflicting) rules of origin into the trading process; (iii) prevent costly duplication of administrative effort; and (iv) reinforce the reform momentum by consolidating the political capital needed to pursue reforms. CBI participants should make every effort to achieve these goals and accelerate the ongoing efforts at trade facilitation.

37. As a practical matter, rationalizing the current multiple RTAs would be facilitated by accelerating reduction of external tariffs on an MFN basis and removing NTBs. Such an action by one country, or group of countries, could increase the pressure on others to follow suit to prevent intraregional trade and investment from being diverted away from them. In addition, more frequent contacts between all the countries in the region might provide a forum for discussion on adopting a common set of objectives, adopting common rules and regulations and reducing administrative complexity, and for resolving policy disagreements. For example, it would be useful to explore the possibility of inviting COMESA and SADC to join the CBI Steering Committee. Rationalization of the multiple RTAs would enlarge markets, improve transparency, and reduce administrative costs, thus providing a better climate for trade and investment.

38. Despite recent progress in several areas, much work also remains to be done to develop the financial systems to achieve the objectives of the CBI. The authorities need to work toward increasing competition in the financial system by accelerating the pace of privatization of banks, in a transparent manner, and by granting further autonomy to central banks—legally and in practice. Further,

macroeconomic stability and the resulting lower inflation rate will ensure that real interest rates are positive and help raise financial savings, and thus the development of money and capital markets. There is also the need to strengthen regulation and supervision to help achieve financial system soundness, which is an important element for macroeconomic stability. The introduction of a transparent safety net, such as a well defined and limited deposit insurance scheme, rather than reliance on blanket government guarantees, would help increase market discipline. It should be pointed out that the prevalence of state-owned banks makes it hard to credibly refuse to bail out such banks in case of failure.

39. Increased investment (both domestic and foreign) in participating countries is crucial for real per capita economic growth and diversification. As mentioned earlier, the Third Ministerial Meeting held in Zimbabwe (February 1998) requested the co-sponsors to prepare a Road Map for Investment Facilitation to be discussed at the Fourth Ministerial Meeting to be held in 1999. The paper outlining this road map, which has now been finalized by the co-sponsors, indicates that while there has been an upturn in the average real per capita growth in recent years, growth in sub-Saharan Africa and the CBI countries needs to be raised and diversified to ensure a significant improvement in living standards in the near future. To this end, gross investment in the CBI countries needs to be increased to at least 25 percent of GDP, as suggested by the Global Coalition for Africa. Foreign direct investment, which had increased only marginally compared to other developing countries, should be allowed to play an important role in this process. The main lessons of experience drawn by the Paper are that investor confidence is linked not only to the perception of the robustness of reforms, but also to their consistent implementation over time; that reform efforts (which usually take a long time) have not been consistent and sustained enough to regain investor confidence; and that a concerted effort is needed, over an extended period, to firmly establish improved general conditions for attracting investment and build a better image. The Paper identified eight essential conditions for attracting investment: political stability, good governance, macroeconomic reform and stability, trade liberalization, exchange system liberalization, market integration, investment deregulation, and consistency in policy application. Since it would not be feasible to tackle all aspects of investment facilitation at one and the same time, the Paper suggests immediate actions in selected priority areas. They consist of actions to accelerate implementation of the CBI trade reform agenda; investment promotion at the regional and national level; selective legal and judicial reforms; selective tax reforms; and steps to raise awareness and spur the private sector to deliver improvements in services and performance.

40. In implementing the remaining agenda, participation of the private sector through the TWGs will continue to be important. Experience under the CBI

suggests that the TWGs have emerged as a crucial part of the CBI process by contributing to ownership and effective implementation of reforms.

ANNEX 1

REGIONAL ORGANIZATIONS IN EASTERN AND SOUTHERN AFRICA, AND THE INDIAN OCEAN

A. The Common Market for Eastern and Southern Africa (COMESA)

41. The COMESA was established in November 1993, superseding the Preferential Trading Agreement (PTA) for Eastern and Southern African states.[20] The aims and objectives of the COMESA Treaty and Protocols are to facilitate the removal of structural and institutional weaknesses of its members through the creation and maintenance of:

- a full free trade area guaranteeing the free movement of goods and services produced within the COMESA region, and the removal of all nontariff barriers;
- a customs union under which goods and services imported from non-COMESA countries will attract a single tariff rate;
- the free movement of capital and investment supported by the adoption of common investment practices;
- a gradual establishment of a payments union based on the COMESA Clearing House, and the eventual establishment of a common monetary union; and
- the adoption of common visa arrangements, leading eventually to the free movement of bona fide persons.

42. The fulfilment of the complete COMESA mandate is regarded as a long-term objective. To become more effective as an institution COMESA has defined its priorities over the next 3—5 years as being "The Promotion of Regional Integration Through Trade and Investment." Under the COMESA program, activities in respect of trade liberalization, trade facilitation, payments systems, institutional support, competition policy, investment road maps, strengthening the private sector, and immigration and free movement of persons will be undertaken.

43. The COMESA program includes the establishment of a Free Trade Area (FTA) by the year 2000, to be achieved by the annual reduction of intra-COMESA tariffs. As of end-December 1998, eight countries had achieved a reduction of 80 percent, and six other countries achieved reductions of 60—70 percent. All COMESA countries have reiterated their commitment to achieve a FTA by October 2000, and over half are in a position to make such a transition without having to effect large additional preferences. Member countries have also

agreed to adopt a formula on the rules of origin for preferential trade that require the local content to be not less than 35 percent of the ex-factory cost of the goods. COMESA member states have further agreed to establish a customs union with a common external tariff (of 0 percent, 5 percent, 15 percent, and 30 percent) by 2004. In the area of trade facilitation, the COMESA Secretariat is implementing a program to improve the transport and communications systems of the region. These include the adoption of Harmonized Road Transit Charges, a Yellow Card (vehicle insurance) Scheme, Customs Bond Guarantee Scheme, and an Advance Cargo Information System. To provide the required financial infrastructure and service support, COMESA has created specialized institutions in the form of a Trade and Development Bank, a Reinsurance company, and the COMESA Clearing House.[21] Institutional support in the form of a Court of Justice, formally created in June 1998, establishes COMESA as an institution with rules which can be enforced through a court of law. The Court will adjudicate and arbitrate on, inter alia, unfair trade practices, interpretation of the treaty, and ensuring that members comply with agreed decisions. In regard to immigration and the free movement of persons, four countries are already in full compliance, while others have committed themselves to fully implementing the protocol. The protocol on the free movement of persons will be implemented in several stages, with the first stage—the removal of visa requirements—to be completed by the year 2000.

B. The Southern African Development Community (SADC)[22]

44. In August 1992, a formal treaty providing for the establishment of SADC was adopted, superseding the Southern African Development Coordination Conference (SADCC).[23] This treaty called for the broadening of cooperation among member states in 20 sectors, including transport, health, tourism, mining, and water.

45. The SADC Trade and Development Protocol, signed in August 1996, seeks to establish a SADC Free Trade Area eight years after ratification and the gradual elimination of tariffs and NTBs to trade in the interim. The Protocol has been ratified by only five member states. Others are in agreement on a tariff liberalization program, currently being negotiated by the 11 original signatories of the Trade Protocol. This program is less ambitious than the one agreed by its own member countries under the CBI and under the COMESA. Current proposals call for the removal of all intraregional tariffs within eight years, but do not cover the liberalization of trade with non-SADC countries. Also, unlike agreements under the CBI, proposals regarding trade liberalization among SADC countries allow for special treatment of so-called "sensitive products" (in agriculture, agro-industry, and manufacturing), involving a slower phase-in for import tariff reductions. Moreover, some of the proposals being considered leave open the possibility of excluding some goods/sectors altogether from the trade liberalization exercise.

46. South Africa, on behalf of its partners in the South African Customs Union (SACU),[24] has offered to reduce its tariffs at a faster pace than non-SACU SADC countries, although a number of "sensitive" goods—dairy products, wheat, sugar, cotton, fabrics, leather footwear, and vehicles—will be subject to a slower liberalization process. Negotiations within SADC are being held each month under a Trade Negotiating Forum framework. The aim is to reach agreement on a full schedule of tariff reductions before the SADC Summit in August 1999.

C. SOUTHERN AFRICAN CUSTOMS UNION (SACU)

47. The Southern African Customs Union (SACU) was established in 1910 between the newly established Union of South Africa and the separate protectorates of Botswana, Lesotho, and Swaziland. The agreement was renegotiated in 1969 to reflect increases in the partner country shares of regional imports. Namibia became a member of SACU in 1990. The aims of the SACU are to encourage economic development and diversification, in particular in the less-advanced member countries, and afford all parties equitable benefits arising from intra-Union and international trade. The Customs Union Commission, comprising representatives of all the contracting parties, is the supreme consultative body of SACU and meets annually.

48. Under the SACU agreement, members apply the customs, excise, sales, antidumping, countervailing and safeguard duties, as well as related laws, set by South Africa, to goods imported to the common customs area from third countries outside the Union. A SACU member may enter separately into, or amend, trade agreements with a country outside the common customs area, provided the terms of such agreements or amendments do not conflict in any way with the provisions of the SACU agreements. Members may not impose duties or quantitative restrictions on goods grown, produced or manufactured in the SACU area and they may not impose any duties on importation, from any other member, of goods which were imported from outside the common customs area. Each member has its own legislation on quantitative restrictions on goods imported from outside the SACU area. Members, other than South Africa, may, following consultations, apply additional duties or increase duties for protection of infant industries. Rebates, refunds, and drawbacks granted by member countries must be identical, except in specified circumstances. Exceptional trade restrictions by a member may also be justified. There are marketing arrangements under which agricultural imports from other SACU countries may be restricted.

49. All customs, excise, sales and additional duties collected by SACU members are pooled and distributed to members. The shares of BLNS countries are determined on the basis of a revenue-sharing formula and the residual is allocated to South Africa. The original 1910 revenue sharing formula was based on the respective contribution of the BLNS countries to total imports into, and

consumption of excisable goods produced within, the SACU area. The 1969 formula provided for an enhancement factor of 42 percent of the shares of the BLNS countries; this factor was introduced to compensate the BLNS countries for negative effects resulting from their participation in SACU. These effects were: (i) the price-increasing effect of the customs union for the BLNS countries and the implicit protection for South African industry; (ii) the industrial polarization resulting from the tendency of industries to locate within the customs union to choose sites in South Africa; and (iii) the loss of fiscal discretion experienced by the BLNS partners because South Africa retained tariff-setting power for the region. Nontariff barriers applied by South Africa also had a negative effect on the size of the revenue pool. Subsequently, the revenue sharing formula was renegotiated in 1975 and a "stabilization factor" was added in 1978, operating retrospectively to 1974/75, to reduce fluctuation in the revenue shares accruing to the BLNS countries. The stabilization factor was centered on a mean of 20 percent of the tax base, with a lower bound of 17 percent and an upper bound of 23 percent. The tax base refers to the sum of duty-inclusive imports, c.i.f., and excise tax-inclusive value of goods produced in the Union and consumed in a particular BLNS country.

D. Commission for East African Cooperation (EAC)

50. The EAC between Kenya, Uganda, and Tanzania was established in November 1993, and is the most recent in a long line of regional integration arrangements between these three countries.[25] Through regional cooperation, the EAC seeks, inter alia, to:

- strengthen and consolidate cooperation in agreed fields with a view to bringing about equitable development among member states;
- establish a single market and investment area in the region; and
- promote sustainable utilization of the region's natural resources and effective protection of the environment.[26]

51. The main policy organs of the EAC are: the Summit of the Heads of State, the Permanent Tripartite Commission, the Coordination Commission, and the Secretariat. Since the launching of the EAC, the Tripartite Commission has concentrated on the identification and elimination of physical and policy related constraints, which could slow progress in the establishment of a single market and investment area. Accordingly, much of the work has focussed on formulation of programs to ease the movement of people, goods, services and capital; provide adequate and reliable basic infrastructure; harmonize standards, specifications, trade documentation and investment policies; harmonize macroeconomic and sectoral policies; provide trade financing and other facilities ancillary to the growth of exports; and achieve convertibility of the three East African currencies.

52. As a result of these activities, the EAC has achieved (i) full convertibility of the three East African currencies within the region; (ii) full liberalization of the external current account, and progress towards liberalization of the capital account; (iii) holding of pre- and post-budget consultations in order to harmonize monetary and fiscal policies; (iv) synchronization of the budget day of the three member countries; (v) development of a macroeconomic framework for the region to guide countries towards economic convergence; (vi) launching of the EAC Development Strategy, 1997—2000, which provides for guidelines for economic and social development; (vii) formation of an East African Securities Regulatory Authority to facilitate the establishment of an East African Stock Exchange and cross-listing of stocks; (viii) formation of East African Business Council, comprising private sector organizations to promote cross-border trade and investments; and (ix) the execution of tripartite agreements for the avoidance of double taxation, road transport, and inland waterways. In addition, efforts are underway to eliminate internal tariffs by July 1, 2000, for the launching of an East African passport, and the identification of a EAC designated transport network.

E. THE INDIAN OCEAN COMMISSION (IOC)

53. The IOC was established in December 1982 by Madagascar, Mauritius, and Seychelles, with the objective of promoting cooperation in trade, agriculture, fishing and ecosystem conservation, as well as cooperation in the cultural, scientific, technical and educational areas. While the IOC has developed a wide variety of regional programs, cooperation in the economic sector has been a priority, as reflected in the implementation of an Integrated Regional Program for Development of Trade (PRIDE)[27].

54. The overall objective of PRIDE is to strengthen regional trade integration, specifically by lifting the technical and financial constraints on the private sector of its members. PRIDE is expected to increase business competitiveness, enhance the quality of traded goods, and improve the availability and reliability of trade data. PRIDE has two main components: a macroeconomic component consisting of a general framework of actions to liberalize trade in goods and services, investment, capital movements, and the movement of people;[28] and a microeconomic component aimed at facilitating business contacts and partnerships such as participating in trade exhibitions and organizing trade missions.

55. As the IOC member states are also members of COMESA, they subscribe to the trade integration strategy of COMESA. The IOC has also been actively involved in all the preparatory meetings of the CBI, and expects to be involved in its implementation, particularly in those areas that fall within its purview.

Bibliography

International Monetary Fund, 1994, "Initiative for Promoting Cross-Border Trade, Investment, and Payments in Eastern and Southern Africa" SM/94/91 (Washington: International Monetary Fund).

——, 1996, "The Cross-Border Initiative in Eastern and Southern Africa" SM/96/94 (Washington: International Monetary Fund).

——, 1997, "Trade Liberalization in Fund-Supported Programs" EBS/97/113 (Washington: International Monetary Fund).

——, 1998, "Revenue Implications of Trade Liberalization" SM/98/254 (Washington: International Monetary Fund).

Mehran, Hassanali, and others, 1998, *Financial Sector Development in Sub-Saharan African Countries*, IMF Occasional Paper No. 169 (Washington: International Monetary Fund).

1 - Detailed background information (including on the principles underlying the CBI) was provided in "The Cross-Border Initiative in Eastern and Southern Africa" (SM/96/94, March 14, 1996), and "Initiative for Promoting Cross-Border Trade, Investment, and Payments in Eastern and Southern Africa" (SM/94/91, April 8, 1994).
2 - Comprising Burundi, Comoros, Kenya, Madagascar, Malawi, Mauritius, Namibia, Rwanda, Seychelles, Swaziland, Tanzania, Uganda, Zambia, and Zimbabwe. Recently, Mozambique has expressed its intention of joining the CBI.
3 - See SM/94/91 (Annex).
4 - The Meeting also requested the co-sponsors to prepare a Road Map for Investment Facilitation to be discussed at the Fourth Ministerial Meeting to be held in October 1999.
5 - The TWGs are to act as advisory committees and complement the policy work of the PICs.
6 - LCBIPs had to be completed before end-1995. However, LCBIPs have been agreed for all member countries, except for Burundi and Rwanda.
7 - The remaining two countries—Burundi and Zambia—have expressed the intention of accepting the obligations under Article VIII in the near future.
8 - Although Namibia and Swaziland, as members of the Common Monetary Area (CMA), peg their respective currencies to the South African Rand, an interbank market exists for the determination of forward rates. Comoros has a fixed exchange rate vis-à-vis the French franc, and since January 1, 1999, the Euro. Burundi's franc, and Seychelles' rupee are pegged to baskets of currencies of their main trading partners.
9 - In contrast to a common external tariff structure, the harmonization of external tariffs implies some flexibility for countries to establish their own tariff schedule, while agreeing with its regional partners on parameters such as the number of tariff bands and maximum and average tariffs.
10 - However, Kenya has "stand-by" tariffs on certain imports on top of regular tariffs.
11 - Since these measures were intended to facilitate land-based transportation, Madagascar, Mauritius, and Seychelles were not required to enact them. As for the SACU countries, the timing for the implementation of these measures depended on discussions with South Africa.
12 - This index combines measurements of the restrictiveness of tariffs and nontariff barriers, with a rating of "1" denoting the most open trade regime, and a rating of "10" the most restrictive. For purposes of analysis, countries with a rating of 7—10 were considered "restrictive"; rating of 5—6 "moderate"; and rating of 1—4 "open." For a more detailed description of the index, see "Trade Liberalization in Fund-Supported Programs," Annex I, EBS/97/113.

13 - The select group included non-CBI African countries which had medium-term adjustment programs supported by the Fund in the early to mid-1990s. Comprehensive estimates of the restrictiveness rating for non-CBI African countries in 1993 are not available.
14 - Five CBI countries have trade regimes that are as or less restrictive than that of the average industrial country.
15 - For a detailed analysis see "Revenue Implications of Trade Liberalization," SM/98/254 (November 17, 1998).
16 - See also "Financial Sector Development in Sub-Saharan African Countries," Occasional Paper 169 (1998), Appendix.
17 - Namibia and Swaziland, as members of the CMA, are heavily influenced by interest rate developments in South Africa, although differentials exist between rates in these two countries and South Africa due to differences in reserve and liquidity requirements.
18 - In practice, however, even the central banks with full autonomy face substantial interference from other branches of government.
19 - The need for its ratification has been overtaken by recent economic reforms such as improvements in investment related legislation which generally removed discrimination against foreign direct investment.
20 - At its inception COMESA had 10 members: Ethiopia, Kenya, Lesotho, Malawi, Mauritius, Somalia, Swaziland, Uganda, Zambia, and Zimbabwe. Since that time its membership has expanded to 21 members with the addition of Angola, Burundi, the Democratic Republic of the Congo, Comoros, Djibouti, Egypt, Eritrea, Madagascar, Rwanda, Sudan, Namibia, Seychelles, and Tanzania, and the withdrawal of Lesotho and Somalia. Mozambique was a member for part of the period.
21 - With the direct availability of foreign exchange to firms and importers, the utilization of the Clearing House has declined. A restructuring of the Clearing House is being considered so that it can improve the management of risk in cross-border payments, including a facility to provide guarantees against political risk.
22 - At its inception SADC had nine members: Angola, Botswana, Lesotho, Malawi, Mozambique, Swaziland, Tanzania, Zambia and Zimbabwe. Since then, five countriesCthe Democratic Republic of the Congo, Mauritius, Seychelles, Namibia, and South Africa have joined the Community.
23 - The SADCC was set up as a rather informal organization by the "frontline" countries with the objective of reducing economic dependence on South Africa. For the most part, the focus of the SADCC activities was on the implementation of projects.
24 - Consisting of South Africa and the BLNS (Botswana, Lesotho, Namibia, and Swaziland) countries.
25 - Consisting of the East African High Commission (1948—1961), the East African Common Services Organization (1961—1967), and the East African Community (1967—1977).
26 - To define in clearer terms how cooperation is to proceed, the Heads of State at the last Summit (April 1997), directed that a Treaty to upgrade the current cooperation agreement be prepared, thereby making regional integration more sustainable. It is expected that this Treaty will be signed by July 1999.
27 - Programme Regional Intégré de Développement des Echanges.
28 - Consensus was recently achieved in agreeing on the rules of origin adapted from the COMESA model.

SUMMARY OF THE ECONOMIC AND SOCIAL SITUATION IN AFRICA

I. INTRODUCTION

1. The present report reviews the performance of the African region in 1998 from the perspective of the capability of the region to attain the developmental objective of reducing poverty by half by the year 2015. This objective derives from the post-independence commitment of African Governments to improve the standard of living of their people. More recently, a consensus has emerged among African Governments and their development partners that this goal is the overarching objective of development in the continent. The latest articulation of this objective was at the Second Tokyo International Conference on African Development held in October 1998.

II. STATE OF THE AFRICAN ECONOMIES

2. For the fourth consecutive year, gross domestic product (GDP) in Africa grew faster than population, contrasting markedly with a decade and a half of declining per capita income. The 3.3 per cent growth in GDP in the region, compared with 2.9 per cent growth in 1997, was the highest in the world.

3. This growth is a very welcome achievement for Africa. However, the level of growth is below that necessary to have a significant impact on poverty. If Africa is to reduce poverty by half over the next decade and a half, it will need to attain and sustain an average growth rate of 7 per cent per annum. This is the major challenge for African policy makers and their development partners.

4. Recent growth of African economies is all the more remarkable considering the declining momentum in global growth. The world economy slowed to 2 per cent growth in 1998, from 4 per cent in 1997. The slowdown in Asia triggered by the East Asian currency crises rippled through the world in three ways. Market economies in emerging countries shrank as Governments pursued restrictive fiscal and monetary policies for curative and protective reasons. Globally, there was reduced demand for exports, and there was downward pressure on commodity prices. In combination, these factors contributed to the reduction of global trade from 6 per cent in 1997 to 2 per cent in 1998.

5. Using continent-wide averages for Africa can be misleading because substantial population and GDP differences exist among the subregions of North Africa, West Africa, Central Africa, East Africa and Southern Africa, and also within subregions. The five biggest economies of the continent (South Africa, Nigeria, Algeria, Egypt and Morocco) account for 37 per cent of the population

and 59 per cent of GDP. The 33 least developed countries have 45 per cent of the population and only 17 per cent of GDP. From another perspective, the 11 oil-exporting countries of Algeria, Egypt, the Libyan Arab Jamahiriya, Tunisia, Côte d'Ivoire, Nigeria, Cameroon, Gabon, the Congo, Angola and Equatorial Guinea account for 49 per cent of GDP and 36 per cent of the population.

6. Africa's positive aggregate economic performance in 1998 (3.3 per cent GDP growth, compared with 2.9 per cent in 1997) was not shared evenly across the continent. Only the North and Central African subregions grew in 1998; there were declines in the eastern, western and southern subregional rates of growth. The oil-exporting countries maintained their growth momentum as a group (3.7 per cent in 1998 versus 3.6 per cent the previous year), but growth in Gabon and Angola declined by half, while it increased in the Congo and Algeria. Largely because of the recovery in agriculture and the decline in oil prices, the non-oil-exporting countries grew at a level of 2.9 per cent, up from 2.3 per cent in 1997. It is encouraging that the 33 least developed countries increased their GDP growth rate from 2.4 per cent in 1997 to 4.1 per cent. Growth in the five largest economies (see para. 5 above) increased from 2.2 per cent to 3.1 per cent.Only two economies (the **Comoros** and the Democratic Republic of the Congo) had negative GDPgrowth in 1998 compared with four (the **Comoros**, the Democratic Republic of the Congo, the Congo and Morocco) in 1997. Still, only three countries (Botswana, the Congo and Equatorial Guinea) grew at levels of 7 per cent or more in 1998, the average growth rate required to reduce poverty by half by the year 2015.

7. Agriculture remains the dominant sector in Africa, and its recovery in 1998 fuelled GDP growth. Good weather and reforms, which improved the availability and distribution of modern inputs, including credit, contributed to the better performance. However, the removal of subsidies and the reduction of public extension services, which resulted from the reforms, negatively affected small producers in the agricultural sector. Constraints in the sector were aggravated by the decline in donor support for rural development projects and the reduction of investment in rural social services. These developments had a negative impact on the drive by African countries to attain food self-sufficiency.

8. The industrial sector grew by 3.2 per cent in 1998, down from 3.8 per cent in 1997. The fall in investment was one of the reasons for the drop in growth of the manufacturing subsector, from 2.5 per cent in 1997 to 2.0 per cent in 1998, although weak competitiveness due largely to relatively low productivity were also factors.

9. The recession in emerging markets was transmitted to Africa mainly through depressed commodity prices. All of Africa's exportable products were affected, with oil experiencing the largest fall. But the decline in oil prices did benefit the oil-importing African countries.

10. There was serious pressure on the balance of payments in 1998. Export revenue declined by 17 per cent. For the first time in the decade of the 1990s, the trade balance turned negative, boosting the current account deficit to a high of $16 billion. The perennial imbalance in the services sector, driven by external debt payments and the cost of transport and financial services, continued to put pressure on the current account balance and to claim an inordinate share of foreign revenue from merchandise exports.

11. Resource flows into Africa declined to $3 billion from $4.5 billion in 1997 as a result of reduced private flows and bilateral credit. For sub-Saharan countries, net transfers declined by nearly 40 per cent. The ratio of debt stock to GDP increased moderately and the ratio to exports grew steeply because of the latter's decline. Debt service increased to $35 billion, or 31 per cent of goods and services exports. Ongoing debt reduction initiatives did not significantly affect the debt burden. Only one country of the 41 potentially eligible has benefited from the Heavily Indebted Poor Countries Debt Initiative. That country, Uganda, had its debt reduced by 20 per cent. Only four additional countries (Burkina Faso, Côte d'Ivoire, Mali and Mozambique) are currently scheduled to receive actual debt reduction in the next three years.

12. Investment as a percentage of GDP increased from 21 per cent in 1997 to 23 per cent, mainly because of a 1 per cent increase in domestic savings. Higher incomes and lower consumption, especially in the public sector, were the major contributory factors in the change in domestic savings.

13. Inflation declined from 15 per cent in 1997 to 12 per cent. Increased agricultural production and the fall in the price of imports helped to contain consumer prices. The decline in external trade resulted in an increase in government deficits due to reduced revenues from international trade taxes.

14. Medium-term prospects are brightened by the past four years of increased GDP growth. However, two key determinants of future growth are weather and the external economic environment, which are both exogenously determined. It is unlikely that good weather can be counted on every year although it has occurred for the last four. And the global economy seems unlikely to change for the better over the medium term.

III. CHALLENGE OF REDUCING POVERTY IN AFRICA

15. Until recently, information to measure the extent and severity of Africa's poverty was inadequate for most countries . The key data used for this purpose are from surveys of household income and expenditure that are time-consuming and expensive to complete. Fortunately, sufficient data now exist for some African countries to make these calculations possible. Data used in the present

report are for countries that have 60 per cent of the total population of Africa, and which accounted for 76 per cent of the continent's GDP in 1998.

16. The relevant measure of standard of living is usually taken as the per capita income of society in advanced countries and per capita consumption expenditure (including the consumption of own production) for developing countries. The poverty line can be calculated and the ratio of poor to the total population (the head-count ratio) can be derived. Alternative approaches combine indicators of well- being, such as per capita income, life expectancy, infant mortality and primary school enrolment.

17. Analysis of income distribution in Africa shows a fairly high degree of inequality. Compared with other regions of the world, Africa has the second most unequal income distribution next to Latin America. The Gini coefficient for Africa as a whole is 44.4 per cent. The highest values for inequality are for South Africa, Kenya and Zimbabwe, the lowest for Egypt, Ghana and Algeria. The picture of relatively high inequality is confirmed by shares of total expenditure by quintiles.

18. Although 44 per cent of Africa's population live below the region-wide poverty line of $39 per capita per month, the depth and incidence of poverty varies between and within subregions. In the North Africa subregion, only 22 per cent are under the poverty line of $54 per capita per month, while sub-Saharan Africa has 51 per cent below the poverty line of $34 per capita per month. Significantly more poor people live in the rural areas. The average income of the rural poor is only $14 per person per month, compared with an average of $27 per month for the urban poor.

19. To reduce poverty by half in Africa by the year 2015 will require a 4 per cent reduction in the ratio of people living in poverty each year. Change in poverty can arise for two reasons: a change due to growth in mean consumption expenditure (appropriately adjusted for the change in the poverty line); and a change in the distribution of income (the inequality measure). For Africa as a whole, GDP growth of about 7 per cent per annum would be required to achieve this annual reduction in poverty. Increases of 5–6 per cent are needed for North Africa and Southern Africa, 6–7 per cent for Central Africa, and 7–8 per cent for the West and East African subregions.

20. For Africa as a whole, investment of 33 per cent of GDP would be needed to reach 7 per cent per annum growth, to be financed partly by domestic savings and the rest by foreign inflows. The current domestic savings rate is about 15 per cent. Thus, a further 18 per cent would be needed from external sources. Official development assistance (ODA) for the continent averages about 9 per cent, which leaves a residual financing gap of about 9 per cent.

21. Africa-wide averages hide large variations among the subregions. North Africa needs only about 5 per cent of GDP in external resources to complete the financing needed to generate a GDP growth rate high enough to halve the poverty level in the subregion by 2015. ODA to the subregion has averaged about 3 per cent of GDP, leaving a financing gap of about 2 per cent of GDP. Financing investment for needed GDP growth is most difficult in Central Africa, where the residual financing gap is about 27 per cent.

22. Recent foreign resource flows to Africa have been far short of the volume needed to meet the poverty reduction objective. Africa must address the key issue of raising domestic savings rates, but in the short run any expectation of significant change is unrealistic in view of the existing low levels of income. Given these rather stark realities, what are the key policy issues for the development of Africa? Clearly, in this globalized world, the international economic environment has an impact on Africa. Commodity prices are beyond the control of African policy makers, and ODA flows and dealing with the debt overhang can be influenced only indirectly by maintaining exemplary domestic economic management. ODA and debt issues require the assistance of Africa's development partners.

23. Policy issues that can be addressed directly by African policy makers relate to domestic savings and external resource inflows other than conventional ODA, such as foreign direct investment, and the causes of capital flight. Stabilization of the macroeconomy will stimulate savings by creating an economic environment where private agents can plan their future with a large measure of confidence. Moreover, prudent government behaviour and fiscal discipline will be expected to contribute to increased savings.

24. Financial liberalization will theoretically lead to higher savings through the effects of high real interest rates on savings. However, most empirical work suggests that the effect of interest rates on gross savings is weak or non-existent. The most important determinant of savings in Africa has been found to be the level of real income. Very poor people save little or nothing, and income must rise above the subsistence level before increases in income result in higher savings. For example, it would take 18 years of 5.3 per cent GDP growth for sub-Saharan Africa to reach the income threshold where further increases result in increased savings rates. More research is needed to advance understanding of the factors determining savings rates in sub-Saharan countries. Current understanding of the linkage between interest rates and savings indicates that African Governments have few policy instruments to increase savings in the medium run and for as long as incomes remain low.

25. Africa has suffered massive capital flight, estimated to total $22 billion between 1982 and 1991. At the end of 1991, the average ratio of capital flight to debt was estimated at over 40 per cent for a sample of 18 countries for which

data were available. For four countries, the rate exceeded 60 per cent (Nigeria: 94.5 per cent; Rwanda: 94.3 per cent; Kenya: 74.4 per cent; and the Sudan: 60.5 per cent).

26. A number of former and current top African officials are thought to hold huge foreign currency denominated accounts outside their continent. Most of these assets are believed to be the result of rent-seeking and corrupt activities. Whatever the sources and wherever they are, these resources need to be invested in Africa. A difficult question is what African Governments can do to obtain the repatriation of those funds, and how the countries in which the accounts are held can be persuaded to be of assistance.

27. Foreign direct investment (FDI) is needed as a non-debt-creating form of resource inflow. But experience shows the share of FDI flows to Africa is very small and is highly biased in favour of mineral-rich countries. FDI in Africa seems to be caught in a vicious circle since it requires a hospitable economic environment and sustained high growth. Yet FDI is needed to help create that environment and achieve that rate of growth.

28. The underdeveloped human resource base — exacerbated by outmigration of skilled Africans — and the weak physical infrastructure of the continent deter foreign direct investment. Yet huge investments are needed to develop a skilled labour force and expand transport, communications, energy and related infrastructure. Domestic private sector resources are inadequate to meet these challenges. Foreign direct investment could help. However, given the large volume of investment needed and the low domestic savings rate, targeted mechanisms and special arrangements may be required to entice FDI into these areas. In addition, strategies need to be devised to increase productivity and make judicious use of whatever domestic and foreign resources Governments can mobilize to enhance investment and growth. African countries will need to deepen and expand their reforms, while making sure that the process supports rather than constrains investment. It is important to recognize that persistently high real interest rates engendered by financial liberalization without sufficient institutional development to foster competition, and exchange rates that do not reflect the true scarcity of foreign exchange or that fluctuate wildly can distort investment incentives and decisions. Similarly, trade liberalization that confers undue advantage on foreign competitors has not been conducive to the expansion of domestic investment in the past.

29. Furthermore, political and civil instability, weak institutional capacity and inefficiencies have not created an investment-friendly climate. These conditions have had important negative implications for resource mobilization and utilization in Africa, including exacerbating capital flight. They will therefore need to be given urgent attention.

IV. PERFORMANCE AND SUSTAINABILITY OF AFRICAN ECONOMIES

30. In 1998, Africa enjoyed its fourth consecutive year of positive GDP growth despite global financial and currency turmoil. But this favourable outcome cannot be assumed to mean that the aggregate African economy has crossed the critical threshold to a self-sustainable poverty-reducing growth path. For this to be true, the global environment and exogenous shocks would have changed permanently for the better and/or the domestic foundations for sustainable development would have been put into place. Unfortunately, the global environment and exogenous shocks are not changing in Africa's favour. ODA is stagnant or declining, little progress has been made in reducing the debt burden, protectionist tendencies continue in Africa's major markets and erratic weather conditions persist.

31. Current growth theory posits a specific group of variables and factors to constitute economic growth fundamentals. Macroeconomic stability and other steps are needed to reduce transaction costs, raise returns on investment, reduce risks to investors, improve human capital, improve international competitiveness and address the problems of poverty and inequality. To test whether or not Africa has built a critical mass of momentum towards sustained poverty-reducing growth requires the use of multiple evaluation criteria. Unfortunately, comprehensive Africa-specific composite indices needed for this purpose are not available.

32. An effective evaluation process requires a broad and consistent framework that reflects the current and future capabilities and aspirations of Africa's people and the functions and constraints of its Governments. The overall economic role of the State, it is generally agreed, is the sustainable improvement of the well-being of its citizens, which subsumes standard functions relating to economic growth and stability. Human well-being is central to the notion and measurement of economic development. Broadly speaking, economic policies and performances are deemed good if their impact on well-being is both positive and sustainable. More specifically, an evaluative framework should focus on three dimensions — the impact of policies and performance on well-being; the consistency of policies with the desirable and feasible economic functions of the State; and the sustainability of policies and performance.

33. The definition and measurement of well-being can be approached in two ways. First, by using the constituents of well-being, such as nutrition levels, educational attainments and life expectancy. The second is by using determinants, such as income levels and the availability of educational and health services. In practice, the simultaneous use of both criteria is required.

34. Four elements are used to measure the quality of life — income levels, health status, educational attainment and political and civil liberties. Thus, economic development can be viewed as a sustainable and sustained increase in real

incomes; improvements in health and educational status; and widening of the freedoms of people.

35. In Africa, one way of summarizing the objective of enhancing well-being, which also translates into the main object of development, is the eradication of poverty. Poverty can be viewed as having two main dimensions — material poverty (measured in levels of income) and human poverty (measured in terms of health, education and liberties).

36. The consensus is that the State can and should promote economic development, and through it the well-being of its citizens. In a market economy, the basic economic functions of the State include maintaining law and order; ensuring macroeconomic stability and an incentives-compatible microeconomic environment; investing in basic social services (health and education) and infrastructure (transport and communications networks); and protecting vulnerable people and the environment. To the extent that these functions enlarge the economic space for efficient and effective enterprise and growth, empower citizens to make choices, protect the environment for future generations, and assist the weak and vulnerable in living a meaningful life, they have a positive impact on well-being.

V. STATE OF WELL-BEING, 1998

37. The well-being of Africans is measured in terms of income, health, education and freedoms — the four factors mentioned above. For the first three of these, per capita income, life expectancy at birth, infant mortality and adult literacy are the proxies measured and compared using Borda rankings. These are ordinal indices, using country scores that are the sums of the rank that a country obtains according to the level of each of the variables in the welfare index (hence, equal weight is given to each variable). The sum of the rankings for each country in terms of real per capita GDP, life expectancy at birth, infant mortality and adult illiteracy yields the Borda rank. The best performer has the highest scores, the worst the lowest. For the 46 countries with complete data, results are used to rank countries by indices and then to test for correlation among rankings. The focus is on the 10 countries with the highest scores and the 10 with the lowest scores.

38. The countries with the lowest Borda scores (in ascending order, Sierra Leone, Mali, Burundi, Mozambique, Malawi, Ethiopia, the Niger, Chad, the Gambia, Guinea-Bissau, Burkina Faso and Uganda)[1] come from all subregions except North Africa. They are mainly tropical countries with relatively low resource endowment. They include both large and small countries. Eight are landlocked (Malawi, Mali, the Niger, Uganda, Ethiopia, Burundi, Burkina Faso and Chad) although the significance of this fact is unclear since there are landlocked countries that have performed well (such as Botswana and

Zimbabwe). Most have experienced recent political instability. Although the precise relationship between conflict and low levels of well-being is not quantifiable, past neglect and destruction of assets are probable factors.

39. The highest-scoring countries (in ascending order, Egypt, Gabon, Morocco, Cameroon, Botswana, Swaziland, Algeria, Cape Verde, Tunisia, the Libyan Arab Jamahiriya, South Africa, Mauritius and Seychelles)[1] are predominantly from the North and Southern African subregions. Two of them — Botswana and Swaziland — are landlocked. Population densities are not particularly high. Eight have enjoyed political stability for long periods (all except South Africa and Algeria).

40. The close relationship between income and well-being is confirmed in reference to these two indices. Eight of the 10 best performers selected by per capita income belong to the top 10 countries in the Borda rankings (the exceptions are Cameroon and Swaziland in the Borda top-10 score, replaced in per capita score by Gabon and Namibia). The sets of bottom-10 countries in the two rankings share five countries (Mozambique, Ethiopia, Sierra Leone, Burundi and Malawi). This relationship suggests that citizens of countries with higher per capita incomes are more likely to achieve better well-being. Also, the results suggest that policies targeted primarily at raising incomes can help to improve the overall well-being of communities.

41. With regard to the relationship between well-being and competitiveness, the Borda rankings are compared with the Africa competitiveness index (ACI), which was computed by the World Economic Forum and the Harvard Institute for International Development. ACI consists of a weighted average of six sub-indices covering openness to international trade, the size and role of government, finance, infrastructure, labour and institutions. The positive statistical correlation between the ACI and Borda rankings confirms that welfare and competitiveness move in the same direction. The implication is that policies that enhance the competitiveness of countries are likely to contribute to improving the welfare of their citizens.

42. It is argued that a major determinant of both FDI and capital flight is the risk perception that investors associate with individual countries and groups of related countries. The status of well-being can be expected to relate to investment through the growth-investment link. Several organizations attempt to measure and publish information on investment risk. One such ranking is the institutional investor country risk ratings (IICRR), which covers 35 African countries. A comparison of the 10 countries at the bottom of the Borda and IICRR rankings reveals only two countries in both (Sierra Leone and Mali). Nevertheless, all the bottom-10 IICRR countries for which there are Borda scores are identified as comparatively poor performers by the latter. By contrast, the two rankings share seven top-10 countries (Mauritius, Botswana, Tunisia, South Africa, Egypt,

Morocco and Seychelles). It appears that countries with higher IICRR scores are also more likely to achieve better welfare outcomes.

VI. PERFORMANCE AND SUSTAINABILITY

43. A central issue in economic performance and policy evaluation is the question of sustainability, which explains why some African countries labelled "high performers" at one time drop out of the club. Sustainability is defined in terms of three attributes: the consistency of the observed short-run outcomes with stated long-term goals; continuing replicability of observed (positive) outcomes in the future; and laying the foundations for take-off and ensuring a stable acceleration path. In the Economic Commission for Africa (ECA) indices, emphasis is given to key elements of sustainability, including macroeconomic indicators, structural diversification, dependency, transaction costs/ competitiveness and human capital development. Outcomes are also affected by non-policy factors, such as the international economic environment, initial resource endowments, external shocks (terms of trade, financial flows, weather), donor preferences and civil political conflicts. Accordingly, the indices used in the present report separate policy and non-policy factors. We plan to refine the indicators further in future reports.

44. Three indicators reported here have been newly created by ECA: the annual performance trend index; the economic sustainability index, and the economic policy stance index.

45. The annual performance trend index (APTI) measures improvement or decline in current account balance, inflation and per capita income (this is only a year-on-year measure). Its results can be presented from two perspectives: country performance, and population benefiting from performance improvements or negatively affected by decline. Thirty-two of the 50 African countries for which data were available experienced some improvement in 1998; only 17 countries were worse off. Yet only the Central and North African subregions experienced significant progress in 1998. Southern Africa was basically unchanged, and the East and West African subregions declined (the latter heavily influenced by Nigeria's performance). Fourteen countries had negative ratings, including five of the 11 oil-exporting countries (Gabon, Libya, Algeria, Angola and Nigeria).

46. It is important to note that 14 of the lowest-scoring countries recently experienced or are currently experiencing some form of civil conflict or social upheaval. From the point of view of shares of the population affected by gains and losses, through cluster analysis APTI paints a mixed picture. For the majority of the population of Africa, there was little if any improvement in economic conditions. This is because a majority of the population lives in countries that score poorly on the index, largely because of negative commodity price

developments. The analysis highlights the vulnerability of African economies to exogenous economic and non-economic shocks.

47. To complement the short-term focus of APTI, the economic sustainability index (ESI) has been constructed as a measure of a country's capacity to maintain long-term economic growth. ESI is currently composed of 21 different indicators covering five categories — human capital development, structural diversification, dependency, transaction costs and macroeconomic aspects of sustainability. More indicators will be added in future reports to enhance its utility as an information resource.

48. Using ESI, Equatorial Guinea, South Africa, Botswana, Mauritius and Tunisia are the top five. Notably, three of those countries (South Africa, Botswana and Mauritius) enjoy a high level of resource endowment. Equatorial Guinea, which has enjoyed impressive performance in recent years due to a sudden oil boom, has yet to deepen and broaden its developmental parameters to confirm its capacity for sustainable growth. More data for Equatorial Guinea and Botswana on structural diversity and transaction costs would make the result more robust.

49. The countries at the bottom of the ESI rankings have some history of civil conflict (Sierra Leone, the Niger, Benin, Uganda, the Central African Republic and Rwanda). Subregionally, the Southern and North African subregions rate considerably higher than Central Africa. The East and West African subregions are at the bottom. Over two thirds of the countries are classified as having low sustainability — including large and small countries, natural resource-rich and natural resource-poor countries, countries with good policies and countries with bad policies — and are found in all parts of Africa except the Maghreb.

50. The economic policy stance index (EPSI) measures the appropriateness of government monetary and fiscal policy. Indicators relate to budgets, taxation, monetary growth and interest rates. Incomplete information has limited coverage to only 33 countries. As with ESI, countries are scored from one to 10 based on how they compare with the average of the three best. Ethiopia, Egypt, the Congo, Seychelles and South Africa fill the top five positions in the ranking. With the exception of the Congo, the policy stance of all of these countries also has relatively high approval ratings from the World Bank. No country achieved the best-practice score of seven. The top two countries scored above five (Seychelles and South Africa). In the cluster analysis, however, nearly a third of the countries scored in the cluster associated with good performance, and only a handful of countries rated as poor. This suggests the emphasis on policy reform in recent years has resulted in significant progress although there is still some distance to go.

VII. INTERRELATIONSHIP BETWEEN INDICES

51. Correlation analysis is used to test the connections among the performance, sustainability and policy stance indices. APTI shows little correlation with the other variables, suggesting that an African economy's performance in a given year is not strongly connected to sustainability or well-being. ESI shows a significant degree of correlation between most of the other variables, implying that long-term sustainability is linked to improved standards of living, reduction in poverty, and an environment more conducive to investment. EPSI correlates significantly with the sustainability, well-being, competitiveness and human development indices, suggesting that policy improvements can lead to improvements in these areas as well.

VIII. SOME OBSERVATIONS ON POLICY IMPLICATIONS

52. The pilot application of indices for 1998 has been limited to variables that are quantifiable and for which there are available data. Even this modest effort has yielded interesting results.

53. While four countries (Botswana, Mauritius, South Africa and Equatorial Guinea) score high on the ESI index, only three of them — Botswana, Mauritius and South Africa — satisfy the minimal requirements to sustain growth and development. These countries enjoy a high degree of human capital development, and have fairly well diversified economies and relatively low transactions cost. Equatorial Guinea scores high on the sustainability index despite the non-diversification of the economy mainly due to high macroeconomic indicators of sustainability driven by the oil revenues since the early 1990s.

54. It is of singular importance to underline the fact that an economy's performance in a particular year is not indicative of its overall strength and long-term potential. This is significant for Africa's economies since many of them are prone to exogenous shocks that could have a negative impact on their positive performance from year to year. African countries therefore need to take effective measures to plan for and mitigate the crippling effects of negative natural and environmental phenomena through better scientific and policy understanding and proactive programmes to apply science and technology in solving environmental and natural resource-based constraints. Africa must also come to grips with natural and man-made human catastrophes, particularly the scourge of civil wars and conflict and the human immunodeficiency virus/acquired immunodeficiency syndrome (HIV/AIDS) pandemic, which have undermined the sustainability of development.

55. The frequency with which countries enter and drop out of the list of "high" or "good" performers has been a cause of concern. While policies are very important, they are by no means sufficient to sustain development. The unfortunate neglect of the sustainability variables — macroeconomic factors

(savings-investment and exports), human capital, institutions, structural diversification, transaction costs and competitiveness, as well as environmental and ecological balance — must have been the major cause of Africa's fragile economic performance over time.

56. For most of the African countries now on the verge of recovery, the capacity to sustain growth and development over time is very low. The key mistake of the past two decades has been the focus on macroeconomic stabilization while capacity, structural and institutional elements were neglected. Achieving stabilization has entailed sacrificing expenditures needed to build the requisite institutions and infrastructure, and invest in human capital development and retention. Policies with the twin goals of macroeconomic stability and sustainability have either not been drawn up and adopted or are not being implemented. These are the urgent tasks at hand.

57. The analysis and process of constructing the indicators of performance, sustainability and policy stance underscore the many challenges facing decision makers in moving forward with the Africa development agenda — implementing and sustaining macroeconomic reforms; human capital development; diversification of the economy; institutional development; competitiveness and the capacity of the economy to internally generate resources etc. These challenges call for appropriate policy response by Africa's decision makers. While the present report focuses on key indicators of economic performance and sustainability, which have been developed by ECA, subsequent reports will, in addition to further refining the indices, address the key policy challenges for Africa underlying a particular sustainability index component or components thereof. The ultimate objective is to help focus policy advice on longer- term structural issues while responding to the shorter- term issues and measures that have tended to dominate economic policy discourse.

ANNUAL ECONOMIC REPORT ON THE OIC COUNTRIES 2001

1. INTRODUCTION

The *Annual Economic Report on the OIC Countries* analyses the economic situation in the OIC countries during the most recent five-year period for which the data are available. It examines the major economic developments in the OIC member countries and investigates the inter-linkages of these developments with those in both developing and developed countries as well as the world economy as a whole. The analysis is usually carried out in the light of the global, regional and national developments, using the Centre's Statistical Data Base (BASEIND) which includes current data on OIC member countries, specially compiled from various national and international sources.

This year's Report analyses the recent trends in the major economic indicators of the OIC countries in the light of the recovery in the world economy in 1999-2000 after the severe slowdown in the wake of the Asian financial crisis of 1997-98. In this context, the Report also considers the signs of weakening economic activity coming late in 2000 and early 2001 in major economies, particularly in the US economy, and, thus, the significantly weakened prospects for global growth in 2001.

In view of this situation, the Report shows that, as a substantial part of the developing countries, the OIC countries as a group followed in general the same trends. However, economic growth and recovery in the OIC countries remained below the levels maintained by the developing countries. This indicates that the OIC countries, unlike the developing countries, were, as a group, unable to benefit enough from the strengthening of world economic activity in 1999-2000. In this regard, the Report shows a mixed picture, with a number of extraordinary challenges confronting the OIC countries in their efforts to further economic progress.

In addition, the Report devotes a special section to discuss the impact of the volatility in world commodity prices on economic performance of the OIC commodity exporting countries, particularly the non-oil commodities. This version of the Report is based on statistical data and information available up to the end of March 2001.

2. RECENT DEVELOPMENTS IN THE WORLD ECONOMY

Given the strength of world economic activity in late 1999 and early 2000, global output grew by 4.8 percent in 2000 compared to 3.5 percent in 1999. However, with the signs of greater than expected weakening coming late in 2000, the prospects for global growth have weakened significantly. In this regard, the IMF expected a slowdown in world economic activity in 2001, with global growth projected at 3.2 percent. According to the same report, this was led by a marked slowdown in the United States by the end of 2000, a stalling recovery in Japan, and a moderate growth in Europe and in a number of emerging market countries.

Over the past several years, the strong expansion in the US economy has been instrumental in stabilizing global activity in the face of weak demand elsewhere. However, after a strong start, economic growth in the United States slowed sharply by the end of 2000. Although, for the year as a whole, real GDP expanded by 5 per cent, growth slowed to a rate of just 1 per cent in the fourth quarter, reflecting mainly the surge in oil prices and the tightening of financial conditions, including the drop in US dollar appreciation. This led to a GDP growth projection of 1.5 percent in 2001, the lowest for a decade. Therefore, if the current slowdown in the US economy is to prove deeper and more prolonged, this would pose several inter-linked risks of spillovers to other countries through financial market and confidence effects, and thus to the global economy as a whole.

On the other hand, after a three-year period of economic stagnation, economic activity in the European Union picked up in 2000 with a 3.4 per cent growth in real GDP compared with 2.6 per cent in 1999. However, growth eased in the second half of the year, mostly reflecting the negative effect of higher oil prices on purchasing power. In early 2001, business confidence has weakened and signs of slowing industrial activity have intensified. Thus, real GDP growth in 2001 is expected to remain relatively well sustained at 2.4 per cent, exceeding growth in the United States for the first time since 1991. However, although the global slowdown and financial market weakness are having an adverse impact on economic activity, growth in the euro area is expected to be lessened mainly by domestic demand.

In Japan, the 1.7 per cent increase in economic activity in 2000 was driven mainly by a strong first quarter. However, by the second half of the year, private consumption was weighed down by uncertainties regarding future economic prospects, and industrial activity was dampened by the slowdown in foreign demand and the downturn in the information technology cycle. Banking lending continued to contract, reflecting weak credit demand and ongoing financial system weaknesses. Low public investment and weak external demand are estimated to have made negative contributions to growth after midyear. Due to all these developments, the growth forecast for 2001 has been marked down to 0.6 per cent.

In Asia, the continuing recovery from the 1997-98 crisis led to a GDP growth of 6.9 per cent in 2000. In particular, growth in the newly industrialised Asian countries exhibited a notable turnaround from a 2.4 per cent contraction in 1998 to a real GDP growth of 8.2 percent in 2000. However, following rapid growth in the first half of the year, the pace of activity has since fallen back markedly. Thus, in 2001 growth is expected to decline to 5.9 per cent in the region as a whole, and to 3.8 per cent in the group of newly industrialised Asian countries. While a slowdown from the high growth rates during the recovery period was expected, this also reflected some other factors, including higher oil prices, slowing growth in the US, the downturn in the global electronics cycle, and the lagging pace of corporate and financial restructuring in a number of countries.

In the case of the developing countries as a group, the slow recovery achieved in 1999 accelerated in 2000, with average real GDP growth recorded at 5.8 per cent compared to 3.8 per cent in 1999. Economic growth picked up, albeit unevenly, in all developing regions in 2000. This was markedly in Latin America and in Middle East and North Africa regions. In Latin America, GDP growth picked up to 4.1 percent in 2000 from a mere 0.2 per cent in 1999. This was aided by active US demand, higher oil prices, and a recovery in domestic demand from the depressed levels of 1999. In the Middle East and North Africa, GDP growth picked up to 4.5 percent in 2000 from 2.7 per cent in 1999. This was aided by higher oil revenues, as oil prices rebounded in 1999-2000, leading to a substantial improvement in fiscal and external imbalances in many countries in the region. However, due to the signs of weakened world economic activity by the end of 2000, particularly in the Asian region, growth in 2001 is expected to decline slightly to 5 per cent in the developing countries as a group.

As a substantial part of the developing countries, the OIC countries as a group followed in general the same trends. However, as we shall see in the next section, economic growth and recovery in the OIC countries remained below the levels maintained by the developing countries. This indicates that the OIC countries, unlike the developing countries, were, as a group, unable to benefit enough from the strengthening of world economic activity.

3. MAJOR DEVELOPMENTS IN THE OIC COUNTRIES

3.1. OVERVIEW

The OIC region is geographically vast. The current 57 OIC member countries are dispersed over a large area on four continents, extending from Albania (Europe) in the north to Mozambique (Africa) in the south, and from Guyana (Latin America) in the west to Indonesia (Asia) in the east. As such, the OIC countries as a group account for one sixth of the world area and one fifth of the world population. The OIC member countries constitute a substantial part of the world developing countries. However, being at different levels of economic development, they do not make up a homogeneous economic group. As a group, the OIC countries are well-endowed with potential economic resources in different fields and sectors, such as agriculture and arable land, energy and mining, human resources, and a vast strategic trading region. Yet, this inherent potential does not manifest itself in the form of reasonable levels of economic and human development in many OIC countries and in the OIC countries as a group.

In 2000, the OIC countries as a group accounted for only 4.5 per cent of the world GDP in current US dollars and 8.1 per cent of the world merchandise exports (see Table A.3 and Table A.8 in the Annex). The average real per capita GDP grew by 2.2 percent, corresponding only to a mere 0.1 percent above the average population growth rate, and still significantly lower than the same rate recorded by the developing countries in the same year (Table 3). The picture becomes worse when we consider the OIC countries' external debt. According to the World Bank's classification of all economies according to their indebtedness in January 2001, 23 OIC countries are classified as severely indebted countries and another 15 countries are classified as moderately indebted countries (World Bank, *Global Development Finance 2001*, pp. 150-51). For more details about the foreign debt problem in the OIC countries, see Table A.14 and SESRTCIC, *The External Debt Situation of Sub-Saharan African OIC Countries: The enhanced HIPC Scheme*.

Against this concise background, the rest of this section examines in detail the trends in major economic indicators of the OIC countries in the five-year period of 1996-2000, in comparison with those of both developing and developed countries as well as the trends in the world economy as a whole. However, it is important to point out in this regard that since the OIC countries, unlike the industrial countries, are not made up of an economically homogeneous group, overall group analysis is rather difficult and may conceal some underlying factors. For this reason, an attempt has been made to divide the OIC countries into 4 sub-groups, which, presumably, would better illustrate the developments and the overall performance within the OIC countries.

The first group includes the least developed member countries of the OIC, which will be named, hereafter, the **OIC-LDC group**. This group is made up of those members of the OIC which are designated as least developed countries by the United Nations, namely Afghanistan, Bangladesh, Benin, Burkina Faso, Chad, Comoros, Djibouti, Gambia, Guinea, Guinea-Bissau, Maldives, Mali, Mauritania, Mozambique, Niger, Sierra Leone, Somalia, Sudan, Togo, Uganda and Yemen.

The second group includes, generally, the middle-income OIC countries, which will be named, hereafter, the **OIC-MIC group**. These are Cameroon, Egypt, Guyana, Indonesia, Ivory Coast (a new member country), Jordan, Lebanon, Malaysia, Morocco, Pakistan, Senegal, Surinam, Syria, Tunisia, and Turkey.

The third group comprises the oil-exporting members of the OIC, which will be named, hereafter, the **OIC-OEC group**. These are Algeria, Bahrain, Brunei, Gabon, Iran, Iraq, Kuwait, Libya, Nigeria, Oman, Qatar, Saudi Arabia, and the United Arab Emirates (U.A.E.).

The last group comprises the Central Asian member countries in transition, which will be named, hereafter, the **OIC-TC group**. These are Albania, Azerbaijan, Kazakhstan, Kyrgyz Republic, Tajikistan, Turkmenistan, and Uzbekistan.

The averages of the major economic indicators for these sub-groups and for the group of the OIC countries as a whole were computed on the basis of percentage changes for individual countries weighted by 1996 GDP values in terms of the US dollar.

3.2. STRUCTURE OF THE ECONOMY

In this sub-section, we present an overall picture of the structure of the OIC economies based on an analysis of the sectoral distribution of the output (GDP) and the reflection of this picture in the structure of the main source of export earnings. Table 1 below displays the averages of sectoral shares in GDP for the different sub-groups of OIC countries and for the OIC countries as a group. The average of the five-year period (1995-99) has been computed in order to avoid the problems resulting from missing data for some countries, and the effects of year-to-year cyclical fluctuations in others.

TABLE 1: STRUCTURE OF OUTPUT
(Value added as % of GDP, average 1995-99)

	Agriculture	Industry: Of which	Services

			Manufacture	
OIC-LDC	30.3	22.0	11.6	50.0
OIC-MIC	17.9	34.0	21.6	46.9
OIC-OEC	12.5	47.5	9.0	39.8
OIC-TC	23.7	30.1	13.8	46.1
OIC countries	**16.7**	**38.4**	**15.9**	**44.2**

Source: Table A.4 in the Annex.

With the highest share in GDP (44.2 per cent), the services sector plays a major role and constitutes an important source of income in almost all the OIC countries. The highest share of services in GDP (50 per cent) was recorded in the OIC-LDC group and the lowest share of services in GDP (39.8 per cent) recorded in the OIC-OEC group. At the individual country level, this share exceeds 50 per cent in 19 countries and 30 per cent in 51 countries, and falls below that level only in 2 countries. The shares vary from 9 per cent in Nigeria to 77 per cent in Djibouti (Table A.4 in the Annex).

With a 38.4 per cent share in the GDP, industry constitutes the second major economic activity in the OIC countries as a group. The highest share of industry in GDP (47.5 per cent) is registered in the OIC-OEC group, and the lowest share (22 per cent) in the OIC-LDC. At the individual country level, the share of industry in GDP varies from 13 per cent in Benin to 56 per cent in Nigeria. This share exceeds 33.0 per cent in 18 OIC countries, of which 13 are oil-exporting countries (Table A.4 in the Annex). Such a significant role of industry in the economies of these countries is to be expected because oil production is classified under industrial activities. Yet, the share of industry in the GDP of an economy, per se, does not reflect the industrialisation level of that economy. Therefore, the performance of the manufacturing sector must also be considered.

Agriculture is widely known to be the primary economic activity and is assumed to play the major role in the economies of most developing countries. However, this argument does not hold in the case of a significant number of OIC countries. The share of agriculture in GDP amounts to 16.7 per cent in the OIC countries as a group.

The highest share of agriculture in GDP (30.3 per cent) recorded in the OIC-LDC group and the lowest share (12.5 per cent) recorded in the OIC-OEC group. At the individual country level, the share of agriculture in GDP varies from only 1 per cent in Bahrain, Kuwait and Qatar to 55.0 per cent in Albania and 52.5 per cent in Guinea-Bissau. It is equal to or greater than 33.0 per cent in 16 countries, of which 11 countries are LDCs. In addition, it is equal to or less than 5.0 per cent in 6 oil-exporting countries (see Table A.4 in the Annex).

The figures on the share of the manufacturing sector in the GDP indicate the weak performance of this sector in most of the OIC economies. Yet, in some countries, particularly in the OIC-MIC group, it is gaining importance. The share of the manufacturing sector in the OIC countries varies from 4.0 per cent in Comoros, Djibouti and Oman to 34 per cent in Malaysia. Although countries belonging mostly to the OIC-MIC group such as Indonesia, Egypt, Turkey, Tunisia, and

Morocco take up the top ranks, a few countries from other sub-groups achieved similar ranks. These include Turkmenistan and the Kyrgyz Republic from the OIC-TC group and Burkina Faso from the OIC-LDC group. Regarding the sub-group averages, the highest share of manufacturing (21.6 per cent) is recorded in the OIC-MIC group and lowest (9 per cent) in the OIC-OEC group.

The picture of the overall structure of the economies of the OIC countries described above in terms of the composition of their output (GDP) reflects clearly the structure of their export earnings. In general, agriculture and oil production are the main productive economic activities that contribute the highest shares to the output of almost half of the OIC countries. Indeed, according to the recent IMF classification of all economies by the main source of export earnings, 15 OIC countries are classified as non-oil primary product exporting countries, almost all of these countries are LDCs in sub-Saharan Africa. In addition, 13 OIC countries in the Middle East and North Africa are classified as oil-exporting countries (IMF 2001: 159).
There is no doubt that the exports of oil and agricultural commodities play a critical role in the prospects of growth and development in these countries, especially in the OIC-OEC and OIC-LDC groups. Yet, the large share of primary commodities in output and exports brings about a significant exposure of the economy to the risks of external shocks such as those due to fluctuating trends in international commodity prices and/or adverse seasonal factors and, thus, affects economic growth and long-term policy making. This issue will be further discussed in section 4 as a special topic.

3.3. Economic Growth

With a total population of 1.3 billion (21.3 per cent of the world population), the combined income (GDP) of the OIC countries in current US dollars amounted in 2000 to $1424.4 billion. This makes up only 4.5 per cent of the world GDP (see Tables A.2 and A.3 in the annex). With a 23.7 per cent share of the total OIC population, the income of the OIC-LDC group (19 countries) amounted to $97 billion or 6.8 per cent of the total OIC income. In contrast, with 48.5 per cent of the total OIC population, the income of the OIC-MIC group (15 countries) stood at $724.5 billion or 50.9 per cent of the total OIC. On the other hand, with 22.6 per cent of the total OIC population, the total income of the OIC-OEC group (12 countries) reached $555.4 billion or 39.0 per cent of the total OIC income. Lastly, with 5.2 per cent of the total OIC population, the OIC-TC group (7 countries) generated $47.5 billion or 3.3 per cent of the total OIC income.

As it may be observed, the share of the OIC-LDC group and the OIC-TC group in the total OIC income is very low, even less than the national income of some individual OIC member countries such as Turkey, Saudi Arabia, or Indonesia. The 26 countries in these two groups accounted for only 10.1 per cent of the total OIC income. In contrast, the share of the OIC-MIC group and the OIC-OEC group is quite high. The 27 countries in these two groups generated 89.9 per cent of the total OIC output. Roughly, this means that only two-thirds of the OIC population generate 90.0 per cent of the OIC income. Moreover, only 6 countries, namely Turkey, Saudi Arabia, Indonesia, Egypt, Iran, and Malaysia contributed 63.8 per cent to the overall OIC income.

Accordingly, growth performance of the OIC countries as a group is highly influenced by the developments in the OIC-MIC and OIC-OEC groups. Similarly, the performance of these two groups is also influenced by the developments in certain countries in these two groups like those mentioned above. This is because average growth rates are computed on the basis of percentage changes for individual countries weighted by the GDP values in US dollars. For this reason, the arguments in the following analysis relating to the average growth rates of OIC countries as a group and the sub-groups of OIC countries must be considered cautiously within this framework.

TABLE 2: REAL GDP GROWTH RATES
(Average annual % change)

	1983-92	1996	1997	1998	1999	2000
OIC-LDC	3.3	5.3	5.8	5.1	4.9	5.0
OIC-MIC	5.2	7.2	5.1	-2.6	1.0	5.5
OIC-OEC	2.0	3.4	4.3	3.5	-6.2	3.3
OIC-TC	-0.2	1.2	1.4	2.1	4.6	8.0
OIC countries	**3.7**	**5.5**	**4.7**	**0.3**	**-1.4**	**4.7**
World (*)	3.4	4.0	4.2	2.8	3.5	4.8
Developed countries (*)	3.3	2.9	3.5	2.7	3.4	4.1
Developing countries (*)	4.7	6.5	5.8	3.5	3.8	5.8

Source: Table A.5 in the Annex.
(*) IMF, *World Economic Outlook*, May 2001, p. 165.

As it may be shown in Table 2 above, the OIC countries as a group achieved the highest average real GDP growth rate of 5.5 per cent in 1996. This rate is significantly higher than the 3.7 per cent average rate achieved in the ten-year period of 1983-92. Moreover, when this rate is compared with the world average and the average rate of the developed countries in the same year, it appears that the OIC countries as a group performed quite better. Yet, in none of the five years of the period under consideration, the growth performance of the OIC countries as a group could reach the average growth performance of the developing countries.

The growth performance of the OIC group deteriorated sharply in 1998 when the average real GDP growth rate dropped to only 0.3 per cent and further down to a negative rate of 1.4 per cent in 1999. However, like everywhere else, the year 2000 witnessed a strong recovery in the economic performance of the OIC countries with an average real GDP growth rate of 4.7 per cent. These trends can be explained, in part, by the negative effects of the Asian crisis in 1997-98 and the fall in world commodity prices in the same period, but later by the improved situation and recovery in the world economy in 1999 and 2000.

In this regard, the economies of the OIC-MIC group seem to be the most negatively affected by the adverse external factors in 1998. They were followed in that by the economies of the OIC-OEC. At the individual country level, it has been observed that the number of countries, which experienced negative rates of growth during the period under consideration, increased from 6 countries in 1997 to 11 countries in 1999, of which 8 countries are related to the OIC-MIC and OIC-OEC groups. However, in 2000, the number of these countries decreased to only 3 countries (see Table A.5 in the Annex).

The OIC-LDC group achieved the highest average growth rate of 5.8 per cent in 1997. However, this rate slowed down in the following two years to reach 4.9 per cent in 1999 but then increased slightly to 5 per cent in 2000. In part, this can be explained by the negative impact of the fall in world commodity prices. In this regard, prices of non-oil commodities weakened steadily over the financial year 1997, resulting in a decline of 14.7 per cent in 1998 and 7.1 per cent in 1999 before increasing slightly by 1.8 per cent in 2000 (Table A.1 in the Annex).

The OIC-MIC group achieved the highest average growth rate of 7.2 per cent in 1996. However, in 1997, the growth performance of the OIC-MIC group started to deteriorate when the average real GDP growth rate decreased to 5.1 per cent, and then dropped sharply in 1998 to record a negative rate of 2.6 per cent. This can be explained by the sharp drop in economic growth of Indonesia and Malaysia, the two countries within this group that have felt the brunt of the Asian financial crisis in mid-1997. In 1998, real GDP dropped in Indonesia to record a negative rate of growth of 13.1 per cent compared to a positive rate of 8.0 per cent in 1996. In Malaysia this rate reached a negative level of 7.4 per cent in the same year, compared to a positive rate of growth of 10.0 per cent in 1996.

Other countries within this group have also been negatively affected by the Asian crisis. For example, the real GDP growth rate in Turkey decreased to 3.1 per cent in 1998 compared to 7.5 per cent in 1997 and dropped more in 1999 to reach a negative rate of 4.7 per cent. The total negative effect of the Asian financial crisis on the economic growth performance of the OIC-MIC group becomes clear when we consider the significant income contribution of these three countries to the total income of the group. In 1997, Indonesia, Malaysia and Turkey produced together almost 35 per cent of the total OIC-MIC group's GDP in terms of the US dollar.

On the other hand, the OIC-OEC group achieved the highest average real GDP growth rate of 4.3 per cent in 1997. However, this rate decreased steadily in the following two years to reach a negative rate of 6.2 percent in 1999, the lowest among all other OIC groups. This can be easily explained by the weakened world oil prices in 1997 and 1998. Lastly, after experiencing a very unfavourable growth record in the first half of the 1990s, the group of OIC-TC countries in transition managed to reverse their growth trends and were quite successful in maintaining positive rates of growth in the second half of the decade. This was so even in the two-year period of the Asian financial crisis. The group achieved the highest average real GDP growth rate of 8.0 per cent in 2000. This rate was much higher than the OIC average and the averages of all other OIC groups.

To enrich the above analysis on the overall economic growth in the OIC countries and to make this picture clearer, we now consider the growth performance of the economy in terms of population. With a total population of the OIC countries growing at a rate of more than 2.0 per cent a year, the economy of these countries as a group must be able to grow at least by the same rate to maintain the same level of per capita income. For this reason, we conclude this section by presenting a brief discussion about the per capita income levels in the OIC countries in terms of both current US dollar value and average growth rate of real per capita income.

TABLE 3: REAL PER CAPITA GDP GROWTH RATES
(Average annual % change)

	1996	1997	1998	1999	2000
OIC-LDC	2.4	2.5	3.0	1.9	2.0
OIC-MIC	3.8	1.9	-1.3	0.5	2.9
OIC-OEC	1.4	1.8	1.6	-3.0	1.5
OIC-TC	3.0	3.5	1.4	7.7	10.0
OIC countries	**2.8**	**2.0**	**0.2**	**-0.7**	**2.2**
Developed countries (*)	2.3	2.8	2.1	2.8	3.6
Developing countries (*)	4.8	4.1	2.0	2.4	4.3
Memo:					
Total OIC Population	2.0	2.4	2.0	2.1	2.1

Source: Derived from Table A.5 and Table A.2 in the Annex.
(*) IMF, *World Economic Outlook*, May 2001, p. 165.

In terms of current US dollar value (see Table A.6 in the Annex), the average OIC per capita GDP amounted to $1232 in 1996, the highest level during the period under consideration. However, it dropped sharply in 1998 to $1075 before increasing again to $1141 in 2000. During the period under consideration, the OIC-LDC group maintained the highest average per capita GDP of $361 in 2000 and the lowest of $345 in 1996. The OIC-MIC group recorded the highest level of $1337 in 1996 and the lowest level of $1067 in 1998. In contrast, the OIC-OEC group maintained the highest level of $2115 in 1997 and the lowest level of $1926 in 1998. Lastly, the OIC-TC group recorded the highest level of $765 in 1998 and the lowest level of $713 in 1996.

These figures reflect a high level of income inequalities and a huge gap between the rich and the poor countries within the OIC community. In this respect, the income per person in 13 OIC oil-exporting countries (22.6 per cent of the total OIC population) was almost six times that in 19 OIC least developed countries (23.7 per cent of the total OIC population) in 2000. At the individual country level, the income per person in the richest country is 294 times that in the poorest country (see Table A.6 in the Annex). In fact these discrepancies may constitute one of the basic factors that hinder intra-OIC economic cooperation.

On the other hand, Table 3 above displays the average real per capita GDP growth rates in OIC countries as a group and in the sub-groups of the OIC countries as well as those of both developing and developed countries in the period 1996-2000. During this period, the OIC countries' average growth rate of real per capita GDP reflects clearly the trends of both real GDP and population growth discussed above. After achieving a relatively high rate of 2.8 per cent in 1996 (higher than the average population growth rate), the OIC countries' average rate of real per capita GDP decreased steadily in the following three years to reach a negative rate of 0.7 per cent in 1999. In 2000, however, the average real per capita GDP growth recorded a positive rate of 2.2 per cent, corresponding to a rate higher than the average population rate in that year by a mere 0.1 per cent. Yet, in none of the five years of the period under consideration, the average real per capita GDP growth rate of the OIC countries as a group could reach that of the developing countries.

3.4. INFLATION

In economic theory, a low level of inflation is regarded as an indication of macroeconomic stability in the economy. In fact, the governments of the industrial countries and many of the developing countries paid special attention and applied different fiscal and monetary policies over the last two decades to control the inflation rates and to maintain price stability in their economies. As a result of these efforts, the average rates of inflation have fallen significantly in developed as well as developing countries.

As it may be shown in Table 4 above, the average inflation rate in the developed countries decreased gradually from 4.6 per cent in the period 1983-92 to 2.4 per cent in 1996 and further down to only 1.4 per cent in 1999. The average inflation rate in developing countries was 46.9 per cent in the period 1983-92. However, in 1996 it declined down to 15.4 per cent and further to 9.9 per cent in 1997, and recently it stood at 6.1 per cent in 2000. Even the countries in transition, which experienced hyperinflation in the early 1990s, started recently to bring it under control. The average inflation rate in these countries fell from more than 600 per cent in 1993 to 133.5 per cent in 1995 (IMF 2001: 176) and further down to 20.1 per cent in 2000.

TABLE 4: AVERAGE INFLATION RATES
(Annual % change in consumer prices)

	1983-92	1996	1997	1998	1999	2000
OIC-LDC	21.1	23.8	9.0	8.2	6.0	5.2
OIC-MIC	20.1	24.4	24.3	39.3	22.6	15.1
OIC-OEC	8.4	10.3	5.5	6.1	5.4	4.5
OIC-TC	0.9	98.4	38.8	15.6	15.4	15.8
OIC countries	**15.4**	**22.0**	**17.2**	**24.9**	**15.3**	**10.8**
Developed countries (*)	4.6	2.4	2.1	1.5	1.4	2.3
Developing countries (*)	46.9	15.4	9.9	10.4	6.7	6.1
Countries in transition (*)	42.4	42.4	27.4	21.8	43.9	20.1

Source: Table A.7 in the Annex.
(*) IMF, *World Economic Outlook*, May 2001, p. 176.

On the other hand, when the average inflation rates in the OIC countries are considered, Table 4 above shows that the annual average inflation rate in the period 1983-92 was significantly lower than that of the developing countries. However, in all the years of the period under consideration, the average inflation rate of the OIC countries was considerably higher than that achieved by the developing countries. In fact, the average rate of inflation in the OIC countries as a group accelerated during the first half of the 1990s where it reached a peak of 84.5 per cent in 1994 (SESRTCIC, *Annual Economic Report*, March 1998). Then, it fell sharply to 22 per cent in 1996 and further decelerated to 17.2 per cent in 1997. However, it climbed up again to 24.9 per cent in 1998 before declining again to 15.3 per cent in 1999 and further to 10.8 percent in 2000, the lowest level reached in the period under consideration.

Similar trends have been observed in the case of the sub-groups of the OIC countries. The average inflation rate had a tendency to increase in all the groups in the early 1990s, and then it commenced to decline in the second half of the decade, particularly in the last three years. During the period under consideration, inflation reached its peak in 1996 in all OIC sub-groups. The average inflation rates realised in 1996 in all the OIC sub-groups and the OIC average were quite higher than the average rate of the ten-year period of 1983-92. Moreover, although towards the end of the period under consideration a declining trend in average inflation rates has been observed in the OIC countries as a group, these rates remained considerably higher than those realised in both developed and developing countries.

Amongst the OIC sub-groups, the OIC-OEC experienced average inflation rates that were below the OIC averages in all the years of the period under consideration. Except in 1996, this was also true for the OIC-LDC, which realised average inflation rates lower than those realised by the developing countries during the same period. In contrast, the average rates in the OIC-MIC group were above the OIC averages. The average inflation rate in the OIC-TC group was considerably higher than the OIC average in 1996 and 1997, but significantly lower in 1998 when the group managed to curb inflation and bring it down to a level of 15.6 per cent. However, this rate was higher than that of the OIC average in 2000. At the individual country level, the OIC countries with the highest inflation rates in 2000 were Mozambique (12.3 per cent) from the OIC-LDC, Turkey (54.9 per cent) from the OIC-MIC, Iran (18.5 per cent) from the OIC-OEC, and Tajikistan (34 per cent) from the OIC-TC (Table A.7 in the Annex).

3.5. Foreign Trade and Payments Balances

Having examined the performance of the main indicators of the domestic economy, this sub-section will now take up the developments in the foreign sector of the OIC countries. It will examine the trends in the exports and imports of merchandise as well as the trade balances. It will also present an overall picture of the situation of the current account balance and the international reserve position.

3.5.1. Exports and Imports of Merchandise

In 2000, the total OIC countries' exports of merchandise amounted to $511.7 billion (Table A.8 in the Annex). However, this accounted only for 8.1 per cent of the world total merchandise exports in that year. In fact, this is the highest share in world exports achieved by the OIC countries in the last decade; the lowest share of 6.3 per cent was recorded in 1998 (see Table 5 below).

As it may be shown in Table 5, the highest average rates of change in merchandise exports were recorded in 2000 while the lowest rates were recorded in 1998. It is clear that export performance deteriorated markedly in 1998 when all the groups, except the group of developed countries, experienced negative rates of growth in exports, the worst of which were recorded in the OIC group. However, a strong recovery took place in the following two years when all the groups managed to reverse the trend and maintained positive rates of growth in exports, the highest of which were recorded in the OIC group.

TABLE 5: MERCHANDISE EXPORTS (Average annual % change)

	1996	1997	1998	1999	2000
OIC-LDC	7.9	2.6	-4.7	10.1	14.1
OIC-MIC	9.0	2.9	-8.7	12.5	13.6
OIC-OEC	16.0	4.1	-38.5	18.2	30.4
OIC-TC	4.3	-0.2	-20.1	5.5	30.9
OIC countries	**12.0**	**3.3**	**-20.9**	**14.6**	**22.0**
Developed countries	2.5	3.0	2.3	6.4	8.5
Developing countries	7.3	6.0	-10.6	1.2	15.1
World	4.1	4.0	-2.1	4.8	10.7
Share in the world total (%)					
OIC countries	**7.5**	**7.5**	**6.3**	**7.0**	**8.1**
Developed countries	64.6	63.9	66.9	68.0	66.4
Developing countries	33.9	34.7	32.0	30.8	32.4

Source: Table A.8 and Table A.9 in the Annex.

During the period under consideration, similar trends in export performance have also been observed in the OIC sub-groups. The average rates of change in exports dropped sharply in 1998 in which all the OIC sub-groups experienced negative rates of growth in exports varying from 4.7 per cent in the OIC-LDC group to 38.5 per cent in the OIC-OEC group. The highest rates of increase in exports were recorded in 2000 in all the OIC sub-groups.

It is then clear that the export performance of the OIC countries has been negatively affected by the world economic recession, which took place in the two-year period of 1997-98, due to the Asian financial crisis in mid-1997. The export performance of many OIC countries has also been negatively affected by the marked fall in world commodity prices in the same period. In particular, this is very clear in the case of the OIC-OEC group, for which the average rate of growth in exports is highly correlated with the rates of change in world oil prices. The average rate of change in exports of this group fell to 4.1 per cent in 1997 and then sharply to a negative rate of 38.5 percent in 1998. This has been matched with the negative rates of change in world oil prices recorded in these two years.

Another important observation about the export performance of the OIC countries is the heavy concentration of exports in a few countries in certain OIC sub-groups. The OIC-MIC group and the OIC-OEC group together accounted for 94.0 per cent of the OIC countries' total exports during the period under consideration leaving the remaining 6.0 per cent to be shared by the OIC-LDC and the OIC-TC groups. At the individual country level, Malaysia, Indonesia and Turkey from the OIC-MIC accounted for about 39 per cent of the total OIC countries' exports in 2000. Together with Saudi Arabia and the U.A.E from the OIC-OEC group, these countries accounted for about 60 per cent of the total OIC countries' exports in the same year (calculated from Table A.8, in the Annex).

Similar to the developments on the export side, the imports of the OIC countries as a group, on the other hand, followed in general the same trend. In 2000, the total OIC countries' imports of merchandise amounted to about $425 billion, which makes up only 6.4 per cent of the world total merchandise imports (Table A.10 in the Annex). The figures in Table 6 below show that the highest average rate of growth in imports of the OIC countries as a group (16.3 per cent) was recorded in 2000 and the lowest rate (-9.8 per cent) in 1998. At the level of the OIC sub-groups, the highest average rate of growth in imports were recorded in 2000 except in the OIC-TC group for which it was in 1996. The lowest level of both the OIC-MIC and the OIC-TC was recorded in 1998, while that of the OIC-LDC was recorded in 1997 and that of the OIC-OEC in 1999 (see Table 6 below).

TABLE 6: MERCHANDISE IMPORTS
(Average annual % change)

	1996	1997	1998	1999	2000
OIC-LDC	6.7	-0.2	7.9	9.1	9.2
OIC-MIC	5.9	1.8	-19.9	5.0	18.9
OIC-OEC	6.8	0.3	3.8	-0.1	12.5
OIC-TC	19.9	-6.8	-10.3	-6.4	17.4
OIC countries	**6.7**	**0.9**	**-9.8**	**3.2**	**16.3**
Developed countries	3.3	2.4	0.6	3.7	8.7
Developing countries	6.8	6.1	-4.1	7.4	19.9
World	4.5	3.6	-1.2	5.1	12.9
Share in the world total (%)					
OIC countries	**6.9**	**6.7**	**6.2**	**6.1**	**6.4**
Developed countries	65.6	64.7	65.9	64.9	61.9
Developing countries	34.7	33.3	33.2	34.1	37.1

Source: Table A.10 and Table A.11 in the Annex.

Similar to exports, the imports of the OIC countries are heavily concentrated in a few countries in certain OIC sub-groups. In 2000, the OIC-MIC group accounted for 60.0 per cent of the OIC countries' total imports, the OIC-OEC accounted for 30.0 per cent, and the remaining 10.0 per cent was shared by both the OIC-LDC and the OIC-TC groups. At the individual country level, Malaysia, Indonesia and Turkey from the OIC-MIC accounted for 41.6 per cent of the total OIC countries' imports in 2000. Together with Saudi Arabia and the U.A.E. from the OIC-OEC group, these countries accounted for almost 60.0 per cent of the total OIC countries' imports in the same year (calculated from Table A.10 in the Annex).

3.5.2. Trade Balance, Current Account and Reserves Positions

As a result of the developments in exports and imports discussed above, the OIC countries as a group recorded a trade balance surplus in all the years of the period under consideration except in 1998. The highest trade balance surplus ($86.6 billion) was recorded in 2000 (calculated using the data in Tables A.8 and A.10 in the Annex). When the OIC sub-groups are considered, the OIC-OEC group recorded a trade balance surplus in all the years of the period under consideration. In contrast, all the other OIC sub-groups experienced trade balance deficits during the same period, except the OIC-MIC group in 1999 and the OIC-TC group in 2000.

On the other hand, Table 7 below summarises the current account balance of the OIC countries in terms of the US dollar and according to the number of deficit or surplus countries in the latest five years for which the data are available. It also summarises the international reserve position in terms of the US dollar and the number of deteriorating and improving countries. The term "deteriorating" indicates a decrease in or depletion of international foreign exchange reserves excluding gold. These reserves are usually used to partially finance the deficit in the current account balance. In contrast, the term "improving" indicates an addition to or accumulation in these reserves. This may occur even when the country has a deficit current account balance, providing that it may manage to finance its deficit through external financing channels such as external borrowing (foreign debt).

During the period under consideration, the OIC countries maintained a surplus in their combined current account balance only in 1999 (amounted to $16.6 billion). In fact this is the second time in a decade that the OIC countries maintained a surplus current account balance. The first time was in 1990, when the combined OIC countries' current account had a surplus balance of $3.3 billion (SESRTCIC, *Annual Economic Report*, March 1998). However, the OIC countries as a group did not succeed in keeping that surplus balance of their current account in the following years. Although a relative improvement has been realised in the volume of the deficit, especially in 1997 when it was reduced to $4.6 billion, the current account of the OIC countries remained in a deficit balance till 1999.

In general, the deterioration in the current account balance is financed through foreign exchange reserves. However, the actual picture does not conform to this assumption.

This implies that many OIC countries managed to finance their current account deficits through external financial channels, particularly through external borrowing (foreign debt). This is obvious, for example, in 1998 when the deficit in the total OIC countries' current account balance increased while the number of countries with a deficit current account balance decreased. Meanwhile, in the same year, both the total external debt and reserves increased while the net foreign direct investment (FDI) flows decreased (see Table 7).

TABLE 7: CURRENT ACCOUNT AND RESERVES POSITION

	1995	1996	1997	1998	1999
CURRENT ACCOUNT BALANCE (billion US $)					
OIC countries	**-34.3**	**-7.8**	**-4.6**	**-17.1**	**16.6**
Developed countries (*)	59.0	42.3	95.1	34.8	-133.1
Developing countries (*)	-96.9	-74.5	-60.5	-92.2	-18.5
Number of OIC countries with:					
(-) current account balance	42	38	42	40	26
(+) current account balance	11	14	10	8	11
RESERVES EXCLUDING GOLD (billion US $)	**144.4**	**151.2**	**155.6**	**174.1**	**181.5**
Number of OIC countries with:					
Deteriorating position	12	13	15	22	14
Improving position	35	34	32	23	30
Memorandum					
Foreign debt (billion US $)	573.1	580.9	583.5	627.6	625.3
As % of developing countries	26.6	25.8	25.0	24.4	24.4
FDI (billion US $)	16.8	18.6	20.1	15.6	12.2
As % of developing countries	15.7	14.2	11.6	8.8	6.6

Source: Table A.12 to Table A.15 in the Annex.
(*) IMF, *World Economic Outlook*, May 2001, p. 200.
(-) Deficit current account balance. (+) Surplus current account balance.

4. COMMODITY PRICES AND OIC COMMODITY EXPORTING COUNTRIES

Although the rapid growth of manufactured exports is a dominant trend and world trade in primary commodities has grown more slowly than manufactures, primary commodities are still very important in world trade, especially for developing countries. According to the recent IMF classification of all economies by the main source of export earnings, 42 developing countries around the world are still depending on non-oil primary commodities for more than 50 per cent of their export earnings (non-fuel primary product exporting countries). The majority of them are least developed countries in sub-Saharan Africa. In addition, another 18 developing countries are classified as oil-exporting countries; most of them are in the Middle East and North Africa regions (IMF 2001: 159).

15 out of the world 42 non-oil primary product exporting countries are OIC members, almost all of them are least developed countries in sub-Saharan Africa depending for their growth and development on exports of no more than two or three non-oil primary commodities, mostly agricultural ones. These include Benin, Burkina Faso, Chad, Gambia, Guinea, Guinea-Bissau, Guyana, Ivory Coast, Mali, Mauritania, Niger, Somalia, Sudan, Suriname, and Togo. In addition, 13 out of the world 18 oil-exporting countries are OIC members, namely Algeria, Bahrain, Brunei, Gabon, Iran, Iraq, Kuwait, Nigeria, Libya, Oman, Qatar, Saudi Arabia, and U.A.E.

It is then clear that almost half of the OIC countries are primary commodity-dependent economies (mostly oil or agricultural commodities). There is no doubt that the exports of these commodities play a critical role in the prospects of growth and development in these countries. This is true particularly for the 15 OIC non-oil commodity exporting countries (the subject of this section), whose livelihood may be jeopardized by low prices and/or adverse seasonal factors, considering the fact that most of them are small land-locked economies with small shares in international commodity markets. Non-oil primary commodities continue to be a large component of these countries' total exports. Countries like Guinea, Guinea-Bissau, Niger, Somalia, Sudan and Uganda still derive more than 90 per cent of their export earnings from non-oil commodities. Since these countries depend for their growth on their capacity to pay for imports of capital goods, intermediate products and fuels, they are understandably concerned about what happens in the world commodity trade, the trends in world commodity prices, and the proceeds from the particular commodities which they export.

In general, the large share of primary commodities in output and exports brings about a significant exposure of the economy to the risks of external shocks such as those due to fluctuating trends in international commodity prices and/or adverse seasonal factors and, thus, affects economic growth and long-term policy making. In particular, commodity prices in the aggregate have typically been much more volatile than prices of manufactures. Therefore, shocks in world commodity prices are likely to create serious challenges for commodity exporting countries and thus to have a marked impact on their economic performance and growth prospects. Since volatility in world commodity prices contributes to export revenue instability, it is not unusual for commodity exporting countries to suffer adverse term-of-trade shocks equal to several percentage points of GNP in a given year. In many cases countries find that their fiscal position and foreign exchange reserves change substantially over short periods as a result of a sudden change in world prices.

TABLE 8: REAL GDP GROWTH RATES AND WORLD COMMODITY PRICES
(Average annual % change)

	1983-92	1996	1997	1998	1999	2000

Non-oil Commodity						
OIC-NOCEC (1)	2.0	6.9	6.4	5.1	3.5	3.0
World NOCEC (2)	2.6	5.9	5.5	3.1	2.1	4.0
OIC-LDC	3.3	5.3	5.8	5.1	4.9	5.0
World prices (3)	0.8	-1.2	-3.2	-14.7	-7.1	1.8
Oil						
OIC-OEC	2.0	3.4	4.3	3.5	-6.2	3.3
World OEC (4)	2.6	3.5	4.6	2.9	1.0	4.3
World prices (3)	-5.2	18.4	-5.4	-32.1	37.5	56.9

Source: (1) OIC non-oil commodity exporting countries, calculated using the data in Table A.5 in the Annex. (2) World non-oil commodity exporting countries, IMF, *World Economic Outlook*, May 2001, p. 165. (3) World trade prices in US dollar, IMF, *World Economic Outlook*, May 2001, p. 193. (4) World oil exporting countries, IMF, *World Economic Outlook*, May 2001, p. 165.

Indeed, there is an apparent relationship between the trend in world commodity prices and the trend in growth performance of these countries, where, in general, a low level of world commodity prices does not provide enough impetus to active growth performance. This can be shown in Table 8 below. Prices of non-oil commodities weakened steadily over the financial year 1997, resulting in a decline of 14.7 per cent in 1998 and 7.1 per cent in 1999 before increasing slightly by 1.8 per cent in 2000. During the same period, the average real GDP growth rate of the OIC non-oil commodity exporting countries as a group declined steadily from 6.9 percent in 1996 to 3 percent in 2000. A similar relationship has also been observed between the trend in world oil prices and the trend in growth performance of the OIC-OEC group.

However, this does not mean that dependence on primary commodities should be associated with slow growth. Some examples around the world suggest that commodity-exporting countries can also be successful in maintaining high growth levels. A good example is Chile in Latin America, which expanded its fruit exports dramatically in the 1980s. Another example is Botswana in sub-Saharan Africa, which maintained the highest average GDP growth in the world from 1970 to 1990, largely depending on the strength of its exports of uncut diamonds. What seemed to matter in both these countries was the government's commitment toward a stable political and macroeconomic climate as well as trade and exchange rate policies that encouraged exports. Moreover, many of the emerging developing countries with diversified export structures and most of the East Asian newly industrialised countries (Indonesia, Korea, Malaysia, the Philippines, and Thailand) were once heavily dependent on primary commodities. Indeed, they are still large producers and exporters of agricultural commodities such as natural rubber, tropical timber, and rice. The experience of these countries suggests that successful diversification away from these commodities tends to occur after productivity rises in the primary commodity sectors and through implementation of appropriate macroeconomic stabilisation policies.

Taking this into account, it seems that commodity-related factors (e.g., volatility of world prices) are not on their own a reason for a slow economic growth even in the least developed primary exporting countries. In this regard, there is a large body of empirical literature, stimulated by the so-called "new growth theory", which attempts to identify by means of cross-country regression analysis the factors that lead to the differences in long-term growth rates between countries and regions. The poor performance of the economies of low-income primary exporting countries, particularly those in sub-Saharan Africa, has recently received some attention in this literature (for a survey of this literature see Dabour, Nabil 1998). A wide range of socio-economic factors have been tested for their effects on income growth. Among other things, these studies have drawn attention to the relative importance of both the structural and policy factors in explaining the poor performance of these countries.

In addition to the high dependence on primary commodities, other poor structural factors have been shown as principal causes of economic under-performance in many of these countries. These include land-locked and small size economies, high population growth rates, lack of openness and diversification in output and exports, and low performance on human development and poverty alleviation. Poor policy variables, such as low levels of savings and investment, real exchange rate variations, inflation and foreign debt burden have also been estimated to play a significant role in underlying growth performance in these countries.

Considering all the above, creation of appropriate structural environment and sound macroeconomic stability policies would most likely play a leading role in managing and directing the economies of OIC primary exporting countries towards sustainable economic growth in the long run. These factors would facilitate long-term planning and investment decisions, and thereby encourage savings, private capital accumulation, and eventually facilitate the diversification in the long run. Therefore, there is an urgent need in these countries for further wide-ranging macroeconomic policy reforms aimed at tackling the structural problems that continue impeding and slowing their economic growth. In this connection, a turnaround in economic policies, to encourage private investment and strengthen market mechanisms, backed by improved macroeconomic management, and changes in the external environment, such as increasing trade liberalisation could be cited as main factors for sustainable economic growth in OIC primary commodity exporting countries.

5. SUMMARY AND CONCLUDING REMARKS

Following the severe recession in 1998, the world economy witnessed a strong recovery in late 1999 and early 2000 in which global trade and output growth in 2000 were the strongest in more than a decade, with all regions benefiting from the stronger world economy. However, with the signs of a greater than expected weakening coming late in 2000, particularly the marked slowdown in the US economy, the prospects for global growth in 2001 have weakened significantly.

The slow recovery achieved by the developing countries as a group in 1999 accelerated in 2000, with average real GDP growth recorded at 5.8 per cent compared to 3.8 per cent in 1999. Economic growth picked up, albeit unevenly, in all developing regions in 2000. This was markedly so in the regions of Latin America, Middle East and North Africa in which growth was stimulated by higher oil revenues, as oil prices rebounded in

1999-2000, leading to a substantial improvement in fiscal and external imbalances in many countries in these regions. However, due to the signs of weakened world economic activity by the end of 2000, growth in 2001 is expected to decline slightly to 5 per cent in the developing countries as a group.

As a substantial part of the developing countries, the OIC countries as a group followed in general the same trends. However, economic growth and recovery in the OIC countries remained below the levels maintained by the developing countries. This indicates that the OIC countries, unlike the developing countries, were, as a group, unable to benefit enough from the strengthening of world economic activity. Moreover, the group of OIC countries was the most negatively affected group among the other groups of the developing countries by the adverse shocks in the world economy such as the financial crises and the fall in world commodity prices.
With more than one fifth of the world population, the OIC countries in 2000 accounted for only 4.5 per cent of the world output in terms of GDP in current US dollars and 8.1 per cent of the world exports of merchandise. They maintained an average real growth rate of 4.7 per cent; the same as the pre-crisis level in 1997. However, although this rate was comparable to the world average, it was still lower than the 5.8 per cent rate maintained by the developing countries in the same year. As a result, although the average real per capita income of the OIC countries grew by 2.2 percent (a mere 0.1 per cent more than the average population growth rate), it was still significantly lower than the level maintained by the developing countries in the same year.

The overall picture indicates a high level of diversity and a huge gap between the rich and the poor countries within the OIC community. While the share of the OIC-LDC group and the OIC-TC group in the total OIC income is very low, even less than the national income of some individual OIC member countries, the share of the OIC-MIC group and the OIC-OEC group is quite high. Roughly, only two-thirds of the OIC population generate 90 per cent of the OIC income. Moreover, only 6 countries, namely Turkey, Saudi Arabia, Indonesia, Egypt, Iran, and Malaysia contributed 64 per cent to the overall OIC income. As a result, the income per person in 13 OIC oil-exporting countries (22.6 per cent of the total OIC population) was almost six times that in 19 OIC least developed countries (23.7 per cent of the total OIC population). At the individual country level, the income per person in the richest OIC country is 294 times that in the poorest country. In fact these discrepancies may constitute one of the basic factors that hinder intra-OIC economic cooperation.

On the other hand, the production and export structures of the OIC countries have hardly changed over the past 20 years. With the highest share in GDP (44.2 per cent), the services sector remained the main source of income in almost all the OIC countries. In contrast, the low share of the manufacturing sector (15.9 per cent) indicates the weak performance of this sector in most of the OIC countries. Yet, in some countries, particularly in the OIC-MIC group, it is gaining importance. In general, agriculture and oil production are the main productive economic activities that contribute the highest shares to the output of almost half of the OIC countries. In this regard, 15 OIC countries are classified as non-oil primary product exporting countries. Almost all of these countries are LDCs in sub-Saharan Africa depending for their growth and development on exports of no more than two or three non-oil primary commodities, mostly agricultural ones. In addition, 13 OIC countries in the Middle East and North Africa are classified as oil-exporting countries.

This means that almost half of the OIC countries are primary commodity-dependent economies (mostly oil or agricultural commodities). There is no doubt that the exports of these commodities play a critical role in the prospects of growth and development in these countries, particularly in the OIC least developed non-oil commodity exporting countries. In general, the large share of primary commodities in output and exports brings about a significant exposure of the economy to the risks of external shocks such as those due to fluctuating trends in international commodity prices and/or adverse seasonal factors and, thus, affects economic growth and long-term policy making.

However, empirical studies show that dependence on primary commodities and commodity-related factors, such as the volatility of world commodity prices are not on their own a reason for a slow economic growth. Some examples around the world suggest that commodity exporters can also be successful in maintaining high levels of economic growth. The experience of these countries shows that successful diversification away from these commodities tends to occur after productivity rises in the primary commodity sectors and through implementation of appropriate macroeconomic stabilisation policies. Therefore, if they are to sustain favourable levels of economic growth and reduce their economies' vulnerability to external shocks, such as the volatility in world commodity prices, the OIC commodity exporting countries need to develop highly productive commodity sectors, possess the capacity to diversify to non-traditional commodity exports (typically, high value-added products) and maintain macroeconomic stability.
Finally, taking all the above into account and noting that:

- **Globalisation and liberalisation have made the external environment for development crucial particularly since the OIC countries have become more vulnerable to the intense competition and unpredictable fluctuations in international trade, instability in financial and monetary flows as well as to the changes in technology;**

- The world economy faces periodical severe fluctuations and crises in some regions the effects of which spill over globally due to the solid linkages between economies and international financial markets;

The following points should be emphasised:

- The need to devise ways and means to minimise the adverse effects of globalisation on the economies of OIC countries as well as to enable them to harness opportunities provided by globalisation.

- Enhancing efforts aimed at strengthening economic cooperation and economic policy coordination among OIC countries so as to maximise the complementarities in their economies and avoid marginalisation.

- Enhancing efforts to set up joint investment projects to achieve and ensure economic integration among the OIC countries with the ultimate objective of establishing an Islamic Common Market or any other form of economic integration.

- Urging the OIC countries to coordinate their efforts aimed at making the necessary contacts with the concerned international parties and organisations so as to safeguard their economic interests.

SOURCES

Dabour, Nabil (1998). *OIC Low-Income Primary Producing Countries: Does Dependence on Primary Commodities Mean Slower Growth?*, Ankara Centre (SESRTCIC), www.sesrtcic.org.
IMF (2000), *Direction of Trade Statistics Yearbook 2000*, IMF, Washington, D.C.

IMF (2001), *Direction of Trade Statistics Quarterly*, IMF, Washington, D.C., June 2001.

IMF (2001), *World Economic Outlook, May 2001*, IMF, Washington, D.C. May 2001.

IMF (2001), *WEO Database*, www.imf.org, May 2001.

SESRTCIC (2001), Data Base (*BASEIND*), Ankara Centre, May 2001.

SESRTCIC (1998), *Annual Economic Report on the OIC Countries*, Ankara Centre, March 1998.

SESRTCIC (2000), *The External Debt Situation of Sub-Saharan African OIC Countries: The Enhanced HIPC Scheme*, Ankara Centre, October 2000.

World Bank (2001), *Global Development Finance 2001*, The World Bank, Washington, D.C.

World Bank, *World Development Reports* 1997 to 2000/2001, The World Bank, Washington, D.C

TOTAL RESERVES EXCLUDING GOLD

(In million US dollars)

	1996	1997	1998	1999	2000
Albania	241.05	280.86	308.50	369.05	352.22
Algeria	4235	8047	6846	4526	12024
Azerbaijan	211.28	466.09	447.33	672.59	679.16
Bahrain	1318.4	1290.3	1079.2	1369	1564.1
Bangladesh	1834.6	1581.5	1905.4	1603.6	1486
Benin	261.8	253.1	261.5	400	458.1
Burkina Faso	338.6	344.8	373.3	295	243.6
Cameroon	2.77	0.86	1.29	4.43	212
Chad	164.48	135.82	120.09	95.02	110.70
Comoros	50.55	40.48	39.14	37.15	43.21
Djibouti	76.97	66.57	66.45	70.61	67.80

Egypt	17398	18665	18124	14484	13118
Gabon	248.72	282.60	15.41	17.95	190.09
Gambia	102.13	96.04	106.36	111.25	
Guinea	87.34	121.63	236.71	199.68	147.91
Guinea-Bissau	11.53	33.70	35.76	35.28	66.73
Guyana	329.68	315.51	276.60	268.28	
Indonesia	18251	16587	22713	26445	22548
Ivory Coast	605.8	618.4	855.5	630.4	667.8
Jordan	1759.3	2200.3	1750.4	2629.1	3331.3
Kazakhstan	1294.7	1697.1	1461.2	1479.2	1594.1
Kuwait	3515.1	3451.8	3947.1	4823.7	7082.4
Kyrgyzstan	94.6	169.8	163.8	229.7	239
Lebanon	5931.9	5976.4	6556.3	7775.6	5943.7
Libya	4600	4100	7270	7280	12461
Malaysia	27009	20788	25559	30588	29523
Maldives	76.17	98.31	118.54	127.12	122.80
Mali	431.5	414.9	402.9	349.7	381.2
Mauritania	141.2	200.8	202.9	224.3	
Morocco	3794	3993	4435	5689	4823
Mozambique	344.06	517.35	608.50	651.60	725.11
Niger	78.5	53.3	53.1	39.2	80.3
Nigeria	4075	7700			
Oman	1389.4	1548.8	1064.1	2767.5	2379.9
Pakistan	548	1195	1028	1511	1513
Qatar	710	1391			
Saudi Arabia	14321	14876	14220	16997	19585
Senegal	288.3	386.2	430.8	402.9	383.5
Sierra Leone	26.6	38.5	44.1	39.5	50.9
Sudan	106.8	81.6	90.6	188.7	
Surinam	96.32	109.11	106.14		
Togo	88.5	118.6	117.7	122	152.3
Tunisia	1897.6	1978.1	1850.1	2261.5	

Turkey	16436	18658	19489	23340	19952
U.A.E.	8055.5	8372.3	9077.1	10675.1	13522.7
Uganda	528.4	633.5	725.4	763.1	808
Yemen	1017.2	1203.1	995.5	1471.5	2900.3
OIC total	144424.4	151178.1	155578.8	174060.3	181533.9

SESRTCIC's Statistical Data Base (BASEIND).

GLOSSARY -- COMOROS (INDIAN OCEAN)

CFA
: Communauté Financière d'Afrique (African Financial Community). The CFA covers those African countries whose currencies are linked with the French Franc at a fixed rate of exchange.

Comoran franc (CF)
: One Comoran franc = 100 centimes; in June 1995 US$1.00 = CF363.98.

crown colony
: A colony of the British Commonwealth over which the crown maintains some control, as through appointment of the governor.

European Community (EC)
: See European Union.

European Currency Unit (ECU)
: Standard currency unit of the European Union; in April 1995 ECU1 = US$0.75.

European Union (EU)
: Formerly the European Community, it was established by the Maastricht Treaty of December 1991 to expand European cooperation from economic and commercial into monetary, security and judicial matters. It officially came into being at the end of 1993.

exclusive economic zone (EEZ)
: A wide belt of sea and seabed adjacent to the national boundaries where the state claims preferential fishing rights and control over the exploitation of mineral and other natural resources. Madagascar claims a 150-nautical-mile exclusive economic zone. Mauritius, Comoros, Seychelles, and Maldives all claim 200 nautical miles. Boundary situations with neighboring states sometimes prevent the extension of the exclusive economic zones to the full limits claimed.

fiscal year (FY)
: Same as the calendar year for all except Mauritius, in which it runs from July 1 to June 30.

Franc Zone
: A monetary union among countries whose currencies are linked to the French franc. Members are France and its overseas appendages and fourteen African countries, including Comoros.

gross domestic product (GDP)
: A value measure of the flow of domestic goods and services produced by an economy over a period of time, such as a year. Only output values of goods for final consumption and intermediate production are assumed to be included in the final prices. GDP is sometimes aggregated and shown at market prices, meaning that indirect taxes and subsidies have been eliminated, the result is GDP at factor cost. The word "gross" indicates that deductions for depreciation of physical assets have not been made. *See also* gross national product.

gross national product (GNP)

Gross domestic product (*q.v.*) plus the net income or loss stemming from transactions with foreign countries. GNP is the broadest measurement of the output of goods and services by an economy. It can be calculated at market prices, which include indirect taxes and subsidies. Because indirect taxes and subsidies are only transfer payments, GNP is often calculated at factor cost, removing indirect taxes and subsidies.

import substitution

The replacement of imports by domestically produced goods, often supported by tariffs or import quotas, and motivated by foreign exchange considerations.

International Development Association (IDA)

See World Bank.

International Finance Corporation (IFC)

See World Bank.

International Monetary Fund (IMF)

Established along with the World Bank (*q.v.*) in 1945, the IMF is a specialized agency affiliated with the United Nations and is responsible for stabilizing international exchange rates and payments. The main business of the IMF is the provision of loans to its members (including industrialized and developing countries) when they experience balance of payments difficulties. These loans frequently carry conditions that require substantial internal economic adjustments by the recipients, most of which are developing countries.

Lomé Convention

The first Lomé Convention (Lomé I) came into force in 1976, Lomé II came into effect in 1981, and Lomé III came into force in 1985; Lomé IV came into effect in 1990. The convention covers economic relations between the members of the European Economic Community (EEC) and their former colonies in Africa, the Caribbean, and the Pacific (ACP). The convention allows most ACP exports to enter the EEC duty-free or at special rates and, among other things, provides funds through the Stabex system (*q.v.*) to offset adverse fluctuations in the prices of ACP exports.

London Club

An informal group of commercial banks that come together to negotiate a debt rescheduling agreement with a country. The group has two committees, an economics committee that develops economic data projections and a negotiating committee. Committee members usually come from the five principal banks that hold the largest amounts of a country's debt.

Malagasy franc (FMG)

1 Malagasy franc (franc malgache-FMG) = 100 centimes; in May 1995 US$1.00 = FMG4,236.9.

Mauritian rupee (MauR)

1 Mauritian rupee = 100 cents; in August 1995 US$1.00 = MauR14.43.

parastatal

A semi-autonomous, quasi-qovernmental, state-owned enterprise.

Paris Club

The informal name for a consortium of Western creditor countries (Belgium, Britain, Canada, France, Germany, Italy, Japan, the Netherlands, Sweden, Switzerland, and the United States) that have made loans or guaranteed export credits to developing nations and that meet in Paris to discuss borrowers' ability to repay debts. Paris Club deliberations often result in the tendering of emergency loans to countries in economic difficulty or in the rescheduling of debts. Formed in October 1962, the organization has no formal or institutional existence. Its secretariat is run by the French treasury. It has a close relationship with the International Monetary Fund (*q.v.*), to which all of its members except Switzerland belong, as well as with the World Bank (*q.v.*) and the United Nations Conference on Trade and Development (UNCTAD). The Paris Club is also known as the Group of Ten (G-10).

rufiyaa (Rf)

Maldives currency; 1 rufiyaa = 100 laari; in June 1995 US$1.00 = Rf11.77.

Seychelles rupee (SRe)

1 Seychelles rupee = 100 cents; in August 1995 US$1.00 = SRe4.25.

Shia (from Shiat Ali, the Party or Ali)

A member of the smaller of the two great divisions of Islam. The Shia supported the claims of Ali and his line to presumptive right to the caliphate and leadership of the Muslim community, and on this issue they divided from the Sunni (*q.v.*) in the major schism within Islam. Later schisms have produced further divisions among the Shia over the identity and number of imams. Most Shia revere Twelve Imams, the last of whom is believed to be hidden from view.

South Asia Association for Regional Cooperation (SAARC)

Comprises the seven nations of South Asia: Bangladesh, Bhutan, India, Maldives, Nepal, Pakistan, and Sri Lanka; founded as South Asia Regional Cooperation (SARC) organization at a meeting of foreign ministers in New Delhi on August 1-2, 1983; a second organizational meeting of foreign ministers was held in Thimphu in May 1985; inaugural meeting of heads of state and government in Dhaka on December 7-8, 1985. The goal is to effect economic, technical, and cultural cooperation and to provide a forum for discussions of South Asia political problems.

special drawing rights (SDRs)

Monetary units of the International Monetary Fund (*q.v.*) based on a basket of international currencies including the United States dollar, the German deutsche mark, the Japanese yen, the British pound sterling, and the French franc.

Stabex system

A system of export earnings stabilization set up by the European Community (EC) in accordance with the African, Caribbean, and Pacific

(ACP) states. Under the system, the EC helps developing countries withstand fluctuations in the price of their agricultural products by paying compensation for lost export earnings.

Sunni

The larger of the two great divisions of Islam. The Sunni, who rejected the claims of Ali's line, believe that they are the true followers of the sunna, the guide to proper behavior set forth by Muhammad's personal deeds and utterances. *See also* Shia.

World Bank

Informal name used to designate a group of four affiliated international institutions: the International Bank for Reconstruction and Development (IBRD), the International Development Association (IDA), the International Finance Corporation (IFC), and the Multilateral Investment Guarantee Agency (MIGA). The IBRD, established in 1945, has the primary purpose of providing loans to developing countries for productive projects. The IDA, a legally separate loan fund but administered by the staff of the IBRD, was set up in 1960 to furnish credits to the poorest developing countries on much easier terms than those of conventional IBRD loans. The IFC, founded in 1956, supplements the activities of the IBRD through loans and assistance specifically designed to encourage the growth of productive private enterprises in the less developed countries. The MIGA, founded in 1988, insures private foreign investment in developing countries against various noncommercial risks. The president and certain senior officers of the IBRD hold the same positions in the IFC. The four institutions are owned by the governments of the countries that subscribe their capital. To participate in the World Bank group, member states must first belong to the International Monetary Fund (IMF-- *q.v.*).

INTERNATIONAL MONETARY FUND

COMORESOS

Recent Economic Developments

Prepared by a staff team consisting of Messrs. H. Snoek (head), J. Cady, A. D'Hoore, and Ms. C. Sancak (all AFR)

Approved by the African Department

July 3, 2001

Contents

II. Statistical Appendix Tables

I. Introduction

1. The Federal Islamic Republic of the Comoros (henceforth, the Comoros), situated in the Indian Ocean between Madagascar and the African continent, is comprised of three islands: Grande Comore, Anjouan, and Mohéli.[1] The population in 2000 was estimated at 568,000, of which about 55 percent live on Grand Comore, 40 percent on Anjouan, and 5 percent on Mohéli. About 70 percent of the population is involved in the agricultural sector, which consists of subsistence agriculture (including fishing) and the production of three export crops: vanilla, cloves, and ylang-ylang (a natural essence). While there is some tourism, this sector is not well-developed. The primary sector accounted for 40 percent of nominal GDP in 2000, the secondary sector for12 percent, and the tertiary sector for 48 percent (Table 1). The population growth rate is high at 2.7 percent, and the increasing population density is becoming a problem, especially on the island of Anjouan. There has been significant out-migration; Comorians from Grand Comore usually migrate to France, and those from Anjouan to Mayotte.[2] Transfers from this "diaspora" provide substantial income for the Comoros, mitigating the effects of declining per capita growth rates. GDP per capita is estimated at US$356 in 2000 and about 60 percent of the population is living below the poverty line, placing the Comoros among the poorest countries in the world.

2. The Comoros has been unable to create a stable political environment since its independence from France in 1975, experiencing frequent coup d'états. The political situation worsened after the secession attempt of Anjouan in September 1997, followed by internal armed conflict on that island in 1998 and 1999. In April 1999, a conference on inter-island reconciliation was held in Madagascar under the auspices of the Organization of African Unity (OAU). Grand Comore and Mohéli reached agreement (the Antananarivo Agreement) on maintaining the territorial integrity of the Comoros, but Anjouan disagreed with the proposed political structure. The failure to reach an agreement led to political unrest and riots in Grand Comore; within a week, the current federal government came to power through a bloodless military coup d'etat (April 30, 1999).

3. Anjouan did not receive any international support for its secession attempt. In addition to the internal unrest, the rupture in services that were previously provided by the federal government, including salary payments for the about 1,900 civil servants on the island, led to a deterioration in the economic situation. The latter was further aggravated following an international embargo imposed by the OAU in early 2000. Renewed negotiations between the islands led to an agreement in August 2000 (the Fomboni Accord), which, however, was not supported by the OAU. The OAU and the Organization for the Francophonie were actively involved in further discussion, which led, in February 2001, to

---

[1] The fourth island in the archipelago, Mayotte, opted to remain a French territory when the Comoros became independent in 1975.

[2] The number of Comorians living abroad is estimated at 100,000–150,000.

an agreement between the federal government, Anjouan, the opposition and the OAU and Organization for the Francophonie on the reunification of the country under a new structure with broader autonomy for each island. This agreement outlines a calendar for constitutional reform, the formation of a transitional government of national unity after a referendum on the new constitution, legislative and presidential elections, and, finally, the reestablishment of democratic political institutions by end-2001. The agreement is supervised by a Steering Commission, including representatives of all signatories to the agreement. A broad-based tri-partite commission (72 members), comprising representatives of the federal government, the islands, opposition parties, and civil society, is responsible for the implementation of this calendar.

4. Although the economic database remains weak (Box1), available information indicates that recent macroeconomic developments have been poor. Real GDP growth has remained below population growth since the mid-1980s. The Comoros is a member of the French Franc zone, and the stable exchange rate has allowed inflation to remain in the low single digits. However, large fiscal imbalances have resulted in the accumulation of large wage and external debt payment arrears.

5. This recent economic developments report (RED) provides background information on economic developments in the Comoros in the 1997–2000 (because of disruptions in government services and the political unrest, there were no Article IV consultation discussions in 1998 and 1999, and the 2000 RED included a statistical appendix only). Because of the political problems and the deterioration in the economic database of Anjouan, the data for the period 1997–2000 include only estimates for Anjouan.

Box 1. Comoros: Statistical Issues

The collection and processing of macroeconomic statistics on the Comoros remain deficient. The disruptions in the civil service and the unavailability of data from Anjouan have further compounded these problems in recent years. The national accounts prepared by the authorities include methodological errors in the calculation of real GDP and the GDP deflator. In 1995, real GDP values were calculated using household and business surveys; however, since then, the authorities' real GDP estimates values are based on extrapolations only. The indicators for calculating GDP deflators reflect only a small part of the concerned economic activity. Because of the incomplete data, the staff has adjusted the national accounts estimates based on a broad range of indicators.

There are also methodological problems with regard to the consumer price index (CPI). In 2000, based on the recommendation of AFRISTAT, the authorities have updated the consumption basket using the 1995 household budget survey. However, in addition to the fact that the important structural changes in recent years brought about by the disruptions in government services may have reduced the relevance of the 1995 date, the revised series does not have an overlap with the old one, resulting in a break in series. The staff estimates attempt to correct for this.

The balance of payments estimates include data on Anjouan; however, over the 1997–2000 period, the data are less reliable due to the lack of actual data from that island. The monetary data also include Anjouan. However, public expenditure management on Anjouan has severely deteriorated in recent years, and there are no comprehensive fiscal data available for the years 1997–2001.

II. Production, Income, and Prices

A. Production and Income

6. Real GDP growth averaged 1.5 percent during 1997–2000, but declined by 1.1 percent in 2000; per capita real GDP declined by 5.8 percent. Growth in the primary sector, which consists mainly of subsistence agriculture and fishing, averaged less than 3 percent during 1997–2000 (Table 2). Food production is estimated to have increased by slightly more than the population growth (Tables 5–7)—which is corroborated by the fact that food imports have not increased, while there are no indications of shortages. The production of export crops, which accounts for about 10 percent of the value added in this sector, is estimated to have stagnated during the last four years (Table 8). In the case of vanilla, production increased in 1997 and 1998, but declined in 1999 and 2000 (Tables 9–10). This decline occurred despite a steady increase in international prices caused by the shortage in world supply after cyclones in 1997 and 2000 damaged a large part of Madagascar's vanilla crop. The production of cloves increased sharply in 1997 and more steadily thereafter, reflecting positive price developments. The latter increase was the result of falling production in Indonesia—one of the world's principal producers (and

consumers)—because of droughts. However, over-harvesting in 1999 damaged the trees, and the combined output of cloves and clove buds is estimated to have declined in 2000.[3] The production of ylang-ylang, which is mainly on Anjouan, sharply increased in 1998, but declined again in 1999 and is estimated to have stagnated in 2000, reflecting limited world demand because of large stocks. The local currency price of ylang-ylang has been relatively steady over the period 1997–1999; it then increased by almost 60 percent in 2000, which is largely explained by the appreciation of the US dollar against the euro and the Comorian franc (ylang-ylang is priced in U.S. dollars in world markets).

7. The secondary sector is not well-developed in the Comoros. Most manufactured goods are imported, and the manufacturing sector consists mainly of food processing, (bakeries and restaurants), some textile manufacturing, wood and paper processing, and the production of construction material. The average annual growth rate for manufacturing industries was –2.3 percent and for construction –2.2 percent over 1997–2000 because of low public and private demand. As a result, value added in the secondary sector declined on average by 1.2 percent annually during 1997–2000.

8. Growth in the tertiary sector stagnated during 1997–2000. Domestic trade and tourism (25 percent of GDP), and public administration (14 percent of GDP) are the most important contributors to the value added in this sector. The former showed a small increase, on average, which was offset by a decline in value added in the government sector, reflecting a reduction in staffing. The tourism sector was adversely affected by the political uncertainty. The number of visitors increased slightly from 26, 200 in 1997 to 27,500 in 1998 but then dropped sharply by 3,000 to 24,500 in 1999; however, these numbers include visits by the large Comorian community abroad (Table 12). While the available number of beds increased slightly from 766 in 1997 to 780 in 1999 (of which 450 are in the only large resort hotel, which opened in 1989), the average occupancy rate for hotels remained below 70 percent in the late 1990s.

B. Domestic Demand

9. The share of consumption in nominal GDP is estimated to have declined considerably in recent years, from 103 percent in 1996 to 93 percent in 2000 (Table 3). The main contribution to the decline derived from the public sector, reflecting the decline in both domestic and foreign financed expenditures in recent years. Reflecting these developments, gross national savings increased from 5 percent of GDP in 1996 to 10 percent in 2000. Over the same period, both private and public sector investment declined as a result of the uncertain political environment and structural problems, and following the completion of an investment program in the electricity company in 1998. Thus, overall investment fell from 13.6 percent of GDP in 1996 to 10.4 percent in 2000. Net factor income declined from the

[3] Cloves and ylang-ylang take five years to harvest after planting, whereas vanilla takes about two years.

already low level of 0.4 percent of GDP in the mid-1990s. However, this does not reflect the income that is brought along by visiting Comorians living abroad (which is included under receipts from tourism in the balance of payments), or transferred outside the official channels; these alternative channels for transfers are estimated to be substantial, although firm data is not available.

C. Prices

10. Inflation remained stable at 3.0–3.5 percent over 1997–1999, but increased slightly to 4.8 percent in 2000 on an end-year basis as a result of increases in petroleum prices (Table 14). In early 2000, on the recommendation of a mission of the African Statistical Institute (AFRISTAT)[4] in 1998, the Planning Directorate revised the basket for the calculation of the consumer price index on the bases of the 1995 household budget survey.

11. The government regulates, to a varying degree, the prices of key export products and some import products. For the three export cash crops (vanilla, cloves, and ylang-ylang), the government, in consultation with producers and exporters, determines the minimum price to be paid to the producers, with a view to protecting farmers from oligopolistic price setting by the few merchants who buy the cash crops. Similarly, the government fixes consumer prices for some import products after discussions with the large merchants. The final consumer price is determined based on the invoice of the suppliers and other applicable costs and taxes; the final price allows, in general, for a 5–10 percent profit margin. The import products whose prices are determined by the government are: petroleum products, certain food products (rice, sugar, oil, meat, chicken, salt, flour, concentrated milk, and bottled tomatoes), certain construction materials (cement, steel, and iron), school supplies (notebooks, pencils, erasers, etc.), and essential pharmaceuticals.[5] Local product prices are not regulated by the government.

D. Environment

12. The government does not have a national environmental policy. However, the depletion of forests and erosion are likely to pose problems for the environment in the future. This is especially acute on Anjouan, with high population pressure and a high demand for firewood for the distillation of ylang-ylang oil. The latter has been further aggravated by the recently increased demand for low grade oils, which requires a distillation process of up to five times as long as for high grade oil.

---

[4] AFRISTAT is an Africa-based statistical institute, supported by EUROSTAT, the European Commission's Statistical Office. African countries must become members, pay dues, and then benefit from direct technical assistance by AFRISTAT.

[5] Petroleum prices and low-grade rice are imported solely by parastatal companies.

III. Fiscal Developments

13. Assessment of fiscal developments over the period 1997–2000 is rendered difficult by a sharp deterioration in the reliability of fiscal data—especially for 1998—because of the deterioration in government services and political crisis. From August 1997, revenues collected on Anjouan and Mohéli were not reported to the federal authorities. In mid-1998, while the provisioning of data from Mohéli was restored, the federal government interrupted payment of wages to federally-employed civil servants on Anjouan, numbering about 1,900 out of the total civil service of about 6,200, thereby effectively ending all fiscal relations with this island.[6] Data on government operations for the period 1998–2000 used in this report (Tables 16–18), cover the federal government only.

14. Overall fiscal developments were mixed over the period. The government made some, albeit limited, progress in tackling long-standing fiscal problems, namely, uneven revenue performance and a high share of wages in expenditures, coupled with poor controls of the wage bill. Given limited access to domestic credit, a decline in donor support in the context of the political problems, and a high burden of debt service obligations, current fiscal imbalances led to the persistent accumulation of arrears on wages, payments to domestic suppliers, and on external debt service. This in turn led to further social discontent and worsening administrative performance, further impeding donor support.

15. Revenue performance deteriorated over much of the period, with total revenues declining from 13.8 percent of GDP in 1997 to 10.2 percent in 2000, though, as indicated earlier, the latter does not include revenues collected on Anjouan since 1998, estimated at about 1.7 percent of GDP in 2000. Tax revenues varied widely between 1997 and 2000, falling by over 2 percent of GDP in 1998 and about 1 percent in 2000, after having recovered by 0.5 percent in 1999. Broad social unrest in 1998 and the political instability no doubt account for a part in the overall decline and year-on-year variations. However, with the share of taxes on international trade accounting directly for about 70 percent of total revenues, revenue performance suffered mostly from persistent weaknesses in customs administration, inadequate efforts to restrict the scope for customs exemptions, and a tariff regime skewed towards specific rates, most of which remained unadjusted over the whole period. Accordingly, the ratio of taxes on international trade to total imports of goods declined from about 35 percent in 1997 to 24 percent in 2000.

16. In 1999, following an effort to improve revenue performance, revenues increased by 11.2 percent, compared with a decline of 15.3 percent in 1998. In May 1999, the new government implemented a number of measures amounting to a revenue effort equivalent to

---

[6] A precise estimate of the gross and net effects of these developments on the federal government fiscal accounts is unavailable. Preliminary calculations suggest a net saving of about CF 1 billion per year, or about 1 percent of GDP, in favor of the federal government for the whole period 1998–2000.

1.5 percent of GDP. The measures included stricter enforcement of tax compliance, intensified collaboration with the import inspection company, an increase in the sales tax from 7 to 10 percent, and an increase in the tax on alcohol and tobacco from 150 to 180 percent. Nevertheless, despite these measures, revenue fell by 8.8 percent to 10.2 percent of GDP in 2000, owing to the granting of tax exemptions for the import of personal effects (to encourage the large Comorian community abroad to increase such imports) in July 2000, continued problems in customs administration, and tax arrears incurred by the parastatal petroleum import company (Société Comorienne des Hydrocarbures—SCH). The SCH's arrears reflected liquidity problems caused by a change in supplier and delays in adjusting domestic prices to higher import costs.

17. Domestic expenditures[7] decreased by 10 percent in 1998 (from 13.5 percent of GDP in 1997 to 11.8 percent) as a result of the halt in wage payments to Anjouan in the second half of the year (equivalent to about 0.5 percent of GDP), and following measures taken in an effort to respond to the fall in revenues. However, the share of the wage bill in total revenues remained very high at about 65 percent, its average level over the first half of the 1990's. In 1999, despite the continued exclusion of Anjouan from the wage bill, domestic expenditure rose by 9 percent, to 12 percent of GDP, as an effort to return to the normal functioning of government services led to a increase of 49 percent in expenditure on goods and services. However, as the government started to improve the management of the payroll and implemented layoffs of staff with irregular documentary backgrounds, wage expenditure fell by 10 percent, to 6.3 percent of GDP, or the equivalent of 53 percent of revenues (Tables 19–21).

18. In July 2000, in response to the revenue shortfall and in order to avoid the accumulation of new wage arrears, the authorities adopted a revised budget, sharply reducing expenditures on goods and services and transfers. In addition, delays in resolving the problems with Anjouan resulted in savings of about 0.5 percent of GDP compared with the original budget; further improvements in the management of the payroll generated an additional 5 percent reduction in the wage bill compared to 1999. As a result, domestic expenditures decreased from 12.0 percent of GDP in 1999 to 11.3 percent in 2000.

19. Grant- and loan-financed current (technical assistance) and capital expenditures declined from 10.4 percent of GDP in 1997 to 5.1 percent in 2000, as donor support fell sharply owing to political instability and persistent accumulation of arrears. Foreign-financed capital expenditures increased by 36 percent in 1998, to 7.4 percent of GDP, mainly as a result of one-time large investments in the power-generating sector, but declined sharply in 1999, to 5.4 percent of GDP, due to the suspension of World Bank assistance following debt-service arrears, and again in 2000, to 3.9 percent of GDP, their lowest level in more than a decade.

[7] Domestic expenditures and balances exclude foreign-financed current and capital expenditures, and payment of interest on foreign debt

20. Revenue and domestic expenditure developments resulted in small overall domestic deficits (on a commitment basis) over much of the period, equivalent of 0.4 percent of GDP in 1998 and declining to 0.2 percent of GDP in both 1999 and 2000. With the exception of 1998, when the government drew down its deposits with the banking sector by about 1 percent of GDP, the scope for domestic financing was limited; as a result, even small domestic deficits have led to substantial financing needs to cover external debt service obligations, which were, on average, equivalent to about 43 percent of revenues over the period.

21. The overall financing need—including amortization on foreign debt of about 4–5 percent of GDP annually—increased sharply in 1998 but declined to below the 1997 level in 1999. While in 1997 debt rescheduling helped to meet part of the financing need, in 1998 and 1999 financing through the accumulation of domestic and external arrears increased. At end-1999, the stock of wage arrears amounted to CF 8.3 billion (8.1 percent of GDP), up from CF 6.2 billion at end-1997. In 1998 and 1999, only 13 percent of external debt service obligations, consisting of obligations to the World Bank and the Fund, were actually paid.

22. In 2000, the overall financing need amounted to 4.9 percent of GDP; in the absence of external budget support, this led to new wage arrears (of 0.3 percent of GDP, or about one month of wages) bringing the total outstanding stock of wage arrears accumulated by the federal government since 1995 to CF 8.7 billion (8.1 percent of GDP), and to new arrears to suppliers (1.1 percent of GDP) and to external creditors (3.2 percent of GDP). At end-2000, the total stock of external debt service arrears was estimated at US$84 million, of which US$55 million was due to multilateral creditors, mainly the African Development Bank and the Arab Bank for the Economic Development of Africa (BADEA).

23. Regarding Anjouan, preliminary data suggest severe fiscal problems on the island. Revenues collected on the island, mostly in the main port, were estimated at about CF 2.4 billion in 1999 (about 2.3 percent of GDP of the Comoros), dropping to CF 1.8 billion in 2000, following the embargo instituted by the OAU. The wage bill (on a commitment basis) was estimated by the Anjouan authorities at about CF 2.5 billion (2.4 percent of GDP) during 1998 to 2000. Little information is available on other government expenditures. Since the interruption of payments of civil servants on Anjouan by the federal government in mid-1998[8], the island administration was unable to fully cover its wage bill. Yet the authorities were reluctant to proceed with massive layoffs, given social and political tensions, and even recruited staff to fill vacant high-ranking positions previously held by personnel from the main island. With no source of financing, domestic or external, the Anjouan authorities accumulated substantial wage arrears, estimated at about 15 months at end-2000, as well as suppliers arrears.

[8] The exact recording of wage payments by the federal government to Anjouan, and the extent of total wage arrears on the island, is in dispute.

IV. Monetary Developments

24. Monetary policy is conducted by the Central Bank of the Comoros (Banque Centrale des Comores—BCC) within the framework of the French franc zone system and related institutional arrangements. The banking system is composed of one commercial bank (Banque pour l'Industrie et le Commerce—BIC), the Development Bank of the Comoros, presently being restructured, and two microfinance networks. After falling by 6.6 percent in 1998, broad money grew by 7 percent in 1999, and by 14.5 percent in 2000, on account of sharply higher cash crop exports and continued growth in private transfers from abroad (Tables 24–26). While net credit to the government slightly declined in 1999 and 2000 (the government having reached the statutory borrowing ceiling at the central bank), credit to the private sector—mainly (foreign) trade related—sharply increased in 2000, after falling in 1999. Net foreign assets also increased sharply in 1999 (12.1 percent) and 2000 (14.7 percent). In May 1999, the BCC imposed a reserve requirement of 30 percent in order to force the BIC to repatriate part of its assets held abroad and sell them to the central bank, thus improving official reserves.

25. In the absence of competition, maximum and minimum deposit and lending interest rates are set by the BCC. Since January 1, 2000 they have been linked to euro-money market rates. Given the little variation in these reference rates throughout 2000, Comorian rates remained constant (Table 27).

26. The financial system remains underdeveloped. The BIC focuses exclusively on short-term commercial lending and trade- and transfer-related transactions. The Development Bank of the Comoros (Banque de Développement des Comores—BDC), the traditional medium- and long-term lender, stopped new lending operations in November 1997 as a result of liquidity and nonperforming loan problems; though inactive, it is kept alive with a view to being restructured, for which donor assistance is being provided. In recent years, two systems of micro-finance—the MECK and the SANDUK—have grown rapidly. Their combined credit portfolio represented about 8 percent of that of the BIC in 2000. However, they have not yet been recognized as financial institutions and are thus not supervised by the BCC.

V. External Sector Developments[9]

A. Balance of Payments

27. Between 1997 and 2000, the current account deficit of the balance of payments (excluding official transfers) narrowed steadily from 24.8 percent of GDP to 4.6 percent, as a result of improvements in the trade and services balances and, to a lesser extent, increased

[9] The external debt situation is discussed in detail in the External Debt Sustainability Analysis in Appendix II of the 2001 Staff Report.

net private transfers (Tables 28 and 29). Official transfers and the capital account declined significantly over the same period, largely due to the political uncertainty in the wake of the secession of Anjouan in 1997 and the military coup in 1999. In 2000, the balance of payments registered a strong improvement, posting the first surplus since 1993.

28. The improvement in the trade deficit, from 19.8 percent of GDP in 1997 to 12.9 percent in 2000, reflected strong export volume increases in 1997 and 1998 and sharp increases in the terms of trade amounting to 91.0 percent in 1999 and 57.1 percent in 2000. While the volume of traditional merchandise exports declined in 1999 and 2000, their value increased significantly due to the sharp increase in unit prices (Table 30).[10] Over 1997–2000, the international price of vanilla increased steadily, as a result of which the value of Comorian vanilla exports increased by almost 124 percent in 2000. The steady increase in the international price of cloves over 1997–2000 and the increase in Comorian production, together led to a sharp rise in the value of Comorian clove exports, especially in 1999 (by 554 percent). The decline in the volume of clove exports in 2000 reflects the lower local production because of the previous year's over-harvesting. The volume of ylang-ylang exports has been steady due to limited world demand. In the 1997–2000 period, imports declined slightly. In 2000, sharp increase in the prices of petroleum and rice were compensated by a decrease in the volume of rice imports and in some other import goods, such as meat (Table 31).

29. The service account improved over the period 1997–2000, moving from a deficit of 4.9 percent of GDP in 1997 to surpluses of 3.4, and 6.8 percent of GDP in 1999, and 2000, respectively. This steady improvement in the service account is the result of increases in service exports and decreases in service payments. Service receipts increased by 49.0 percent between 1997 and 2000, as travel receipts increased by 68 percent; this large growth is mainly explained by increasing expenditure by visiting expatriate Comorians. Imports of nonfactor services, however, decreased by 25.8 percent between 1997 and 2000 and 13.4 percent alone in 2000, largely due to decreased donor assistance in the wake of political instability.

30. Official transfers declined by 45.7 percent between 1997 and 2000 due to political instability and accumulating debt-service arrears. Net private transfers—mainly from the Comorian community abroad—declined sharply from their highest level in more than a decade in 1996 to nearly zero in 1997 because of a statistical reclassification (to travel receipts), but increased gradually again in 2000.

31. The surplus on the capital account of the balance of payments declined by 82.1 percent between 1997 and 2000. A large part of the overall decline is accounted for by the sharp decrease in short-term capital inflows (including errors and omissions), which is

---

[10] Due to a lack of reliable trade data from Anjouan over the 1997–2000 period, the balance of payments estimates are less reliable than in previous years.

related to the disruptions caused by the secession of Anjouan and the subsequent political unrest. For the first time since 1993, the overall balance of payments registered a surplus, and the net international reserves of the central bank rose by 9.3 million U.S. dollars, bringing reserve cover to 8 months of imports, up from an average of 6 months in 1997–99.

B. External Debt[11]

32. The Comoros has had long-standing external debt difficulties. In 1990, the stock of external debt amounted to US$197 million (76 percent of 1990 GDP), including US$44 million (17 percent of 1990 GDP) in arrears (Tables 33–35). In 1991 debt restructuring and rescheduling operations were concluded with the Islamic Development Bank. The Comoros has never benefited from Paris Club debt rescheduling. However, since 1993, the Comoros has benefited from restructuring and rescheduling operations from bilateral creditors, including from Saudi Arabia, Abu Dhabi, and Kuwait as well as a complete write-off of official French loans in support of the 1994 devaluation of the Comorian franc. With minimal commercial debts, the Comoros has never benefited from London Club rescheduling.

33. At end-2000, the external debt of the Comoros, including arrears, amounted to US$225 million (or 111 percent of GDP). About 78 percent of total nominal debt was owed to multilateral institutions and some 22 percent to official bilateral creditors (with just over 1 percent owed to the sole Paris Club creditor). Debt service payments arrears amounted to US$84 million at end-2000, of which US$54.5 million was due to multilateral creditors. Significant payments arrears were due to the African Development Bank (AfDB), the Arab Bank for Economic Development in Africa (BADEA), as well as to most official bilateral creditors; there were, however, no payments arrears to the IMF or the World Bank. Debt service due in 2000 amounted to the equivalent of 18 percent of exports of goods and nonfactor services.

34. At end-2000, the World Bank represented the largest external creditor, accounting for over 30 percent of total nominal claims and some 40 percent of multilateral claims . The African Development Bank was the second largest creditor, with claims amounting to 23 percent of total nominal debt, followed by the BADEA with about 11 percent. Claims by the IMF were equivalent to US$1.5 million in nominal, amounting to less than 1 percent of the total debt.

C. Exchange Rate

35. The Comoros is a member of the French Franc zone and continues to maintain a fixed exchange rate vis-à-vis the Euro. After a 33 percent devaluation in January 1994, the

[11] Due to the lack of reliable trade data from Anjouan over the 1997–2000 period, the balance of payments estimates are less reliable than in previous years.

Comorian franc was pegged to the French franc (FF) at the rate of 1 FF = CF 75. Since January 1999, with the establishment of the Euro, the Comorian franc has been pegged to the this currency at the rate of 1 Euro = CF 492. The exchange system has generally remained free of restrictions on current payments and, for countries in the franc zone, free of capital controls. Since 1996, the real effective exchange rate has generally been stable, implying no significant change in international competitiveness of the Comoros since then (Figure 1). The nominal exchange rate has also generally remained stable until 1999, when it started depreciating following the depreciation of the Euro vis-à-vis the U.S. dollar.

D. Regional Cooperation

36. The Comoros is a member of three regional trade groupings: the Indian Ocean Commission (IOC), the Common Market for Eastern and Southern Africa (COMESA), the Cross-Border Initiative (CBI) and its successor, the Regional Integration Facility Forum (RIFF). The Comoros has made some progress in trade liberalization over the course of the last decade. During 1991–94, state trading monopolies were reduced to two: the Société Comorienne des Hydrocarbures (SCH), which imports petroleum products, and the Office National d'Importation et de Commercialisation du Riz (ONICOR), which imports ordinary rice (import of high grade rice is liberalized).

37. Over the period 1996–1997, the external tariff regime was revised to a system of three non-zero bands with rates of 20, 30, and 40 percent (with the exception of alcohol and tobacco, which were taxed at 180 percent)[12], an average unweighted tariff of 30 percent, and a significant number of goods subject to specific import taxes. In 2000, the ratio of tariff revenue to imports was 38 percent, indicating that a very high proportion of imports were subject to the 40 percent rate or higher specific rates.[13] In addition, there is a statistical fee of 1 percent, a presumptive tax on imports, and a withholding tax, the latter serving as a prepayment of domestic income taxes and professional licenses due from importers. The trading system generally does not have non-tariff barriers, apart from the state trading monopolies mentioned above. Import licenses for goods originating outside the French franc zone and export licenses were required until early 2000 for statistical purposes only. Effective January 31, 2000, both licensing requirements were suspended; however, a notification requirement remains for statistical purposes. France is the Comoros' largest trading partner (Table 32). In 2000, the share of Comorian exports to France is 38.6 percent, followed by 19.9 percent to the United States. The share of Comorian imports from France is 36.6 percent, followed by 13.7 percent from Pakistan and 9.0 percent from South Africa.

---

[12] The tax on alcohol and tobacco was raised from 150 percent to 180 percent in August 1999. The tax on alcohol was further raised to 200 percent, in the 2001 budget, effective March 2001.

[13] Budgetary projections for 2001 suggest that over 80 percent of imported products are subject to the 40 percent or higher specific duty rates.

VI. STRUCTURAL REFORMS

38. The government has recently embarked on an ambitious public enterprise privatization program. Accordingly, the government has drafted regulations to liberalize the postal service and telecommunications company, SNPT (Société Nationale des Postes et Télécommunications) and allow the participation of the private sector in the postal services and telecommunications sector. The government is also preparing regulations to separate the savings bank physically and financially from the SNPT. In addition, an agreement has been signed in 2000 with ComoreTel, a new venture with private foreign participation, for the lease of the Comoros' international telephone access code. This agreement would allow private clients to use the code as a world-wide free access number.

39. The government intends to complete the privatization of the port and maritime transport company Société Comorienne des Ports et des Transports Maritime (SOCOPOTRAM) before end-2002; three international operators have expressed interest in operating the port of Moroni. With the assistance of the international financial advisor responsible with assisting the privatization commission, a schedule for the bidding process for the operation of ports has been put in place.

VII. SOCIAL REFORMS: POVERTY

40. Based on a per capita GDP of US$356 in 2000, the Comoros remains one of the poorest countries in the world. According to the United Nations Human Development Index, the country is also among the least advanced in terms of human development. Since independence, the Comoros has experienced numerous challenges on the road to development: its limited natural resources, limited human capital, and the weakness of its infrastructure are some of these challenges. In addition, poor economic management, coupled with political instability, resulted in a real growth rate which has remained generally below the population growth rate.

41. Poverty can be measured by a number of different approaches, which complement each other. Different approaches not only point to the varied nature of poverty in the Comoros, but they also highlight that each of the three islands presents a diverse picture in terms of its level of poverty.[14] The 1995 household survey allows poverty to be measured at the household and the individual level in each island. In the more traditional approach to poverty, it is considered that household expenses are an approximate measure of well-being. This approach uses the monetary description of poverty, which defines a poverty line based on the cost of basic needs. A second approach assumes that well-being is a multidimensional concept. The UN human development index follows a multidimensional approach to measuring poverty, based on essential needs. According to the monetary definition of

[14] A detailed discussion of poverty in the Comoros is presented in *Poverty in Comoros: Concepts, Measure and Analysis*, UNDP, 2000.

poverty, 47 per cent of households or 50 per cent of the population live under the poverty line, which is defined as US$1 per day. According to the human development index, which is based on an index including life expectancy, education, and living conditions, the rate of national poverty is estimated at 49 percent. Compared to the national averages, Grand Comore has a relatively low rate of monetary poverty, but a moderate rate of poverty in terms of human development, based on poor literacy rates and nonaccess to potable water. In contrast, Mohéli has a high rate of monetary poverty but a moderate rate of human development. In Anjouan both definitions of poverty indicate high rates. Both measures indicate increasing rate of national poverty between 1995 and 2000.

42. When households are grouped based on participation of the head in the labour market, it is found that the incidence of national poverty among households where the head is involved in agriculture (70 percent) is higher compared to other groups. More than 50 percent of these households are involved in subsistence agriculture. The incidence of poverty is higher in Anjouan and Mohéli, where 50–60 percent of households are considered poor, compared to Grand Comore, where only a little less than a third of households are poor. However, more than three quarters of the incidence of poverty is explained by poverty in the rural sectors of Grand Comore and Anjouan.

43. Within the context of the National Program of Reconstruction and Reconciliation, which was prepared by the government in September 2000, the Comoros is preparing a national strategy to reduce poverty and increase economic growth. The United Nations Development Program (UNDP) is supporting this strategy under a project which is expected to be completed by the end-2002 (February 2001–December 2002). The preliminary report is to be submitted to the representatives of political parties, the representative groups in the society, and donors in 2002. In addition, the World Bank has recently approved financing of a project on the methods to increase economic growth in the Comoros. This project is expected to be completed before the end-2001.

Figure 1. Comoros: Effective Exchange Rates, January 1993-December 2000
(Average 1995=100)

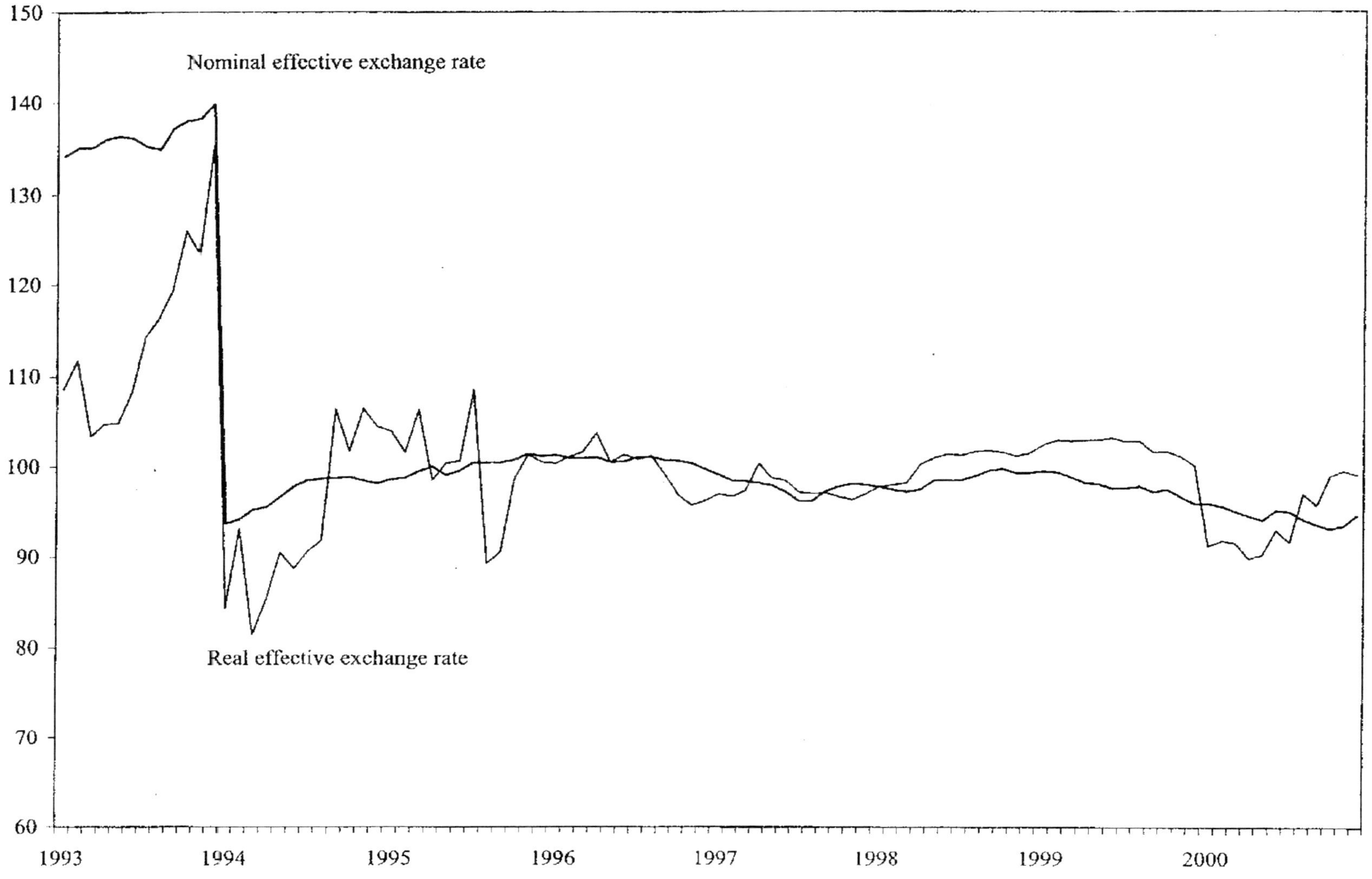

Comoros: Summary of Tax System, 1999

Tax	Nature of Tax	Exemptions an Deductions	Rates
1.Taxes on net income and profits			
1.1 Taxes on miscellaneous profits (*impôts sur les bénéfices divers* -IBD)	Tax levied on all individuals and corporations involved in commercial activities or in other lucrative activities.	Agricultural cooperatives and credit unions, government agencies and offices, managers of low-cost housing, and enterprises eligible under the provisions of the Investment Code.	35 percent for individuals and companies with turnover < CF 500,000,000 50 percent with turnover > CF 500,000,000
	Advance tax payment levied by customs on imports.	International organizations and diplomats. Noncommercial imports.	1 percent of import value, c.i.f., and 5 percent for occasional imports.
1.2 Taxes on capital income (IRCM)	Tax on distributed dividends and interest paid.	Interest on loans contracted or granted by the Development Bank, government low-cost housing offices, loan companies, agricultural credit unions, and the Caisse Française de Développement.	15 percent.
1.3 General income tax (IGR)	General tax on income of any type, payable by all individuals habitually resident in the Comoros or not resident but receiving income in the Comoros.		CF 150,001- 500,000 5 percent CF 500,001-1,000,000 10 percent CF 1,000,001-1,500,000 15 percent CF 1,500,001-2,000,000 20 percent CF 2,500,001-3,500,000 25 percent Over CF 3,500,000: 30 percent
1.4 Single Professional Tax (TPU)	Tax levied on all individuals or corporations involved in commercial activities or any other lucrative operations and whose turnover is less than CF 20,000,000.	In the event that the provisions of the Investment Code are approved.	10 percent of rental value of premises.

Comoros: Summary of Tax System, 1999 (continued)

Tax	Nature of Tax	Exemptions an Deductions	Rates
2. Property tax			
2.1 Tax on developed or rented property (IPBL)	Annual tax on dwellings and commercial and industrial premises.	New properties used as dwellings for the first two years, and properties belonging to the government or to communes.	Dwellings: 20 percent of rental value; commercial and industrial premises: 30 percent.
2.2 Tax on registered property	Tax levied on sold properties	No exemption	10 percent of sales price. 5 percent of acquisition price.
3. Taxes on goods and services			
3.1 Business license	Tax on any individual or corporation involved in trade, industry, or a liberal profession.	Public or private sector employees, for their wage-earning activity only, manual workers, artists, farmers, agricultural cooperatives, agricultural credit unions, insurance companies, midwives, and the Caisse Française de Développement.	CF 5,000-300,000 fixed tax, depending on the activity; 10 percent proportional tax, calculated on the rental value of the premises and the value of all means of production.
3.2 Consumption Tax (TC) [1]	VAT-type tax on imports (base: c.i.f. plus single import tax) and domestic production and services, including wholesale trade (base: turnover).	Medical services are exempt. Enterprises with turnover of CF 20 million or less are exempt. Exports and bunkering/petroleum products as well as journals and newspapers are example.	Four rates: base rate, 10 percent; basic necessities, 0 percent; water, private schools, and airline tickets, 3 percent; percent; electricity, telephone and banking services, 5 percent.

[1] Replaces former General sales tax, TGV.

Comoros: Summary of Tax System, 1999 (continued)

Tax	Nature of Tax	Exemptions an Deductions	Rates
3.3 Visa fee	Annual tax payable by all foreigners over 18 years of age residing in the Comoros.		1- 5-day tourist visa CF 3,000 1-15-day tourist visa CF 10,000 1-45-day tourist visa CF 15,000 Long-term tourist visa CF 30,000 Residency card CF 60,000 One-time exit visa CF 500 Exit-entry visa CF 2,000 Multiple-exit visa CF 20,000
3.4 Motor vehicle tax	Annual tax on vehicles in use.	Vehicles owned by the central government or local governments, and foreign vehicles if kept in the Comoros less than three months or belonging to diplomats.	CF 9,000-22,500, depending on the age and power of the vehicle.
3.5 Special tax on diesel engine vehicles	Annual tax on vehicles in use.	Vehicles owned by the central government or local governments, and vehicles used in agricultural activities.	CF 25,000 per unit of horsepower.
4.Taxes on international trade			
4.1 Single import tax (TUI)	All imported goods.	Goods imported by the central government under grants, and imports by diplomatic missions.	Rates of 20 percent, 30 percent, or 40 percent of import value, c.i.f.
4.2 Single specific tax on imports (TUS)	Selected imports.	Goods imported by the central government under grants, and imports by diplomatic missions.	CF 10-150 per kilo, CF 8-200 per liter.
4.3 Special fiscal duty (TSVF)	Levied on alcoholic beverages and tobacco products.		Alcoholic beverages: 200 percent; tobacco products, 180 percent; c.i.f.
4.4 Statistical levy (RI)	All imported goods.	Goods imported by the central government under grants, and imports by diplomatic missions.	1 percent of customs receipts on taxable imports; 3 percent of c.i.f. value of exempt imports.

Comoros: Summary of Tax System, 1999 (concluded)

Tax	Nature of Tax	Exemptions an Deductions	Rates
4.5 Single tax on petroleum products (TPP)		Reduced rate applied to diplomatic missions, ships, and aircraft.	Gasoline (normal rate) CF 215/l Gasoline (reduced rate) CF 196/l Diesel oil (normal rate) CF 80/l Diesel oil (reduced rate) CF 55/l Aircraft fuel (normal rate) CF 10/l Kerosene CF CF 8/l Revenue earmarking: 10 percent to Road Fund
4.6 Single tax on rice			CF 100/kg for high-grade rice; CF 60/kg for ordinary rice.
4.7 Withholding tax (ASDI)	Levied on all commercial imports.	Immediately deductible from payments of domestic taxes (IBD and TPV).	1 percent of c.i.f. value.
4.8 Export duty			Ylang-ylang and other perfume oils: 11.6 percent; vanilla (2000-01 crop season): 5 percent
5. Additional centime	Levied on behalf of the Chamber of Commerce (UCCIA).		1 percent of export value, f.o.b., less export duties.

Table 1. Comoros: Gross Domestic Product by Sector at Current Market Prices, 1995-2000

(In millions of Comorian francs)

Economic Activity	1995	1996	1997	1998	1999	2000
Agriculture, livestock, fishing, and forestry	35,499	36,161	37,962	38,971	42,029	44,082
Manufacturing	3,614	3,681	3,865	3,968	4,279	4,488
Electricity, gas, and water	1,332	1,357	1,424	1,462	1,577	1,654
Construction and public works	5,422	5,523	5,798	5,952	6,419	6,733
Trade, hotels, bars, and restaurants 1/	21,868	22,276	23,385	24,007	25,891	27,155
Banks, insurance, REB, and STE 2/	3,743	3,813	4,003	4,109	4,432	4,648
Transportation and communications	4,602	4,688	4,921	5,052	5,449	5,715
Government departments	12,418	12,650	13,280	13,633	14,702	15,420
Other services	479	488	512	526	567	595
Imputed banking production	2,165	2,205	2,315	2,377	2,563	2,688
GDP at market prices	86,812	88,432	92,836	95,304	102,781	107,801

Sources: Directorate of Statistics; and IMF staff estimates.

1/ Including import duties and taxes.
2/ REB = real estate business and STE = services to enterprises.

Table 2. Comoros: Gross Domestic Product by Sector at 1990 Constant Prices, 1995-2000

Economic Activity	1995	1996	1997	1998	1999	2000
			(In millions of Comorian francs)			
Agriculture, livestock, fishing, and forestry	28,713	28,651	30,913	30,931	32,294	32,614
Manufacturing	3,344	3,142	3,163	3,076	3,076	2,860
Electricity, gas, and water	963	927	475	947	1,140	1,144
Construction and public works	4,662	4,604	4,605	4,567	4,622	4,205
Trade, hotels, bars, and restaurants 1/	18,765	18,338	19,142	19,116	18,945	19,281
Banks, insurance, REB, and STE 2/	3,293	3,268	3,255	3,255	3,287	3,063
Transportation and communications	2,993	2,993	3,038	2,993	3,023	3,009
Government departments	9,376	9,133	9,090	9,454	9,209	8,772
Other services	361	336	398	336	339	325
Imputed banking production	1,811	1,680	1,428	1,187	1,033	1,215
GDP at market prices	70,659	69,712	72,651	73,488	74,902	74,058
			(Annual percent change)			
Agriculture, livestock, fishing, and forestry	9.6	-0.2	7.9	0.1	4.4	1.0
Manufacturing	8.2	-6.0	0.7	-2.8	0.0	-7.0
Electricity, gas, and water	5.4	-3.7	-48.8	99.4	20.4	0.4
Construction and public works	9.8	-1.2	0.0	-0.8	1.2	-9.0
Trade, hotels, bars, and restaurants 1/	9.3	-2.3	4.4	-0.1	-0.9	1.8
Banks, insurance, REB, and STE 2/	2.9	-0.8	-0.4	0.0	1.0	-6.8
Transportation and communications	9.9	0.0	1.5	-1.5	1.0	-0.5
Government departments	8.3	-2.6	-0.5	4.0	-2.6	-4.7
Other services	8.7	-6.9	18.4	-15.5	0.9	-4.1
Imputed banking production	9.1	-7.2	-15.0	-16.9	-13.0	17.6
GDP at market prices	3.6	-1.3	4.2	1.2	1.9	-1.1
Primary sector	9.6	-0.2	7.9	0.1	4.4	1.0
Secondary sector	8.7	-3.3	-4.9	4.2	2.9	-7.1
Tertiary sector	8.5	-2.1	2.5	0.7	-1.0	-1.0

Sources: Directorate of Statistics; and IMF staff estimates.

1/ Including import duties and taxes.
2/ REB = real estate business and STE = services to enterprises.

Table 3. Comoros: Source and Use of Resources at Current Market Prices, 1995-2000

(In millions of Comorian francs)

	1995	1996	1997	1998	1999	2000
Public consumption	19,338	16,800	16,950	14,832	14,975	14,547
Private consumption	72,116	74,849	84,273	76,492	84,871	85,726
Gross fixed capital formation	13,480	12,058	12,414	14,048	12,256	11,257
Change in stocks	3,411	5,116	2,300	3,063	3,120	3,000
Exports of goods and services	17,157	16,204	16,845	21,682	23,738	27,638
Imports of goods and services	-38,689	-36,594	-39,946	-34,814	-36,178	-34,367
GDP at market prices	86,812	88,432	92,836	95,304	102,781	107,801
Factor income	381	140	102	-163	93	178
Gross national product	87,193	88,572	92,938	95,141	102,874	107,979

Sources: Directorate of Statistics; and IMF staff estimates.

Table 4. Comoros: Source and Use of Resources at 1990 Constant Prices, 1995-2000

(In millions of Comorian francs)

	1995	1996	1997	1998	1999	2000
Public consumption	15,729	13,601	13,703	12,282	12,082	11,892
Private consumption	58,705	58,338	66,884	60,673	65,520	62,640
Gross fixed capital formation	10,965	9,979	9,766	10,656	8,524	7,504
Change in stocks	2,774	4,099	1,795	2,372	2,276	2,121
Exports of goods and services	13,955	13,303	13,873	18,347	18,470	21,419
Imports of goods and services	-31,469	-29,608	-33,370	-30,843	-31,969	-31,518
GDP at market prices	70,659	69,712	72,651	73,488	74,902	74,058
Factor income	310	110	81	-130	72	132
Gross national product	70,969	69,822	72,732	73,358	74,975	74,190

Sources: Directorate of Statistics; and IMF staff estimates.

Table 5. Comoros: Food Crop Production, 1995-2000 1/

(In metric tons)

	1995	1996	1997	1998	1999	2000
Cereals						
Paddy	3000	3000	2965	2960	2960	2955
Maize	3709	3700	2695	2690	2690	2685
Tubers						
Cassava	49000	49700	50396	51100	51820	52540
Taro	8102	8300	8499	8700	8910	9125
Yams	3434	3500	3567	3635	3700	3770
Sweet potatoes	1355	1390	1426	1460	1495	1530
Legumes						
Ambrevade beans	7387	7600	7820	8045	8275	8515
Ambérique beans	276	280	284	288	290	295
Tomatoes	423	430	437	445	455	465
Potatoes	292	300	308	315	325	335
Peanuts	769	790	811	835	860	885
Onions	142	150	158	165	175	185
Miscellaneous	1116	1190	1269	1340	1430	1525
Fruits						
Bananas	55969	57000	58026	59070	60130	61210
Coconuts (thousands)	70636	72500	74385	76320	78304	80340
Miscellaneous	3050	3100	3150	3200	3250	3300

Source: Directorate of Agriculture, Ministry of Agricultural Production, Marine Resources and Environment.

1/ Except paddy rice (which is linked directly to the import of white rice) and maïs; other food crops, in particular tubers tended to increase since 1980.

Table 6. Comoros: Livestock, 1995-2000

(In number of head)

	1995	1996	1997	1998	1999	2000
Cattle	43,200	43,300	48,200	49,500	50,000	50,000
Sheep	19,000	19,500	18,900	19,100	20,000	20,000
Goats	172,000	174,500	119,110	140,600	170,000	170,000
Poultry	162,000	164,000	184,600	184,600	207,700	207,700
Semi-industrial aviculture						
Meat	11,000	11,500	18,000	18,000	41,000	41,000
Eggs	5,000	5,100	6,500	6,500	6,600	6,600

Source: Directorate of Breeding, Ministry of Agricultural Production, Marine Resources, and Environment.

Table 7. Comoros: Production of Meat, Fish, and Dairy Products, 1995-2000

	1995	1996	1997	1998	1999	2000
Meat and fish (in metric tons)						
Cattle	603	828	846	1,053	1,260	1,660
Sheep and goats	210	215	219	253	314	314
Poultry	190	191	189	190	190	192
Fresh fish	12,766	13,146	12,956	13,330	13,430	13,730
Miscellaneous						
Milk (in thousands of liters)	970	980	990	995	1,005	1,015
Eggs (in thousands)	8,450	8,450	8,450	8,450	8,580	13,000

Source: Directorate of Breeding, Ministry of Agricultural Production, Marine Resources, and Environment.

Table 8. Comoros: Export Crop Production, 1995-2000

(In metric tons)

	1995	1996	1997	1998	1999	2000
Vanilla (green)	600	625	815	943	600	685
Cloves 1/	500	884	1,965	2,010	3,210	3,884
Clove buds 1/	420	1500	1,707	1,700	2,500	714
Ylang-ylang 2/						
Flowers (units) 1/	3,180	2,650	2,491	3,551	2,650	525
Essence 1/	60	50	47	67	50	10

Sources: Comorian Office of Vanilla; and Directorate of Projects, Ministry of Agricultural Production, Marine Resources, and Environment.

1/ In 2000, includes only the production of Grande Comore and Moheli.
2/ Conversion rate for ylang-ylang: 1/53

Table 9. Comoros: Prices of Export Crops, 1995-2000

(In Comorian francs per kilogram)

	1995	1996	1997	1998	1999	2000
Vanilla 1/						
Producer price (green vanilla) 2/	1,350	1,250	750	1,000	1,250	2000-2500
Export price, f.o.b. (dried vanilla)	15,085	11,325	6,819	8,015	9,973	25,818
Ylang-ylang						
Producer price (flowers)	110	75-100	75-100	100-125	150	217
Export price, f.o.b. (essence)	19,700	18,160	16,884	14,195	14,075	22,175
Cloves						
Producer price	190	75-100	150-200	225-275	1000-1250	900-1200
Export price, f.o.b.	276	255	227	249	1,130	1,293

Sources: Comorian Office of Vanilla; and General Directorate of Customs.

1/ The yield from 5 kilograms of green vanilla is about 1 kilogram of dried vanilla.
2/ Floor prices.

Table 10. Comoros: Cost Structure of Vanilla Exports, 1995-2000

(In Comorian francs per kilogram of dried vanilla) 1/

Cost elements	1995	1996	1997	1998	1999	2000
1. Producer price 2/	6,250	2,500	....	....	6,250	18,750
2. Collection fees 2/	500	250	....	....	500	500
3. Preparation of green vanilla	2,200	1,700	....	....	2,200	2,250
4. Financial and miscellaneous costs	1,916	1,262	....	....	1,377	1,889
5. Total ex-warehouse costs	10,866	5,712	....	....	10,327	23,389
6. Customs duties and other taxes 3/	1,572	1,031	....	....	...	1,291
7. Transportation and insurance	131	80	....	....	105	168
8. Total f.o.b. cost at Moroni Port	12,569	6,823	....	....	10,432	24,848

Sources: Comorian Office of Vanilla; and General Directorate of Customs.

1/ The yield from 5 kilograms of green vanilla is about 1 kilogram of dried vanilla.
2/ Equivalent dried vanilla.
3/ From 1992, includes contributions to the Fonds de Solidarité Vanille.

Table 11. Comoros: Production and Consumption of Electricity, 1995-2000

	1995	1996	1997 2/	1998	1999	2000
Production (in millions of kilowatts/hour) 1/	32.0	30.9	12.3	29.0	34.9	35.0
Consumption (in millions of kilowatts/hour) 1/	22.9	21.4	....	18.0	22.0	18.0
Installed capacity (in megawatts)	9.5	9.8	....	12.7	12.7	12.7
Anjouan	2.0	2.0	....	1.3	1.3	1.3
Ntrenani 2/	1.9	1.9	....	1.3	1.3	1.3
Domoni	...	0.0	0.0	0.0	0.0	0.0
Dima	0.1	0.0	....	0.0	0.0	0.0
Mohéli	0.8	0.8	....	0.0	0.0	0.0
Grande Comore	6.7	7.0	....	12.7	12.7	12.7
Foumbouni et M'Beni	0.4	0.6	....	2.4	2.4	2.4
Voidjou	6.0	6.0	....	0.6	0.6	0.6
Ouzioini	0.1	0.2	....	9.4	9.4	9.4
Dembéni	0.2	0.2	....	0.3	0.3	0.3

Source: Electricity and water company (CEE).

1/ The difference between production and consumption reflects power losses and fraud.

2/ In 1997, strong disruptions at establishment level (long and frequent powercuts) have not permitted to produce data on consumption.

Table 12. Comoros: Indicators of Tourism Activity, 1995-2000

	1995	1996	1997	1998	1999	2000 1/
Tourist accommodation available 2/						
(number of beds)	615	715	766	766	780	....
Number of visitors	22838	23775	26219	27474	24479	....
By origin (in percent of total)						
Europe	62.0	44.7	52.0	51.3	49.0	....
of which: France	41.4	33.6	30.0	22.6	30.8	....
Africa and Indian Ocean	34.8	47.8	41.0	39.0	44.0	....
of which: South Africa	28.6	33.6	36.0	24.8	33.0	....
Other countries	3.2	7.6	7.0	9.7	7.0	....
of which: Gulf states	...	6.1	2.0	3.5	4.0	....
Visitor overnights	130600	127200	209752	219792	195832	....
of which: COMOTEL 3/	....	....	....	....	....	....
Galawa 4/	103200	99200	167801	176833	156665	....
Other 5/	27400	28000	41951	43959	39167	....
Average length of stay						
(in days)	9	9	7	7	7	....
of which: COMOTEL	10	10	7	7	7	....
Galawa	8	8	7	7	7	....
Average room occupancy rate (in percent)	75	91	60	71	70	....
COMOTEL	25	31	15	23	17	....
Galawa	70	64	65	48	53	....
Turnover						
(in billions of Comorian francs)	3.6	3.5	9.5	8.3	11.4	....
of which: COMOTEL	0.5	0.4	1.9	1.7	2.3	....
Galawa	3.1	3.1	7.6	6.6	9.1	....

Source: General Directorate of Tourism, Ministry of Transportation and Tourism.

1/ 2000 data not yet available.
2/ No official data have been provided by the Galawa Hotel.
3/ Includes the Ylang-Ylang, Coelacanthe, and Al Amal hotels.
4/ The Sun Resorts Group includes the Galawa, Maloudja, and Itsandra hotels.
5/ Includes the Kartala, and, since 1986, the Relais de Singali hotels.

Table 13. Comoros: Indicators of Population, Employment, and Education, 1995-2000

	1995	1996	1997	1998	1999	2000
Population and employment						
Total population (in thousands)	497.0	506.7	517.3	527.9	538.5	549.3
Labor force (in thousands)	140.7	144.5	146.9	149.9	152.9	156.0
of which: wage earners	....	....	....	....	....	....
Unemployed (in thousands)	28.0	29.0	30.0	30.0	31.0	31.2
Unemployed (in percent of labor force)	19.9	20.1	20.4	20.0	20.3	20.0
Education						
Primary enrollment (number of pupils)	78,527	....	....	....	82,789	....
of which: public	31,916	....	....	....	72,522	....
private	46,611	....	....	....	10,267	....
Secondary enrollment	21,192	....	....	....	28,718	....
Vocational schools 1/	437	....	....	....	232	....
Higher education 2/	1,101	....	....	....	649	....

Sources: Directorate of Statistics; Ministry of Health, Social Affairs, and Education.

1/ For education, the 1999 data correspond to 1998/99. The data for 1999/2000 are not available.
2/ Includes the training school for teachers.

Table 14a. Comoros: Consumer Price Index, 1995-99 1/

(For 1989-93, index 1986 = 100; for 1994-96, index 1993 = 100)

	Weight	1995	1997	1998	1999
Foodstuffs and tobacco	71.4	133.2	139.2	139.1	147.5
Cereals and starches	21.2	150.8	145.7	145.4	146.9
Fruits and vegetables	12.0	133.9	136.9	128.8	159.2
Milk and fats 2/	7.7	95.2	126.5	133.5	143.2
Meat and fish	17.9	110.3	129.2	130.8	137.8
Groceries 3/	8.5	173.6	145.7	145.6	142.9
Tobacco and cigarettes	4.1	127.9	167.1	170.4	175.9
Other products	28.6	129.6	132.7	138.8	123.0
Clothing	11.6	146.3	163.1	159.0	124.0
Energy	3.8	116.4	111.0	121.9	122.7
Household capital goods	3.0	150.9	110.4	141.6	130.8
Health care 4/	3.2	53.8	50.6	81.3	82.7
Transportation	2.2	143.2	141.3	163.0	140.7
Education and leisure	2.5	147.2	135.9	109.0	137.4
Rent	2.3	121.7	147.5	151.4	131.7
Total	100.0	132.2	137.4	139.0	140.5
		(Annual change in percent)			
Memorandum item:					
Consumer price index	...	...	1.5	1.2	1.1

Sources: Directorate of Statistics; and Fund staff estimates.

1/ For Moroni only.
2/ Imports from the members of the Cooperation Council for the Arab States of the Gulf in 1995.
3/ Sharp increase in spice prices in 1995.
4/ Introduction of generic medicines in 1995.

Table 14b. Comoros: Consumer Price Index, 2000 1/

(index 1999 = 100)

	Weight	1999	2000
Foodstuffs, drinks and tobacco	6803	100.0	102.7
of which:			
Unprocessed cereals	11	100.0	103.5
Flours, semolina	1	100.0	101.2
Meat	9	100.0	95.2
Fish	10	100.0	102.5
Milk and dairy products	5	100.0	104.7
Edible oils	3	100.0	98.5
Fruits	3	100.0	86.2
Vegetables	6	100.0	107.0
Potatoes, manioc, other tubercules	8	100.0	99.2
Clothing and footware	470	100.0	103.6
Rent, water, electricity, gas and other combus	1552	100.0	110.9
of which:			
Other combustibles	264	100.0	130.4
Furniture, electric appliances	208	100.0	129.3
Health care	135	100.0	94.1
Transportation	246	100.0	94.8
Entertainment	14	100.0	98.5
Education	423	100.0	105.3
Hotels, coffee shops and restaurants	6	100.0	124.4
Other good and services	143	100.0	115.3
Total	10000	100.0	104.6
	(Annual change in percent)		
Memorandum item:			
Consumer price index			4.6

Source: Directorate of Statistics.

1/ CPI prior to 2000 not available due to change in the consumption basket in 2000.

Table 15. Comoros: Prices of Essential Goods, 1995-2000 1/

(In Comorian francs per unit, unless otherwise indicated)

	1995	1996	1997	1998	1999	2000
Rice (kilogram)						
Unit value of imports	126	109	115	120	110	122
Retail price	225	254	235	250	250	250
Annual change (in percent)	0.0	12.9	-7.5	6.4	0.0	0.0
Retail/import price	1.78	2.34	2.04	2.08	2.27	2.05
Sugar (kilogram)						
Unit value of imports	229	222	....	235	215	270
Retail price	450	375	....	400	400	500
Annual change (in percent)	0.0	-16.7	....	....	0.0	25.0
Retail/import price	1.96	1.69	....	....	1.86	1.85
Flour (kilogram)						
Retail price	250	303	....	250	250	300
Annual change (in percent)	0.0	21.2	....	....	0.0	20.0
Salt (kilogram)						
Retail price	90-100	150	150	150	150	150
Cement (metric ton)						
Unit value of imports	38,137	36,529	35,000	34,000	35,000	36,000
Retail price	75,000	70,920	70,100	70,000	75,000	70,000
Annual change (in percent)	15.4	-5.4	-1.2	-0.1	7.1	-6.7
Retail/import price	1.97	1.94	2.00	2.06	2.14	1.94
Petroleum products (liter) 2/						
Regular gasoline	325	325	360	360	390	390-450
Diesel 3/	125-295	125-295	205	230	230	230-250
Kerosene 4/	125-190	125-190	100	130	130	130-200
Electricity (kilowatt-hour) 5/						
Retail price	100-110	100-110	....	110	110	120
Water (cubic meter)						
Retail price	205-220	205-220	....	200-220	200-250	200-250

Source: Directorate of Statistics.

1/ Unit values of imports are calculated on the basis of imports, c.i.f.
2/ Average retail price per liter at new stations.
3/ The lower price is the tax exempt price paid by the electricity and water company.
4/ The higher price is for jet kerosene, sold only to civil aviation.
5/ It is the rate imposed on households and the industries.

Table 16. Comoros: Consolidated Government Financial Operations, 1995-2000
(In millions of Comorian francs, unless otherwise indicated)

	1995	1996	1997	1998 Est. 1/ 2/	1999 Est. 1/	2000 Est. 1/
Total revenue and grants	20,950	18,195	21,011	17,812	18,885	15,557
Revenues	11,478	10,909	12,828	10,865	12,079	11,018
Tax revenues	9,901	9,568	11,968	9,277	10,509	9,724
Nontax revenues	1,577	1,341	860	1,588	1,570	1,294
Exceptional revenue	--	--	--	--	--	--
External grants	9,472	7,286	8,182	6,947	6,806	4,539
Budgetary assistance	793	1,380	250	--	--	--
Project financing (incl. TA)	8,679	5,906	7,932	6,947	6,359	4,513
Other nonbudgetary aid	--	--	--	--	447	26
Total expenditure and net lending	27,310	23,353	23,076	21,038	19,669	17,614
Current expenditure	21,765	18,239	17,512	13,648	14,138	13,493
Budgetary	15,977	13,875	13,012	11,886	13,055	12,066
Wages and salaries	7,728	8,285	8,553	7,190	6,430	6,093
Goods and services	6,110	4,149	3,307	3,121	4,642	4,169
Transfers	1,327	662	265	615	1,033	844
Interest payments	812	777	887	960	950	960
External debt						890
Domestic debt						70
Technical assistance	5,500	4,366	4,500	1,762	1,083	1,427
Other expenditures 3/	288	--	--	--	--	--
Priority rehabilitation expenditures	--	--	--	--	--	--
Transition	--	--	--	--	--	--
Inter-regional Transfers	--	--	--	--	--	--
Retrenchment	288	--	--	--	--	--
Post-conflict	--	--	--	--	--	--
Capital expenditure	5,545	5,115	5,564	7,390	5,531	4,157
Budgetary	475	703	400	360	192	130
Financed externally	5,070	4,411	5,164	7,030	5,339	4,027
Priority rehabilitation expenditures	--	--	--	--	--	--
Net lending	--	--	--	--	--	-35
Overall balance (payment order)	-6,359	-5,159	-2,065	-3,226	-784	-2,057
Excluding grants	-15,831	-12,444	-10,247	-10,173	-7,590	-6,596
Change in net arrears	2,903	2,755	404	2,677	624	1,965
Interest on external debt	630	590	122	887	534	551
Domestic arrears 4/	2,273	2,166	281	1,790	90	1,413
Others (unidentified residuals) 5/	--	--	--	-3,191	495	395
Overall balance (cash basis)	-3,456	-2,403	-1,661	-3,740	336	302
Financing	3,456	2,403	1,661	3,740	-336	-302
Foreign (net)	2,961	2,536	1,695	1,593	-504	108
Drawings, PIP (identified)	1,891	2,872	1,731	1,845	63	940
Drawings, adjustment loans	1,199	--	118	--	--	--
Amortization	-3,544	-6,138	-4,045	-3,782	-4,367	-3,766
Exceptional financing	807	3,434	2,220	--	--	--
Arrears (principal)	2,609	2,369	1,671	3,530	3,801	2,933
Domestic (net)	495	-133	-34	2,147	168	-410
Bank financing 6/	897	-133	-34	1,615	-21	-210
of which: IMF (SAF)	--	--	--	--	--	-172
Deposits and claims on Treasury	--	--	--	532	-11	--
Nonbank financing	-402	--	--	--	200	-200
Asset sales			--	--	--	--
Financing need	--	--	--	--	--	--
Fiscal balances 7/						
Domestic primary current balance	-3,686	-2,186	703	-61	-26	-88
Current balance (excluding grants)	-4,498	-2,964	-184	-1,021	-976	-1,048
Overall domestic balance before exceptional expenditures	-4,161	-2,889	303	-421	-218	-253
Overall domestic balance (commitment basis)	-4,449	-2,889	303	-421	-218	-253

Sources: Ministry of Finance; and IMF staff estimates.

1/ Excludes Anjouan (for the second half of 2001 and for 2002, inter-regional transfers reflect an estimate of the financing requirement for the island budget)
2/ December 1998 estimates
3/ Includes costs of election, rehabilitation expenditures, civil service reform and inter-regional transfers
4/ Net arrears accumulation (preliminary estimates)
5/ Unidentified receipts (+)/payments (-)
6/ Financing from BCC and BIC
7/ Domestic balances exclude foreign grants, foreign-funded project spending (TA and capital expenditures), and foreign debt service

Table 17. Comoros: Consolidated Government Revenue and Grants, 1995-2000
(in millions of Comorian francs)

	1995	1996	1997	1998 Est.1/ 2/	1999 Est.1/	2000 Est. 1/
Tax revenue	9,901	9,568	11,968	9,277	10,509	9,724
Taxes on income and profits	1,403	1,044	1,436	1,598	2,084	1,895
Corporate (IBD)	880	477	923	1,025	1,556	1,348
TPU	21	19	24	25	20	16
Social Security Payments	478	464	479	524	477	514
IRVM	24	84	10	24	31	17
Taxes on property	122	119	125	62	58	65
Buildings	78	65	50	17	22	17
Registration	44	54	75	45	36	48
Taxes on goods and services	1,090	973	912	1,108	1,266	1,205
Turnover (TGV/ASDI)	946	765	605	646	736	817
Business and profit licenses	144	208	307	202	273	263
Other	--	--	--	5	13	27
AIT	--	--	--	255	244	98
Taxes on international trade	7,009	7,401	9,434	6,481	6,852	6,367
Import taxes and duties	3,006	3,435	5,039	2,458	3,663	3,010
Customs duties on exports	309	123	132	123	12	--
Other	390	279	364	1,021	159	226
Unified tax 2/	3,303	3,565	3,899	2,879	3,018	3,131
Petroleum products (90% budget)	2,240	2,377	2,376	2,225	2,225	1,772
Rice	1,063	1,188	1,523	654	793	1,359
Other taxes	277	31	61	28	249	192
Nontax revenue	1,577	1,341	860	1,589	1,570	1,294
Rental income 4/	219	14	48	61	97	127
Proceeds from services	442	572	129	681	406	284
Other nontax revenue	916	755	684	847	1,067	883
Total revenue	11,478	10,909	12,828	10,866	12,079	11,018
Exceptional revenue	--	--	--	--	--	--
External grants	9,472	7,286	8,182	6,947	6,806	4,539
Budgetary assistance	793	1,380	250	--	--	--
Project financing (incl. TA)	8,679	5,906	7,932	6,947	6,359	4,513
Other nonbudgetary aid	--	--	--	--	447	26
Total revenue and grants	20,950	18,195	21,011	17,813	18,885	15,557

Sources: Ministry of Finance; and IMF staff estimates.

1/ Excludes Anjouan (for the second half of 2001 and for 2002, inter-regional transfers reflect an estimate of the financing requirement for the island budget)
2/ December 1998 estimates

Table 18. Comoros: Consolidated Government Expenditure, 1995-2000
(in millions of Comorian francs)

	1995	1996	1997	1998 Est.1/ 2/	1999 Est.1/	2000 Est. 1/
Total expenditure and net lending	27,310	23,353	23,076	21,038	19,669	17,614
Current expenditure	21,477	18,239	17,512	13,648	14,138	13,493
Budget	15,977	13,873	13,012	11,886	13,055	12,066
Wages and salaries	7,728	8,285	8,553	7,190	6,430	6,093
Goods and services	6,110	4,149	3,307	3,121	4,642	4,169
Transfers	1,327	662	265	615	1,033	844
Interest payments 2/	812	777	887	960	950	960
External	812	777	887	960	950	890
Domestic	--	--	--	--	--	70
Technical assistance 3/	5,500	4,366	4,500	1,762	1,083	1,427
Capital expenditure	5,545	5,115	5,564	7,390	5,531	4,157
Budgetary	475	703	400	360	192	130
Financed externally	5,070	4,411	5,164	7,030	5,339	4,027
Grants	3,179	1,540	3,432	5,185	5,276	3,493
Loans	1,891	2,872	1,731	1,845	63	534
Net lending	--	--	--	--	--	-35
Budget	--	--	--	--	--	-35
Extrabudgetary	--	--	--	--	--	--

Sources: Ministry of Finance; and IMF staff estimates.

1/ Excludes Anjouan
2/ December 1998 estimates

Table 19. Comoros: Wage Bill Developments by Ministry, 1995-2000 1/

(In millions of Comorian francs)

	1995	1996	1997	1998	1999	2000
Federal Assembly	322	135	....	377	189	131
Constitutional Council	52	18	....	120	42	15
Office of the President 2/	173	288	....	956	284	200
Defense	....	....	....	...	...	1,009
Office of the Prime Minister	248	239	....	327	177	160
Foreign Affairs 3/	315	343	....	418	403	286
Embassies	...	...	....	...	...	...
National Security	80	86	....	174	166	128
Finance and Budget	525	471	....	559	514	495
Economy, Planning, and Commerce	81	...	....	42	48	51
Infrastructure, Urbanism, and Housing	147	...	....	129	101	96
National Education	3,024	3,316	....	2,861	2,021	2,230
Rural Development	255	259	....	191	176	158
Social Affairs, Labor, and Employment	31	0	....	0	0	...
Health	618	739	....	596	487	511
Transportation and Tourism	118	126	....	156	161	102
Information, Youth, Culture, and Sport	124	0	....	...	...	63
Justice and Islamic Affairs 4/	118	0	....	...	...	184
Civil Service and Justice	100	0	....	278	284	85
Provinces	212	223	....	...	...	132
Other ministries	0	721	....	7	140	56
Total	6,330	6,741	....	7,189	5,190	6,093

Source: General Directorate of Budget/ Civil Service, Ministry of Finance; and Fund staff estimates.

1/ Only includes budgeted expenditures on wages and salaries, which are paid by the Ministry of Civil Service. Protectorats are excluded.

2/ For 1998 defense is included in the figure for Presidency.

3/ Includes embassies.

4/ Before 2000, figures for Justice reported together with Civil Service

5/ Excluding Anjouan for the last quarter of 1998 onwards.

Table 20. Comoros: Breakdown of Staffing Levels by Ministry, 1995-2000 1/ 2/ 3/

	1995	1996	1997	1998	1999	2000
Federal Assembly	82	26	53	51	37	36
Constitutional Council	8	--	31	37	5	5
Office of the President (excludes Defense)	108	180	82	144	77	102
Foreign Affairs (excludes embassies)	76	92	95	93	84	83
National Security	122	129	185	199	172	118
Finance and Budget	439	465	467	464	445	343
Economy, Planning, and Commerce	76	1	62	68	65	35
Infrastructure, Urbanism, and Housing	151	--	130	133	122	83
National Education	2,791	2,889	3,003	2,972	2,794	1,965
Rural Development	224	--	200	201	182	0
Production	--	--	--	--	--	115
Health	636	723	725	751	695	463
Transportation and Tourism	122	131	136	129	122	84
Information, Youth, Culture, and Sport	110	--	--	43	56	40
Justice and Islamic Affairs 3/	168	--	121	125	127	107
Civil Service	42	--	64	73	77	66
Office of the Prime Minister	61	59	52	53	40	51
Ngazidja province	148	154	124	121	114	111
Ndzouani province	110	108	47	49	47	0
Mohéli province	45	46	84	84	84	46
Public enterprises	--	792	--	--	--	--
Contractuals paid manually	--	--	123	338	464	
Other ministries	--	--	--	12	--	--
Total of civil servants paid by Ministry of Civil Service	5,544	5,795	5,784	6,140	5,809	3,866
Other public employees	1,064	123	505	504	784	....
Total of public employees	6,608	5,918	6,289	6,644	6,593	....

Source: General Directorate of Budget/ Civil Service, Ministry of Finance.

1/ Staff paid by the Treasury
2/ 1998 and 1999 figures include an estimated value for Anjouan; 2000 figures exclude Anjouan.
3/ Before 2000, figures for Justice reported together with Civil Service

Table 21. Comoros: Breakdown of the Goverment Wage Bill, 1995-2000

(In Comorian francs)

	1995 1/	1996 1/	1997 1/	1998 2/	1999 2/	2000 2/
Basic salaries	4,589	4,930	5,206	4,633	3,819	3,666
Allowances	1,585	1,635	1,197	967	1,344	950
Function	203	176	96	82	136	141
Housing	758	823	654	626	798	459
Teaching (teachers)	233	242	232	156	198	166
Indemnité de sujétion	120	115	15	27	25	19
Indemnité de remise	68	71	75	70	60	63
Geographic	75	88	--	--	--	63
Other	129	120	125	211	127	39
Employer contributions	369	398	418	347	291	286
Total	6,543	6,963	6,821	5,947	5,454	4,934

Source: General Directorate of Budget/ Civil Service, Ministry of Finance.

1/ 1995-97 figures exclude embassies and defense.
2/ Including embassies.

Table 22. Comoros: Consolidated Net Statement of Public Enterprises, 1995-2000
(In millions of Comorian francs)

	Turnover	Change in Stocks	Wages and Salaries	Pur-chases	Taxes	Financial Charges	Other Expen-ditures	Total Expen-ditures	Surplus or Loss 1/
Import monopolies									
SCH									
1995	6,893	-153	293	2,346	209	217	3,697	6,609	284
1996	7,554	-248	264	3,502	0	46	3,789	7,353	201
1997	7,314	431	267	2,764	82	26	3,608	7,178	136
1998	6,739	-215	241	2,428	2,985	46	3,783	6,490	22
1999	7,079	-75	267	3,122	2,795	40	3,805	7,125	43
2000	8,106	-59	211	3,830	2,577	47	....	....	20
ONICOR									
1995	4,048	0	33	2,720	117	5	1,282	4,217	-169
1996	....	....	....	....	....	....	....	....	....
1997	....	....	....	....	....	....	....	....	....
1998	....	....	....	....	....	....	....	....	....
1999	....	....	....	....	....	....	....	....	....
2000	4,388	0	52	4,135	2	8	126	4,327	72
Airport Hahaya (AIMPSI)									
1995	657	1	172	166	3	0	102	444	213
1996	740	4	182	163	4	41	169	561	177
1997	748	9	192	150	7	40	114	513	236
1998	749	-8	190	159	6	41	161	549	200
1999	849	12	210	167	35	41	195	660	189
2000	....	....	....	....	....	....	....	....	....
Public utilities									
SNPT									
1995	2,524	22	358	375	106	135	417	1,412	1,112
1996	2,984	4	400	399	449	95	503	1,849	1,135
1997	3,330	29	466	428	438	118	504	1,982	1,348
1998	3,383	-133	536	603	371	119	512	2,008	1,375
1999	4,057	22	595	549	373	236	479	2,254	1,803
2000	4,754	21	550	869	497	328	386	2,652	2,102
SOCOPOTRAM									
1995	....	....	....	....	....	....	....	....	....
1996	....	....	....	....	....	....	....	....	....
1997	....	....	....	....	....	....	....	....	....
1998	543	....	545	34	37	5	50	630	-87
1999	899	....	728	53	1	2	90	873	25
2000	985	....	628	61	18	9	248	957	28

Sources: Public enterprises listed below; and IMF staff estimates.

Notes: SCH (Comorian Hydrocarbons Company); ONICOR (National Rice Imports and Marketing Office); SNPT (Post and Telecommunications Office); SOCOPOTRAM (Comorian Ports Establishment); and IBD is taxes on miscellaneous profits.
Data on CEE (Compagnie d'Eau et d'Electricité) not available.

1/ Before provision for amortization.

Table 23. Comoros: Consolidated Financial Statement of Public Enterprises, 1995-2000

(In millions of Comorian francs)

	Share Capital	Total Long-term Debt	Turnover	Net Profit Before IBD	IBD	Net Profit After IBD	Accu-mulated Losses	Long-term External Debt	Interest on Gross Debt	Gross Fixed Investment	Govern-ment Arrears 1/	Profit Rate (in per-cent) 2/	Profit Rate (in per-cent) 3/
Import monopolies													
SCH													
1995	650	190	6,893	419	209	210	0	190	....	235	2,447	64.5	6.1
1996	650	0	7,554	-2	0	0	0	0	....	59	2,774	....	....
1997	650	0	7,314	164	82	0	0	0	....	32	1,625	....	....
1998	650	0	6,728	434	217	0	0	0	....	90	1,463	....	....
1999	650	0	7,177	146	73	0	0	0	....	351	1,029	....	....
2000													
ONICOR													
1995	504	0	4,048	...	117	...	...	0	0	0	0	0	0
1996	....	....	....	....	....	....	....	....	....	....	....	....	....
1997	....	....	....	....	....	....	....	....	....	....	....	....	....
1998	....	....	....	....	....	....	....	....	....	....	....	....	....
1999	....	....	....	....	....	....	....	....	....	....	....	....	....
2000	360	0	4,388	72	36	36	0	0	0	0	0	0	0
AEROPORT HAHAYA (AIMPSI)													
1995	4,186	464	667	-175	0	-175	2,499	464	....	....	....	....	....
1996	4,186	1,270	740	-63	0	-63	2,675	1,270	....	....	....	....	....
1997	4,186	1,350	748	-158	0	-158	2,738	1,350	....	....	....	....	....
1998	4,186	1,350	749	-227	0	-227	2,896	1,350	....	....	....	....	....
1999	4,186	1,316	849	-176	0	-176	3,122	1,316	....	....	....	....	....
2000	4,186	1,316	849	-176	8	-176	3,122	1,316	....	....	....	....	....
Public services													
SNPT													
1995	1,257	3,161	2,524	127	51	76	1,270	1,694	....	....	115	4.8	5.2
1996	1,257	3,016	2,984	763	381	381	1,270	1,547	....	....	328	....	....
1997	1,257	3,033	3,330	768	384	384	1,270	1,542	....	....	592	....	....
1998	1,257	3,029	3,383	577	288	288	1,270	1,562	....	....	832	....	....
1999	1,257	4,356	4,057	601	300	300	1,270	2,889	....	....	645	....	....
2000*	1,257	4,489	4,754	800	400	400	1,270	3,024	883	....	862	....	....

Sources: Public enterprises listed below; and IMF staff estimates.

Notes: SCH (Comorian Hydrocarbons Company); ONICOR (National Rice Imports and Marketing Office); SNPT (Post and Telecommunications Office); and IBD = taxes on miscellaneous profits. Data on CEE (Compagnie d'Eau et d'Electricité) and Comorian Ports Establishment (SOCOPOTRAM) not available.

1/ At year's end

2/ Net profits before IBD over social capital.

3/ Net profit before IBD over turnover.

Table 24. Comoros: Monetary Survey, 1995-2000

(In millions of Comorian francs; end of period)

	1995	1996	1997	1998	1999	2000
Net foreign assets	15,697	19,339	18,765	17,737	19,890	22,813
Central bank	14,901	18,499	16,838	15,398	17,124	22,102
Assets	16,422	19,950	18,298	16,581	18,295	23,017
Liabilities	-1,521	-1,451	-1,460	-1,183	-1,171	-915
Commercial bank	796	840	1,927	2,339	2,766	711
Assets	889	848	1,927	2,373	3,966	3,009
Liabilities	-93	-8	0	-34	-1,200	-2,298
Net domestic assets	1,041	-1,523	-391	-579	-1,529	-1,794
Domestic credit	11,705	9,674	10,474	12,528	12,087	12,661
Net credit to government	2,183	2,050	2,016	3,631	3,610	3,272
Credit to government	3,519	3,905	3,740	4,307	4,368	4,158
Government deposits	-1,336	-1,855	-1,724	-676	-758	-886
Claims on public enterprises	772	107	426	165	335	74
Credit to private sector 2/	8,750	7,517	8,032	8,732	8,142	9,315
Other items (net)	-10,664	-11,197	-10,865	-13,107	-13,616	-14,455
Broad money	16,738	17,816	18,374	17,158	18,361	21,019
Money	11,296	11,649	10,603	10,175	11,662	14,115
Currency in circulation	5,782	5,639	5,433	5,418	6,310	7,564
Demand deposits	5,514	6,010	5,170	4,757	5,352	6,551
Quasi-money	5,442	6,167	7,771	6,983	6,699	6,904

Sources: Central Bank of the Comoros; and Fund staff estimates and projections.

1/ Includes *Fonds particuliers* (special funds).
2/ As of 1993, excludes bankers' acceptances.

Table 25. Comoros: Summary Statement of the Central Bank, 1995-2000

(In millions of Comorian francs; end of period)

	1995	1996	1997	1998	1999	2000
Foreign assets	16,422	19,950	18,298	16,581	18,295	23,017
of which						
Operations account with French Treasury	15,492	18,857	16,410	14,847	16,382	20,568
Bank notes (CFA franc area)	522	672	1,383	1,334	1,367	1,819
Gold	82	84	79	70	82	83
SDR holdings	39	21	52	2	80	87
Correspondents	-8	11	46	6	7	76
Reserve position with IMF	295	305	327	320	363	372
Claims on Government	3,589	3,569	3,646	3,806	3,814	3,858
Statutory advances	1,991	1,981	2,034	2,226	2,234	2,278
Other claims on Treasury	5	8	0	0	0	0
Treasury (IMF account)	1,593	1,580	1,612	1,580	1,580	1,580
Claims on deposit money bank	--	--	--	50	50	50
Other assets	722	796	860	689	523	499
Assets=liabilities	20,733	24,315	22,804	21,126	22,682	27,424
Reserve money	8,870	11,936	10,454	9,323	11,104	13,980
Currency in circulation	5,782	5,639	5,433	5,418	6,310	7,564
Cash in banks	53	123	137	129	99	263
Bank for Industry and Commerce deposits	1,691	4,651	4,232	3,432	3,729	5,228
Development Bank deposits	1,223	874	17	309	938	888
Public enterprise deposits	121	649	635	35	28	37
Government deposits	1,169	1,723	1,515	542	518	508
Treasury account	20	63	38	30	61	37
Government bodies	920	1,182	663	386	365	399
Food aid services	124	186	147	....	....	....
STABEX account 1/	6	126	107	81	47	27
Cash at Treasury	99	166	560	45	45	45
Counterpart fund for Chinese aid	--	--	--	--	--	--
Foreign liabilities	192	122	131	61	112	128
Other correspondents	191	119	118	56	74	128
Transactions under way	1	3	13	5	38	0
IMF credit	--	--	--	--	--	--
Other liabilities	10,502	10,534	10,704	11,200	10,948	12,808

Sources: Central bank of the Comoros; and IMF staff estimates.

Table 26. Comoros: Summary Statement of the Bank for Industry and Commerce, 1995-2000

(In millions of Comorian francs; end of period)

	1995	1996	1997	1998	1999	2000
Reserves	1,631	4,719	4,024	3,511	3,796	5,257
Cash	53	123	137	152	99	263
Deposits at the Central bank	1,578	4,596	3,887	3,359	3,697	4,994
Foreign assets	889	848	1,927	2,373	3,966	3,009
Claims on government	--	415	94	501	554	300
Claims on private sector	8,680	7,438	8,032	8,682	8,142	9,315
Unclassified assets	1,365	467	923	490	743	1,675
of which						
Bills to be collected	--	--	--	--	--	1,189
Assets=liabilities	12,565	13,887	15,000	15,557	17,201	19,556
Demand deposits	4,170	4,487	4,518	4,413	4,386	5,626
Time and savings deposits	5,442	6,167	7,771	6,983	6,699	6,904
Time deposits	550	239	305	--	--	--
Savings deposits	4,708	5,531	5,975	6,871	6,469	6,612
Blocked account 1/	184	397	1,491	112	230	292
Government deposits 2/	167	132	209	134	240	378
Foreign liabilities	93	8	--	34	1,200	2,298
Unclassified liabilities	2,693	3,093	2,502	3,993	4,676	4,350

Source: Central Bank of the Comoros.

1/ Deposits required by the Bank for Industry and Commerce for imports under letter of credit.
2/ Principally the Stabilization Fund for Export Earnings.

Table 27: Comoros: Structure of Interest Rates, 1996-2000

(In percent)

	1996	1997	1998	1999	2000
Central bank rates					
Advances to government	5.5	4.8	4.8	3.7	6.4
Deposits from Treasury	5.5	4.5	4.5	3.1	4.9
Discount rate	8.5	7.0	7.0	5.9	6.4
Commercial bank lending rate	11.0/18.0	11.0/18.0	11.0/18.0	9.0/15.0	9.0/15.0
Deposit rates					
Demand deposits	0.0	0.0	0.0	0.0	0.0
Time deposits	5.0	3.0/4.0	3.0/4.0	3.0	3.0
Savings deposits	5.0-5.5	3.0	3.0	3.0	3.0

Source: Central Bank of the Comoros.

Table 28. Comoros: Balance of Payments, 1995-2000
(In millions of Comorian francs)

	1995	1996	1997	1998	1999	2000
Trade balance	-15,791	-16,357	-18,446	-16,099	-15,823	-13,903
Exports, f.o.b.	4,235	2,436	2,630	2,632	4,181	6,464
Vanilla	2,320	1,035	1,119	1,058	1,835	4,105
Cloves	133	210	360	180	1,177	1,213
Ylang-ylang	855	645	716	582	563	887
Other	927	546	435	812	606	259
Imports, f.o.b.	-20,026	-18,793	-21,077	-18,731	-20,004	-20,367
Services balance (net)	-5,361	-3,894	-4,553	2,804	3,476	7,352
Freight and insurance	-5,385	-5,056	-5,699	-5,100	-5,447	-6,084
Other transportation	-1,855	-2,027	-2,056	-69	-183	-59
Travel	5,363	6,806	7,010	11,464	12,341	14,137
Investment income	1,193	918	989	815	1,057	1,068
Interest payments	-812	-777	-887	-978	-964	-890
Other services	-3,865	-3,756	-3,909	-3,328	-3,328	-819
Private transfers (net)	3,260	4,626	--	100	907	1,546
Current account (excluding official transfers)	-17,892	-15,625	-22,999	-13,195	-11,440	-5,005
Official transfers	10,183	7,898	8,362	7,405	7,216	4,539
Current account (including official transfers)	-7,708	-7,727	-14,637	-5,790	-4,225	-466
Direct investment	333	360	100	170	125	50
Medium- and long-term borrowing	439	-2,797	-2,115	-1,698	-2,796	-2,826
Gross borrowing	3,983	3,341	1,930	2,272	1,571	940
Amortization	-3,544	-6,138	-4,045	-3,970	-4,367	-3,766
Trade-related credits	448	59	683	-737	18	-321
Commercial banks	-684	-44	-1,087	-412	-427	2,055
Foreign assets	-774	41	-1,079	-446	-1,593	2,055
Foreign liabilities	90	-85	-8	34	1,166	0
Short-term capital (including errors & omissions)	1,739	7,355	11,382	2,610	4,596	2,648
Capital account	2,275	4,932	8,963	-67	1,516	1,607
Overall balance	-5,433	-2,794	-5,674	-5,857	-2,708	1,141
Financing	5,433	2,794	5,674	5,857	2,708	-1,141
Central bank	1,388	-3,598	1,661	1,440	-1,727	-4,978
Gross foreign assets of Central Bank	1,307	-3,528	1,652	1,717	-1,714	-4,722
Net use of Fund credit	--	--	-108	-108	-199	-172
Others (net)	81	-70	117	-169	186	-84
Valuation change	--	--	--	--	--	--
Change in arrears	3,239	2,958	1,793	4,417	4,435	3,837
Exceptional financing	807	3,434	2,220	--	--	--
Financing gap	--	--	--	--	--	--
Memorandum items:						
Gross foreign assets of the Central Bank	16,422	19,950	18,298	16,581	18,295	23,017
In months of imports of goods and nonfactor services	5	7	6	6	6	8
Nominal stock of debt in percent of GDP 1/	87	91	86	86	80	111
Debt service in percent of exports of goods and nonfactor services	25	43	29	23	22	18

Sources: Central Bank of the Comoros; Ministry of Finance; and IMF staff estimates.

Table 29. Comoros: Balance of Payments, 1995-2000
(In millions of US Dollars)

	1995	1996	1997	1998	1999	2000
Trade balance	-42.2	-42.6	-42.1	-36.4	-34.3	-26.0
Exports, f.o.b.	11.3	6.3	6.0	5.9	9.1	12.1
Vanilla	6.2	2.7	2.6	2.4	4.0	7.7
Cloves	0.4	0.5	0.8	0.4	2.5	2.3
Ylang-ylang	2.3	1.7	1.6	1.3	1.2	1.7
Other	2.5	1.4	1.0	1.8	1.3	0.5
Imports, f.o.b.	-53.5	-49.0	-48.1	-42.3	-43.3	-38.1
Services balance (net)	-14.3	-10.1	-10.4	6.3	7.5	13.8
Freight and insurance	-14.4	-13.2	-13.0	-11.5	-11.8	-11.4
Other transportation	-5.0	-5.3	-4.7	-0.2	-0.4	-0.1
Travel	14.3	17.7	16.0	25.9	26.7	26.5
Investment income	3.2	2.4	2.3	1.8	2.3	2.0
Interest payments	-2.2	-2.0	-2.0	-2.2	-2.1	-1.7
Other services	-10.3	-9.8	-8.9	-7.5	-7.2	-1.5
Private transfers (net)	8.7	12.1	--	0.2	2.0	2.9
Current account (excluding official transfers)	-47.8	-40.7	-52.5	-29.8	-24.8	-9.4
Official transfers	27.2	20.6	19.1	16.7	15.6	8.5
Current account (including official transfers)	-20.6	-20.1	-33.4	-13.1	-9.1	-0.9
Direct investment	0.9	0.9	0.2	0.4	0.3	0.1
Medium- and long-term borrowing	1.2	-7.3	-4.8	-3.8	-6.1	-5.3
Gross borrowing	10.6	8.7	4.4	5.1	3.4	1.8
Amortization	-9.5	-16.0	-9.2	-9.0	-9.5	-7.1
Trade-related credits	1.2	0.2	1.6	-1.7	0.0	-0.6
Commercial banks	-1.8	-0.1	-2.5	-0.9	-0.9	3.8
Foreign assets	-2.1	0.1	-2.5	-1.0	-3.4	3.8
Foreign liabilities	0.2	-0.2	0.0	0.1	2.5	0.0
Short-term capital (including errors & omissions)	4.6	19.2	26.0	5.9	10.0	5.0
Capital account	6.1	12.9	20.5	-0.2	3.3	3.0
Overall balance	-14.5	-7.3	-13.0	-13.2	-5.9	2.1
Financing	14.5	7.3	13.0	13.2	5.9	-2.1
Central bank	3.7	-9.4	3.8	3.3	-3.7	-9.3
Gross foreign assets of Central Bank	3.5	-9.2	3.8	3.9	-3.7	-8.8
Net use of Fund credit	--	--	-0.2	-0.2	-0.4	-0.3
Others (net)	0.2	-0.2	0.3	-0.4	0.4	-0.2
Valuation change	--	--	--	--	--	--
Change in arrears	8.7	7.7	4.1	10.0	9.6	7.2
Exceptional financing	2.2	8.9	5.1	--	--	--
Financing gap	--	--	--	--	--	--
Memorandum items:						
Gross foreign assets of the Central Bank	44	52	42	37	40	43
In months of imports of goods and nonfactor services	5	7	6	6	6	8
Nominal stock of debt in percent of GDP 1/	87	91	86	86	80	111
Debt service in percent of exports of goods and nonfactor services	25	43	30	24	22	18

Sources: Central Bank of the Comoros; Ministry of Finance; and Fund staff estimates and projections.

Table 30. Comoros: Volume and Value of Principal Exports, f.o.b., 1995-2000

(Value in millions of Comorian francs; volume in metric tons; unit value in Comorian francs per kilogram)

	1995	1996	1997	1998	1999	2000
Vanilla						
Value	2,320	1,035	1,119	1,058	1,835	4,105
Volume	154	91	164	132	184	159
Unit value	15,085	11,325	6,819	8,015	9,973	25,818
Clove buds						
Value	133	210	360	180	1,177	1,213
Volume	483	822	1,583	722	1,042	938
Unit value	276	255	227	249	1,130	1,293
Ylang-ylang						
Value	855	645	716	582	563	887
Volume	43	36	42	41	40	40
Unit value	19,700	18,160	16,884	14,195	14,075	22,175
Other products						
Value	927	546	435	812	606	259
Total value	4,235	2,436	2,630	2,632	4,181	6,464
Memorandum item:						
Export price index 1/	73.0	61.7	49.2	45.0	92.7	155.8

Source: General Directorate of Customs.

1/ Index 1990=100; calculated by the Fund staff.

Table 31. Comoros: Volume and Value of Principal Imports, c.i.f., 1995-2000

(Value in millions of Comorian francs; volume in metric tons; unit value in Comorian francs per kilogram)

	1995	1996	1997	1998	1999	2000
Rice						
Value	5,252	3,318	3,947	4,076	3,536	4,710
Volume	41,650	30,538	34,323	34,718	35,353	30,000
Unit value	126	109	115	117	100	157
Meat						
Value	1,617	1,456	2,469	2,357	2,671	1,587
Volume	2,574	2,373	3,205	3,261	3,327	2,150
Unit value	628	613	770	723	803	738
Petroleum products						
Value	2,897	1,509	1,384	965	1,426	2,703
Volume	33,962	15,663	16,380	16,663	17,144	17,893
Unit value	85	96	84	58	83	151
Cement						
Value	1,652	880	843	833	878	1,454
Volume	43,315	24,088	24,088	24,504	25,094	41,542
Unit value	38	37	35	34	35	35
Iron and steel 1/						
Value	804	858	668	711	691	708
Volume	3,461	3,299	3,168	3,223	3,300	2,633
Unit value	232	260	211	221	209	269
Other products						
Value 2/	13,189	15,828	17,464	17,405	19,344	15,289
Total value 2/	25,411	23,849	26,776	23,831	25,451	26,451
Memorandum item:						
Import price index 3/	153.8	149.3	159.6	172.2	185.8	198.8

Source: General Directorate of Customs.

1/ Including fabrications.
2/ Balance of payments basis, including adjustments for coverage, valuation and recording errors.
3/ Index 1990=100; calculated by the Fund staff.

Table 32. Comoros: Geographical Distribution of Trade, 1995-2000

(In percent)

	1995	1996	1997	1998	1999 1/	2000
Exports	100	100	100	100	100	100
European Union	45.5	60.1	52.3	68.7	43.4	50.3
of which						
France	36.9	48.5	42.5	54.7	29.1	38.6
Germany	8.1	14.9	12.0	12.6	14.0	6.6
Netherlands	0.4	2.5	1.7	0.2	1.5	0.0
Africa	18.6	18.6	16.5	18.3	6.3	8.7
United States	34.7	11.5	19.3	5.4	33.8	19.9
Rest of the world	1.1	9.8	11.9	7.7	16.5	21.1
Imports	100	100	100	100	100	100
European Union	35.3	46.4	42.4	44.8	45.8	44.3
of which						
Belgium-Luxembourg	0.7	2.0	2.3	1.4	3.1	3.8
France	31.7	41.8	34.9	36.1	37.6	36.6
Germany	0.5	1.2	2.0	2.3	1.0	1.5
Netherlands	0.7	0.8	1.4	2.1	1.2	0.9
Other European countries	2.0	4.5	2.9	1.8	0.8	1.0
of which						
Romania	1.1	1.5	2.1	0.3	0.0	0.0
Switzerland	0.4	1.1	0.7	0.9	0.7	0.4
Africa	18.3	20.2	23.7	22.2	31.6	26.2
of which						
Kenya	4.3	7.0	6.9	7.5	7.7	10.8
Madagascar	1.1	1.4	1.4	1.7	2.4	1.8
Mauritius	1.3	1.3	0.9	1.0	1.3	1.5
Réunion	3.4	2.9	3.6	2.1	9.8	2.0
South Africa	6.9	7.0	10.6	9.0	9.7	9.0
Asia	43.1	28.3	30.8	30.7	21.4	28.0
of which						
China	5.1	0.7	0.3	0.0	0.2	1.1
Japan	1.3	0.4	0.1	3.8	4.1	0.7
Kuwait	0.0	0.2	0.0	0.0	0.0	0.0
Pakistan	4.0	8.1	10.1	12.1	0.1	13.7
Saudi Arabia	9.4	3.2	2.4	1.0	0.9	1.2
Singapore	2.2	1.8	1.2	1.9	0.3	0.6
Thailand	0.1	0.0	0.0	0.0	0.1	0.2
Vietnam	0.0	6.1	5.0	0.0	3.2	0.0
United States	0.8	0.1	0.1	0.4	0.2	0.3
Rest of the world	0.4	0.4	0.1	0.1	0.3	0.2

Source: General Directorate of Customs.

1/ Data for the first 11 months.

Table 33. Comoros: External Debt Outstanding by Creditors, 1995-2000

(In millions of U.S. dollars)

	1995	1996	1997	1998	1999	2000
Multilateral loans	149.3	135.7	131.5	134.2	123.9	120.8
International Development Association	59.7	61.1	64.1	68.6	65.6	70.6
International Fund for Agricultural Development	3.4	2.9	2.7	2.6	2.4	5.8
African Development Fund	46.4	40.3	37.1	35.5	33.0	1.7
African Development Bank	12.6	9.6	7.4	6.8	5.9	34.6
Arab Bank for Economic Development in Africa	5.0	3.5	3.0	3.1	1.9	0.7
International Monetary Fund	3.3	3.2	2.9	2.7	2.6	1.5
Islamic Development Bank	9.8	8.8	8.5	8.6	8.2	4.8
Organization of Petroleum Exporting Countries Special Fund	2.9	2.1	1.9	2.0	1.5	0.2
Arab Fund for Economic and Social Development	6.2	4.3	3.9	4.2	2.8	--
European Development Fund/European Investment Bank	--	--	--	--	--	0.9
Bilateral loans	39.7	31.0	28.0	27.1	21.1	20.1
Abu Dhabi	0.8	0.7	0.6	0.7	0.6	--
China	0.8	0.4	0.5	0.7	0.5	2.7
France	--	--	--	--	--	2.4
Kuwait	24.9	20.2	18.6	18.2	14.9	13.4
Saudi Arabia	13.2	9.7	8.2	7.5	5.0	1.6
Total 1/	189.0	166.7	159.5	161.3	145.0	140.9
Arrears						
Principal	22.1	25.6	30.4	37.6	40.0	57.1
Interest	7.2	8.1	9.3	11.1	12.0	26.6
Total arrears	29.3	33.6	39.7	48.7	52.0	83.7
Stock of debt	218.3	200.3	199.1	210.0	197.0	224.6

Source: Ministry of Finance.

1/ Disbursed, outstanding, and not yet due.

Table 34. Comoros: External Debt Payment Arrears by Creditors, 1995-2000

(In millions of U.S. dollars)

	1995	1996	1997	1998	1999	2000
Multilateral creditors	**25.7**	**27.1**	**30.0**	**34.6**	**35.9**	**54.5**
International Development Association	0.2	0.2	0.2	0.1	0.7	0.0
International Monetary Fund	0.0	0.0	0.0	0.0	0.0	0.0
African Development Bank	5.3	6.4	7.4	8.6	9.5	15.5
of which: African Development Fund	1.6	2.0	2.4	2.9	3.2	3.9
Arab Bank for Economic Development in Africa	7.8	7.7	8.5	10.1	10.0	24.4
International Fund for Agricultural Development	0.0	0.0	0.0	0.0	0.1	0.0
OPEC Special Fund	2.9	2.8	3.1	3.4	3.2	3.4
Islamic Development Bank	0.4	0.8	0.7	0.6	0.6	11.2
Arab Fund for Economic and Social Development	7.6	7.3	7.8	9.0	8.7	....
Bilateral creditors	**3.6**	**6.6**	**9.7**	**14.1**	**16.2**	**29.2**
France	0.0	0.0	0.0	0.0	0.0	0.3
China	1.1	1.2	1.2	1.3	1.2	3.6
Kuwait	1.0	2.2	3.6	5.3	6.3	10.1
Saudi Arabia	1.5	3.2	4.9	7.5	8.7	14.1
United Arab Emirates	0.0	0.0	0.0	0.0	0.0	1.1
Total 1/	**29.3**	**33.6**	**39.7**	**48.7**	**52.0**	**83.7**
Of which:						
Principal	22.1	25.6	30.4	37.6	40.0	57.1
Interest	7.2	8.1	9.3	11.1	12.0	26.6

Sources: For 1995-1999, Ministère des Finances; for 2000, Comorian authorities, creditor records, and IMF staff estimates.

Table 35. Comoros: External Debt-Service Payments by Creditors, 1995-2000

(In millions of U.S. dollars)

	1995	1996	1997	1998	1999	2000
Principal due	9.37	9.51	9.51	8.79	9.71	....
of which: paid	0.45	0.96	0.89	0.57	1.18	....
Multilateral creditors	4.47	4.55	4.21	4.04	5.00	....
International Development Association	0.38	0.39	0.47	0.45	0.58	0.60
International Monetary Fund	0.00	0.00	0.25	0.24	0.43	0.32
African Development Bank	1.12	1.16	0.69	0.68	1.05	....
of which: African Development Fund	0.32	0.29	0.26	0.28	0.47	....
Arab Bank for Economic Development in Africa	0.63	0.68	0.72	0.70	0.78	....
International Fund for Agricultural Development	0.06	0.07	0.06	0.06	0.06	0.05
Organization of Petroleum Exporting Countries Special Fund	0.30	0.31	0.29	0.23	0.06	....
Islamic Development Bank 1/	0.97	0.93	0.76	0.73	0.84	0.13
Arab Fund for Economic and Social Development	0.69	0.72	0.72	0.67	0.71	....
Bilateral creditors	4.90	4.96	5.30	4.75	4.71	....
France 2/	0.00	0.00	0.00	0.00	0.00	....
China	0.24	0.02	0.03	0.03	0.03	....
Kuwait	1.19	1.37	1.48	1.49	1.75	....
Saudi Arabia	3.41	3.51	3.71	3.23	2.93	....
United Arab Emirates	0.07	0.08	0.08	0.00	0.00	....
Interest due	2.45	2.46	2.26	2.18	2.12	....
of which: paid	0.47	0.52	0.55	0.16	0.97	....
Multilateral creditors	2.11	2.15	1.98	1.95	1.91	....
International Development Association	0.46	0.57	0.51	0.52	0.56	0.58
International Monetary Fund	0.02	0.02	0.01	0.01	0.01	0.00
African Development Bank	0.77	0.73	0.68	0.67	0.52	....
of which: African Development Fund	0.35	0.33	0.29	0.28	0.29	....
Arab Bank for Economic Development in Africa	0.35	0.37	0.37	0.34	0.37	....
International Fund for Agricultural Development	0.03	0.04	0.04	0.05	0.06	0.05
OPEC Special Fund	0.03	0.02	0.02	0.02	0.06	....
Islamic Development Bank	0.05	0.04	0.03	0.03	0.03	0.00
Arab Fund for Economic and Social Development	0.04	0.04	0.03	0.02	0.02	....
Bilateral creditors	0.34	0.32	0.28	0.23	0.21	....
France	0.00	0.00	0.00	0.00	0.00	....
China	0.01	0.01	0.01	0.01	0.01	....
Kuwait	0.18	0.17	0.17	0.15	0.15	....
Saudi Arabia	0.15	0.13	0.11	0.07	0.05	....
United Arab Emirates	0.00	0.00	0.00	0.00	0.00	....
Total debt service due	11.82	11.98	11.78	10.97	11.83	....
of which: paid	0.92	1.48	1.44	0.74	2.15	....
Multilateral creditors	6.57	6.70	6.19	5.99	6.91	....
International Development Association	0.84	0.95	0.98	0.97	1.14	1.18
International Monetary Fund	0.02	0.02	0.26	0.26	0.44	0.32
African Development Bank	1.89	1.89	1.37	1.35	1.57	....
of which: African Development Fund	0.67	0.62	0.55	0.57	0.76	....
Arab Bank for Economic Development in Africa	0.98	1.05	1.09	1.04	1.15	....
International Fund for Agricultural Development	0.10	0.10	0.10	0.11	0.13	0.11
OPEC Special Fund	0.33	0.34	0.31	0.24	0.13	....
Islamic Development Bank 1/	1.02	0.98	0.79	0.76	0.87	0.13
Arab Fund for Economic and Social Development	0.73	0.75	0.75	0.69	0.73	....
Bilateral creditors	5.25	5.28	5.59	4.98	4.91	....
France	0.00	0.00	0.00	0.00	0.00	....
China	0.24	0.03	0.04	0.04	0.04	....
Kuwait	1.37	1.54	1.65	1.64	1.90	....
Saudi Arabia	3.56	3.63	3.82	3.31	2.98	....
United Arab Emirates	0.07	0.08	0.08	0.00	0.00	....

Source: Ministry of Finance.

1/ Includes debt rescheduled in 1996.
2/ Includes debt cancellations in 1994.

VIII/112/97-EN

FEDERAL ISLAMIC REPUBLIC OF THE COMOROS

EUROPEAN COMMISSION

NATIONAL INDICATIVE PROGRAMME

8th EDF

FRAMEWORK OF COOPERATION BETWEEN THE COMOROS AND THE EUROPEAN COMMUNITY NATIONAL INDICATIVE PROGRAMME

I - GENERAL FRAMEWORK

1. The Government of the Federal Islamic Republic of the Comoros, represented by Mr Mohamed Ali Soilihi, Minister for Finance, the Budget, the Economy and Home Trade, EDF National Authorizing Officer, and the European Commission represented by Mr ...., met in Moroni from ...... to ...... with a view to determining the general guidelines of cooperation between the Comoros and the European Community (EC).

2. During these discussions, the Indicative Programme of Community aid to the Comoros was drawn up in accordance with Article 282 of the Fourth Lomé Convention, as revised by the agreement signed in Mauritius on 4 November 1995, hereinafter referred to as "the Lomé IV Convention", in respect of the implementation of the Second Financial Protocol.

3. The representatives of the Government and of the European Commission stress that their cooperation is based on the following priorities:

   . the consolidation of democracy and the rule of law and respect for human rights and fundamental freedoms;

   . poverty alleviation;

   . sustainable economic and social development, with a particular emphasis on human resources development, especially gender issues and environmental protection;

   . integration into the world economy, in particular through the promotion of the private sector and the development of trade.

4. Within this framework, the overall objective of cooperation under the Indicative Programme is the long-term sustainable development of the Comoros through strong growth and the equitable distribution of the fruits of that growth.

5. Under programmable financial and technical cooperation (Article 281 of the Lomé IV Convention) the Community intends to make available to the Comoros an indicative allocation of ECU 27.5 million for the duration of the Second Financial Protocol. An initial tranche of 70%, corresponding to ECU 19.25 million, will be made available immediately. A second tranche may be made available in accordance with the provisions set out under point VI.1 below (Entry into force, implementation and review).

6. This Indicative Programme is concerned mainly with programmable financial resources, although care has been taken to ensure coherence with other resources for which the Comoros might also be eligible under the various Community instruments, e.g. the other financing facilities provided for by the Convention, including the structural adjustment facilities (SAF), STABEX, the new facility to support institutional and administrative reforms, and traditional support from the Community budget.

7. Resources administered by the European Investment Bank could also be used to finance productive investment projects which comply with the Bank's statutory rules and regulations and the provisions of Articles 233 to 237 of the Convention, as detailed in Annex 1.

8. The effectiveness of any development initiative depends on the existence of a stable macroeconomic framework which encourages private initiative and promotes sustained economic growth in the medium term.

In 1990, in response to a marked deterioration in the economic situation in the late 1980s, the Government of the Comoros adopted an economic reform programme with the support, from 1991 onwards, of the International Monetary Fund (IMF) under the structural adjustment facility and the World Bank in the form of a loan to assist macroeconomic and institutional capacity reform (MERCAP). Despite some progress in 1992 and 1993, the objectives of this initial programme were not achieved and the talks with the IMF and World Bank are at a standstill. The new Government intends to do its utmost to re-open the dialogue and reach an early agreement with the Bretton Woods institutions. The main measures and expected results of this macroeconomic programme, otherwise known as the "Community Support Framework", are outlined in Annex 3.

Action financed under this Indicative Programme and possibly also under the other instruments covered by the Convention will dovetail with and consolidate the country's macroeconomic reconstruction efforts.

II - FOCAL AREAS OF COOPERATION

Within this general framework the parties have agreed on the main priorities for cooperation and on the sectors on which Community aid will focus. They have identified the reciprocal commitments to be entered into by the Community and the Comoros to achieve the desired objectives in accordance with the conditions detailed below.

Two interdependent focal areas of cooperation were selected based on the principle of sustainable development:

- Improving the transport and communications infrastructure (48-52% of the NIP)
- Environmental protection (28-32% of the NIP)

The operations identified in the environment and infrastructure fields are designed to establish conditions conducive to the development of a form of tourism suited to the social and cultural context of the Comoros. Particular attention will be paid in each area to the cross-sector issues of human resource development, poverty alleviation and the participation of women in overall economic development.

The early implementation of the 8th EDF requires the country to build up institutional capacity. Provision will therefore be made for technical assistance to:

- the National Authorizing Officer, to help coordinate and monitor the whole of the programme;
- the Directorate-General for the Environment, which is currently short of staff, equipment and finances;
- the Directorate-General for Public Works (DGTP).

II/1 - FOCAL AREA No 1:

Improving transport and communications infrastructure (48-52% of the NIP)

1.1. Background and definition

The flow of trade and social exchanges on and between islands and the development of ecotourism are largely dependent on the modernization and maintenance of a basic transport and communications network of roads, ports and airports. Over the years the Government has therefore endeavoured to pursue a policy designed to open up the country using own resources and aid from foreign donors, in particular the World Bank and the European Community.

1.2 Specific objectives

The specific objectives in this sector involve the following:

- maintenance of the road infrastructure;
- rationalizing and improving port facilities in Moroni;
- safety improvements to the secondary airports at Anjouan and Mohéli;
- institutional support to the Directorate-General for Public Works.

1.3 Sectoral policy and Government commitments

The Government's sectoral policy on transport and communications infrastructure puts the emphasis on safeguarding and improving existing infrastructure. An investment policy of this nature must be accompanied by a policy to transfer public services to the private sector.

The Government undertakes, pursuant to its policy, to:

- increase the resources available to the DGTP for routine maintenance by raising the amount allocated to the road maintenance fund (FER) from the tax on mineral oils from 10% to 13%;
- ensure that users comply with the decree on maximum axle loads;
- carry out a policy of transferring all roadworks, including routine road maintenance, from the state to the private sector;
- similarly, confer responsibility for the management of public works equipment stocks to the private sector after invitation to tender;
- privatize management of sea ports, port handling facilities and warehouses following international invitations to tender;
- make the transhipment of goods between ships in port and between quays more competitive and efficient;
- increase revenues from the secondary airports to ensure adequate resources for their maintenance and smooth operation;
- improve the maintenance of secondary airports by entrusting it to the private sector following invitation to tender.

1.4 European Community support

Subject to the provisions of the Convention on the appraisal and approval of projects and programmes, Community aid will be used to support the above sectoral policy in coordination with the funds earmarked in the national budget and those provided by other donors through the following activities:

1.4.1. Specific objective 1: road infrastructure maintenance

Some roads are liable to deteriorate rapidly without early maintenance.

1.4.2 Specific objective 2: construction of tracks to open up rural areas

Construction of tracks to open up rural areas so as to afford permanent access to potentially productive agricultural areas.

1.4.3 Specific objective 3: rationalizing and improving port facilities in Moroni

Contribution to:
- improving traffic management in the port

1.4.4 Specific objective 4: safety improvements to secondary airports at Anjouan and Mohéli

Contribution to:
- modernizing air safety equipment;
- constructing protective fencing to improve safety in the area of airports.

II/2 - FOCAL AREA No 2: Environment (28-32% of the NIP)

2.1. Background and definition

The extent of the deterioration of the environment in the Comoros is such that the country's economic and social stability is seriously threatened by it.

In 1994 the Government of the Comoros laid the foundations of an Environmental Action Plan and presented the main priorities of its environmental strategy for the period 1995-2000 to donors at the Geneva Conference. The strategy was to be implemented by the country's Directorate-General for the Environment.

The aims of the 8th EDF Programme are to build up institutional capacity in programming, management and monitoring of operations and to support the Government's efforts to promote the conservation and development of the national heritage and, by preventing unplanned and ill-considered use of resources, put a halt to their widespread destruction.

2.2 Specific objectives

The Community's strategy is geared to the rational management of natural resources to achieve sustainable development. To that end the Government of the Comoros and the Community have selected the following specific objectives from among the programmes included in the national strategy:

- the conservation, development and restoration of forest resources and appropriate management of sea and coastal areas;

- preventing pollution through the introduction of an urban waste management system and improving sanitation in major towns through rain-water drainage and wastewater treatment in the most affected areas;

- institutional support to the services responsible for implementing national environmental policy;
- identifying alternative solutions to help relieve population pressure on the environment and on natural resources, in particular sea sand and firewood.

2.3. Sectoral policy and Government commitments

Two features are currently illustrative of the Government's policy on the environment:

- the 1994 framework environment law designed to:
- preserve the diversity and integrity of the environment of the Comoros which is especially vulnerable on account of the country's insularity;
  - create conditions conducive to the sustainable utilization of natural resources;
  - guarantee all Comorians environmentally sound and balanced living conditions.

- the Environmental Action Plan.

In view of the worsening environmental problems and the urgent need to improve natural resource management as a prerequisite to the improvement of living conditions for inhabitants of the islands, the Comorian Government undertakes to take the following measures:

- build up the design and planning capacities of the technical services responsible for the environment;
- enforce the framework environment law by setting up an operations division to be responsible for monitoring its application and imposing penalties;
- enforce the law on environmental impact studies for development projects, in particular private or public investment projects involving reconstruction or building works;
- adopt appropriate tax measures with a view to promoting private initiatives relating to alternative crops;
- give the Production Ministry's Forestry Service operational status by providing it with the resources necessary for its efficient operation;
- speed up the processes for defining and officially classifying protected land and sea areas;
- boost cross-sector cooperation by relaunching the Inter-Ministry Environment Advisory Committee.

2.4. European Community support

The European Community is still one of the main donors directly involved in the environment field in the Comoros under the IOC regional environment programme and through local improvement schemes under the micro-projects programme. There is an increasingly urgent need to set up practical initiatives based on the key priorities fixed by the Government in order to provide the women of the Comoros with income earning opportunities. They currently make up for the lack of employment by informal activities based on freely available natural resources such as sea sand and coral.

Subject to the provisions of the Convention on the appraisal and approval of projects and programmes, Community aid will be used to support the above sectoral policy in coordination with the funds earmarked in the national budget from own resources and those provided by other donors through the following activities corresponding to the three specific objectives adopted:

2.4.1. Specific Objective 1: national heritage conservation and development

2.4.1.1 Conservation and restoration of forest resources

Setting up a project covering two main areas:

- Conservation and development of existing resources:

1. development of the Khartala National Park on Grande Comore through the establishment of a protected area with the cooperation of neighbouring communities. The project will involve development of the area's eco-tourism potential;
2. consolidation of forestry management in those forest areas which remain and information campaign on firewood saving;

- restoration and consolidation of permanent tree cover on ridges, in critical drainage basins and along water-courses and dissemination of agro-forestry techniques for erosion control.

2.4.1.2 Appropriate management of sea and coastal areas

Participation in the implementation of an appropriate sea and coastal area management programme geared to the priorities identified in the IOC-EDF Regional Environment programme, in particular:

- the creation of a marine reserve on the south-west coast of Grande Comore. The project will involve:
  - assistance to village fishermen's groups in the reserve to improve fisheries management and thereby reduce the pressure on the reef;
- aid to coastal village communities to help improve management of resources and areas at risk.

2.4.2. Specific Objective 2: pollution control measures

2.4.2.1 Household waste management in the principal towns

The disposal of household and hospital waste by fly-tipping or at sea is currently a critical factor in pollution and gives rise to serious public health problems. A facility is therefore to be set up with a contribution from the European Community for the collection, disposal and processing of urban waste from Moroni, Mitsamiouli, Mutsamudu, Domoni and Fomboni.

2.4.2.2 Sanitation in the principal towns

The disposal of untreated sewage and runoff water in the sea is leading to its pollution. The EU is to help combat the problem therefore by contributing to the construction of drainage works and small-scale treatment plants in the principal towns.

2.4.3. Specific Objective 3: finding alternative solutions:

2.4.3.1 Construction materials

The use of sea sand is resulting in the gradual but inevitable disappearance of beaches. Coercive measures alone are unable to put an end to this blight and therefore action is needed to:

- encourage public authorities and local communities to use replacement materials: crushed pozzolana sand, lava stone, plant materials, etc.;
- promote the setting-up of groups for the purchase and supply of crushed sand;
- coordinate with other ongoing programmes so as to identify alternative economic activities to those resulting from the systematic destruction of beaches and reefs.

2.4.3.2 Alternative energy sources and developing hydroelectric potential

One possible solution would be to renovate or construct small hydro-power plants on the islands of Anjouan and Mohéli. This might also encourage local communities to become aware of the need to protect forests.

III - OPERATIONS OUTSIDE THE FOCAL SECTORS (20%)

3.1. DECENTRALIZED COOPERATION (15%)

This operation will be implemented by decentralized cooperation in the form of a programme of micro-projects in perfect keeping with the geographical and social context of the Comoros. The broad success both with the community and local authorities of the programme financed under the 7th EDF bears witness to this.

A project to support the health services is also planned with the aim of underpinning assistance already given to this sector under the 7th EDF (AIDS, SAP, micro-projects) cofinanced with other donors, notably France and the World Bank.

3.2 Private sector support (4%)

This operation represents the continuation of another undertaken under the 7th EDF and will be implemented in conjunction with the PRIDE programme. Account will be taken of the lessons learnt from past experience when adopting the proposed operations which include projects to bolster microenterprises and small businesses by increasing the financial resources available to them and to reorganize the intermediary organizations which are meant to represent them.

3.3 Training (1%)

Related training activities will be provided in the two focal sectors. Other non-related training activities will also be undertaken particularly in the field of justice with a view to consolidating democracy and the rule of law.

IV - CONVERGENCE AND CONSISTENCY OF INSTRUMENTS

The Community aid policy will pursue a limited number of objectives using the various instruments (STABEX, SAF, NIP) at its disposal in a harmonious manner and with due respect to the nature of the instruments. The SAF and NIP should continue to be used in a complementary manner.

STABEX funds will be used in keeping with the aim to develop traditional exports, which is also backed by a 7th EDF project.

V - REGIONAL COOPERATION

In relation to regional cooperation, the Comoros and the European Commission are due to sign the 8th EDF Regional Indicative Programme (RIP) for the Indian Ocean. This programme is currently being finalized.

VI - ENTRY INTO FORCE, IMPLEMENTATION AND REVIEW

1. When about 80% of the first tranche has been committed, the parties will carry out a joint review of the implementation of the Indicative Programme, in accordance with Article 282(3) of Lomé IV. The following aspects will be examined:

- implementation of sectoral policies and their relevance in the context of macroeconomic policy, in fulfilment of the Government's commitments, which are set out in Annexes 2 and 3;

- adherence to the implementation timetable, especially the commitment and payment forecasts in Annex 4;

- adherence to the timetable set out in the financing agreement for each operation;

- implementation of cooperation under previous EDFs, especially the balances remaining from previous NIPs;

- the preparation of operations that the Government of the Comoros intends to carry out in the period covered by the Second Financial Protocol and the corresponding financial requirements;

- the overall coherence of the country's development efforts, to be evaluated on the basis of the quality of the management of public finances and the structure of budget expenditure;

- any unforeseen changes occurring after the signing of this Indicative Programme that are beyond the control of the parties.

- In any event, the review of the first tranche must be carried out by 31 December 1999, regardless of the primary commitment rate achieved.

- In the light of the findings of the review, all or part of the balance of the indicative allocation may be used for the financing of the operations provided for in this Indicative Programme until the end of the period covered by the Second Financial Protocol of the Lomé IV Convention.

2. In accordance with Article 284(3) of the Lomé IV Convention and in the interests of speedy implementation of the Indicative Programme and facilitating the review referred to above, the National Authorizing Officer and the Head of Delegation will draw up an annual progress report within 90 days of the end of each calendar year. They will take all necessary measures to ensure that the Indicative Programme is adhered to. To this end, they will determine the causes of any delays and propose appropriate measures to deal with them.

3. Subject to the ratification and entry into force of the Lomé IV Convention, the agreement between the two parties to this Indicative Programme will be considered final six weeks after its signing, unless one party notifies the other of its decision to the contrary before the end of this period.

Done at Moroni, ...1997

For the European Commission

For the Federal Islamic Republic of the Comoros

ANNEXES

1. EIB

2. SECTORAL POLICIES AND GOVERNMENT COMMITMENTS

   2.1 SECTOR: ENVIRONMENT
   2.2 SECTOR: INFRASTRUCTURE

3. MACROECONOMIC POLICY SHORT AND MEDIUM-TERM OBJECTIVES AND STRATEGY / THE COMMUNITY SUPPORT FRAMEWORK

4. IMPLEMENTATION TIMETABLE

Federal Islamic Republic of the Comoros

EUROPEAN INVESTMENT BANK DEVELOPMENT-FINANCING OPERATIONS

With reference to paragraph 7, the EIB may contribute to the financing of productive projects and programmes - or other investment aimed at promoting the private sector - particularly in industry, food processing, tourism, mining, energy, transport and telecommunications.

The amounts and financing arrangements for each project will be determined in the light of a detailed appraisal carried out in accordance with the Bank's procedures.

In the present circumstances, the Bank would provisionally put the indicative volume of assistance it could provide under the Second Financial Protocol of the Lomé IV Convention at ECU 3 million.

The Bank has taken note that Government of the Federal Islamic Republic of the Comoros intends to present, or authorize the presentation of, financing proposals in the following areas:

- private sector: support for private investment in manufacturing industries, processing of raw materials and tourism; assistance in the development of small- and medium-sized businesses by direct financing or through local, regional or EU financial institutions.

- Infrastructure: incoming generating infrastructure in the fields of energy, water and sanitation, telecommunications, solid waste treatment, etc.

- transport: improvements to airport infrastructure and national air navigation facilities, maritime transport.

The Government undertakes that private-sector operations financed by the Bank from its own resources or from risk capital, whether directly or through an intermediary, will enjoy all the advantages laid down in Article 237 and other relevant provisions of the Convention. In accordance with the spirit of cooperation that informs Article 236(c), the Government undertakes to provide the Bank within a reasonable period with confirmation that the advantages set out in Article 237 apply to the operation in question.

The Bank points out that its financial assistance could be suspended in the event of the Federal Islamic Republic of the Comoros failing in its financial obligations to the Bank.

Done at Moroni, ...

For the Government of the Federal Islamic Republic of the Comoros	For the European Investment Bank

NEW WORLD POLITICAL LEADERS LIBRARY-2002

ULTIMATE INFORMATION ON LOLITICAL AND BUSINESS LEADERS OF FOREING COUNTRIES

The ultimate handbook with detailed information on foreign leaders, including biographic data, position on domestic and international issues, economic policy and more

Price: $79.95 each

TITLE	ISBN
1. Albania President Rexhep Meidani Handbook	07397-2762-8
2. Armenia President Robert Kocharian Handbook	07397-1180-6
3. Austria President Dr. Thomas Klestil Handbook	07397-05997
4. Azerbaijan President Heydar Aliyev Handbook	07397-1072-9
5. Bangladesh Prime Minister Khaleda Zia Handbook	07397-1181-4
6. Belarus President Alexander LUKASHENKO Handbook	07397-1073-7
7. Brunei Sultan Haji Hassanal Bolkiah Mu'izzaddin Waddaulah Handbook	07397-1190-3
8. Canada Prime Minister Joseph Jacques Jean Chrétien Handbook	07397-09488
9. China President Jiang, Zemin Handbook	07397-09976
10. Cuba President Fidel Castro Handbook	07397-1183-0
11. Egypt President Hosny Mubarak Handbook	07397-1185-7
12. France President Jacques Chirac Handbook	07397-1188-1
13. Germany President Johannes Rau Handbook	07397-09968
14. Iran President Hojjatoleslam Seyed Mohammad Khatami Handbook	07397-1178-4
15. Iraq President Saddam Hussein Handbook	07397-1179-2
16. Israel Prime Minister Ariel Sharon Handbook	07397-1192-X
17. Japan Prime Minister Junichiro Koizumi Handbook	07397-1194-6
18. Korea North General Secretary Kim Jong Il Handbook	07397-1197-0
19. Korea South President Kim Dae-jung Handbook	07397-1198-9
20. Libya President Muammar Muhammad Abd as-Salam al-Gaddafi Handbook	07397-1175-X
21. Norway Queen Sonja Handbook	07397-2699-4
22. Pakistan President Pervez Musharraf Handbook	07397-2735-4
23. Palestine President Yasser Arafat Handbook	07397-2766-0
24. Philippines President Gloria Macapagal Arroyo Handbook	07397-2737-0
25. Poland President Aleksander Kwasniewski Handbook	07397-2738-9
26. Russia President Vladimir Putin Handbook	07397-0999-2
27. Saudi Arabia King Fahd bin Abdul Aziz Handbook	07397-2740-0
28. Syria President Bashar Hafez Al-Assad Handbook	07397-2744-3
29. Thailand King Bhumibol Adulyadej Handbook	07397-2747-8
30. United Arab Emirates Ruler Sheikh Zayed bin Sultan Al Nahyan Handbook	07397-2736-2
31. United States President George W. Bush Handbook	07397-0998-4
32. Uzbekistan President Islam Karimov Handbook	07397-2764-4
33. Yugoslavia President Vojislav Koštunica Handbook	07397-0995X

To order and for additional analytical and marketing information, please contacrt
<u>International Business Publications, USA at:</u>
P.O. Box 15343, Washington, DC 20003, USA. Phone: (202) 546-2103. Fax: (202) 546-3275.
E-mail: rusric@erols.com
World Business Catalog on Line: http://www.wworld.mirhouse.com

Printed in the United States
1490500001B/147